Christianity in Hitler's Ideology

How did Hitler's personal religious beliefs help shape the development of National Socialism? Through a close analysis of primary sources, Mikael Nilsson argues that Hitler's admiration of Jesus was central to both his public and private life, playing a key role throughout his entire political career. *Christianity in Hitler's Ideology* reexamines the roots of National Socialism, exploring how antisemitic forms of Christian nationalism de-Judaized Jesus and rendered him as an Aryan. In turn, the study analyzes how Hitler's religious and ideological teachers, especially *Völkisch*-Christian writers Houston Stewart Chamberlain and Dietrich Eckart, weaponized these ideas. Nilsson challenges the established understanding that Hitler only used religion as a tool of propaganda. Instead, he argues that religious faith and deeply held convictions were at the core of National Socialism, its racism, the Second World War, and the Holocaust.

Mikael Nilsson is an independent Swedish scholar and historian with research interests in Hitler, National Socialism, and Nazi Germany, along with the Cold War. His previous publications include *Hitler Redux: The Incredible History of Hitler's So-Called Table Talks* (2021).

Christianity in Hitler's Ideology

The Role of Jesus in National Socialism

Mikael Nilsson

Shaftesbury Road, Cambridge CB2 8EA, United Kingdom

One Liberty Plaza, 20th Floor, New York, NY 10006, USA

477 Williamstown Road, Port Melbourne, VIC 3207, Australia

314–321, 3rd Floor, Plot 3, Splendor Forum, Jasola District Centre, New Delhi – 110025, India

103 Penang Road, #05-06/07, Visioncrest Commercial, Singapore 238467

Cambridge University Press is part of Cambridge University Press & Assessment, a department of the University of Cambridge.

We share the University's mission to contribute to society through the pursuit of education, learning and research at the highest international levels of excellence.

www.cambridge.org
Information on this title: www.cambridge.org/9781009314954

DOI: 10.1017/9781009314961

© Mikael Nilsson 2024

This publication is in copyright. Subject to statutory exception and to the provisions of relevant collective licensing agreements, no reproduction of any part may take place without the written permission of Cambridge University Press & Assessment.

When citing this work, please include a reference to the DOI 10.1017/9781009314961

First published 2024

A catalogue record for this publication is available from the British Library.

A Cataloging-in-Publication data record for this book is available from the Library of Congress

ISBN 978-1-009-31495-4 Hardback
ISBN 978-1-009-31497-8 Paperback

Cambridge University Press & Assessment has no responsibility for the persistence or accuracy of URLs for external or third-party internet websites referred to in this publication and does not guarantee that any content on such websites is, or will remain, accurate or appropriate.

For Ilse, William, Robert, and Morris

CONTENTS

Acknowledgements viii

Introduction 1

1 Christ on the Crooked Cross, Part I: Jesus as an Aryan, Antisemitic Warrior 32

2 Hitler's Religious Teachers: Dietrich Eckart and Houston Stewart Chamberlain 85

3 Christ on the Crooked Cross, Part II: Did Hitler Believe That Jesus Was Divine? 134

4 Hitler's Damascus Road Experience: How Hitler Modeled His Political Conversion Narrative in *Mein Kampf* on the Apostle Paul's Religious Conversion in Acts 9 160

5 Jesus as an Ideological Inspiration for Hitler and the NSDAP 180

Conclusion 234

Bibliography 243
Index 258

ACKNOWLEDGMENTS

As a historian, I am used to isolating myself either in the archives or at home as I do my reading and writing. Like so many other historians, I quite enjoy being on my own, thinking about and tinkering with various ideas. Writing a book is indeed in many ways a lonely job. Yet there are many people who I need to thank and credit for their invaluable assistance and support in making this book a reality. One of the most important people on this list is Professor Brendan Simms: without him, this book would not have been possible. His guidance through the process of finding a publisher for my manuscript was invaluable. He believed in me and selflessly helped me realize an academic goal I had set for myself twenty years ago as I was writing and researching my dissertation, and for that I will forever be in his debt. I have also been given immense support from Professor Thomas Weber and Associate Professor Richard Steigmann-Gall. Their readings of, and comments on, my manuscript made sure that the text was improved in a way that I hardly thought possible. They believed in my ideas and gave me constructive criticism and remained encouraging even when they had differing views. Without them, this book would not have become a reality.

I also want to express my never-ending love and gratitude to my mother and father, who brought me into this world, who raised me, and who gave me the love and support necessary to grow up to be the man I am today. I give thanks to my wonderful sister, who is a true fighter and

ix / Acknowledgments

an inspiration to me. Other people I wish to thank are (in no particular order) Magnus Brechtken, Niklas Stenlås, Lars M. Andersson, Marco Wyss, Timothy Ryback, Anders Wiberg (BB), Henrik Arnstad, Wolfram Pyta, and Sir Ian Kershaw.

I want to direct a warm and special "thank you" to my editor at Cambridge University Press, Liz Friend-Smith, for believing in my book and for being so kind and so helpful on this journey. I know my emails with questions must have been demanding at times, but she handled them with both kindness and great professionalism.

Last, but certainly not least, I want to thank my beloved wife Ilse for believing in me through the years that I spent late nights, early mornings, and far too many weekends writing and researching this book. I love you always.

INTRODUCTION

Why is yet another book about Hitler necessary? Has not Hitler, the Third Reich, and National Socialism already been sufficiently mapped and described so that another book about these historical phenomena cannot but be superfluous? Judging by the constant stream of new books on the topic every year, the obvious answer is "no." There does not seem to be a limit for the number of books that can be produced and consumed. The market appears to be insatiable. Granted, not every book written has been either necessary, or helpful when it comes to increasing our understanding of this part of our common history. Nonetheless, there may be a more interesting question to be answered here, namely: Are there aspects of this topic that have not yet been given quite the attention in the literature that they deserve? The answer to this question is an equally obvious "yes." There are many issues and aspects of National Socialism that are in need of further research. Among them is the topic of this book: Hitler's and National Socialism's relationship to the central figure of Christianity – Jesus Christ.[1] Hitler's relationship to Christianity has been hotly debated.

[1] Recently, the French historian Johann Chapoutot has touched on this theme, but his book is more about the Nazi cultural revolution in general. The focus is not on Hitler's ideology but rather on the ideas on which National Socialism was built as they were espoused by other ideologues, lawyers, and politicians; see Chapoutot, Johann, *La révolution culturelle nazie* (Paris: Gallimard, 2017), pp. 135–177. The book only contains a few references to Hitler's writings and speeches.

2 / Christianity in Hitler's Ideology

It has been claimed that he resented Christianity in all its forms, although much of that scholarship is built on poor sources and reasoning.

In his book *Humanity*, Jonathan Glover quotes Hitler talking about what he thought about Christianity:

> I shall never come personally to terms with the Christian lie. . . . Our epoch will certainly see the end of the disease of Christianity. It will last another hundred years, two hundred years perhaps. My regret will have been that I couldn't, like whoever the prophet was, behold the promised land from afar.[2]

This is an oft-quoted passage from the famous source *Hitler's Table Talk*.[3] It certainly seems to confirm that Hitler was a staunch non-believer and completely anti-Christian. There is only one problem with it: it is based on a forgery. The English text was translated not from the German original (despite historian H. R. Trevor-Roper's claim to the contrary), which is problematic from a source-critical perspective, but from a French version of that text produced by the Swiss Nazi sympathizer (and owner of one of the German source texts) François Genoud and published a year prior to *Hitler's Table Talk* in 1952.[4] Genoud not only rewrote the German original text, but he also inserted completely new phrases into it. I reviewed the unreliability of the "table talk" texts in great detail in my book *Hitler Redux*.[5]

---

[2] Glover, Jonathan, *Humanity: A Moral History of the Twentieth Century* (London: Jonathan Cape, 1999), p. 355.

[3] Hitler, A., *Hitler's Table Talk: His Private Conversations 1941–1944. With an introductory essay on the mind of Adolf Hitler by H. R. Trevor-Roper* (London: Weidenfeld & Nicolson, 1953), p. 343.

[4] Genoud, François, *Libres propos sur la Guerre et la Paix: Recueillis sur l'ordre de Martin Bormann. Préface de Robert d'Harcourt de l'Academie française. Version française de François Genoud*, Vol. I (Paris: Flammarion, 1952), p. 332.

[5] Nilsson, Mikael, *Hitler Redux: The Incredible History of Hitler's So-Called Table Talks* (London: Routledge, 2021); for a dissection of this part, see pp. 2–4. This fact has not stopped David Redles from citing the table talks in a recent publication. Redles refers to my research and acknowledges the problematic nature of these sources but thinks I go "too far in largely dismissing them as a legitimate source." He cites the corrupted English edition and says he has "consulted both German editions to verify the English translations," but this does nothing at all to offset the real problem with these sources, which is that the German texts cannot be trusted to provide an accurate record either. Redles then makes an obviously

3 / Introduction

To discover Hitler's true attitudes toward Jesus and to really understand what he himself understood true Christianity to be, historians must move beyond this and other similarly unreliable and questionable sources. Instead, we need to delve into the core beliefs of National Socialism. In this book, I do this by examining the foundational texts of National Socialism, as well as the more reliable sources for Hitler's personal beliefs. In the process, I show that the character of Jesus, the central figure in Christianity, also held a central place within Hitler's ideology. This suggests that Hitler and the other National Socialists understood true Christianity to be something entirely different than what we are used to imagining. Instead of rejecting Christianity as a whole, it turns out that Hitler and his followers were seeking to reestablish the original teachings of Jesus, which they thought had been lost over the centuries due to the manipulations of the apostle Paul and then the Catholic Church.

This book thus argues that Hitler's religious beliefs were of central importance for how National Socialism as an ideology developed from 1920 onwards, for how the Third Reich was organized, and for why Hitler and his henchmen developed policies designed to inflict so much suffering and death. There can be doubt that this is an argument that has thus far not taken center stage when historians have studied Hitler's Germany. Of course, one may argue that it was only *the way Hitler used religious beliefs* that was important and that he therefore did not really believe what he said. But by studying the ideological history of National Socialism and its foundational texts, even those written before Hitler became a National Socialist, we can trace the roots of the central position held by Jesus within National Socialism. A careful reading of the primary sources shows without a doubt that religious faith and deeply held convictions regarding what plan God had

---

false claim, namely, that the table talks never were considered verbatim sources (Redles, David, "The Apocalypse of Adolf Hitler: *Mein Kampf* and the Eschatological Origins of the Holocaust," in John J. Michalczyk, Michael S. Bryant, and Susan A. Michalczyk (eds.), *Hitler's* Mein Kampf *and the Holocaust: A Prelude to Genocide* [London: Bloomsbury Academic, 2022], p. 318, n60). But the table talk notes were indeed considered verbatim records because they were for a very long time claimed to be, and accepted as, the work of a stenographer. I prove and debunk this very notion in my book *Hitler Redux*, which Redles refers to in his text.

4 / Christianity in Hitler's Ideology

for humankind and the universe were at the very core of National Socialism, its racism, the Second World War, and – not least – the Holocaust. This may at first appear to be a controversial statement. It is my conviction, however, that when the reader finishes this book, this opinion will no longer be present – instead, it will be obvious to the reader that my argument is worth taking very seriously.

It is important to understand that National Socialism was not an invention of Hitler and the National Socialist German Workers' Party (NSDAP). Its history began many decades before 1919/20. For example, the Czech National Socialist Party was founded already in 1898, and in 1903 the German Workers' Party (DAP) [*not* the one that Hitler would join in 1919] in Bohemia saw the light of day. The latter renamed itself the "German National Socialist Workers' Party" (DNSAP) in 1918 and then split into one Austrian and one German branch. National Socialism was therefore not at all born out of the chaos of the First World War, writes Thomas Weber. Even the Zionists had their own dream of a National Socialist homeland, he notes. Furthermore, the first country to have a National Socialist elected to parliament was neither Germany nor Austria, but Great Britain. This happened when John Joseph "Jack" Jones of the British National Socialist Party got elected to the House of Commons on December 14, 1918. In Germany, however, the roots went even further back. National Socialism developed on the political right shortly after the German unification in 1871 as a reaction against Marxism and Social Democracy, as Asaf Kedar shows. There were various forms already from the beginning – a liberal-Christian bourgeois strain (represented by Friedrich Naumann), a moderate conservative-Christian lineage (represented by Adolf Stoecker), and a more radical extreme-right (mostly) Christian strain (represented by the ideologue and NSDAP member Theodor Fritsch).[6]

This means that the argument put forth in this book should not necessarily be interpreted as one aligning with the German *Sonderweg*

---

[6] Kedar, Asaf, "National Socialism before Nazism: Friedrich Naumann and Theodor Fritsch, 1890–1914," PhD diss. (University of California, Berkeley, 2010); Weber, Thomas, *Becoming Hitler: The Making of a Nazi* (Oxford: Oxford University Press, 2017), pp. xiii–xiv.

5 / Introduction

(special path) hypothesis. Although Hitler and the NSDAP naturally emerged out of a specifically German historical context and their ideologies can be traced back to the National Socialist discourses that immediately preceded them in the German-speaking world, similar ideas were afloat also in other parts of Europe at the same time. Fascism, then, was not a German *Sonderweg* but instead a part of a general ideological trend in Europe and elsewhere in the world. Yet, the form that National Socialism took in Germany was not mirrored in other countries. In this sense, every country had its own *Sonderweg* due to the unique circumstances they each found themselves in.

While a lot has been written about National Socialism's connection to, and Hitler's view of, religion in general and Christianity in particular, no study has yet investigated the role of Jesus in National Socialist ideology. This book therefore plugs a significant hole in the literature in the field. It argues that Hitler was an honest admirer of Jesus – or rather, the Nazi interpretation of Jesus, who should not be confused with the Jesus of orthodox Christianity – and that he viewed him as an inspiration both for a National Socialist's moral and ethical development as well as for the political struggle against the Jews.

Chapter 1 shows that the ideological roots of National Socialism's connection to Jesus go back much further than 1919. National Socialism arose from a conservative religious milieu in Germany already in the 1870s–1890s. Because of the racial antisemitism[7] that grew stronger and stronger from the mid-1800s onwards, more and more Christian theologians started to question the racial status of the central figure in their faith – Jesus – turning him into an Aryan. In Nazi Germany, this development would culminate in the theology of the Protestant church movement *Deutsche Christen*. Hitler tapped into, and drew from, this tradition, and it became the foundation for his understanding of Jesus.

Chapter 2 deals with Dietrich Eckart and Houston Stewart Chamberlain, the two most central figures in Hitler's religious and ideological development in the early 1920s. Eckart appears to have been the most important for Hitler's political schooling. Eckart's book

---

[7] I follow the International Holocaust Remembrance Alliance's (IHRA) recommendation for the spelling, which is "antisemitism" instead of "anti-Semitism" because of the antisemitic roots of the derived construct "Semite."

6 / Christianity in Hitler's Ideology

Der Bolschewismus von Moses bis Lenin,[8] which contained a fictional conversation between himself and Hitler on religious and political topics, offers us a view into the religious universe that Eckart and Hitler coinhabited. The book is also a clear testament to the fact that religious beliefs had a central place within National Socialism. Chamberlain's views of Jesus as an Aryan warrior became a vital part of Hitler's theology. Still, Hitler did not simply copy Eckart's or Chamberlain's ideas. A good example of this is that Hitler rejected the apostle Paul while Chamberlain accepted him. The early 1920s were indeed formative years for Hitler's political ideology and understanding of himself and his place in the world, and it was at this time that Eckart convinced him that he was the one that was destined to bring salvation to Germany.

In Chapter 3, I deal with the issue of whether Hitler considered Jesus to have been divine. This is certainly not a trivial issue. It is pertinent to the question of whether Hitler considered his mission to be from God and thereby have divine sanction. The explicit references to Jesus are not very frequent, and most of them appear during the 1920s and, to a lesser extent, in the early 1930s. Yet Hitler made these statements both in public and in private. Therefore, I maintain that the claim that his comments about Jesus and Christianity were just intended for public consumption and propaganda purposes cannot be sustained. Granted that the evidence is a bit ambiguous, and at times even contradictory, we nonetheless have several examples of Hitler clearly referring to Jesus as divine. This has not been noticed by historians before and should be considered very significant.

Chapter 4 argues that Hitler modeled his own political conversion story as presented in *Mein Kampf* on the narrative about the apostle Paul's conversion in Acts 9. We find too many parallels between this story and the one that Hitler offered in *Mein Kampf* for the connection to be purely accidental. Hitler includes a period of temporary blindness, a conversation with the divine, and an awakening experience that gave him his sight back, and he portrays himself as the founder of a great and revolutionizing movement. Just like Paul, Hitler

---

[8] Eckart, Dietrich, *Der Bolschewismus von Moses bis Lenin: Zweigespräch zwischen Adolf Hitler und mir* (Munich: Franz Eher Verlag, 1924).

7 / Introduction

emphasizes that he went from being completely unknown to someone who was recognized all over, and he also claims to have received a mission from God. It was also a convenient narrative device that Hitler could be certain would be familiar to his readers. In Chapter 5, finally, I show how Hitler's admiration – and National Socialism's more generally – for Jesus inspired the politics of Nazi Germany up until the very end in the bunker in Berlin in April 1945. In the example of Jesus, Hitler found the inspiration for fighting the Jews, and it was in the former's footsteps that he felt he and his party were following. He considered himself chosen by God to fulfill the mission that Jesus had not been able to complete: the eradication of the Jewish people from the face of the earth. In the Conclusion, I then summarize my findings and end with suggestions and recommendations for future research.

Sources and Source Criticism

The last twenty years have seen a steady stream of books in both English and German (as well as many other languages of course) about Hitler's religiosity. It is therefore not possible to argue that this is a theme that has not received any attention by historians. Nonetheless, this aspect of Hitler's personality remains one of the least known to the public. One major reason for this omission is that the biographies of Hitler refer to this topic only in passing (if that) and that his religious faith is not given any weight at all in that literature. But there is also a clear flaw in the literature that does deal with Hitler's religiosity, namely, that proper source criticism is often lacking. These works tend to cite every available source without exception and without using any apparent historical epistemological principles according to which the unreliable information can be separated from the reliable. This is the case not least regarding what is perhaps the most famous source for Hitler's anti-Christian statements: the so-called table talks.[9] But Hitler's

---

[9] I have investigated the history of the table talks in detail in Nilsson, M., *Hitler Redux . . .* See also Nilsson, Mikael, "Hitler Redivivus: Hitlers 'Tischgespräche' and 'Monologe im Führerhauptquartier': eine kritische Untersuchung," *Vierteljahrshefte für Zeitgeschichte*, Vol. 67, No. 1 (2019), pp. 105–146; Nilsson, Mikael, "Constructing a Pseudo-Hitler? The Question of the Authenticity of *Hitlers politisches* Testament," *European Review of*

8 / Christianity in Hitler's Ideology

table talks are far from the only source that is cited uncritically by historians; the same goes for the memoirs of former Nazis.

This book started as a summary of the state of research on the topic of Hitler's religious beliefs, but soon I realized that I would have to go through the primary sources anew and not only (perhaps) reinterpret what other historians had already done, but also weed out the sources and literature that are not trustworthy. Therefore, the writing turned into a multiyear research project conducted on evenings and weekends. One of the most central problems with large parts of the previous literature is the reliance on "contemporary eyewitnesses," that is, Nazis that had spent a longer or shorter period of time in Hitler's entourage and who, often many years or even several decades after the war, decided to tell "their story," often to journalists. These eyewitnesses, of whom the most (in)famous must no doubt be Albert Speer, have subsequently been able to spread their version of reality virtually unopposed to historians and journalists who have relied on their "memories" when writing about Hitler and the Third Reich. These memories are always affected by these Nazis' wish to clear their own names – or whatever other agenda they may have had – and to more often than not blame everything that happened in Nazi Germany on Hitler's almost magical powers of persuasion.

Instead of assuming that these witnesses are telling the truth, the opposite approach should be taken, that is, what they say should always be considered suspect until proven otherwise. Speer's lies were introduced almost at the very beginning through the British historian Hugh Trevor-Roper and his book *The Last Days of Hitler* from 1947 (which built on interviews with Speer) and his countryman Alan Bullock's *Hitler: A Study of Tyranny* from 1952.[10] German historians were not much better. The first thorough German Hitler biography, written by the journalist Joachim Fest and published in 1973,[11] was to a significant

---

History–Revue Européenne d'histoire, Vol. 26, No. 5 (2018), pp. 871–891; Nilsson, Mikael, "Hugh Trevor-Roper and the English Editions of Hitler's Table Talk and Testament," *Journal of Contemporary History*, Vol. 51, No. 4 (2015), pp. 788–812; Carrier, Richard, "Hitler's Table Talk: Troubling Finds," *German Studies Review*, Vol. 26, No. 3 (2003), pp. 561–576.

[10] Trevor-Roper, Hugh, *The Last Days of Hitler* (London: Macmillan & Co., 1947); Bullock, Alan, *Hitler: A Study in Tyranny* (London: Odhams Press, 1952).

[11] Fest, Joachim, *Hitler: Eine Biographie* (Berlin: Propyläen, 1973).

9 / Introduction

degree based on his many conversations with Speer since they had first met in August 1967. Fest had then been given the task by the publisher Wolf Jobst Siedler to edit and rewrite (effectively ghostwrite) Speer's manuscript for his *Erinnerungen* (Memoirs – later published in English as *Inside the Third Reich*).[12] After the publication of his Hitler biography, Fest came to take on a similar role during the publication of Speer's *Spandauer Tagebücher* (Diaries from Spandau) in 1975.[13] During this work, Fest made Speer write down Hitler quotations for him, which Speer dutifully did. In this way, "genuine" Hitler quotes were created no less than twenty-two years after the end of the war, which have subsequently found their way into basically all history books about the Third Reich.[14] Nonetheless, Speer's two books received glowing reviews both in Germany and elsewhere. For example, the historian Klaus Hildebrand declared that Speer's diaries were a very important *contemporary* source out of which direct citations of Hitler could be mined.[15] Not even after Speer was exposed as a relentless liar did historians seem to change their mind about him. Therefore, Speer cannot be used to corroborate anything except how he wished to portray himself and the events and people he spoke about. As a source for knowledge about the realities of Hitler and the Third Reich, Speer's books are worthless. The main takeaway from all of this is that a lot in the previous literature has in fact been shown to be incorrect, or at least in need of serious nuancing, by newer research. But far from all prior scholarship has been vetted in this way to see how much flawed or incorrect information from these eyewitnesses it contains.

For this reason, I have as far as possible refrained from referring to, and from supporting my argumentation with, such eyewitness

---

[12] Speer, Albert, *Erinnerungen* (Berlin: Propyläen, 1969).

[13] Speer, Albert, *Spandauer Tagebücher* (Berlin: Propyläen, 1975).

[14] For more on Fest's and Siedlers' role in the publication of Speer's books, as well as a review of the state of research on the topic, see Brechtken, Magnus, *Albert Speer: Eine deutsche Karriere* (Munich: Siedler, 2017), passim, but especially pp. 9–15, 365–576. Fest also received part of the revenues from the sales of Speer's books, which already in the case of *Erinnerungen* had made him a wealthy man.

[15] Brechtken, M., *Albert Speer ...*, pp. 407–410, 485–491. Certain criticism did occur, but this never managed to drown out the celebratory reviews or Speer's defenders. For a detailed review of the reception of Speer's books, see Trommer, Isabell, *Rechtfertigung und Entlassung: Albert Speer in der Bundesrepublik* (Frankfurt: Campus Verlag, 2016).

10 / Christianity in Hitler's Ideology

accounts (both directly and indirectly via other literature) if I have been unable to corroborate the information with independent, reliable sources. An obvious exception to this rule is where I have wished to show how these eyewitnesses wanted to portray their own role post facto. Instead, I have based my analysis on the available primary contemporary source material in addition to the existing scholarship. This does not mean that these primary sources are unproblematic. The editions of Hitler's speeches and writings present the historian with several delicate problems. We can, for example, never be certain that Hitler formulated his words in exactly the way that the transcripts show (except in the cases where we have audio recordings that can be compared to the text). Hitler did not read a completed manuscript when he spoke; rather, he improvised from a set of supporting notes and a core of established themes that he returned to repeatedly. In many cases, the speeches were taken down by the NSDAP stenographer and then transcribed and published in the *Völkischer Beobachter*. These notes then follow Hitler's actual words very well, but they still do contain occasional corrections made afterwards, as well as a few transcription mistakes. Moreover, we far from always have access to full verbatim transcripts. Often what we have are summaries made by police observers or journalists, for example, who then published their notes in the newspapers. Sometimes, however, we have dictations by Hitler made for speeches that were to be read by someone else, for instance by Goebbels. This happened on several occasions, especially toward the end of the war as Hitler's public appearances became few and far between. Even though we can then be rather sure that the wording is correct, there are examples where the speech was shortened by Goebbels due to time constraints.

The period 1905–24 is covered by the source volume *Hitler: Sämtliche Aufzeichnungen* (Hitler's Collected Notes) published in 1980. It contains not only transcribed speeches, but also speech notes, summaries in the form of police reports and newspaper articles, interviews, and letters.[16] However, this volume contains no less than seventy-five forgeries made by the con artist Konrad Kujau, who also forged the

---

[16] Jäckel, Eberhard (ed.), *Hitler: Sämtliche Aufzeichnungen 1905–1924* (Stuttgart: Deutsche Verlags-Anstalt, 1980). Henceforth: *SA*.

11 / Introduction

infamous Hitler Diaries. Ever since this scandal was revealed in 1983, these forgeries have been well known to historians, but this has not stopped some scholars less familiar with the field from using them. One example is the Swedish historian Svante Nordin, who based several conclusions in his 2018 book *Hitlers München* (Hitler's Munich), which was widely celebrated by reviewers in the Swedish press, on many of these forgeries. I was the only one to discover his mistake and to make the public aware of it (as well as several other inaccuracies).[17] Friedrich Tomberg also cites one of Kujau's forged poems in his book.[18]

Regarding the period 1925–33, we have the fourteen-volume series from the *Institut für Zeitgeschichte* (IfZ) (Leibniz Institute for Contemporary History) in Munich (four of these volumes contain the court transcripts from Hitler's trial in 1924, and one contains the manuscript for Hitler's unpublished second book from 1928).[19] Here, too, we are often dealing with summaries of his speeches made by police observers or journalists. They also contain the preserved letters that Hitler wrote during this period of his life. As far as we know, none of these documents are forgeries, but as historians we should always be careful enough to tell our readers whenever we cite a summary of a speech made by someone else. What we are quoting in these instances is someone else's memory of what Hitler said, and not the speech itself. Fortunately, the volumes include several summaries of the same speech, and therefore one can spot biases and variations of themes quite well. Still, we must keep in mind that we cannot know for sure what Hitler really said on these occasions.

But when we get to the period 1932–45, the four volumes pertaining to which were published by Max Domarus in 1965, we are considerably worse off.[20] Domarus' volumes do not contain all the speeches, and often contains only parts of them. Moreover, he also

---

[17] Nilsson, Mikael, "Pinsamt: Förfalskade dokument om Führern tas för sanna i Svante Nordins bok 'Hitlers München'," *Dagens Nyheter*, June 4, 2018, p. 7.

[18] Tomberg, Friedrich, *Das Christentum in Hitlers Weltanschauung* (Munich: Wilhelm Fink Verlag, 2012), pp. 195–196.

[19] Hitler, Adolf, *Hitler: Reden, Schriften, Anordnungen. Februar 1925 bis Januar 1933* [14 volumes with different editors] (Munich: K. G. Saur, 1992–2003). Henceforth: RSA.

[20] Domarus, Max (ed.), *Hitler: Reden und Proklamationen 1932–1945. Kommentiert von einem deutschen Zeitgenossen* (Band I–IV) (Munich: Süddeutscher Verlag, 1965). Henceforth: HRP.

12 / Christianity in Hitler's Ideology

included his own commentary. These volumes are mostly based on the version that was published in *Völkischer Beobachter*. An even greater problem is that the comparisons between these transcripts and the available audio recordings of these speeches that the IfZ has now made, recordings that were not available to Domarus, show that the transcribed versions contain many inaccuracies that often affect the meaning of what was said and therefore directly impact the interpretation and understanding of what Hitler said (note that this is therefore likely to be the case also of the earlier periods). It is because of this fact that the IfZ is currently working on a new edition of Hitler's speeches and writings during the period 1933–45 that will include all the known texts in their entirety. This project was begun in August of 2017, and it is not known when it will be finished.[21] This means that the documentary evidence for this later period is worse than the time from 1905 to 1932. Obviously, then, my book suffers from the fact that I did not have access to complete transcriptions from the later period. This means that parts of the speeches that I build my analysis on could have been different, and it may or may not affect some of the conclusions I draw from them. Of course, this problem runs both ways, which means that Hitler may have made even more statements of a religious character than are available in Domarus' version; this is perhaps even likely to be the case. Either way, it is not a problem that would in any serious way affect the conclusions in this book considering that the type and number of sources that I use are so varied and so great.

There are also other published sources that have been helpful to me when writing this book. For example, the very extensive diaries of the *Gau* leader of Berlin and later Propaganda Minister, Joseph Goebbels. These are now available almost in their entirety courtesy of the IfZ; the only exceptions are the extremely few cases where the glass plate negatives (on which the diaries had been photographed) have degenerated over time and become illegible.[22] Goebbels' diaries are,

---

[21] Brechtken, Magnus and Becker, Maximilian, "Die Edition der Reden Adolf Hitlers von 1933 bis 1945," *Vierteljahrshefte für Zeitgeschichte*, Vol. 67, No. 1 (2019), p. 157.

[22] Goebbels, Joseph, *Die Tagebücher von Joseph Goebbels 1924–1945. Im Auftrag des Instituts für Zeitgeschichte und mit Unterstützung des Staatlichen Archivdienstes Rußlands. Herausgegeben von Elke Frölich, Band I–IV & I–XV* (Munich: K. G. Saur, 1987–1995). Henceforth: *TBJG*.

13 / Introduction

however, sometimes very difficult from a source-critical perspective, since he intended to publish at least parts of them. He did so even during his lifetime, and the published version (*Vom Kaiserhof zur Reichskanzlei* from 1933) is indeed a bit different compared to the original entries in the diaries. This means that it is not easy to know what was meant for public consumption and what (if anything) was meant for private use. However, Goebbels sometimes criticizes or disagrees with Hitler in the diaries, thereby showing that he had at least some form of independent mind. These diaries thus prove that Konrad Heiden was wrong in his contemporary judgment of Goebbels when he assumed that he was both the least independent and the most dishonest Nazi in that he never believed in what he was saying publicly.[23] In Heiden's defense, we must remember that he did not have access to Goebbels' diaries when making this assessment. When I make use of Goebbels' diaries, I always try to corroborate, or contrast, their content with other independent sources.

Other leading Nazis have also left diaries and private correspondence behind that have been of great use to me while writing this book. Among these, one ought first and foremost to mention the letters of Rudolf Heß, which were published already in 1987 by his son Wolf Rüdiger Heß and the historian Dirk Bavendamm.[24] The letters cover the period 1908–33, but even though they have been available to historians for a long time – and even though they are filled with interesting information about Hitler, Heß, and the early NSDAP – surprisingly few historians have made use of them. Another important source consists of the diaries of Alfred Rosenberg, which only rather recently became available in their entirety to historians.[25] Rosenberg's diaries are of course problematic, just like the rest of these sources, and the utterances ascribed to Hitler simply cannot be uncritically cited as being correct

---

[23] Heiden, Konrad, *Adolf Hitler: Das Zeitalter der Verantwortungslosigkeit. Eine Biographie*, Vol. I (Zurich: Europa Verlag, 1936), p. 379. It is clear that Heiden interprets Goebbels in this way partly because he wants to make a polemical point against Goebbels. By claiming that Goebbels really was not a convinced National Socialist, Heiden was trying to shame and insult him. In those days, Heiden thought there were political reasons to point out every potential contradiction or embarrassment with regard to the leading Nazis.

[24] *Rudolf Heß. Briefe 1908–1933*. Herausgegeben von Wolf Rüdiger Heß. Mit einer Einführung und Kommentaren von Dirk Bavendamm (Munich: Langen Müller, 1987).

[25] Jürgen Matthäus & Frank Bajohr (Hg.), *Alfred Rosenberg. Die Tagebücher von 1934 bis 1944* (Munich: S. Fischer Verlag, 2015)

14 / Christianity in Hitler's Ideology

and verbatim. Nonetheless, together with other independent sources they offer important insights into Hitler's mind (and of course into the minds of the authors themselves) and his thinking on religious matters.

Then there is, of course, Hitler's own *Mein Kampf*, which is a central source for his religious *Weltanschauung* (worldview) and the role that religious beliefs played in National Socialism. Fortunately, too, since 2016 there has been an edition with commentary by experts, published by the IfZ, and this is the edition that I have made use of.[26] A rather cumbersome problem has been the fact that historians have previously cited so many different versions, translations, and editions of *Mein Kampf*. This has resulted not only in references to many different pages for the same quotes, but also to differences in the wording, since various translators have rendered the text differently not only due to their choice of words, but because the various editions changed the wording in many places. The IfZ volume, however, notes all the various changes in the text in the margin of the book. It also contains a standard for page references by including the original pagination from the first edition of *Mein Kampf*. It is of course true that *Mein Kampf* contains a lot of lies, but this is mostly only a real problem for historians when it comes to the autobiographical details. In the IfZ edition, most of this work has already been done for the reader. But regarding National Socialist ideology, the book is nonetheless a reliable source of Hitler's true views – to spread the ideology was after all the whole intention of the book.

Last, but certainly not least, are the published books and pamphlets, including so-called grey literature written by National Socialist ideologues, which serve as important primary source material in this book.[27] While the primary source material that I have relied on for this book to a large extent consists of these published sources, I have also made use of documents from German, British, American, and French archives (both public and private). With regard to citations of secondary literature, I have only cited that which can be corroborated

---

[26] Hitler, Adolf, *Hitler, Mein Kampf: Eine kritische Edition, Band I & II. Herausgegeben von Christian Hartmann, Thomas Vordermayer, Othmar Plöckinger, und Roman Töppel* (Munich: Institut für Zeitgeschichte, 2016). Henceforth: *Hitler, Mein Kampf* ...

[27] The term "grey literature" denotes material published outside of traditional publishing channels.

15 / Introduction

by trustworthy sources. Sometimes, I have cited a source secondhand via scholarly literature, but then I have always made sure to mention this in the footnotes. As far as has been possible, I have always checked that information contained in the literature is correct and reliable. Consequently, I have often ended up correcting the previous research on this topic.

An otherwise commonly used collection of sources that I do not use that much at all are the abovementioned so-called Hitler table talks. This is likely to surprise, and perhaps upset, many readers that are at least a little familiar with these sources, which up until very recently were thought to be extremely reliable renditions of conversations that Hitler held in private in his wartime military headquarters. All historians that have written about Hitler, National Socialism, or the Third Reich have cited the table talks frequently and uncritically. The reason for why I do not use them – with only a few exceptions, and then only when their content can be corroborated by independent sources – is, as mentioned above, their very problematic nature and reliability. The English and French translations should never be used, since they are highly corrupted compared to the German texts and contain forged utterances. As I have shown elsewhere, the table talks are *not* verbatim transcripts of Hitler's statements but carefully edited notes made from memory by several different people after the fact. They also contain statements that Hitler cannot have made. In the few cases when we have access to parallel independent notes, historians should cite *both* versions, so that the differences between them are revealed to the reader. The table talk notes were proofread and edited before they attained their final form; moreover, the originals are no longer available to us, and therefore we do not know what they looked like.[28] The published table talks exist in two different versions based on two distinct German manuscripts (that only partly overlap in time and content), originally published as *Hitlers Tischgespräche im Führerhauptquartier 1941–1942* in 1951 and *Monologe im Führerhauptquartier 1941–1944* in 1980.[29]

---

[28] For this, see Nilsson, M., *Hitler Redux* ...

[29] Picker, Henry, *Hitlers Tischgespräche im Führerhauptquartier 1941–42. Im Auftrage des Deutschen Instituts für Geschichte der nationalsozialistischen Zeit geordnet, eingeleitet und veröffentlicht von Gerhard Ritter* (Bonn: Athenäum Verlag, 1951); *Monologe im Führerhauptquartier 1941–1944: Die Aufzeichnungen Heinrich Heims herausgegeben von*

16 / Christianity in Hitler's Ideology

I have also opted, as far as possible, to cite from literature and sources in their original language, which in this case often means either German or English (but I have also used French and Italian literature). The only exception to this rule is when books have originally been published in English and then been translated to another language (e.g. German, French, or Polish); this exception has been made so as to always try to cite and translate the original wording and language. This is to avoid translation in several steps, that is, to not translate someone else's translation. All translations are my own, unless otherwise stated. This also includes quotes from *Mein Kampf*, even though they have been translated several times into English before. However, these translations are not always exact; either way, no translation is definite and should ever be treated as an authority on how to translate a certain passage. Translators must often take certain liberties with a text in order for it to flow well and to be idiomatic in the new language.

The German historian Ludolf Herbst has correctly observed that what historians can conclude without a doubt is that from 1925 onward the NSDAP in its propaganda cultivated an image of Hitler as a savior-leader appointed by God. However, at the moment we do not have access to the kind of sources that could tell us with any degree of confidence how successful this propaganda was on the German population.[30] This book, therefore, is not trying to give an answer to that question, but instead focuses on Hitler's personal religious faith; how he portrayed this faith in his speeches, his writings, and his private conversations; how the NSDAP propaganda used this

---

Werner Jochmann (Hamburg: Albrecht Knaus, 1980). Before *Monologe* was published in 1980, two other translations of the same manuscript had been published. First, a French edition in two volumes, which came out in 1952 and 1954, respectively, and thereafter the most famous English translation in 1953: Genoud, F., *Libres propos sur la Guerre et la Paix*, ... (Vol. I); Hitler, Adolf, *Hitler's Table Talk 1941–1944, with an introductory essay on the mind of Adolf Hitler by H. R. Trevor-Roper* (London: Weidenfeld & Nicolson, 1953); Genoud, François, *Libres propos sur la Guerre et la Paix: Recueillis sur l'ordre de Martin Bormann. Préface de Robert d'Harcourt de l'Academie française. Version française de François Genoud*, Vol. II (Paris: Flammarion, 1954).

[30] Herbst, Ludolf, *Hitlers Charisma: Die Erfindung eines deutschen Messias* (Frankfurt am Main: S. Fischer Verlag, 2010), p. 270.

17 / Introduction

religious symbolism to convey its message; and how Hitler's closest entourage viewed him in this respect.

The sources show that Hitler interpreted all major events – not only in his own life, but in history generally – in religious terms as being a result of God's intervention in human history. But that is not all. There are, in fact, good reasons to believe that Hitler's morals and ethics, and his views on race, were grounded in his conviction that these were all ordained by God and manifested in the laws of the universe. This is also something that has thus far been almost entirely ignored in the mainstream literature on Hitler and National Socialism,[31] although Michael Burleigh touches upon it when he notes that Hitler's race laws were "revealed by God and in turn invested with sacred properties."[32] In fact, National Socialist morals and ethics are usually, if they are addressed at all, portrayed as a consequence of their racism, which is most often tied to a purported idolizing of science and cold social Darwinist rationality,[33] rather than the other way around – that is, that Hitler's racism was a consequence of his ethics and morality, which in turn followed from his religious beliefs. Hitler was an outspoken enemy of scientific reason and rationality, and was of the opinion that if science should ever contradict National Socialist ideology, then it was science that would have to give way, not the other way around.[34] Without a proper understanding of Hitler's religious beliefs, we simply cannot fully understand why he used morally laden terms such as "racial shaming" (*Rassenschande*) and "sin against the blood" (*Blutsünde*) when condemning miscegenation.

---

[31] For some of the few studies devoted to this topic, see Bialas, Wolfgang and Fritze, Lothar, *Nazi Ideology and Ethics* (Newcastle upon Tyne: Cambridge Scholars Publishing, 2014); Bialas, Wolfgang, "The Eternal Voice of the Blood: Racial Science and Nazi Ethics," in Anton Weiss-Wendt and Rory Yeomans (eds.), *Racial Science in Hitler's New Europe 1938–1945* (Lincoln, NE: University of Nebraska Press, 2013).

[32] Burleigh, Michael, *The Third Reich: A New History* (New York: Hill and Wang, 2000), p. 13.

[33] See, e.g., Weikart, Richard, *From Darwin to Hitler: Evolutionary Ethics, Eugenics and Racism in Germany* (Houndmills, UK: Palgrave Macmillan, 2004).

[34] See, e.g., *Hitler, Mein Kampf* ... (Band II), pp. 1161–1165 [98–100]. The bold type refers to the page numbers in the original first edition.

18 / Christianity in Hitler's Ideology

Previous Research

It will come as no surprise that a lot has been written in both English and German, since the end of the war, on Hitler's religiosity and his attitude toward Christianity, as well as the relationship between the Nazi regime and the Christian churches generally. Despite this, not many of these books give a good overview of the research on the topic. Moreover, it is not all that common to see references to this scholarship in the mainstream and best-selling biographies of Hitler; his religiosity simply does not seem to have been taken seriously by these authors. It is not only that older works like Friedrich Heer's *Das Glaube des Adolf Hitler* from 1968 and Ernst Klee's *"Die SA Jesu Christi"* from 1989 remain almost unknown, it is also that newer and very interesting research such as Richard Steigmann-Gall's *The Holy Reich* from 2003 and Derek Hastings' *Catholicism and the Roots of Nazism* from 2009 only rarely appear in the mainstream and popular general literature on Hitler, National Socialism, and the Third Reich.[35]

One scholar who does not engage with this research at all is Peter Longerich, who in the introduction to his Hitler biography talks about how Hitler did not manage to implement "his radical anti-church policies."[36] One could therefore get the impression that Longerich would delve deep into this issue later on in the book, but even though he includes a chapter with the title "Church Struggle and Cultural Politics," only eleven pages are dedicated to Hitler's attitude toward religion. None of the books mentioned above, nor any other newer scholarly works on the same topic are included by Longerich. Kevin Spicer's research on Catholic priests who were Nazi sympathizers is not brought up; Michael Phayer's scholarship is not included; the important books by Doris L. Bergen and Susannah Heschel are not referred to either. Instead, Longerich chooses to cite research from the 1980s and even the 1970s (and then only if this scholarship supports his

---

[35] Heer, Friedrich, *Der Glaube des Adolf Hitler: Anatomie einer politischen Religiosität* (Munich: Bechtle Verlag, 1968); Klee, Ernst, *"Die SA Jesu Christi": Die Kirche im Banne Hitlers* (Frankfurt am Main: Fischer, 1989); Steigmann-Gall, Richard, *The Holy Reich: Nazi Conceptions of Christianity, 1919–1945* (Cambridge: Cambridge University Press, 2003); Hastings, Derek, *Catholicism and the Roots of Nazism: Religious Identity and National Socialism* (Oxford: Oxford University Press, 2010).

[36] Longerich, Peter, *Hitler: Biographie* (Munich: Siedler, 2015), p. 12.

19 / Introduction

conclusions), which is really before the critical studies in this field were published.[37]

Still, although all good Hitler biographies address some of the religious connections, even the explicitly Christian, no one has thus far treated them as a major explanatory factor. This is the case even though Sir Ian Kershaw in a shorter biography analyzed Hitler using Max Weber's concept of the "charismatic leader," which is tremendously apt for understanding Hitler in religious terms. Concepts like these are simply often used without a deeper analysis of their meaning. It is as if they still do not have a fundamental role to play in the authors' narratives. How are we to understand this phenomenon? I believe that there are several explanations for why the religious aspect is not to a significant degree emphasized in the big best-selling biographies. First, it could be that this aspect is generally not understood as being important enough to warrant attention. Second, I suspect that many historians have a certain psychological opposition to ascribe to religious beliefs any responsibility for this extremely violent and negative part of modern European history. Possibly, this is also why there has been clear resistance to taking the religious, and quasi-religious, elements of National Socialism and its various expressions (mass rallies, rituals, myths, etc.) seriously.[38]

Hannah Arendt remarked on the religious component in National Socialism already in 1951 in her famous book *The Origins of Totalitarianism* in connection to what she called the "tribal nationalism" in the pan-Germanic movement in Germany. Arendt was among the first to point out that at the basis of National Socialism "lies a veritable theology" and that this "kind of fanaticism does not simply

---

[37] Ibid., pp. 501–507, 520–523; for the references, see pp. 1117–1121. The fact is that Hitler's cultural policies are treated just as off-handedly by Longerich, who only devotes twelve pages to the topic. Several of the latest books on the matter – such as Jonathan Petropoulos' *Artists under Hitler: Collaboration and Survival in Nazi Germany* (New Haven, CT: Yale University Press, 2014), Wolfgang Ruppert's *Künstler im Nationalsozialismus: Die "deutsche Kunst," die Kunstpolitik und die Berliner Kunsthochschule* (Cologne: Böhlau Verlag, 2015), and Hans Sarkowicz's *Hitlers Künstler: Die Kultur im Dienst des Nationalsozialismus* (Frankfurt am Main: Insel Verlag, 2004) – are missing.

[38] For a discussion of this topic, see Steigmann-Gall, Richard, "Was National Socialism a Political Religion or a Religious Politics?" in Michael Geyer and Hartmut Lehmann (eds.), *Religion und Nation, Nation und Religion: Beiträge zu einer unbewältigten Geschichte* (Göttingen: Wallstein Verlag, 2004), pp. 395, 401–405.

20 / Christianity in Hitler's Ideology

abuse religious language" but made evident a deeply felt religious conviction that the German people and nation had been chosen by God to achieve greatness. This is, however, one of the least noticed aspects of Arendt's analysis of National Socialism. But Arendt did not care a lot about, or spend a lot of time on, analyzing the religious basis for National Socialism's ethics. The fact is that she insisted that the horror of the SS concentration and death camps, just as the Holocaust, essentially built on "the nihilistic principle that "everything is permitted" and, significantly, possible. She insisted that National Socialism strove toward "creating a society in which the nihilistic banality" degraded human morals and ethics to such a degree that it turned people psychologically into zombies.[39] Arendt was not alone in drawing this conclusion. In his famous lectures from 1964, Erich Voegelin argued that Nazism caused a moral collapse in Germany.[40] Arendt went even further than that and declared that National Socialism was a "radical evil" and that its foundations were therefore the very opposite of morality.[41] It is easy to understand why they would come to this conclusion, but that does not mean that they were correct.

In fact, the question of Hitler's religious beliefs, which includes his idolizing of Jesus, and the religious basis for National Socialist ethics and morality is absolutely central if we wish to understand Hitler in particular and National Socialism in general. This goes also for the ultimate crime of National Socialism: the Holocaust. Even though it may be provocative to even imply that the Holocaust grew out of ethical principles grounded in an absolute morality, namely God, which were based on the religious beliefs of Hitler and other Nazi leaders, we cannot as historians refrain from asking such questions and, when warranted by the available sources, from making such statements. The intention is not to offend anyone, but to shed light on this horrific period of our common history and to, hopefully, contribute to the

---

[39] Arendt, Hannah, *The Origins of Totalitarianism*, new ed. with added prefaces (New York: Harcourt Brace Jovanovich, 1973, originally published in 1951), pp. 227–243, 459, quotes on pp. 233, 440, 459.

[40] Clemens, Detlev and Purcell, Brendan (eds.) and (trans.), *The Collected Works of Erich Voegelin*, Vol. XXXI: *Hitler and the Germans* (Columbia, MI: University of Missouri Press, 1999), p. 156.

[41] Arendt, H., *The Origins . . .* , p. 459.

21 / Introduction

efforts of preventing history from repeating itself through similar genocidal acts. As this book is being written, the war in Ukraine is still raging, once again showing that Europe has not yet escaped its history of atrocities and genocidal violence.

The Religious Roots of Hitler's Racist Antisemitism

Götz Aly argues in a recent study that the "modern" secular antisemitism (the start of which he ascribes to around 1880, the year that the word "antisemitism" was invented in Germany by Wilhelm Marr) was based in "theories" about race and was therefore substantially different from the much older religious version. This is obviously true. But then he also includes another, rather contradictory, explanation, namely, that modern antisemitism was based on greed and resentment, that is, envy of Jewish success in society and in the economy. Religion was only used as a cover for this hatred, he concludes. The secular antisemitism instead gathered its strength from social and economic problems, and this is what gave it its enormous destructive power. He also reasons that the combination of democracy and nationalism resulted in increased antisemitism, and that this can be explained by assuming that it was only in the modern industrial society that the "stranger" in the shape of the wandering "trader" (*Händler*) became a problem (as if xenophobia has not been a serious problem all through human history). Aly says that the modern antisemites very often referred to socioeconomic tensions and very seldom used explicitly racial arguments in their critique of the Jews.[42]

But this dichotomy between a secular and a religious, between a modern and traditional, antisemitism does not stand up to scrutiny. Certainly, socioeconomic arguments for oppressing the Jews were important throughout Europe and in Nazi Germany too, yet no one would even imagine trying to argue that racism was not central to the Nazis' hatred of the Jews. Racial ideas about Jewish inferiority were at the core of Nazi propaganda against the Jews, and the voluminous research on National Socialism and the Holocaust has in painstaking

---

[42] Aly, Götz, *Europa gegen die Juden 1880–1945* (Frankfurt am Main: S. Fischer, 2017), pp. 20–21, 346–365.

22 / Christianity in Hitler's Ideology

detail showed this to be a fact.[43] The so-called Jewish Question in Nazi Germany to a large extent was a question related to the view that the Jews were another race that had to be removed.[44] Christopher R. Browning also highlights the centrality of racial hatred against the Jews in the events leading up to, and during, the Holocaust in his seminal *The Origins of the Final Solution*.[45] Aly's statements are therefore very hard to comprehend, and one is tempted to interpret them as a mistaken emphasis on his part.

How racial antisemitism is not much more important than greed and resentment for explaining modern antisemitism is also never explained by Aly. Moreover, one still cannot possibly understand modern antisemitism without reference to the more than 1,000-year-old roots of Christian theological antisemitism. It is a fact that *all* the ideas about the Jews that were brought forth by the modern racial antisemites had existed in some form already within the religious antisemitism at least since the Middle Ages. Many historians have shown this, of course, but Saul Friedländer makes this point very well in the first volume of his *Nazi Germany and the Jews*, where he points to the significance of the continuing importance of traditional Christian antisemitism.[46] Strangely, this is exactly the very thing that Aly argues was *not* very prominent, that is, racial antisemitism.[47] Frankly, in the light of all the research on antisemitism and the Holocaust, Aly's conclusion that racism played a very small role is absurd.

So is the imaginary discontinuity between Christian religious anti-Judaism and racial antisemitism. Even the idea of the Jews as a separate race whose blood was foreign and threatened to infect non-Jews (i.e. miscegenation) if the latter intermingled with the Jews was

---

[43] See, e.g., Herf, Jeffrey, *The Jewish Enemy: Nazi Propaganda during World War II and the Holocaust* (Cambridge, MA: The Belknap Press of Harvard University Press, 2006), pp. 6–49.

[44] This too has been documented in thousands of studies. For a summary, see, e.g., Kershaw, Ian, *Hitler, the Germans, and the Final Solution* (New Haven, CT: Yale University Press, 2008), pp. 210–234.

[45] Browning, Christopher R., *The Origins of the Final Solution: The Evolution of Nazi Jewish Policy, September 1939–March 1942*, with contributions by Jürgen Matthäus (Lincoln, NE: University of Nebraska Press, 2004), pp. 25–35, 169–193.

[46] Friedländer, Saul, *Nazi Germany and the Jews*, Vol. I: *The Years of Persecution, 1933–1939* (New York: Harper Perennial, 1997), pp. 73–112.

[47] For this argument, see Aly, G., *Europa gegen die Juden . . .*, p. 365.

23 / Introduction

already hundreds of years old by 1933. One obvious proof of this is the doctrine within Spanish Catholicism of *limpezia de sangre* (purity of blood) back in the 1400s.[48] This melting together of theological and racial/ethnic antisemitism was evident already in the patristic era, says New Testament scholar Adele Reinhartz. These writers thought that the Jews were "by their nature evil, and their rejection/killing of Christ is evidence of that evil nature."[49] Moreover, nationalism and democracy did not create anything new, but at most amplified the antisemitic resentment and hatred that was already prevalent and pervasive in society. At the same time, Aly is right when he points out that the Holocaust cannot be understood by only focusing on Germany and German antisemitism. Civilians and military, state, and local governmental administrative structures in all the occupied countries assisted (to varying degrees from country to country) in the destruction of European Jewry during the war, and this rested upon a very long tradition of antisemitism and hatred of Jews.

According to Susannah Heschel, there is:

> a growing number of scholars who no longer find the distinction between theological anti-Judaism and antisemitism to be helpful, particularly when studying the German Christian Movement of the Third Reich.[50]

Moreover, she adds:

> I do not know when the effort to distinguish between anti-Judaism and antisemitism arose. I have encountered the distinction almost exclusively in the writings of theologians, rather than historians, and I wonder if it came into use during the post-World War II era in connection with studies attempting to disclaim Christian responsibility for Nazi antisemitism and the

---

[48] Carroll, James, *Constantine's Sword: The Church and the Jews. A History* (Boston, MA: Houghton Mifflin Company, 2001), pp. 343–362.

[49] Quoted in Heschel, Susannah, "Historiography of Antisemitism versus Anti-Judaism: A Response to Robert Morgan," *Journal for the Study of the New Testament*, Vol. 33, No. 3 (2011), p. 260.

[50] Ibid., p. 258.

24 / Christianity in Hitler's Ideology

Holocaust. General historians seem to agree that "antisemitism" is the acceptable term.[51]

It is important to keep these things in mind when we study the Holocaust. Daniel Jonah Goldhagen was right in focusing on Christian antisemitism as an enormously important factor in this catastrophe, but he was wrong when he argued that there was a specifically German eliminationist antisemitism, that is, a German *Sonderweg* argument. Furthermore, he did not to a necessary degree make it clear in his book that there were both collaborators and resistors in the German population, as well as bystanders, and that it was not at all a fact that all, or even most, Germans wanted to murder their Jewish neighbors.[52] Goldhagen could only reach this conclusion by essentially ignoring the Holocaust in the rest of Europe and all the volunteers that participated in the looting and murdering. German antisemitism, and the Holocaust, was obviously part of a much broader European historical context at the same time as specifically German components were involved, one of the most important, arguably, being Hitler himself, the individual that led the NSDAP and one of the main originators and initiators of the Holocaust.

It is therefore of utmost importance that we understand Hitler and his ideological influences if we are to completely understand the Holocaust, because Hitler was both a product and a creator of the necessary factors that led to the establishment of the Third Reich, the Second World War, and the Holocaust. National Socialism as an ideology must of course also take center stage, and even in this aspect Hitler is completely indispensable since he was one of the most important intellectuals within the movement. Hitler was a man animated by ideas and ideology, and we must make sure we take these ideas seriously if we want to understand the horrific crime syndicate that was the Nazi state, which he created and built. Historians must therefore analyze Hitler's ideology very carefully and not make the mistake, which was very common even long after the end of the war, of not taking him at his

---

[51] Ibid., p. 258 n2. For the same point, see p. 263. Anti-Judaism is, in this view, simply a term for antisemitism dressed in theological language.

[52] Goldhagen, Daniel Jonah, *Hitler's Willing Executioners: Ordinary Germans and the Holocaust* (New York: Alfred A. Knopf, 1996).

25 / Introduction

word – except, of course, when we should not, but those occasions are fortunately rather easy to tease out and separate from the rest. To categorically and without further reflection dismiss his words as mere propaganda and rhetoric would be a horrible mistake. This book thus addresses a part of Hitler's ideology and belief system that has so far been almost completely ignored by historians analyzing the Third Reich and the Holocaust: Hitler's religious ideas, especially about the role and nature of Jesus, and what role they played in his *Weltanschauung*.

National Socialist Morals and Ethics: Secular or Religious in Origin?

When taking on such a controversial subject, it is vital that we keep the following wisdom of the German theologian Rainer Bucher in mind: when studying "Hitler's theology," we cannot only include in this category such ideas about God that we agree on and share. In the case of Hitler, however, we are not dealing with the academic discipline of theology but instead with theology in the meaning "ideas about God," explicitly "conversations about God" (*Rede von Gott*).[53] Bucher published the book *Hitlers Theologie* in 2008, and it is a stringent analysis and presentation (the best ever made, I would argue) of the theological content of Hitler's religious beliefs.[54] The book is therefore too recent for it to have had time to become a classic in the field. But not even Richard Weikart, who published his book *Hitler's Religion* in 2016, gives Bucher any more than a short reference in his

---

[53] Bucher, Rainer, "Hitlers Theologie? Einige Voraussetzungen," in Lucia Scherzberg (ed.), *Theologie und Vergangenheitsbewältigung: Eine kritische Bestandsaufnahme im interdiziplinären Vergleich* (Munich: Ferdinand Schöningh, 2005), pp. 71–72. See also Bucher, Rainer, *Hitlers Theologie* (Würzburg: Echter Verlag, 2008), pp. 32–34.

[54] Bucher, R., *Hitlers Theologie*. The English translation (by Rebecca Pohl) published by Continuum in 2011 was given the title *Hitler's Theology: A Study in Political Religion*, which is a bit misleading since Bucher expressly states that his book is *not* about applying Eric Voegelin's concept of "political religion" on either National Socialism or Hitler's own faith (see Bucher, R., *Hitlers Theologie*, p. 31). Michael Rißmann argues that Hitler's way of governing went far beyond Voegelin's definition of political religion; see Rißmann, Michael, *Hitlers Gott: Vorsehungsglaube und Sendungsbewusstsein des deutschen Diktators* (Zurich: Pendo, 2001), pp. 194–195. For Rißmann's discussion of the concept, see ibid., pp. 191–197.

26 / Christianity in Hitler's Ideology

endnotes.[55] This is possibly because Bucher's serious analysis contradicts many of the central points in Weikart's conclusion.

The question of Hitler's religiosity continues to be an issue that constitutes a major problem for historians that study the dictator and the movement that he led. The absolute majority of them have wished to see Hitler as a secular phenomenon in the same sense that Alan Bullock did in *Hitler: A Study of Tyranny*, where Hitler is said to have been a rational materialist. This is a conclusion that is astonishing, considering how often Hitler condemned materialism, which he thought was the basis for so-called Judeo-Bolshevism. This view is also paralleled by the idea that National Socialism was antireligious.

This way of approaching these issues disregards the essential aspects and properties of Hitler's and of National Socialism's religiosity, according to historian Richard Landes. He argues that there are four basic types of counterarguments to looking at Hitler and National Socialism in that way: (1) they are entirely viewed as secular phenomena that do not even allow for the suggestion that they had a religious dimension, (2) some view National Socialism as something that replaced Christianity but deny that there were connections between them or that Nazism had any religious content, (3) some admit that many Christians did become devout followers of National Socialism but at the same time claim emphatically that this enthusiasm was not returned by Nazism, and (4) a few historians can see that National Socialism contained some Christian aspects, but they do not connect this to the millenarian dimension of this religion.[56]

It has also often been pointed out that Hitler harbored a deep resentment toward organized Christianity and that he, and other leading Nazis, spoke about wanting to crush the churches and that the Church was the most heinous organization imaginable. National

---

[55] Weikart, Richard, *Hitler's Religion: The Twisted Beliefs that Drove the Third Reich* (Washington, DC: Regnery History, 2016), p. 309. Weikart is an Evangelical Christian, and this is apparent throughout his book in several places, not least in the fact that he writes "He" instead of "he" when referring to Jesus in the third person singular (ibid., pp. 80–83). It seems as if Weikart considers it blasphemous not to use a capital "H" in this case. One could therefore perhaps question whether Weikart is capable of remaining sufficiently objective in his analysis of Hitler's relationship to Jesus.

[56] Landes, Richard, *Heaven on Earth: The Varieties of the Millennial Experience* (Oxford: Oxford University Press, 2011), pp. 365–367.

27 / Introduction

Socialism and the Church were forever diametrically opposed to each other, Hitler supposedly said. However, Hitler did also say, as late as 1937, that the time had not yet come for a struggle against the Church. The fact that attacks against the churches continued often had to do with the fact that the NSDAP grassroots often initiated them. This hatred originated in the Nazi idea of organized Christianity as a Jewish religion that poisoned the minds of the German people. But on the other hand, Hitler also stated that as far as the Christian hostility toward the Jews was concerned, he was 100 percent Christian. Even Richard J. Evans admits that both Hitler's and Goebbels' religiosity kept some elements of Christianity, although they mixed it up with many other eccentric elements. The fact that National Socialism lacked a plan for what would happen to the churches after the Nazi victory, as well as the fact that Hitler did not let the heathens of the NSDAP develop an intricate religious liturgy and practice, is also not denied by these historians. Many Nazis in fact dreamed about the establishment of an all-German church under one Reich bishop.[57]

In the preface of the new edition of his Hitler biography, Joachim Fest describes the danger in, and the insufficiency of, describing Hitler as a maniac lacking in moral and ideological principles who is only obsessed with power, as so many previous biographies had done. Hitler, wrote Fest, and the system that he represented and established, can only be understood if we realize and accept that Hitler was guided by an ideological conviction characterized by a will and desire to go to the very end in order to make this conviction a reality.[58] The question one must then ask is what characterizes such an ideology and the kind of people who are willing to go to any length in order to reach the goals they have set up for themselves and the world? The answer is, I believe, that the only thing that could achieve this result is a conviction built on a religious ideology – that is, an ideology whose basis is in principle, if

---

[57] Fischer, Klaus P., *Nazi Germany: A New History* (London: Constable, 1995), pp. 358–360; Bullock, Alan, *Hitler: A Study in Tyranny* (London: Odhams Press Limited, 1952), pp. 207, 616; Kershaw, Ian, *Hitler 1936–45: Nemesis* (London: Allen Lane, 2000), pp. 39–40, 130, 235, 424, 428–429, 449; Kershaw, Ian, *Hitler 1889–1936: Hubris* (New York: W. W. Norton & Company, 1998), pp. 435, 582, 562; Evans, Richard J., *The Third Reich in Power 1933–1939* (London: Allen Lane, 2005), p. 249; Speer, Albert, *Inside the Third Reich: Memoirs by Albert Speer* (London: Weidenfeld and Nicolson, 1970), pp. 95, 123.

[58] Fest, J., *Hitler . . .*, pp. vi–vii.

28 / Christianity in Hitler's Ideology

not directly, assumed to be given by God. The doctrinal content of such an ideology is the central point here: the idea that there is an ultimate truth that never can be, and is not allowed to be, questioned and that morality is not something that develops through a series of explicit or implicit negotiations and discussions between members of societies over time through history, but rather a doctrine that is just as immutable as the laws of nature that humans have to abide by no matter what the consequences are. Claudia Koonz has formulated this point in the following way:

> The Final Solution did not develop as evil incarnate but rather as the dark side of ethnic righteousness. Conscience, originally seen to protect the integrity of the individual from the inhumane demands of the group, in the Third Reich became a means of underwriting the attack by the strong against the weak. To Germans caught up in a simulacrum of high moral purpose, purification of racial aliens became a difficult but necessary duty. ... In offering the faithful a vision of sanctified life in the *Volk*, it [the Nazi ideology] resembled a religion. Its condemnation of egotism and celebration of self-denial had much in common with ethical postulates elsewhere.[59]

Fest also touches upon the same point when he writes that the German people, having been caught up in the chaos of the interwar period, longed for a "faith" to hang their hopes for the future on, and in this longing there was a propensity for "grandiose liturgy" and an expectation "to overcome the dreary, materialist circumstances" that resulted in massive support for National Socialism and gave the latter a "quasi-religious, Adventist aura and that provided a sort of Messianic expectation on Hitler."[60] Koonz draws the conclusion that ethnic fundamentalism brings politics and religion together "within a crusade to defend values and authentic traditions that appear to be endangered." In times that many people think are characterized by moral depravity, political leaders that appear to represent moral values of a bygone era tend to be

---

[59] Koonz, Claudia, *The Nazi Conscience* (Cambridge, MA: The Belknap Press of Harvard University Press, 2003), p. 273.

[60] Fest, J., *Hitler* ... , pp. iv–vi.

seen "as beacons of moral rectitude in a sea of sin."[61] This, too, thus stands in sharp contrast to Aly's flawed conclusions.

National Socialism and Hitler's person united this longing and expectation with the ruthlessness and unrepentant attitude of a religious truth, a doctrine that demands complete obedience and dedication but whose origin remains hidden to the faithful believer and that for precisely that reason is so effective and has such a powerful attraction to the individual. The leader who represents this doctrine, who has received the Gospel of Truth and transmits and nurtures it here on earth, is transformed from a human being of flesh and blood into a representative of a higher power whose word becomes law and whose law is written in stone.

The larger purpose of this book, beyond studying Hitler's relationship to Jesus, is to argue that we must understand the National Socialist movement and its revolution not as "quasi-religious," as Fest and others have put it, but as an ideology that was religious to its core. Only by making this argument can we hope to understand how so many people, not only in Germany, could be so gripped by the urge to implement the most radical and, for all intents and purposes, insane ideas that they were ready and willing to throw all their previous moral and ethical principles aside for a higher aim that they had never seen or even been close to.

Ideology, especially one formulated in such a form, is, as Steven Pinker has pointed out, one of the transcendent factors that can get humans to walk over mountains of corpses to reach the promised Utopia at the end of the rainbow.[62] The role of ideology is also something that has been frequently discussed with regard to Hitler and how we explain his actions psychologically. I adhere to the now almost completely dominant interpretation that ideology is central to understanding Hitler and National Socialism as a mass movement. The ideological explanation of Hitler as a convinced National Socialist was established already in 1947 by British historian Hugh Trevor-Roper in the book *The Last Days of Hitler*.[63] Against this idea stood for many years Trevor-Roper's rival Alan Bullock, who had published

---

[61] Koonz, C., *The Nazi Conscience*, p. 274.

[62] Pinker, Steven, *The Better Angels of Our Nature: The Decline of Violence in History and Its Causes* (London: Allen Lane, 2011), pp. 556–570.

[63] Trevor-Roper, H. R., *The Last Days* ...

30 / Christianity in Hitler's Ideology

his hugely influential biography *Hitler: A Study of Tyranny* in 1952 and who instead argued that Hitler was basically a cynic who just did and said anything to gain power.[64] This view was no doubt highly indebted to Hermann Rauschning's ideas expressed in *Die Revolution des Nihilismus* (The Nihilist Revolution).[65] Eberhard Jäckel has sharply criticized the absurd conclusion that National Socialism and Hitler lacked an ideological goal and purpose.[66] Bullock later changed his view and became convinced that Hitler was indeed honest in his Jew-hating rhetoric, that is, he was ideologically convinced that what he was saying was true. This is what Bullock said in an interview with the historian Ron Rosenbaum in the late 1990s:

> I changed my mind about Hitler in that I originally took him as solely interested in power. ... I now think the ideology *is* central. I think it's what armors Hitler against remorse, guilt, anything. Hitler was unmovable on this ideology, this belief that he was a man sent by providence.[67]

Note what Bullock says in the end of the last sentence regarding Hitler believing he was sent by Providence. Amazingly, Bullock never made much of this insight, and most historians have not done so either, as we have already seen.

[64] These two historians' positions are well described in Rosenbaum, Ron, *Explaining Hitler: The Search for the Origins of His Evil* (London: Papermac, 1999), pp. 63–96.

[65] Rauschning, Hermann, *Die Revolution des Nihilismus: Kulisse und Werklichkeit im Dritten Reich* (Zurich: Europa Verlag, 1938), passim. Rauschning's thesis is that National Socialism was a nihilist ideology, a revolution without a doctrine, as he formulates it. The only thing that mattered was the lust for power. Everything else was a sideshow, even the worldview of the ideology (how could it have been an ideology if it had no content?) was supposedly a sideshow. The last chapter in the book is called "The Tendency to Maximize Reign and Power" (ibid., pp. 451–495). Ironically, Trevor-Roper also pushes the nihilist argument in his book. He claims not only that Speer was a nihilist, but also that the party also showed such features. He even refers to Rauschning when speaking of Hitler's purported nihilism. However, he did not do it as often or thoroughly as Rauschning, and perhaps that is why it seems to have been forgotten (Trevor-Roper, H. R., *The Last Days ...*, pp. 78, 85–87). The issue of whether such a will to power is compatible with nihilism is a question that was left unanswered by both Rauschning and Trevor-Roper. This has been noted by others too; see Schreiber, Gerhard, *Hitler. Interpretationen 1923–1983: Ergebnisse, Methoden und Probleme der Forschung* (Darmstadt: Wissenschaftliche Buchgesellschaft, 1984), pp. 147–148.

[66] Jäckel, Eberhard, *Hitlers Weltanschauung: Entwurf einer Herrschaft*, new revised ed. (Stuttgart: Deutsche Verlags-Anstalt, 1991), pp. 14–19.

[67] Quoted in Rosenbaum, R., *Explaining Hitler ...*, p. 89.

31 / Introduction

In Bullock's realization lies the key to understanding Hitler and National Socialism. It was only by being convinced that they were on a divine mission that the Nazis were able to orchestrate the single greatest genocidal event in world history thus far. Anyone who really believes that he is acting out God's will on earth – that he is the material and spiritual instrument of God – will naturally feel justified in any action he feels is necessary to ensure that God's plan for humankind is realized. History has provided us with far too many examples of this for us to doubt the truth of this statement. In the following chapters, I present a case for the argument that Hitler and the National Socialists were convinced their actions were divinely ordained and that Hitler's admiration for, and belief in, Jesus was a central aspect of the actions.

Historians such as Michael Burleigh have, as has already been noted, begun to explore the religious dimensions of National Socialism, remarking for instance that Nazi ideology "was politics as a biological mission, but conceived in a religious way." The laws of race that Hitler followed were, Burleigh correctly writes, "revealed by God and in turn invested with sacred properties."[68] But as Richard Steigmann-Gall has pointed out, Burleigh has not drawn out the full implications of this insight either. Steigmann-Gall has suggested, in an argument that anticipated my own, that National Socialism should perhaps be viewed as "a politics with a religious dimension" rather than the opposite, as most "political religion" theorists have thus far done. Steigmann-Gall has also noted that "Hitler unequivocally wished to cast Nazism as a religious politics rather than a political religion" and that "the religious ideology in question would be Christian" of sorts. He goes on to argue that Hitler's professed belief in a God, or Providence as he often called it, who actively intervened in the world; the references to himself as a true Christian; and even statements expressing a deep admiration for Jesus as an Aryan warrior against the Jews should all be taken seriously by scholars of National Socialism. "However much Hitler claimed to be an enemy of organized religion, this conception of Jesus displayed a clear limit to his apostasy and the retention of a specifically Christian dimension to his beliefs," summarizes Steigmann-Gall.[69] I believe that this is ultimately the correct way to view National Socialism.

[68] Burleigh, M., *The Third Reich* ... , p. 13.
[69] Steigmann-Gall, R., "Was National Socialism a Political Religion ... ," pp. 395, 401–405.

1 CHRIST ON THE CROOKED CROSS, PART I
Jesus as an Aryan, Antisemitic Warrior

1.1 Introduction

When establishing the importance of Jesus for Hitler, it is necessary to understand that Hitler expressed his admiration for Jesus with a rather remarkable consistency over time. Many sources show this to be a fact. But it is equally important to understand what characteristics Hitler (and many other antisemites both before and contemporary with him) ascribed to Jesus to properly interpret what role Jesus played within his worldview. These characteristics ascribed to Jesus were also consistent over time. In this chapter, therefore, I will present the background to the development of this view, which Hitler did not originate, to set the stage for the rest of the book.

1.2 Like a Foolish Man Who Built His House on Sand

Friedrich Tomberg has somewhat contradictorily claimed that while Hitler strove to "in a way" eradicate Christianity from history and replace the mainstream Christian view of Jesus with one where the latter had been transformed into an Aryan, Hitler also at the same time explicitly claimed that the NSDAP continued in "Jesus' footsteps" with the intention of finally achieving the aim that Jesus had originally set for himself and the world.[1] I write "contradictorily" because it is hard to

---

[1] Tomberg, F., *Das Christentum* ... , pp. 14, 115.

33 / Christ on the Crooked Cross, Part I

understand why Hitler would have had any interest at all in turning Jesus the Jew into Jesus the Aryan if his intention was to eradicate Christianity. Viewing this as a propaganda trick designed to win over millions of Christian voters to the side of National Socialism does not hold water. If that was Hitler's intention, then it would of course have been much easier, and less time-consuming, to simply adopt a mainstream Christian understanding of Jesus as a tool for getting away with that trick. The fact that Hitler had a divergent view of what Christianity really was, and of who Jesus was, and that National Socialism spent so much time and energy on trying to spread this view shows us that we should at least consider taking these claims seriously. Tomberg's investigation is also flawed in the sense that he uses only a small fraction of the available modern scholarship about Hitler and National Socialism's relationship to Christianity. This means that his conclusions are often dubious and untrustworthy.

In his book, Tomberg further undermines his own arguments by explicitly stating that he does not intend to show "what actually happened." The book is instead intended to be a philosophical and literary interpretation, and he says that it is up to the historians to show whether the view that he presents is commensurate with reality.[2] This attitude is also evident in the way that Tomberg treats his sources, which is almost completely void of source criticism, and the critical methods that he does apply are flawed and invalid. For example, he refers to *Tischgespräche* without mentioning that the quality of this source had not been established at the time.[3] He uses Rauschning's *Gespräche mit Hitler* (Conversations with Hitler) from 1940, even though he admits that historians do not think they are genuine; he apparently thinks that he can cite this source anyway because he "corroborates" what Rauschning says using "other" sources (it is unclear which sources he is referring to).[4] Moreover, he refers to the so-called Bormann dictations (Tomberg is referring to *Hitlers politisches Testament*, or *The Testament of Adolf Hitler*), which are said to be continuations of the conversations in *Tischgespräche*, quoting them extensively, even though he has already noted that historians have

---

[2] Ibid., p. 17. [3] Ibid., p. 64. The quality of this source has only recently been established.
[4] Ibid., p. 31.

34 / Christianity in Hitler's Ideology

doubted the veracity of this source too (I have since proven that these notes are forgeries).[5] On another occasion, he cites Hitler based on Dietrich Eckart's book *Der Bolschevismus von Moses bis Lenin* (Bolshevism from Moses to Lenin) without mentioning that this is a fictional conversation fabricated by Eckart.[6] We therefore cannot look to Tomberg to get a reliable description of Hitler's ideas about Jesus and Christianity.

1.3 The Long Tradition of Christian Socialism and Jesus Worship in National Socialism

The idea of Jesus as a fighter and champion for National Socialist ideals and principles was not something that Hitler or the NSDAP concocted. It in fact had a long tradition within German Christian conservative circles already by 1920. A central figure in the early development of this line of thought was the Protestant pastor and politician Friedrich Naumann (1860–1919). He had become very influenced by the court chaplain Adolf Stoecker (1878–1918), the founder of the antisemitic Christian Social Workers' Party (*Christlich-Soziale Arbeiterpartei*), in the early 1880s and his approach to addressing the so-called social question, which was the bourgeois retort to Marxism. The social question was about how to manage social relations in the age of industrialism in a way that would counter the Social Democratic agitation of the day. The solution was to offer an alternative based on an ethical, and explicitly antimaterialist, Christian ideology. It was a purposeful effort to hijack the term "Socialism" and to redefine it in a way that suited a right-wing political agenda. Albrecht Tyrell notes that Naumann explicitly considered himself to be a socialist on the right.[7]

Naumann was explicitly mentioned as a forerunner of National Socialism in NSDAP ideologue Rudolf Jung's book *Der nationale*

---

[5] Ibid., p. 71. For it being a forgery, see Nilsson, M., *Hitler Redux* ... , pp. 279–339.

[6] Tomberg, F., *Das Christentum* ... , p. 21.

[7] Tyrell, Albrecht, *Vom "Trommler" zum "Führer": Der Wandel von Hitlers Selbstverständnis zwischen 1919 und 1924 und die Entwicklung der NSDAP* (Munich: Wilhelm Fink Verlag, 1975), pp. 18–19; Kedar, A., "National Socialism before Nazism ...," pp. 26–27. Naumann is cited and translated by Kedar.

35 / Christ on the Crooked Cross, Part I

Sozialismus from 1922.[8] Jung was a Sudeten German refugee from Bohemia and a member of the Austrian parliament representing the *Deutsche Arbeiterpartei* (DAP – German Workers' Party), which was formed in 1910 and renamed the *Deutsche Nationalsozialistischen Arbeiterpartei* (DNSAP – German National Socialist Workers' Party) in 1918. It is Jung who has been credited with being the one who suggested to Hitler to include "National Socialist" in the party's name. Hitler, on the other hand, apparently had the more combative "Social Revolutionary Party" in mind originally.[9] But the term "revolutionary" did not suit the taste of Anton Drexler, founder of the DAP, which was the party Hitler would later lead.[10] After the creation of Czechoslovakia in the wake of the breakup of the Austro-Hungarian double monarchy after the First World War, the DNSAP set up one branch office in Vienna led by Walter Riehl and one in the Sudetenland under Jung. It makes sense to think that Jung and the DNSAP were the inspirational sources for the creation of the new name NSDAP because it occurred shortly after the Munich National Socialists in the DAP/DNSAP had

---

[8] Jung, Rudolf, *Der nationale Sozialismus: seine Grundlagen, sein Werdegang und seine Ziele*, 3rd ed. (Munich: Deutscher Volksverlag, Dr. E. Boepple, 1922), p. 66. This was a rewritten version (more than doubled in size) of a work that Jung had published in 1919 under the title *Der nationale Sozialismus: eine Erläuterung seiner Grundlagen und Ziele* (Tyrell, A., *Vom "Trommler"* . . . , p. 250 n266). Jung obviously felt he had to expand on his book after Hitler had become the leader of the NSDAP and once a party program was available.

[9] Kuehnelt-Leddin, Erik R. von, "The Bohemian Background of German National Socialism: The D.A.P., D.N.S.A.P., and N.S.D.A.P.," *Journal of the History of Ideas*, Vol. 9, No. 3 (1948), p. 356. One could of course be skeptical about this information, which is based on an article by Konrad Heiden from 1933 and which seems rather anecdotal. It is also not mentioned in the main biographies of Hitler, although it is mentioned in Heiden's biography from 1936 of course (Heiden, K., *Hitler* . . . [Vol. I], pp. 125–126). But it was apparently corroborated by Nazi lawyer, NSDAP member, and propagandist Hans Fabricius (from 1933 onward the personal adjutant to Reich Minister of the Interior, Wilhelm Frick) in his book *Geschichte der nationalsozialistischen Bewegung* in 1937 (pp. 125–126, n72). Tyrell does not mention this in his otherwise very diligent work, and neither do Joachim Fest, Ian Kershaw, Peter Longerich, Volker Ullrich, or Thomas Weber. Sven Felix Kellerhoff does refer to this, however, but he does not mention Jung specifically and bases the information on Heiden (Kellerhoff, Sven Felix, *Die NSDAP: Eine Partei und ihre Mitglieder* [Stuttgart: Klett-Cotta, 2017], p. 49).

[10] Heiden, K., *Hitler* . . . (Vol. I), p. 126. Toland tells another tale, according to which Drexler had suggested the name "German National Socialist Workers' Party" already at the founding meeting of the DAP in January 1919, but that the meeting objected that "the word 'socialist' might be misinterpreted" (Toland, John, *Adolf Hitler* [New York: Doubleday & Company, 1976], pp. 85–86).

36 / Christianity in Hitler's Ideology

visited Salzburg for a joint international National Socialist meeting. Add to this the fact that the DNSAP had begun using the swastika in May 1918, a symbol that the NSDAP also started using after the name change.[11]

It may not be a coincidence that Jung rewrote history in his book, the third edition of which he dedicated to "Adolf Hitler and his own," and claimed that the party that had been founded on January 5, 1919, was not the German Workers' Party (DAP) but the National Socialist German Workers' Party (NSDAP).[12] Jung visited Hitler in the Landsberg fortress[13] (in Landsberg am Lech) on April 5, 1924, and was in fact among the people that spent the longest time speaking to Hitler (they spoke for one hour). This tells us that Jung was certainly

---

[11] Bullock, A., *Hitler* ... , pp. 59–60. Interestingly, we do not know exactly how the NSDAP came to appropriate the swastika or even when they used it for the first time. The swastika was not an all-that-uncommon symbol within *völkisch* circles, however, and it was also used by the Munich-based *Thule Gesellschaft* (Thule Society). But it does not seem as if *Thule Gesellschaft* was the main inspiration after all, since they then ought to have adopted it much earlier (after all, DAP cofounder Karl Harrer was a member of this society). Kershaw states that the NSDAP started to use the swastika in mid-1920, which would mean that it occurred simultaneously with the change of name. Strangely, Kershaw accepts Hitler's claim in *Mein Kampf* that the latter designed the new party emblem (Kershaw, I., *Hitler 1889–1936* ... , p. 147). It makes sense that Hitler would be too narcissistic and too stubbornly proud to ever admit that it was plagiarized from the DNSAP. The first known leaflet from the NSDAP (although the police report still referred to the party as the DAP), printed sometime before April 12, 1920, did *not* contain a swastika, and neither did the prior invitation to the Hitler and Dingfelder evening at the Hofbräuhaus on February 24, 1920. An NSDAP admission slip from December 1920 does not contain this symbol either. Not even an NSDAP membership book from 1921 had the swastika on it. The certificate of debt for the purchase of the *Völkischer Beobachter* in December 1920, however, *does* contain the swastika (a row of swastikas frame the document), and on January 5, 1921, the newly founded local NSDAP group in Esslingen (completely on their own accord, it seems) used it too on a leaflet (I want to thank Sven Felix Kellerhoff for sharing his deep knowledge of this topic with me, as well as some pictures of early NSDAP documents from various German archives [in an email dated August 15, 2021]). Regarding the Esslinger Ortsgruppe, see Kellerhoff, S. F., *Die NSDAP* ... , p. 56. It appears therefore that the adoption occurred *after* the name change but that the usage of the swastika, much like the usage of the new name NSDAP, was rather unorganized and perhaps even a bit spontaneous. This is yet another subject, it would seem, that Hitler lied about in *Mein Kampf*.

[12] Jung, R., *Der nationale Sozialismus* ... , p. 70. Jung committed suicide in Prague in 1945.

[13] The term "fortress" does not signify a particular form of fortification but rather a particular form of incarceration for those convicted of the crime of high treason (Weber, T., *Becoming Hitler* ... , p. 307).

37 / Christ on the Crooked Cross, Part I

a central person in the NSDAP at this time.[14] After the visit, Jung wrote a newspaper article in which he compared Hitler to none other than Jesus.[15] This is even more interesting when we consider the fact that Jung celebrated Jesus in *Der nationale Sozialismus*. Jung stated that "one of the most important demands of the National Socialist doctrines" was the "moral renewal of our people" and the "development of its religious life according to the German spirit." Jesus was portrayed as standing in total contradiction to the Jews, and Jung stressed that Jesus had condemned the Jewish God Jahveh as being Satan, referring to John 8:44, where Jesus says to the Pharisees: "You belong to your father, the Devil" (NIV). He also remarked that Jesus had not founded a church or a cast of priests, and proclaimed that the "centralism" within "the Roman and Bible-believing Lutheran Church is the explicitly Jewish trait in church Christianity."[16] Another one of the Austrian DNSAP's leading figures that saw Hitler as a Christ-like leader was one of its cofounders, Walter Riehl, who also was a sort of ideological inspiration for Hitler after Eckart's death. Riehl thought of himself as a John the Baptist whose task it was to prepare the way for "Hitler the Savior."[17]

Although he was an antisemite, Stoecker (Naumann's inspiration) did not go as far as to claim that Jesus was not a Jew. He could accept Jesus' Jewishness, because he was not a racial antisemite. He was against the Jews because of their rejection of Jesus and viewed the struggle against the Jews in spiritual and not racial terms

---

[14] Fleischmann, Peter, *Hitler als Häftling in Landsberg am Lech 1923/24: Der Gefangenen-Personalakt Hitler nebst weiteren Quellen aus der Schutzhaft-, Untersuchungshaft-, und Festungshaftanstalt* (Neustadt: Verlag PH. C. W. Schmidt, 2015), pp. 44, 55, 251. Othmar Plöckinger writes that Jung visited Hitler also in January 1924 while Hitler was still in jail awaiting trial, but no documentation of that visit has been found (Plöckinger, Othmar, *Geschichte eines Buches: Adolf Hitlers "Mein Kampf" 1922–1945. Eine Veröffentlichung des Instituts für Zeitgeschichte*, 2nd updated ed. (Munich: Oldenburg Verlag, 2011), p. 32; Fleischmann, P., *Hitler als Häftling . . .* , pp. 35, 244). In 1936, a Social Democratic anti-Nazi pamphlet by Alexander Stein called "Adolf Hitler: Schüler der Weisen von Zion" ("Adolf Hitler, a Student of the Elders of Zion") claimed that it was Jung rather than Eckart that had turned Hitler into a rabid antisemite (Heer, F., *Der Glaude des Adolf Hitler . . .* , p. 303). The point here is not whether this is true or not, but that Jung was seen as important enough by people in the 1930s for this to possibly be true.
[15] Longerich, P., *Hitler . . .* , p. 140.   [16] Jung, R., *Der nationale Sozialismus . . .* , pp. 86–87.
[17] Pyta, Wolfram, *Hitler: Der Künstler als Politiker und Feldherr. Eine Herrschaftanalyse* (Munich: Siedler Verlag, 2015), pp. 116–117.

38 / Christianity in Hitler's Ideology

(this view was common also among Hitler's closest supporters, which was why people such as his benefactor, Elsa Bruckmann, simultaneously had Jewish friends and saved some of them from being murdered in the Holocaust).[18] He feared that those who saw this issue in purely racial terms ran the risk of reaching for hate and brutality, which would hurt Christians more than the Jews. There were several strands of thought about Jesus circulating within the German theological and philosophical spheres already during the 1870s and 1880s. Both Johann Gottlieb Fichte (1762–1814) and Friedrich Hegel (1770–1831) considered it impossible that Jesus was a Jew – Hegel because of how he understood Jesus' teachings and Fichte because of his ideas about Jesus' character, or *Wesen*. The antisemitic theologian and philosopher Bruno Bauer (1809–82) argued in the 1840s that Jesus was not a Jew but of Hellenistic descent. Ernest Renan (1823–92) had argued in *Leben Jesu* (The Life of Jesus) in 1863 that Jesus, whose racial descent he thought impossible to establish, had been a revolutionary who had fought against the Jews. The orientalist, philologist, and theologian Paul de Lagarde (1827–91) posited that Jesus was in total opposition to, and the contradiction of, everything Jewish; Jesus was not to be considered Jewish but as the Son of God. Lagarde also emphasized the "masculine" Jesus. Then, perhaps most notably in this context, Richard Wagner (1813–83) and his son-in-law Houston Stewart Chamberlain (1855–1927) both argued that Jesus was not a Jew.[19]

Nonetheless, when the world's first international antisemitic congress was held in Dresden, Germany, in September 1882, Stoecker was one of the attendees. The Vatican's own journal, *Civiltà Cattolica*, reported approvingly that "many violent speeches had been made denouncing the Jews." Stoecker had presented several resolutions to

---

[18] Weber, T., *Becoming Hitler . . .*, pp. 174–176.

[19] Fenske, Wolfgang, *Wie Jesus zum "Arier" wurde: Auswirkungen der Entjudaisierung Christi im 19. und zu Beginn des 20. Jahrhunderts* (Darmstadt: Wissenschaftliche Buchgesellschaft, 2005), pp. 72–73, 81–86, 105–110, 130. Another author who emphasized the masculinity of Jesus and saw him as having a privileged relationship with the white race was Jack London. He built his image of Jesus on his readings of Friedrich Nietzsche, Ernst Haeckel, Herbert Spencer, and Thomas Huxley. London also illustrates well how widespread these ideas were in the early twentieth century. See Bembridge, Steven, "Jesus as a Cultural Weapon in the Work of Jack London," *Studies in American Naturalism*, Vol. 10, No. 1 (2015), pp. 22–40.

39 / Christ on the Crooked Cross, Part I

the congress that, according to the journal, were "relatively moderate," all of which had been approved by the other delegates. The Jews were considered a people that could never be assimilated into any national society, and the emancipation of the Jews "had been a 'fatal mistake' and new restrictive legislation was urgently needed."[20]

1.4 Right-Wing Socialism: Anti-Marxist, Christian, Antisemitic, and Nationalistic

The bourgeois-liberal National Socialism of Naumann and the extreme-right National Socialism of Theodor Fritsch (1852–1933), whose real name was Thomas Frey, sprang from an ethical-conservative tradition that became prominent after German unification in 1871. It was a conservative socialism visible already in the writings of the economist Carl Rodbertus-Jagetzow in the mid-1800s. In 1872, a group of leading Protestant conservative intellectuals had founded the Association for Social Policy (*Verein für Sozialpolitik*). They soon came to be referred to as *Katedersozialisten* ("socialists of the lectern"). While it originally was a derogatory term applied by their opponents, it soon came to a term proudly self-applied by the group. The *Katedersozialisten* were absolutely not left-wingers, and they were not Marxists. They defined themselves by their absolute rejection of Marxist Socialism and laissez-faire liberalism alike. Stoecker became involved with the Association, and in 1877 the Protestant-conservative Central Association for Social Reform (*Centralverein für Sozialreform*) was formed, an organization that also published the journal *Der Staatssozialist* (*The State Socialist*). A year later, Stoecker formed his party, which was characterized by a strong antisemitism. This was a socialism on the right, a socialism not rooted in Marxism, that was not concerned with correcting perceived social injustices through progressive politics and social reforms, but that was instead intended to "preserve an ontologically conceived ethical-holistic social order" in Germany. These were right-wing conservatives who happily self-applied the term "socialist." National Socialists like Naumann and

---

[20] Kertzer, David I., *The Popes against the Jews: The Vatican's Role in the Rise of Modern Anti-Semitism* (New York: Alfred A. Knopf, 2001), p. 142.

40 / Christianity in Hitler's Ideology

Stoecker passionately opposed not only the materialist (and in their view Jewish) Marxist Socialism, but also liberalism in both its economic and philosophical forms. Materialism constituted nothing less than a direct denial of the existence of God.[21] Stoecker was mentioned with respect in the Nazi ideologue Rudolf von Sebottendorff's (his real name was Adam Glauer) 1933 book *Bevor Hitler kam* (Before Hitler Came).[22] It was therefore a socialism that was completely different both in origin and content from the Marxist Socialism of the left that we normally think of when we hear the term today.

The National Socialism of the NSDAP was also influenced by the wave of right-wing "anti-capitalist" thought that emerged within the *völkisch* movement from the late 1880s and early 1890s. In 1889–1890, older groups of antisemites who opposed both "Jewish Marxism" and "Jewish capitalism" began using the term "German Socialism" (*Deutscher Sozialismus*) in their defense of lower-middle-class and bourgeois interests to get people of the lower and middle classes of the population to join the Antisemitic People's Party (*Antisemitische Volkspartei*), renamed as the German Reform Party in 1893 (*Deutsche Reformpartei*), and the German Social Party (*Deutsch-Soziale Partei*). The term "German Socialism" signified "a moderate, conservative, and middle-class antisemitism, which originated in an anti-Liberal or Christian orthodox standpoint and whose aims were the limitation of the civil rights of Jews as well as economic and social reforms to the benefit of small businesses and small farmers." It combined extreme or ultranationalism and racial antisemitism with a particular form of emotional, rather than rational, anti-capitalism that was *not* a refutation of capitalism as such but only a certain aspect of it, which was claimed to be the Jewish "unproductive" international finance capital. Marxist Socialism was seen as a corruption of true German Socialism, and the German sociologist Oswald Spengler (1880–1936) argued in the pamphlet *Preußentum und Sozialismus* (Prussianism and Socialism) in 1919 that socialism had to be liberated from Marx. It was this Socialism

---

[21] Kedar, A., "National Socialism before Nazism ...," pp. 9–10, 19–21, 28; Fenske, W., *Wie Jesus zum "Arier" wurde ...* , p. 96.

[22] Sebottendorff, Rudolf von, *Bevor Hitler kam: Urkundliches aus der Frühzeit der nationalsozialistischen Bewegung* (Munich: Deukula-Verlag Graffinger & Co., 1933), p. 30.

41 / Christ on the Crooked Cross, Part I

that DAP party founder and leader Anton Drexler embraced, agitated for, and included in the NSDAP party program of February 24, 1920.[23] In fact, contrary to popular belief, instead of nationalizing key industries the National Socialists started a massive privatization drive once they came into power. They even reprivatized entities that had been nationalized prior to 1933. The Hitler regime pioneered privatization in a time when the governments in the West were nationalizing.[24]

What all National Socialisms had in common was their understanding of the nation as the central and only relevant social unit. It was the nation that was the object of all economic, political, and social activity, and it was therefore also the nation – which was seen as an organic entity – that was the object of all ethical considerations. What this meant was that all actions were evaluated based on whether they benefited the nation, and *not* the people that made up the nation. The nation was an organism and was not simply the sum of its constituent parts. The nation was simultaneously theologized, and Stoecker argued that every nation (or *Volk*) was "endowed by God with a singular disposition, with special gifts, and that it must hold on to these peculiarities, for they belong to the essence of its existence." Liberalism, Stoecker argued, had atomized the *Volk*. The individualism entailed in the liberal worldview was rejected completely by the National Socialists. Liberalism had destroyed Germany, it had led to the *Kulturkampf* against the churches and religion, and this individualism was to be replaced by a total subordination of the individual to the will of the nation and by a pious willingness to sacrifice oneself for that nation.[25] God and country became one and the same in this view.

The similarities aside, there were certainly also differences between National Socialists like Naumann and Stoecker on the one hand and Hitler and the NSDAP on the other. There were differences between the former two as well, even though they had started out as ideological friends. Stoecker was more focused on nationalism, while

---

[23] Tyrell, A., *Vom "Trommler"* ..., pp. 19–21.
[24] Bel, Germà, "Against the Mainstream: Nazi privatization in 1930s Germany," *The Economic History Review*, Vol. 63, No. 1 (2010), pp. 34–55.
[25] Kedar, A., "National Socialism before Nazism ...," pp. 11–13.

42 / Christianity in Hitler's Ideology

Naumann, although still a fervent nationalist, was more focused on the Christian social agenda. Stoecker was more conservative and less concerned with the issue of social reform. Naumann was less hostile toward Social Democracy than Stoecker and instead more negative toward the large landowners. They also differed in that Naumann thought that social reformism would eventually gain traction in the bourgeois political parties, even (or even especially) in the Conservative Party. It was also Stoecker's conservatism that would lead to the break between him and Naumann.[26] Hitler could be seen as having combined traits reminiscent of both Naumann's and Stoecker's Christianity-inspired National Socialism. He was certainly very concerned with social reform at the same time as he regarded nationalism to be of central importance. But Hitler was not a conservative, although he was part of an ideological heritage that grew out of conservative circles – he was a revolutionary right-wing ultranationalistic socialist. Conservatives, in Hitler's view, were reactionaries who did not understand what Germany needed to survive – that is, a thorough rebirth of the nation and (equally) thorough moral reform.[27]

Interestingly, Jung denied that National Socialism was a revolutionary movement and ideology. It was not through violent revolution but through reform that the current private capitalist system should be overturned. Due to its craving for private profits, the current system had become "soulless materialism." It could therefore never be the "spiritual basis" for true Socialism. This was the opposite of what is commonly thought of as Socialism, which was nothing but "Communism of a Marxist type" in Jung's eyes. Both Communism (which included Social Democracy) and the grubbing finance capitalism were the tools of the Jews to enslave the peoples of the world.[28] Jung may of course be

---

[26] Ibid., p. 28.

[27] Hitler's anti-Conservativism slant is perhaps best illustrated by his well-known hatred of the monarchy as both a system and a symbol. Hitler's vendetta against the Habsburg family, whom he saw as a symptom of all that was wrong with the multi-ethnic double monarchy in which he was born and grew up, is perhaps the most obvious example of this (Longo, James, *Hitler and the Habsburgs: The Vendetta Against the Austrian Royals* [New York: Diversion Books, 2018]). Hitler scorned the German Hohenzollern family just as much.

[28] Jung, R., *Der nationale Sozialismus* ... , pp. 104–105, 110–111. Jung also discusses the ideas of Marx and Engels in some detail, which was rather uncommon for National Socialist ideologues (ibid., 106–107).

43 / Christ on the Crooked Cross, Part I

forgiven for not thinking of National Socialism as a revolutionary ideology, because he wrote his book before Mussolini had come to power in Italy in 1922 after the March on Rome. It was only after this point that Hitler realized that this was even a possibility – he was so inspired by Italian Fascism's revolution that he decided to attempt his own in Munich.[29]

1.5 Antisemitism: The Key to Understanding the NSDAP Party Program

Issues frequently derogatorily associated with the Jews, such as the prohibition of usury and land rent, and productive versus unproductive capital and labor, are to be found in the NSDAP party program in points 11, 13, and 17–18. Point 11 demanded the abolition of effortless income. Point 13 demanded the expropriation by the state of "trusts" (*not* of companies in general, which is how this has often been interpreted by those who wish to portray National Socialism as a leftist movement), which were understood as nonproductive concentrations of capital where price-fixing was used to defraud the *Volk*. Point 17 demanded land reform "suited to our national needs," the prohibition on land speculation and land interest, and a law allowing for the expropriation of land that was not used for the benefit of the *Volk*. Point 18 demanded relentless struggle against, and the death penalty for, usurers (*Wucherer*), smugglers, and "lousy criminals against the *Volk*" (*gemeine Volksverbrecher*) "regardless of religion or race." Indeed, the entire program can only be understood correctly within the Christian, ultranationalist, and antisemitic historical context described above. This connection was made explicitly by Jung in *Der nationale Sozialismus*, in which he claimed that the persecution of the Jews in Germany during the Middle Ages was not due to religious differences but to the Jewish activity of usury through land rent and interest on loans. The trusts were just the

---

[29] Hitler's admiration for Mussolini and his modeling of his own political movement upon the latter has been the subject of several books. See, e.g., Wiskemann, Elizabeth, *Rome-Berlin Axis: A History of the Relations between Hitler and Mussolini* (Oxford: Oxford University Press, 1949); Schneider, Wolfgang, *Adolf Hitler: Politischer Zauberlehrling Mussolinis* (Oldenburg: De Gruyter, 2017); Goeschel, Christian, *Mussolini and Hitler: The Forging of the Fascist Alliance* (New Haven, CT: Yale University Press, 2018).

44 / Christianity in Hitler's Ideology

last developmental stage in modern finance capitalism and an expression of "the mammonism" and "the materialism of our time, whose driving force is none other than the Jewish spirit!"[30] The phrase "regardless of religion or race" in point 18 is a testament to that. In fact, this was explicitly stated by Gottfried Feder in a commentary on this point in 1933.[31] The words "Jew" and "Jewish" get only a single mention, in points 4 and 24, respectively, in the entire program, but it was *precisely because* the rest of the program was almost entirely aimed against the Jews, and understood as such by those whom the NSDAP wished to attract to the then highly exclusive party (remember that this was before it was decided to make it into a popular mass party in order to win election) that the authors of the program here had to make explicitly clear that this applied to everyone and not only the Jews.

Later in his book, Jung described the NSDAP desire for "socialization" (*Vergesellschaftung*) in the following way: "We unreservedly advocate for the transfer of all capitalistic large companies [*Großbetriebe*], which effectively are private monopolies, into the hands of the state, land [a body of *völkisch* self-administration], or local community." But in contrast to the Marxist position, said Jung, it was a question of "nationalizing," that is, of "transfer into our people's hands," rather than "socialization." Jung contrasted the National Socialist wish to nationalize only the large private monopolies to the Marxists' wish to socialize *all* private enterprises regardless of their size or nationalistic character. Furthermore, the only companies and areas affected by this nationalizing were those engaged in mining the "treasures of the earth" (*Bodenschätze*) such as "coal [and] waterpower." Everything else was not a target for socialization, wrote Jung. This was combined with the demand that no others than German nationals, a category that explicitly excluded the Jews, could be allowed to own land.[32]

---

[30] Jung, R., *Der nationale Sozialismus . . .* , pp. 25–28, 40.

[31] Koehne, Samuel, "The Racial Yardstick: 'Ethnotheism' and Official Nazi Views on Religion," *German Studies Review*, Vol. 37, No. 3 (2014), p. 588. Feder also mentioned point 23, which demanded that newspapers that spread "lies" and "un-Germanness" should be banned. This shows that this point too was aimed against the Jews, even though it did not mention them.

[32] Jung, R., *Der nationale Sozialismus . . .* , pp. 133–136, 150.

45 / Christ on the Crooked Cross, Part I

It is thus obvious that this demand had to do with making sure that the *Volk* had full control over the natural resources on the territory under its possession. This, in turn, was rooted in the ultranationalism that provided the foundation for National Socialist ideology. It was a way for the Nazis to secure the much-coveted autarchy for Germany. Any attempt to understand the party program without interpreting it through the lens of National Socialism's particular brand of antisemitism will lead to grave misunderstandings of the ideology. The term "nationalization" really meant "Aryanization." It was not the state, that is, the government, that was to own and operate these businesses and assets, but Aryan Germans, who were considered members of the German nation. This is also exactly what happened after 1933. The Jews were of course forced to sell. The expropriation was done by government decree, by law, or through violent harassment, and the property was sold – in actuality, handed out – to private non-Jewish Germans at a fraction of its real value. And because of the corrupt nature of the Nazi regime, it was often party officials that "purchased" the best and most valuable goods and properties. It was government-backed robbery on a massive scale.[33]

As Drexler started working on the party program of the DAP sometime in 1918, he did so to a large extent based on the ideas of Alfred Brunner of the *Deutschsozialistische Partei* (DSP – German Socialist Party), which had been founded the same year, although he was also inspired by Gottfried Feder and Dietrich Eckart. Many of the points in the DAP program are basically copied from Brunner and the DSP, and there was a considerable overlap in membership between the DSP and the DAP (the DSP was dissolved in 1922, and many of its members instead joined the NSDAP). However, there were also points in the DAP/NSDAP program that did not have direct precursors in the DSP program. Points 4–8 were explicitly directed against the Jews and their civil rights. Points 10–11 were implicitly directed against the Jews too in their focus on the demand that every citizen must be engaged in either intellectual or physical productive work, and on the abolition of workless and effortless income. These types of activities and income were considered typical of

---

[33] For a great overview of Aryanization, see Friedländer, S., *Nazi Germany and the Jews*, Vol. I: ... , pp. 232–239, 242–244, 247, 257–261, 280–298, 316–330.

46 / Christianity in Hitler's Ideology

the Jews. Point 14, demanding profit sharing in large companies (*Großbetrieben*), referred to large companies and was certainly not demanding profit sharing for the workers in these companies, but rather for the *Volk* – that is, the nation. The DSP program expressly stated that craftsmen, small businesses, and small industries were exempted. The distinction between the productive and unproductive concentration of capital must be kept in mind here. It is the same distinction as the one made in point 16 in the NSDAP program, that is, the demand for the creation and maintenance of a "healthy middle class" by the communalization of "big department stores" (*Groß-Warenhäuser*). This was also a euphemism for Jewish department stores and the leasing of these spaces at low rents to small traders. The latter was certainly not a demand that any Marxist, that is, leftist, Socialist would ever make. But it made perfect sense within an ultranationalist *Weltanschauung* that made the distinction between productive and unproductive companies and individuals, and that was simultaneously informed by a vitriolic antisemitism that in every case put the Jews in the latter category.[34]

The often somewhat cryptically formulated points in the DAP/NSDAP program are thus often explained by their close relation to the DSP program – the latter was like a hidden matrix on top of which Drexler's program was placed. Gottfried Feder's influence can be seen in point 11, and Dietrich Eckart was obviously the inspiration for point 24 with its demand for religious freedom and for the party to be based on "positive Christianity," parts of it being taken verbatim from him. That Hitler took part in the formulation of the program appears apparent, according to historian Albrecht Tyrell, although the extent of his involvement remains uncertain. It might be that the short and sharp formulations of the program points are due to Hitler's influence.[35]

---

[34] Tyrell, A., *Vom "Trommler"* ... , pp. 76–82; Koehne, Samuel, "Religion in the Early Nazi Milieu: Towards a Greater Understanding of 'Racist Culture'," *Journal of Contemporary History*, Vol. 53, No. 4 (2018), pp. 670–676, 679–683, 688–690. See also *Grundsätzliches Programm der Nationalsozialistischen Deutschen Arbeiter-Partei*, http://jgsaufgab.de/intranet2/geschichte/geschichte/natsoz/programm_nsdap_20.htm.

[35] Tyrell, A., "*Vom Trommler*" ... , pp. 84–85. Konrad Heiden, who wrote already in the mid-1930s, assigns a much larger role to Hitler in the creation of the program. On the other hand, he mistakenly states that the program was only a matter of propaganda for Hitler, i.e., that he did not really believe in the points listed in it (Heiden, K., *Hitler* ... [Vol. I], p. 87).

47 / Christ on the Crooked Cross, Part I

Samuel Koehne has also shown that the NSDAP's two official party program commentaries, one by Alfred Rosenberg from 1923 and one by Gottfried Feder from 1927, confirm that point 24 heavily targeted the Jews and their supposed destructive influence on German morality and the German race. Feder thought "it was obvious that Point 24 was an antisemitic point, as did others who examined the program."[36]

The ground elements of Hitler's and the NSDAP's National Socialism were therefore more or less all present already in Naumann's and Stoecker's Christian National Socialism of the 1880s and 1890s. However, the main impulse for Hitler's antisemitism did not come from Naumann's religiously motivated arguments, but from arguments based in ideas about biological race and culture in the tradition of Wilhelm Marr, Eugen Dühring, and Theodor Fritsch. Marr, a thorough secularist, was the author of one of the foundational texts of modern antisemitism, namely *Der Sieg des Judentums über das Germanenthum* (The Victory of Judaism over Germanism) from 1879. Marr, who was dubbed "the patriarch of antisemitism" by Moshe Zimmerman in a 1986 book, and who has been credited with coining the phrase itself, claimed that the Jews had disguised themselves and that they had "lodged themselves in Germany as a 'state within a state'," an expression literally used by Hitler in *Mein Kampf*, and that their aim was total world domination and the destruction of the German nation. Notably, also, Marr presents the productivist idea about the Jews as a people who shun "real labour." Marr argued that the Jews had by the 1800s almost entirely defeated the Germans, and saw "only one last, desperate 'popular expression' of anti-Jewish struggle: namely, the 'agitation against usury' at a time when 'the poor people [*Volk*] of all estates [*Stände*] remain a victim of the [Jewish] usurers and their ... Germanic helpers'."[37]

This is a formulation that is basically identical to what we find in point 18 of the NSDAP party program; it is almost as if the authors of the program had Marr's text in mind when they formulated the part

---

[36] Koehne, S., "The Racial Yardstick ... ," p. 588.
[37] Kedar, A., "National Socialism before Nazism ... ," pp. 95–99. Quotes and translation by Kedar. For the "a state within the state" quote, see *Hitler, Mein Kampf* ... (Band I), p. 427 [158]. The editors of the critical volume do not note this similarity with Dühring on this occasion, although they do in other places.

48 / Christianity in Hitler's Ideology

about the death penalty for usurers regardless of their religion or race, that is, whether they were Jewish usurers or their treasonous German helpers. In the chapter "The Career of the Jews" in *Mein Kampf*, Hitler made it clear that the Jew never ever worked in society as a "producer" but as a "moneylender," always charging "exorbitant interest," and that the Jew was the inventor of interest as such.[38] This was essentially a comment on the party program's demand for the death penalty against usurers confirming that the reason why it applied to all religions and races was because of the inherent antisemitic content throughout the whole NSDAP program.

1.6 Blending Racial Antisemitism and Christian Productivist Ideology

Another parallel between the National Socialism of Naumann on the one hand and that of Hitler on the other is the focus on "Christian productivism." This was a view that elevated so-called productive work to a status of a "morally sanctioned organizing principle for society," one that viewed society as a dichotomy consisting of "producers" and "nonproducers." The latter were considered "parasites" who lived on the productive work of the former. This view was the centerpiece of the extreme right-wing Theodor Fritsch's *Weltanschauung* as well. It was, in short, something that was characteristic of modern antisemitism in its entirety. Productivism also became a way for Naumann and Fritsch to reject the ethical conservatism of Stoecker. It was consequentially also a main pillar in the National Socialism of Hitler and the NSDAP, and Hitler would write at length about how the Jews were parasites living in the "body" (*Körper*) of other peoples in *Mein Kampf*. Fritsch is of course even more central to this form of National Socialism, since he was not only an ideological inspiration for the Nazis, but also an enthusiastic party member from the 1920s until his death in 1933. Hitler explicitly mentioned the great influence that Fritsch had had on him, especially on his antisemitism.[39]

---

[38] Hitler, *Mein Kampf* ... (Band I), p. 805 [327].
[39] Kedar, A., "National Socialism before Nazism ... ," pp. 29–31, 92–93; *Hitler, Mein Kampf* ... (Band I), pp. 791–793 [322–323].

49 / Christ on the Crooked Cross, Part I

The National Socialists (i.e., right-wing Socialism) were not against private property per se, not if it was used for "honest work" and did not damage the public interest or the national community, Jung explained. With biblical imagery, he described who qualified as "productive" workers. It was not only "the artist, in whom the divine spark glimmers in his soul, the inventor, the far-sighted entrepreneur, the daring merchant" who fell into this category. So did "also the farmer" and "the forester" who worked the soil and forest to earn a living from Mother Earth "in the sweat from his brow." The latter is a line taken directly from the tale in the book of Genesis about original sin and the fall from grace leading to humans being banished from the Garden of Eden. Also "the official, who cares about the well-being of the general public" counted as a "productive" worker, Jung explained.[40] It would of course be rather dim-witted to define matters in such a way that one finds oneself among the unproductive lot.

Fritsch, or Frey, was not a theologian or even a philosopher, but an engineer. However, he founded the publishing house *Hammer Verlag*, which published a lot of antisemitic literature (including the forgery *The Protocols of the Elders of Zion*) as well as the *Deutsch-Soziale Partei* (German Social Party – not to be confused with the *Deutschsozialistische Partei* mentioned above) in 1889. He even sat in the *Reichstag* for a short period in 1924. According to Fritsch, Jesus was an Aryan of Galilean descent whose father had been a Roman soldier, and his whole life was a constant battle against the Jews. Fritsch argued that Christianity "was an Aryan protest against the inhuman spirit of the Jews" and that, contrary to Jewish materialism, (true) Christianity was pure idealism. Fritsch argued that Jesus was a genius (*Genie*) character and that, as such, he could, by definition, not be a Jew. The idea of the "creative genius" had an almost mythological status in racist right-wing circles during this time period, and every great historic personality was interpreted in terms of having been such a genius. This included Hitler as well, whose self-image was to a large degree built upon this concept. This meant that the ideologues who followed

---

[40] Jung, R., *Der nationale Sozialismus . . .* , pp. 90–91.

50 / Christianity in Hitler's Ideology

Fritsch could simply add some pseudoscientific ornamentation to this argument to make it seem like a solid fact.[41]

However, during the mid-1890s Naumann came to abandon his Christian Socialism for a more pronounced National Socialism that replaced the ethical ideal of social reform with a national existentialism that trumped all ethical imperatives, and, simultaneously, his Christian productivism for a nationalist productivism. Naumann's National Socialism now explicitly rejected the idea that private property was to be abolished, yet it took aim at the "abuse of property" and at the immeasurable growth of capital. Here too, it was the concept of productive work that took precedence; capital carried with it interest, and income from interest was not considered productive, since it produced no useful goods. Despite this, Naumann did *not* reject concentration of capital per se, because he explicitly celebrated it when it was combined with great concentration of enterprise, as in the case of big entrepreneurs like Krupp and Stumm. However, when it was the result of "land rent," such as mortgage interest and house rent – and Naumann connected this idea to his antisemitism by explicitly mentioning "Rothschild, Bleichbröder, and company" as examples of interest-accumulating, nonproductive capitalists – then it was anathema. This was nothing other than a form of usury law (*Wuchergesetz* in German), and Naumann claimed that his Christian Social form of "practical anti-capitalism" had been informed by "Conservatives and Antisemites." The prohibition on interest, or income acquired without labor, has a long history in Christianity and was condemned already by Thomas Aquinas, who also threw commercial capital into the same despicable category.[42] This "practical anti-capitalism" was really nothing other than nationalistic capitalist protectionism.

Fritsch was very influenced by Marr when he claimed that the Jews were the source of all the misery of the German people since "they drain the blood of the national body [*Volkskörper*]." However, Fritsch went beyond even Marr when he declared that the Jews were physically

---

[41] Fenske, W., *Wie Jesus zum "Arier" wurde* . . . , pp. 96–97. For the importance of the concept of "genius" for Hitler, see Pyta, W., *Hitler* . . . , pp. 219–260.

[42] Kedar, A., "National Socialism before Nazism . . . ," pp. 25, 28–30, 42. Quotations and translation by Kedar.

51 / Christ on the Crooked Cross, Part I

incapable of bodily labor (the terrible and tragic irony being that the Nazis would enslave the Jews and murder them, to a large extent, through precisely such physical labor in the concentration camp system and, in so doing, prove this assumption wrong in the process, although they no doubt viewed the high death rates among the Jewish slave laborers as a confirmation of Fritsch's idea). They therefore spent their time haggling, trading, and charging exorbitant interest. The Jews possessed a "nomadic nature," claimed Fritsch, and were "cosmopolitan." They were therefore also incapable of nationalist feelings, and consequently a Jew could never be a true German patriot no matter how assimilated he was. In addition, Fritsch was also very much influenced by Eugen Dühring, who claimed that the Jews, whom he accused of being "the most evil manifestation of the entire Semitic race," could not be defined as a religious community but only as a race (this idea was also echoed by Hitler in his letter to Adolf Gemlich on September 16, 1919, the first written evidence we have of Hitler's National Socialist antisemitism, and later in *Mein Kampf*, where he claimed that the Jews were only a race, or a people, and not a religious community, and that they only used religion as a tool to spread as a destructive decease under the guise of religious freedom). Marr had not seen race as being so important and constitutive of the so-called Jewish question as Dühring and, following him, Fritsch did. Dühring introduced the idea that it was racial mixing, not religious intermarriage, that threatened the German people. It was a Manichean worldview characterized by a battle between absolute good and absolute evil, manifested in the flesh as the German and Jewish people, respectively. It is also noteworthy that Dühring, as Hitler later would, also considered established Christianity to be "a spiritual manifestation of the Jewish racial qualities." In Dühring's philosophy, productivism and capital were split up "into healthy ('natural') and pernicious, usurious ('Jewish') forms." Social injustice and class conflict were therefore not structurally embedded in capitalism itself but were the result of seditious Jewish activity.[43] Where the views of the anti-Marxist Dühring and Hitler diverged, however, was in

---

[43] Ibid., pp. 97–102. Quotes and translation by Kedar. See also *Hitler, Mein Kampf . . .* (Band I), pp. 427, 795, 799 [158, 324–325]. See also Lüdicke, Lars, *Hitlers Weltanschauung: Von "Mein Kampf" bis zum "Nero-Befehl"* (Paderborn: Ferdinand Schöningh, 2016), p. 43.

52 / Christianity in Hitler's Ideology

Dühring's rejection of Jesus precisely because he was a Jew.[44] This was in a sense a more logical attitude than the one adhered to by Hitler.

However, the productivist ideology that Hitler and the NSDAP espoused probably cannot be as separated from the religious, or Christian, world of ideas as, for example, Asaf Kedar assumes. It was no doubt also informed by specifically Christian ideas from the New Testament. Kedar also overemphasizes, it seems, the degree to which Dühring's views really were secular in nature. On the face of it, that was certainly true, as he rejected outright any religious foundations for his antisemitism. But it is at the same time equally true that this racial and so-called biological antisemitism contained the very spiritual and religious concepts that Susannah Heschel has pointed to in her book *The Aryan Jesus*, concepts such as blood and spirit, as well as how blood and spirit interacted with each other.[45] The metaphysics in Alfred Rosenberg's *Der Mythos des 20 Jahrhunderts* stated "that race is the image of soul." "Soul means race seen from within. And, conversely," he wrote, "race is the external side of a soul."[46] In this vein, the Berlin pastor Siegfried Nobiling created a creed in 1932 that contained the phrase "We see in the Jews the spiritual and physical poisoning of our race."[47] These ideas were not secular but thoroughly mythological, spiritual, and even outright religious in character. Even Kedar speaks about Dühring's complex of ideas as being "underpinned by a Manichean cosmology that views good and evil as ontological entities" that existed in the world and acted throughout world history – hardly secular concepts and ideas. He also notes that this dynamic was then *retheologized* by Fritsch, who brought back God and Satan into the discussion about the German and Jewish people. He believed that God had created the Jews to torment humanity just as God had created parasites and vermin to do the same, and that it therefore was human-

---

[44] Fenske, W., *Wie Jesus zum "Arier" wurde ...* , p. 87.

[45] Heschel, Susannah, *The Aryan Jesus: Christian Theologians and the Bible in Nazi Germany* (Princeton, NJ: Princeton University Press, 2008), pp. 18–23.

[46] Quoted in Varshizky, Amit, "Alfred Rosenberg: The Nazi *Weltanschauung* as Modern Gnosis," *Politics, Religion & Ideology*, Vol. 13, No. 3 (2012), p. 320.

[47] Heschel, S., "Historiography of Antisemitism ... ," p. 263.

53 / Christ on the Crooked Cross, Part I

ity's mission to trample and destroy the Jews. The Jews were, in his words, "the legitimate heirs of Satan."[48]

1.7 The Aryan Warrior Christ: Christian Racial Theology Meets National Socialism

The fact that the early National Socialists like Naumann, Marr, and Fritsch were believing Christians naturally also meant that their concept of who Jesus was had to be influenced by their ideological development. Naumann, for example, argued that Jesus was "on ethical grounds a radical adversary of capital accumulation" and that the "antimammonistic thrust is characteristic of the entire thought of Jesus." He claimed that when the *Volk* would finally wake up from the fog of materialism, whose spell they were currently under, they would find Jesus. It was indeed morally wrong for anyone to "exploit their brothers through interest and compound interest while they have abundantly enough" and to "hoard treasures on earth even though Jesus has forbidden it." The ethical dimension, and the need for ethical reform, was an important part of both Naumann's and Stoecker's National Socialism, yet both came to repudiate the ethical-conservative side of this early National Socialism.[49] In the book *Jesus als Volksman* from 1894, Naumann claimed that Christ was deeply engraved in the spirit of the German people and argued that he was in fact "German" and a "contemporary" of the German people in Naumann's own time.[50] These parts of Naumann's conception of Jesus to some extent also appear in Hitler's rendition of Jesus, which is perhaps no surprise considering that Hitler was a huge admirer of the extremely antisemitic mayor of Vienna, Karl Lueger, who was also the leader of the Christian Social Party (*Christlich-Soziale Partei*). Hitler would later celebrate Lueger in *Mein Kampf* as perhaps the greatest *German* (although Lueger was of course Austrian) mayor of all time.[51]

---

[48] Kedar, A., "National Socialism before Nazism ... ," pp. 99, 101.

[49] Ibid., pp. 27–28, 30 n30. Quotes and translation by Kedar.

[50] Fenske, W., *Wie Jesus zum "Arier" wurde ...* , pp. 99–100.

[51] *Hitler, Mein Kampf ...* (Band I), p. 207 [55]; Hamann, Brigitte, *Hitlers Wien: Lehrjahre eines Diktators* (Munich: Piper, 1996), pp. 333–336, 393–425. For more on Lueger, see Wladika, M., *Hitlers Vätergeneration ...*, pp. 184–190.

54 / Christianity in Hitler's Ideology

However, Naumann had at least as late as 1891 argued that "racial antisemitism is basically also anti-Christian, and the Christian knows that he cannot conduct a racial struggle on the basis of the Gospel."[52] Naumann also still thought by June 1895 that Socialism should not be based on Darwinism "but is to be clarified, purified, and energized by Jesus Christ." But just a few months later, he shrugged off this view and fully embraced the idea that struggle was "a benign, divinely ordained motor of world history" and that therefore struggle was the key to true progress. He thought it strange that God had created nature on the premise that only he who fights will survive only to then turn around and proclaim that the same principle ought not to apply to humans, human society, and human history. If struggle were to end, Naumann now declared, then world history, culture, and humanity would inevitably come to an end with it. God had blessed struggle, he argued, and stated that Jesus would never demand that Germany destroy its weapons with which it defended its *Volkskörper* and its very existence. It was during the last months of 1895 that Naumann was shedding the last vestiges of his Christian Socialism, turning away from the ethical approach, and instead fully embracing a National Socialism built on the social Darwinist idea of struggle and national existentialism. He also noted that Jesus had *not* told his followers to have no enemies, but instead to love them (this was of course a principle that was not very hard to harmonize with the social Darwinist principle of the struggle for survival – in a way one should be thankful to one's enemy, because it was after all due to the existence of the enemy that historical progress was possible, according to this view). Ironically, Naumann embraced social Darwinism under direct influence from church historian and fellow Christian Rudolf Sohm. Much like Hitler would later do, Sohm criticized the attempts of some political parties to monopolize Christ and declared that "Christ belongs to no political, indeed to no ecclesiastical party." It was at the same time a critique that argued for a secular state and the separation of church and state.[53]

Naumann's new view of the world as a perpetual racial struggle and, concomitant with this change, his new understanding of Jesus had

---

[52] Fenske, W., *Wie Jesus zum "Arier" wurde ...* , p. 101.
[53] Kedar, A., "National Socialism before Nazism ... ," pp. 39–40.

55 / Christ on the Crooked Cross, Part I

some even further consequences. By 1902, after a visit to Palestine and having seen the social situation there, Naumann also abandoned the idea of Jesus as a social reformer and believed that one should not ask Jesus for advice when it came to social and economic issues. He also claimed that wherever a state had made Christianity into official religion this was not in the image of Christ.[54] Whether this change also meant that Naumann began to consider Jesus to have been an Aryan is unknown. Hitler would of course essentially include these very same ideas in chapter 11, "People and Race" (*Volk und Rasse*), of the first volume of *Mein Kampf* in a section under the header "Life Is Struggle" (*Leben ist Kampf*).[55] This idea formed the backbone of Hitler's National Socialism, as well as his religious beliefs, during the rest of his life.

It is precisely the "love your enemy" passage (Matthew 5:43–48) that Eckart comments on in his *Der Bolschewismus von Moses bis Lenin*. In this conversation, it is Eckart who brings the passage up and Hitler that has the role of explaining Jesus' statement to the readers. Hitler is made to say:

> He who is a real enemy, an open one, and therefore much more brutal, him can one also love. One can at least respect him, and that is also what Christ meant. But that we should let into our hearts people who are pure monsters, who could not be stopped from poisoning our body and soul by no amount of love in the world; to suffer that would not even have occurred to Christ in a dream. After all, he does not do so himself. On the contrary, he strikes [back] as hard as he can.[56]

The latter was a reference by Hitler to the often-used story of how Jesus chased the moneylenders out of the temple with his whip in hand.[57]

Hitler would later accuse, for example, the Catholic *Zentrum* party for politicizing religion, and so the Eckart-inspired point 24 in the NSDAP party program, which spoke not only of the party being

---

[54] Gärtner, Sandro, *Die Synthese des Nationalen und des Sozialen bei Friedrich Naumann* (Studienarbeit GRIN, 2001), pp. 6–7.

[55] *Hitler, Mein Kampf* ... (Band I), p. 755 [306].

[56] Quoted in Heer, F., *Der Glaube des Adolf Hitler* ..., p. 205. My translation.

[57] See Matthew 21:12–13; Mark 11:15–18; Luke 19:45–46; John 2:15–16.

56 / Christianity in Hitler's Ideology

founded on "positive Christianity" but also of "freedom of religion," must be understood and interpreted in this light. It could of course be argued that the efforts during the mid-1930s to create a Protestant German state church modeled on the Anglican Church of England contradicts this principle, but the fact that Hitler gave this up when it turned out to be more difficult than he had anticipated suggests that what he had in mind was more a marriage of convenience than of true love. The intention appears to have been to gather all denominations of Protestant Christians under one roof.

But what did the term "positive Christianity" mean? It was, in fact, not a term invented by the National Socialists themselves. It had a longer history within Christianity and "meant[,] according to Protestant terminology of the time, conservative, fundamentalist and nationalistic Protestantism." But this was not the whole story, because the established meaning did not catch the racial element that was so essential in Nazi religiosity. Antisemitism was the main element in National Socialism as a political ideology, and the same was true regarding the movement's Christian faith. Alfred Rosenberg described it as "an extreme anti-Jewish Christianity." The religious freedom that was talked about in point 24 was of course not really a freedom as much as a limitation – it included the caveat that religion was not allowed to offend the law and morality of the *Volk*. Morality was here tied directly to a people's spirit and race, excluding the Jews by definition. But it could also readily be applied against any Christian dogma that went against National Socialist beliefs and ideology.[58]

Hitler shared his view of the conflicts between the various religious confessions in a speech delivered in Munich on September 27, 1923, when he stated that the NSDAP rested upon "the teaching that *Christ* had once proclaimed to the world, *but what type of Christian each individual is, that is up to each and every one.*" In one's home, one may be Catholic or Protestant, but as a politician one must first and foremost be a German, Hitler said. He continued: "We want to be respectful to each other in the conviction that we are all Germans, and we are all the more Christian when we do this."[59] Four years later, in a speech delivered on

---

[58] Koehne, S., "The Racial Yardstick ... ," pp. 580, 582–583, 587.
[59] *SA*, p. 1018 (Document 574).

57 / Christ on the Crooked Cross, Part I

May 24, 1927, Hitler stated that, when the NSDAP did not tolerate any infighting in the party, "we believe that we are acting in accordance with the intention of our most high Lord. We serve Christ more than those who enter election alliances with Marxists, Atheists, and Jews." Hitler was referring to the Catholic parties *Zentrum* and BVP, and he continued to berate them for having voted in ways in the *Reichstag* that made them effective allies of the atheist Marxists.[60]

The idea that all confessions should be able to coexist in the NSDAP was also expressed in point 24 of the party program, where it was also said that the party was founded on "positive Christianity" and that it remained stable over time. For example, Goebbels noted in his diary on February 23, 1937, that the party should not go to war with Christianity and that, instead, the NSDAP should declare themselves to be the only true Christians. Hitler had explained that Christ had also fought against Jewish world domination, Goebbels wrote, but the Jew Paul had corrupted Christ's teachings and had thereby done to Christianity what Marx had done to Socialism. However, this fact could not hinder the NSDAP from being true Socialists.[61] Richard Steigmann-Gall has pointed out that this also implicitly meant that the NSDAP could not allow itself not to be Christians just because Paul had corrupted Jesus' ideas.[62] Goebbels ended this paragraph by writing: "The *Führer* is truly a genius. With the power of a prophet, he gives meaning and content to this age. I am euphoric. May God let us keep him many decades still."[63]

Goebbels expressed the same wish in his eulogy to Hitler on the latter's 52nd birthday on April 20, 1943: "We thus ask a merciful God to keep him in good health for a long time still, and to grant His blessing to his work to free our people from all chains."[64] The same theme was repeated again in Goebbels' birthday eulogy the following year, but

---

[60] *RSA*, II/1, pp. 317–319 (Document 129). See also Weikart, R., *Hitler's Religion . . .* , p. 78.

[61] Goebbels, J., *TBJG*, I/3, p. 55 (February 23, 1937).

[62] Steigmann-Gall, R., *The Holy Reich . . .* , pp. 118–119.

[63] *TBJG*, I/3, p. 55 (February 23, 1937). The particular passage belonged to a part of the manuscript that due to time constraints was not in the actual speech, but it was included in the newspapers' publication of it afterwards.

[64] *GR* II, p. 57 (April 19, 1941). See also ibid., pp. 170, 216 (January 30 and April 19, 1943).

58 / Christianity in Hitler's Ideology

then with added details concerning the God who Goebbels wished should bless Hitler:

> One calls the eternal power that rules over us the Almighty, or God, or Providence, or the loving Father, who – as it says in the final chorus of the Ninth Symphony, must dwell above the starry canopy. We ask this Almighty to keep the *Führer* for us, to give him strength and blessings, to heighten and further his work, and to confirm in us our faith, to give us perseverance in our hearts and strength in our soul, to – albeit after struggle and sacrifice – give our people victory and thereby fulfil the age that we have been able to begin![65]

The symphony that Goebbels was referring to is Beethoven's Ninth, whose final movement, "Ode to Joy," is a celebration of the Christian God. The text was originally a poem written by Friedrich Schiller in 1785, which Beethoven reworked and included in his symphony from 1824. Goebbels even cited the text when he mentioned "the loving Father ... must dwell above the starry canopy," a phrase that in both Schiller's original and in Beethoven's edited version read "above the starry canopy a loving father must dwell."[66] Goebbels here expressed his religiosity and faith in God, a belief that never left him and that remained with him until the end in Berlin in May 1945.

The imperialist-expansionist trait in Hitler's *Weltanschauung* is also visible in Naumann's National Socialism where nationalism became synonymous with the urge to extend Germany's influence over the world. This was just a natural state of things in a world in which God had ordained struggle to be the highest organizing principle for living organisms. This led Naumann to turn the Malthusian angst over rising populations and a nation's ability to feed its people into a positive drive for expansion. The nation with the largest and healthiest population stood a better chance to win the international struggle between

---

[65] Ibid., p. 119 (April 19, 1943).
[66] Goebbels uses the word *guten* about God (or the Father), which is synonymous with the word *lieber* (which also means "dear" or "loved") used by Schiller and Beethoven.

59 / Christ on the Crooked Cross, Part I

nations. Germany needed higher birth rates and "men, men so we can wage war! The masses are decisive in modern war."[67]

The idea that Jesus was in fact not at all a Jew but a Galilean Aryan was advanced by Franz Schrönghamer-Heimdal in a series of five articles entitled "Was Jesus a Jew?" in *Völkischer Beobachter* already in early 1920, soon after he had joined the party. Schrönghamer-Heimdal also considered the Jews to be the literal embodiment of the Antichrist in the form of materialist Judeo-Marxist Bolshevism. Another influential party member that also expressed his admiration for Jesus was Alfred Rosenberg. In his book *Die Spur des Juden im Wandel der Zeiten* (The Track of the Jew through the Ages) from 1920, he argued for a clear separation between the Christ and the Antichrist.[68] The Aryan warrior Jesus of National Socialism, the antisemitic hero, was also presented in great detail in Hans Hauptmann's book *Jesus der Arier* (Jesus the Aryan) from 1930.[69] Hauptmann argued that Jesus was a Galilean and a warrior by nature (*eine Kampfnatur*), but he denied that Jesus was divine. The Jesus that Hauptmann wrote about had not come to establish a new religion but to bring a very old one back to life.[70] The word *Kampfnatur* had in fact been used about Jesus by Hitler in a speech to an NSDAP rally on December 18, 1926, in Munich.[71]

In his book *Der nationale Sozialismus*, Rudolf Jung wrote about Jesus and how he had chased the money changers out of the temple. He also pointed out how Jesus had criticized the Pharisees and quoted the Gospel of John where it said that the Devil was the father of both the Jews and lying and that the Jews were doing their father's

---

[67] Kedar, A., "National Socialism before Nazism ... ," pp. 51–53. Quotes and translation by Kedar.

[68] Hastings, D., *Catholicism and the Roots of Nazism* ... , pp. 56–57, 79–80. Others, including Houston Stewart Chamberlain, had expressed similar ideas earlier than that (ibid., p. 206). See also Kellogg, Michael, *The Russian Roots of Nazism: White Émigrés and the Making of National Socialism 1917–1945* (Cambridge: Cambridge University Press, 2005), pp. 238–242; Gentile, Emilio, *Contro Cesare: Cristianesimo e totalitarismo nell'epoca dei fascism* (Milan: Feltrinelli Editori, 2010), pp. 248–258.

[69] Piper, Ernst, "Steigmann-Gall, *The Holy Reich*," *Journal of Contemporary History*, Vol. 42, No. 1 (2007), p. 50.

[70] Hauptmann, Hans, *Jesus der Arier: Ein Heldenleben* (Munich: Deutscher Volksverlag Dr. E. Boepple, 1930), pp. 5–6, 9–10.

[71] RSA, II/1, pp. 105–106 (Document 59). See also Tomberg, F., *Das Christentum* ... , pp. 125–126.

60 / Christianity in Hitler's Ideology

work. Because Jesus had seen through the Jews and their lies, they had him murdered and crucified. Rather than becoming the Messiah of the Jews, Christ became "the Saviour of the non-Jews." The Jews have hated Christ with a passion to this day, wrote Jung, because the idealism of Jesus – manifested in the practice of sacrificing one's own life for the realization of a higher idea and principle – was unintelligible to them. This was what Jesus had done, and this in and by itself constituted proof that he was not a Jew but of Nordic blood. What managed to keep the Aryans in Christianity, a religion that in reality was against the Aryan nature and that they had no real use for, was precisely the heroic death of Jesus Christ: "This act was spirit of our spirit, blood of our blood."[72] This portrayed Jesus as a clear inspiration for and leader of the Aryans and the National Socialists, and these are the very same ideas that Hitler expressed as well.

"The masculine character of Jesus" was also addressed by Alfred Rosenberg in his book *Der Mythos des 20 Jahrbunderts*. It had been in the interest of the Roman Catholic Church to portray Jesus as characterized by "submissive humility" and to proclaim it an ideal in order to draw followers. "To correct this portrayal is yet another indispensable task for the German movement of renewal," Rosenberg wrote.[73] He continued:

> Jesus appears to us today as a self-confident Lord in the highest and best sense of the word. It is his life that is of importance for the Germanic people, not his suffering death .... The violent preacher and the angry one in the temple; the man who carried away, and whom "they all" followed, not the sacrificial lamb of the Jewish prophesy, not the crucified, is the ideal of today, which shines through to us from the Gospels. And if that does not shine through, then the Gospels too are dead.[74]

Rosenberg stressed that the inner recalibration of the Christian believers to Christ the fighter must also necessarily be accompanied by an

---

[72] Jung, R., *Der nationale Sozialismus* ... , pp. 46–47.
[73] Rosenberg, Alfred, *Der Mythos des 20 Jahrhunderts: Eine Wertung der seelich-geistigen Gestaltenkämpfe unserer Zeit*, 3rd ed. (Munich: Hoheneichen-Verlag, 1934), p. 604.
[74] Ibid.

61 / Christ on the Crooked Cross, Part I

outward harmonization of expressions. A case in point was the Christian crucifix, which manifested the teaching of Christ as a sacrificial lamb. This was an image that could only contribute to making the German people unwilling to face evil head-on. A German church would have to replace the crucified and defeated Jesus with "the teaching fire spirit, represented by heroes in the highest sense." He noted that almost all artists in Europe had painted Jesus as an Aryan – blond and thin – and Raphael's (1513–14) *Sistine Madonna* "showed the blond Jesus 'downright heroic' in the world." This was because "the love of Christ," Rosenberg wrote, "was the love of a man who was aware of his spiritual nobility and his strong personality." This was "Jesus as Lord," according to him: "Jesus sacrificed himself as Lord, not as a slave."[75] This made perfect sense within a context where Jesus had been turned into an Aryan with "Nordic" features, something that was the topic of Franz Wolter's book *Wie sah Christus aus?* (What Did Christ Look Like?) published simultaneously with Rosenberg's *Der Mythos des 20 Jahrhunderts* in 1930. Consequently, in 1937, at the exhibition of *Entartete Kunst* (degenerate art), the regime displayed images of Christ suffering on the cross as examples of images that were banned. This was because "agony and crucifixion were unheroic and thus unsuitable to the Nazi movement," writes Susannah Heschel. Focus was to be on Christ's life and resurrection, not on his death.[76]

Hitler adopted the reinterpreted Jesus that had made him into an Aryan warrior, a glowing example of masculinity who waged holy war on the Jews, who were the offspring of Satan. This demanded some intellectual acrobatics, considering that most of the things that Jesus says and does in the Gospels were not commensurable with National Socialism. But Hitler apparently chose to hold on to the few passages that he felt spoke to him on a more profound level. The advice to turn the other cheek was not among these, however, and this adage was

---

[75] Ibid., pp. 617, 622.
[76] Heschel, Susannah, "Confronting the Past: Post-1945 German Protestant Theology and the Fate of the Jews," in Jonathan Frankel and Ezra Mendelsohn (eds.), *The Protestant-Jewish Conundrum: Studies in Contemporary Jewry*, Vol. XXIV (Oxford: Oxford University Press, 2010), p. 46. "Nordic" was simply just synonymous with "Aryan." Wolter's book was discussed at length by the racial anthropologist Hans F. K. Günther in the journal *Volk und Rasse (People and Race)* in 1932 (ibid., p. 65).

62 / Christianity in Hitler's Ideology

therefore assumed to have been forged by the Jew Paul. Instead, as Hitler told his audience in Augsburg on July 6, 1923, the state was to be built upon "true Christianity" and a true Christian did not simply turn the other cheek like a coward, but instead chose to combat injustice and fight for what was right.[77]

Rosenberg proclaimed that scholarly textual criticism had now come far enough for such a renewal of the New Testament to be feasible. Remarkably, Rosenberg too acknowledged the divine nature of Jesus. It was the Gospel of Mark, he wrote, that likely contained "the real core of the message of the child of God against the Semitic doctrine of the servant of God." The Gospel of John was "the first genial interpretation" of the "experience of the eternal polarity between good and evil against the delusion of the Old Testament" and the Jewish God contained in it. In Mark, where Jesus scolded Peter for calling him the Messiah, there was no trace of "Jesus as the 'fulfiller' of the Jewish idea of the Messiah, whom Matthew and Paul brought to us to the calamity of the entire Western culture," Rosenberg preached. All of this showed, he argued, that "the Pauline churches are thus essentially not Christian, but rather a product of the Jewish-Syrian Apostle activity, such as it was begun by the Jerusalemitic [*jerusalemitisch*] author of the Gospel of Matthew and, independently of him, completed by Paul." Rosenberg then cited several paragraphs from the Pauline epistles to demonstrate the Jewish nature of these texts. To infect the nations and peoples with a theocracy, such was "the Pauline forgery of the great figure of Christ." John, on the other hand, "interpreted Jesus brilliantly, but his realization that he was dealing with an anti-Jewish spirit hostile to the Old Testament had been overgrown by Jewish lore."[78] He continued:

> The "Christian" churches are but a monstrous conscious and unconscious forgery of the simple, joyful news of the Kingdom of Heaven within us, of the child of God [*Gotteskindschaft*], of the service for good and of the flaming defence against evil. In the original Gospel [*Urevangelium*] of Mark we also find the legendary features of the possessed, which we can trace back to

---

[77] *SA*, p. 947 (Document 544, July 6, 1923).
[78] Rosenberg, A., *Der Mythos ...* , pp. 605–607.

63 / Christ on the Crooked Cross, Part I

popular tales as well as the embellishing additions to the adventures of Friedrich the Great and Francisco the Holy, for example, who is said to have preached even to the birds. But original Mark [*Ur-Markus*] is far away from all the raptures in which parts of the Sermon on the Mount exceed one another. To not oppose evil, to give the left cheek when you are hit on the right and so on, these are feminist exacerbations that are not to be found in Mark. These are forged additions by other people. Jesus' entire being was a fiery "oppositionist." Because of this he had to die. … Jesus' religion was undoubtedly the preaching of love. All religiosity is actually primarily a mental excitement that is at least internally related to love. … But to develop a German religious movement, which wants to become a Peoples' Church, one must explain that the ideal of loving one's neighbour is subordinated the teaching of nationalism; that no action may be approved by a German Peoples' Church, which does not first and foremost aim at preserving the people.[79]

Rosenberg is here writing as a theologian just as much as a National Socialist ideologue. The Rosenberg that we meet in the pages of *Der Mythos des 20 Jahrhunderts* is thus far from an atheist hell-bent on destroying Christianity. On the contrary, he thought of himself and the NSDAP as the harbingers of real Christianity. I think it is safe to say that the National Socialists took the claim to represent "true" Christianity in the form of Christ's original teachings seriously.

Derek Hastings observes that the people attending the rallies during the early 1920s were reminded again and again of the fact that Jesus had not come to bring peace but a sword. Hitler and the other leading Nazis were constantly portrayed as heroic Christian fighters representing a party that did not ascribe to a "Christianity of words," but to a Christianity of "deeds" or of "action."[80] The traditional Protestant Christianity of "good works" or "deeds" was a central part of the *Führer* cult in general. The head of the *Ahnenerbe*, the philologist

---

[79] Ibid., pp. 607–608.
[80] Hastings, D., *Catholicism and the Roots of Nazism* … , pp. 111–136. For the same, see Sebottendorff, R. von, *Bevor Hitler kam* … , p. 26.

64 / Christianity in Hitler's Ideology

and philosopher of religion Walther Wüst, stressed this point in a lecture about the Aryan worldview in *Mein Kampf* in *Hackenbräukeller* in Munich on March 10, 1937.[81] But the roots of this idea of the Aryan Jesus went much further back than this. Thus, it was not as if National Socialism infected Christianity with its foreign racist ideas, but rather the other way around, as Richard Steigmann-Gall has pointed out. These ideas had been developed by Christian theologians for a long time before National Socialism was a historical reality.[82]

The idea of an Aryan Jesus was in a way a natural theological development of the racist discourse from the mid-1800s onward. It was only a matter of time before this would infiltrate the theological discussions within Christianity. It was not very hard to introduce these ideas either, as Susannah Heschel has shown in her book *The Aryan Jesus*, because of the theological antisemitism that had existed within Christianity for many centuries. Ernest Renan – a French Catholic, linguist, and religion scholar – was the first to give this movement the concepts with which to complete the racial transformation of Jesus from Jew to Aryan. According to Renan, Jesus had been born a Jew, but his racial status had changed when he became the destroyer of Judaism. He had transcended his own Jewishness, Renan argued, and shed his Jewish nature. These ideas where then picked up by Hitler's idol, Houston Stewart Chamberlain, (we will get back to him later) and presented to the world in his *Die Grundlagen des neunzehnten Jahrhunderts* (The Foundations of the Nineteenth Century) from 1899. Chamberlain wholeheartedly believed in the Aryan Jesus and considered himself to be a true Christian. Furthermore, he argued that only Jesus' teachings which could be made to agree with his Aryan heritage should be kept in the Bible; the rest, which he considered to be Jewish interpolations, would have to be cleansed from Scripture. This view later became

---

[81] Junginger, Horst, "From Buddha to Adolf Hitler: Walther Wüst and the Aryan Tradition," in Horst Junginger (ed.), *The Study of Religion under the Impact of Fascism* (Leiden: Brill, 2008), pp. 121–125.

[82] Steigmann-Gall, Richard, "Christianity and the Nazi Movement: A Response," *Journal of Contemporary History*, Vol. 42, No. 2 (2007), p. 187.

65 / Christ on the Crooked Cross, Part I

dogma for the pro-Nazi *Deutsche Christen* (German Christians) movement and their theology.[83]

Many famous Christian theologians were involved in the transformation of Jesus from a Jew into an Aryan. Here, we find professors at well-known theological institutions at prestigious German universities such as Gerhard Kittel and Paul Althaus, William Wrede, Emanuel Hirsch, Walter Grundmann, Wilhelm Bousset, Walter Bauer (a prominent historian of early Christianity), and Paul Fiebig. In 1927, Bauer, in his article "Jesus der Galiläer" ("Jesus the Galilean"), argued that Jesus was an Aryan. Far from a majority of German theologians accepted the *Deutsche Christen* view of course, but enough of them did for it to become an accepted mainstream view that millions of German Christians adhered to, and it was preached to the faithful from the pulpit in tens of thousands of (mostly Protestant) churches in Germany. This included the idea of the nondivine Jesus, that is, the "Son of Man" who was not also at the same time God's son or the Messiah.[84] Note that this means that it is not possible to argue that those who did not accept Jesus as divine were by definition not Christians.

The *Deutsche Christen* were not a marginal sect but were the dominant denomination within German Christianity in the mid-1930s, and they controlled most theological faculties, women's organizations, and, during the war, also managed to infiltrate the organization of military priests. The *Protestant Soldier's Song Book* , which was distributed in millions of copies to the soldiers of the *Wehrmacht*, followed the *Deutsche Christen* in their aim to eradicate all Jewish influences from the Bible and from church music. The organization had its

---

[83] Heschel, S., *The Aryan Jesus . . .* , pp. 30, 33–37, 41–44, 48–55; Gutteridge, Richard, *Open Thy Mouth for the Dumb! The German Evangelical Church and the Jews, 1879–1950* (Oxford: Basil Blackwell, 1976), pp. 22–23; *Hitler, Mein Kampf . . .* (Band I), p. 896 [353]. For more background to the theological development, see also Kelley, Shawn, *Racializing Jesus: Race, Ideology and the Formation of Modern Biblical Scholarship* (London: Routledge, 2002). The German word for "resurrection" is *Auferstehung*, a word that Hitler did not use, but the implication is still the same, namely that a spiritually dead Germany had become spiritually alive again.

[84] Ericksen, Robert P., *Theologians under Hitler: Gerhard Kittel, Paul Althaus, and Emanuel Hirsch* (New Haven: Yale University Press, 1985); Heschel, Susannah, "Jewish Studies in the Third Reich: A Brief Glance at Viktor Christian and Kurt Schubert," in *Review of Rabbinic Judaism*, Vol. 13, No. 2 (2010), p. 238. See also Kelley, S., *Racializing Jesus . . .* , pp. 64–88, 129–164; Heschel, S., *The Aryan Jesus . . .* , pp. 58–66.

66 / Christianity in Hitler's Ideology

headquarters in Eisenach in Thuringia in central Germany and was led by Siegfried Leffler. The professor of theology at the University of Jena (1936–45), Walter Grundmann, was the head of its research department.[85] Theology students in Jena were in fact required to read *Mein Kampf*, and the professor of practical theology Wolf Meyer-Erlach told his students that they had to read not only Hitler's epos, but Rosenberg's too, before their examinations.[86]

The idea of an Aryan Jesus had been well established within theological circles in German Protestant Christianity by 1918 at the latest, writes Elisabeth Lorenz. Grundmann, however, never went as far as to explicitly say that Jesus was an Aryan. Instead, he argued, in what can only be described as an intellectual cop-out, that Jesus, as a divine creature, stood above this human category. Jesus was raceless, he claimed, even if he by 1940 in the book *Jesus der Galiläer und das Judentum* (Jesus the Galilean and Judaism/the Jews), note the title's similarity to Bauer's article from 1927, wrote with the utmost certainty that Jesus was not a Jew. But Grundmann's view of Jesus was based on arguments coming from theology and the history of religion, not from race biology.[87] In fact, the study of Judaism did not diminish during National Socialist rule. Instead, it flourished, albeit in its ideological and antisemitic form, and produced thirty-two dissertations in the years 1939–42 alone.[88] Grundmann's book was a huge success that sold 200,000 copies in the first six months.[89]

---

[85] Bergen, Doris L., *Twisted Cross: The German Christian Movement in the Third Reich* (Chapel Hill, NC: University of North Carolina Press, 1996), pp. 1–8, 98–100, 148–149; Heschel, S., *The Aryan Jesus* ... , pp. 3–6, 26–66, 88–91; Lorenz, Elisabeth, *Ein Jesusbild im Horizont des Nationalsozialismus: Studien zum Neuen Testament des "Instituts zur Erforschung und Beseitigung des jüdischen Einflusses auf das deutsche kirchliche Leben"* (Tübingen: Mohr Siebeck, 2017), pp. 29–34.

[86] Heschel, Susannah, "Being Adolf Hitler: Mein Kampf as Anti-Semitic Bildungsroman," in John J. Muchalczyk et al. (eds.), *Hitler's Mein Kampf and the Holocaust: A Prelude to Genocide* (London: Bloomsbury Academic, 2022), p. 189.

[87] Lorenz, E., *Ein Jesusbild im Horizont des Nationalsozialismus* ... , pp. 35–37. For a detailed history of Grundmann and his role in Aryanizing Jesus, see Deines, Roland, "Jesus der Galiläer: Traditionsgeschichte und Genese eines antisemitischen Konstrukts bei Walter Grundmann," in Roland Deines, Volker Leppin, and Karl-Wilhelm Niebuhr (eds.), *Walter Grundmann: Ein Neutestamentler in Dritten Reich* (Leipzig: Evangelische Verlagsanstalt, 2007), pp. 43–131.

[88] Heschel, S., "Jewish Studies in the Third Reich ... ," pp. 240–241.

[89] Head, Peter, "The Nazi Quest for an Aryan Jesus," *Journal for the Study of the Historical Jesus*, Vol. 2, No. 1 (2004), pp. 79–80.

67 / Christ on the Crooked Cross, Part I

Conservatism in Germany, not least in its northeastern parts such as Prussia, was closely tied to the churches, and Shelley Baranowski underlines that it is not possible to understand this conservatism unless one investigates the role of the Evangelical churches in society.[90] What the *Deutsche Christen* tried to do was not really at all new, and it was not at all alien to Christianity. In fact, it was essentially the same as what the early church father Marcion of Sinope (circa 85 BCE–circa 160 BCE) tried to do. He has been credited with creating the first Christian canon, which consisted of eleven "books." Only one of the Gospels in the New Testament, namely that which later was ascribed to Luke (although absent the history of Jesus' birth and all references to the Old Testament), was part of that canon, and all the rest were texts ascribed to Paul. Marcion, who has been classified as a Gnostic, thought that the Old Testament was in complete contradiction to the message of Jesus. Not only was the Old Testament filled with internal contradictions, but it was also deeply immoral and barbaric. The Jewish God in the Old Testament was simply not the same God as that which Jesus had spoken about, according to him, but the Demiurge. Marcion's project was not successful, however, and he came to be seen by Catholic orthodoxy as one of the first heretics. Yet, his gift to church history was his contribution to the creation of the canon that is still accepted today.[91] The *Deutsche Christen* thus in a sense wanted to return to Marcion's opposition to the Old Testament influences in the Christian canon.

This was the same view as that which Houston Stewart Chamberlain espoused in his *Mensch und Gott* (Human and God) from 1922. There, he hailed Marcion as a Gnostic role model because he had proclaimed that the materialist Jewish God Jahveh was not the father of Jesus. The Jewish God was the evil creator God, the Demiurge, who ruled over the material world. The Aryan God, whose son was Jesus, was the God of love. The Jewish Jahveh was the one who saw to it that the Jews killed Christ. Marcion then devoted his life to liberating

---

[90] Baranowski, Shelley, *The Sanctity of Rural Life: Nobility, Protestantism, and Nazism in Weimar Prussia* (Oxford: Oxford University Press, 1995), p. 83.

[91] Freeman, Charles, *A New History of Early Christianity* (New Haven, CT: Yale University Press, 2009), pp. 134–136.

68 / Christianity in Hitler's Ideology

Christianity from the Old Testament, he proclaimed. It was in essence a Manichean Christianity where the God of evil stood against the God of goodness. Jewish Christianity was a religion of laws and a "religion of sin"; true Aryan Christians were in no need of churches or even religious dogmas. All that Aryans needed to encounter God were Wagner's works of art.[92]

The theology and cosmology expressed here, where a God who created the material world (the Demiurge) stands in total contrast to a transcendental God, is indeed, as Amit Varshizky points out, a Gnostic concept. Alfred Rosenberg also held up Marcion as a religious pioneer, and he may have picked this view up from Adolf von Harnack, who published a book entitled *Marcion: Das Evangelium vom fremden Gott* (Marcion: A Gospel from the Foreign God) in 1920.[93] We do not know when, or even if, Hitler read Chamberlain's book, but his views overlap frequently with those of Chamberlain's also in this case. This was a view of the relationship between man and God that suited Hitler perfectly, considering that he had long since used Wagner's operas, as well as other pieces of art, to gain access to transcendent, religious-like experiences.

It is in this context that one has to understand the massive violence inflicted upon the Hebrew Bible or Tanakh (תֶּנַ״ךְ) – that is, the scrolls containing the Torah (תּוֹרָה), Nevi'im (נְבִיאִים), and Ketuvim (כְּתוּבִים) – by the Nazis during the Pogrom of November 9–10, 1938. Thousands of copies of these books were burned in hundreds of German cities, large and small, and 1,400 synagogues were set ablaze in a frenzy of antisemitic hatred. Alon Confino points out that these burnings are often forgotten when the history of the November Pogrom is written. He asks why the Nazis would go to such lengths and expend so much energy on burning religious items.[94] Part of the answer may be the desire to purge a National Socialist Christian Germany of what was considered Jewish contamination of the Christian Bible.

---

[92] Hesemann, Michael, *Hitlers Religion: Die fatale Heilslehre des Nationalsozialismus* (Munich: Pattloch Verlag, 2004), pp. 200–201.

[93] Varshizky, A., "Alfred Rosenberg ... ," pp. 316, 323–324.

[94] Confino, Alon, "Why Did the Nazis Burn the Hebrew Bible? Nazi Germany, Representations of the Past, and the Holocaust," *The Journal of Modern History*, Vol. 84, No. 2 (2012), pp. 369–370.

69 / Christ on the Crooked Cross, Part I

Rosenberg celebrated Chamberlain's book in *Der Mythos des 20 Jahrhunderts*, where he stressed that the National Socialist fight for a renewal of German religious life was "the search for an immediate path to the personality of Christ." He continued by stating that the philosopher Johann Gottfried Herder "demanded once, that the religion towards Jesus [*Religion an Jesum*] should become the religion *of Jesus* [*Religion Jesu*]. This is precisely what Chamberlain intended. A completely free man, who inwardly dominates the overall culture of our time, who has shown the finest feeling for the great superhuman simplicity of Christ and portrayed Jesus as he once appeared: as the mediator between man and God" [emphasis in original].[95] This undeniably sounds like a clear recognition of Jesus' divinity on Rosenberg's part. He thus continued his celebration of Jesus from *Die Spur des Juden im Wandel der Zeiten* from 1920.

The same idea was expressed by Jung in *Der nationale Sozialismus*, where he stated that it would be a mistake, as some *völkisch* groups had done, to reject the original Christianity of Jesus just because church Christianity had been corrupted by Jewish influences and teachings. What the National Socialists were striving for could be summarized in the term "people's church" (*Volkskirche*), Jung wrote. This, however, did not imply an actual centralized church organization, nor did it mean that Christianity should be replaced by a revived "Wotan faith." Here, Jung made an argument that Hitler would make later on, and he did so again when he stated that Luther's reformation of the church was only half successful since he did not free the church from its "centralist" (i.e., Jewish) trait. The National Socialist "people's church" would be a nonconfessional amalgamation of the Protestant and Catholic churches in Germany. This would free them from international "centralism" and make them truly nationalistic and German. A prerequisite for the formation of a free "People's Church" was "the separation of church and state," wrote Jung. It was simply not possible for any German religious community to be free if it was associated with the state, he argued, and he exemplified this by referring to the situation in his native Sudetenland.[96] It is obvious that Jung did not yet envision the National Socialist takeover of power in Germany, since Hitler actually made an

---

[95] Rosenberg, A., *Der Mythos* ... , pp. 623–624.
[96] Jung, R., *Der nationale Sozialismus* ... , pp. 88–90.

70 / Christianity in Hitler's Ideology

effort to do the exact opposite, that is, to create a state church as in England. Jung argued within an assumed context where the National Socialists would be living under a non-National Socialist government, as was the case in Weimar Germany when he wrote his book.

Alfred Rosenberg also wrote about how a German *Volkskirche* "was the longing of millions" of Germans. Rosenberg claimed that science could defeat the Christian churches' faulty dogmas but that it could never destroy "true religion." The People's Church would gather all believers in God regardless of confession if their faith remained loyal to the nation and did not contradict "national honour." Religion was a personal matter that was up to everyone to decide for themselves – in contradiction to the current churchly dogmas of Christianity. Dogmas in religion were a Jewish creation and ought to be shunned. The Old Testament had to be cast aside. It represented the failed effort of the last 1,500 years to make the Germans into Jews in spirit. It was an attempt that was intimately tied to the "horrible material domination of the Jews," Rosenberg stated. Another important effort was to revise the New Testament and free it from "superstitious stories" (*abergläubische Berichte*). Rosenberg then stated that "the necessary fifth Gospel" would not be decided upon by a synodic meeting, but "will be the creation of a man who experiences the longing for purification just as deeply as he has researched the scholarship on the New Testament."[97]

Every member of the *Deutsche Christen* was of course a more or less rabid antisemite. Leffler, the leader of this group, stated to a conference in 1936 that he knew that he had a moral obligation to kill Jews, even though this appeared to contradict the prohibition on murder in Christianity, since it was a defensive act intended to save the German nation from its destruction. Leffler said:

> Even if I know "thou shalt not kill" is a commandment of God or "thou shalt love the Jew" because he too is a child of the eternal Father, I am able to know as well that I have to kill him, I have to shoot him, and I can only do that if I am permitted to say: "Christ."[98]

---

[97] Rosenberg, A., *Der Mythos* ... , pp. 599–604.
[98] Heschel, S., "Historiography of Antisemitism ... ," pp. 258–259.

71 / Christ on the Crooked Cross, Part I

No one at the conference seems to have had anything to say against Leffler's statement – even though this was before the Nazis themselves arrived at this conclusion. On April 4, 1939, the *Deutsche Christen* founded a research and propaganda center with the cumbersome name The Institute for the Study and Eradication of Jewish Influence in German Church Life (*Institut zur Erforschung und Beseitigung des jüdischen Einflusses auf das deutsche kirchliche Leben*). The Institute was extremely successful and active, and arranged many conferences and publicized its own "research" in the form of books and articles. The *Deutsche Christen* had about 600,000 pastors, bishops, theology professors, and religion teachers as members by the middle of the 1930s, and eventually came to attract between a quarter and a third of all the members of the Protestant churches in Germany. It was therefore a true mass movement. The opposing *Bekennende Kirche* never managed to gather more than about 20 percent of the Protestant pastors and remained a minority group during the short but horrible history of the Third Reich.[99] Ernst Klee has described the close collaboration between the Evangelical clergy and the Nazi regime in his book *"Die SA Jesu Christi."* He shows that National Socialism took over Evangelical Christianity to such a degree that the *Landesverein für Innere Mission* (Country Association for the Inner Mission) in Hamburg took over, and then ran, the concentration camp Kuhlen from the SA in July 1933. Many other clergy personnel served as guards in other concentration camps, for example, in Hannover and in Esterwegen (until 1936 the largest concentration camp after Dachau), and many were also SA members. No wonder Klee talks about these clerics as the SA and SS of Jesus Christ.[100]

Susannah Heschel writes in *The Aryan Jesus* that if Hitler's antisemitism got a good and wide reception in Germany then this was because of the echo chamber created by the relentless anti-Jewish theological discourse that dominated the country, which linked Nazi antisemitism and Christianity's antisemitism with the churches' moral authority. Antisemitism also tied together the two fighting factions

---

[99] Bergen, D. L., *Twisted Cross: . . .* , p. 7; Heschel, S., *The Aryan Jesus . . .* , pp. 3–4, 10–17, 101–104.

[100] Klee, E., *"Die SA Jesu Christi" . . .* , pp. 61–74.

72 / Christianity in Hitler's Ideology

within the Protestant church, that is, the *Deutsche Christen* and the *Bekennende Kirche*. Anti-Judaism was, Heschel writes, the most frequent theme within Christianity, just as antisemitism was the most frequent theme within National Socialism. Nazism could not completely reject Christianity, not least because of the long history of antisemitism within this religion; but it did combat the churches' influence in the political and moral arenas. Siegfried Hermle notes that not one single Protestant bishop, church directorate, or synod protested the boycott against German Jews and their businesses in 1933, and that this can be explained by reference to both theology and political pragmatism. They kept silent about the Jews, writes Hermle, but on the other hand explicitly voiced their support for the regime in their communication with foreign churches, minimizing the abuse and discrimination that the Jews were exposed to, when their foreign counterparts wondered what was going on in Germany. But while Nazism battled the churches, Heschel notes, Nazism also played on Christian ideas and tradition in its own propaganda to get more Germans to join the NSDAP and the National Socialist project. On the other hand, the *Deutsche Christen* played on the National Socialist *Weltanschauung* to make themselves more attractive in the eyes of the regime. Both the *Deutsche Christen* and the NSDAP viewed Hitler as a reincarnation of the Messiah, writes Heschel. The antisemitism of the *Deutsche Christen* aimed to actively support and to lend moral authority to the Nazi regime's oppression of the Jewish people, and even if the regime's goals did not always align with those of the *Deutsche Christen*, the support of the latter was nonetheless important for Hitler.[101]

However, there apparently were limits to how far the regime wished to go when returning the love for National Socialism that the *Deutsche Christen* and the Institute exhibited. Peter Head cites Martin Bormann, who made it clear to Grundmann in September 1942 that the regime was not prepared to lend official recognition to the Institute. Grundmann's efforts were "well meant," Bormann wrote, but there was

---

[101] Heschel, S., *The Aryan Jesus . . .*, pp. 6–9; Hermle, Siegfried, "Die antijudische NS-Politik als Herausforderung des Protestantismus," in Thomas Brechenmacher and Harry Oelke (eds.), *Die Kirchen und die Verbrechen im nationalsozialistischen Staat* (Göttingen: Wallstein Verlag, 2011), pp. 177–178.

73 / Christ on the Crooked Cross, Part I

no official interest on the part of the government to either assimilate Christianity into National Socialism or in proving that a reformed Christianity was free of Jewish influences. This likely did not come as a surprise to Grundmann, who already in March 1941 concluded at a conference organized by the Institute that the German *Volk*, which was involved in "a struggle against the satanic powers of world Judaism for the order and life of this world, dismisses Jesus, because it cannot struggle against the Jews and open its heart to the king of the Jews."[102]

Head's quotation of Grundmann ends there. This makes it appear as if Grundmann equated the regime's unwillingness to endorse the Institute with a rejection of Jesus. But Susannah Heschel, who also cites Grundmann's statement, shows that he then went on to argue that there was no need to worry because the "struggle against the satanic Jews can be carried forth without having to abandon Jesus" because Jesus was indeed *not* the king of the Jews. The Jews have persecuted Jesus and everyone who follows him to this very day, Grundmann wrote, but the Aryan people could put their faith in Jesus Christ to save them.[103] This makes one wonder whether Head does not include this last part because he wants to make it appear as though Hitler's Germany rejected Jesus and Christianity. This suspicion is especially warranted because Head, a New Testament scholar and a Christian, has defended both Grundmann and Christianity in a critical review of Heschel's book *The Aryan Jesus*.[104]

Considering this issue, it also becomes clear why Head uses Rauschning uncritically in his own article from 2004 about the Aryan Christ – it panders to his own sentiments about the issue and confirms his prejudiced view that Hitler and the Nazis rejected both Christianity and the Jesus figure. But Bormann's statements are still significant. There were other such displays of the government's wish for the churches in Germany to remain aloof from the state too. For example, in 1936 the NSDAP demanded that the churches should remove the

---

[102] Head, P., "The Nazi Quest . . . ," p. 78. The term "king of the Jews" was an odd one to use for someone like Grundmann, who argued that Jesus was not a Jew (see ibid., p. 85).

[103] Heschel, Susannah, "Reading Jesus as a Nazi," in Tod Linafelt (ed.), *A Shadow of Glory: Reading the New Testament after the Holocaust* (New York: Routledge, 2002), p. 34.

[104] Head, Peter, "Susannah Heschel's *The Aryan Jesus*: A Response," *Journal for the Study of the New Testament*, Vol. 32, No. 4 (2010), pp. 421–430.

74 / Christianity in Hitler's Ideology

swastikas from their altars and newspapers. This caused loud protests from pastors and church leaders who "claimed that the swastika was a key element in the religious life of their congregants."[105] Bormann's letter and the example from 1936, however, are probably among the best evidence we have that Hitler, and the other leading Nazis, were not using Christian ideas simply for propaganda purposes. One could argue that the regime acted in this way because it did not want to be associated with Christianity or the churches – whether Catholic or Protestant. But one could also argue that this was an instance of the Nazi leadership taking point 24 of the NSDAP program seriously, that is, that no denomination should be officially favored over another. The latter interpretation is supported for instance by Gerhard Besier, who concludes that "among the National Socialist, or Nazi, political leadership, there was a broad spectrum of opinion with regard to the traditional churches. In reality, the Nazi Party … never really pursued an official propaganda policy of encouraging people to leave the church. Instead, they constantly aligned themselves with Article 24 of the party program."[106]

That Christian anti-Judaism really can be a breeding ground for racial antisemitism, so-called *praeparatio antisemitica*, has been established by several scholars.[107] This is supported also by Doris L. Bergen in her book *Twisted Cross*. Bergen, like James M. Rhodes, Robert A. Pois, and Richard L. Rubenstein, points to the central place of Christianity in National Socialist Germany, and cites Rubenstein, who writes that the culture that made the death camps possible was not only endemic to the West but was a result (albeit an unintended one) of the fundamental religious traditions in the West. Christianity's hostility toward Jews and Judaism played a necessary, if not a sufficient, role

---

[105] Ericksen, Robert P. and Heschel, Susannah, "The German Churches and the Holocaust," in Dan Stone (ed.), *Historiography of the Holocaust* (London: Palgrave Macmillan, 2004), p. 298.

[106] Besier, Gerhard, "The Churches and National Socialism between Hitler's Religious Equivocation and Rosenberg's Myth: Ambiguities, Fascination and Self-Assertion," in Martin Nykvist, David Gudmundsson, and Alexander Maurits (eds.), *Classics in Northern European Church History over 500 Years: Essays in Honour of Anders Jarlert* (Frankfurt am Main: Peter Lang, 2017), p. 153.

[107] See, e.g., Gerdmar, Anders, *Roots of Theological Anti-Semitism: German Biblical Interpretation and the Jews, from Herder and Semler to Kittel and Bultmann* (Leiden: Brill, 2009), p. 594.

75 / Christ on the Crooked Cross, Part I

in National Socialism's ability to turn a whole nation (a slight exaggeration, of course, considering that there were a lot of Germans who were prepared to risk their lives to help the Jews) against the Jews. Bergen stresses how Christian influences and imagery flooded Nazi Germany through Nazi propaganda campaigns. For example, the iconography that the regime used to its benefit was full of references to "self-sacrifice" and "redemption." As was the case in Croatia during the same period, Christianity's history in Nazi Germany shows that religious, national, and personal identities reinforce each other in a (sometimes) deadly way, according to Bergen.[108]

Far from everyone in Germany shared the view of Jesus as an Aryan, of course. Victor Klemperer tells of a legend that made its way through Germany during 1938: a man comes to the hospital in Berlin to have his and his wife's baby delivered. Over the hospital bed, there is an image of the infant Jesus. The man tells the nurse that the image must be taken down because his newborn baby should not have to see a Jewish baby as it opens its eyes for the first time. The nurse tells him that she cannot do anything about this, but she promises to bring his views to those in charge. The man goes away. In the evening, the doctor sends him a telegram telling him: "You have gotten a son. The image does not have to removed, however, because the child is blind."[109] Dark humor as criticism of dictatorial oppression was not unique to Nazi Germany. We find the same in Stalin's USSR and every other brutal dictatorship.

Although more and more scholars now argue that National Socialism was a thoroughly spiritual and religious movement, there are still many who do not ascribe to this view and instead believe that Nazism was based on secular ideas about race. For the Nazi ideologues, however, religion was intimately tied to the concept of race. The Aryan's idealism was considered to be the most conducive to religious feeling, and this was contrasted with the Jewish materialist inability to

---

[108] Bergen, D. L., *Twisted Cross . . .* , pp. 8–10. For similar arguments, see also Rhodes, James M., *The Hitler Movement: A Modern Millenarian Revolution* (Stanford, CA: Stanford University Press, 1980); Pois, Robert A., *National Socialism and the Religion of Nature* (New York: St. Martin's, 1986); Rubenstein, Richard L., *The Cunning of History: Mass Death and the American Future* (Baltimore: Johns Hopkins University Press, 1992).

[109] Klemperer, Victor, *Ich will Zeugnis ablegen bis zum letzten: Tagebücher 1933–1941. Herausgegeben von Walter Nowojski unter Mitarbeit von Hadwig Klemperer* (Berlin: Aufbau Verlag, 1995). Entry for March 30, 1938.

76 / Christianity in Hitler's Ideology

house any real religious belief. The Jew wore religion as a cloak, while the Aryan lived and breathed it. The Aryan possessed a "racial soul," and the important thing for National Socialists was not a specific theology, religious dogma, or tradition. Rather, it should be something that changes with the times but always remains true to the Nordic Germanic spirit. "Blood and faith" were closely tied together. Whatever the particularities of the specific religious beliefs held by the Nazis, they had to agree with their ultra-antisemitic and racist ideology.[110] According to the theologian Hugo Delff (1840–98), it was precisely the idealism of Jesus that had brought him into such sharp conflict with the materialistic Jews. The Germans, on the other hand, were characterized by the same pure idealism as Jesus and could therefore intuitively understand his teachings.[111]

Obviously, the move to de-Judaize Jesus was to a large degree motivated by ideological and racist concerns about him being Jewish; this was a change that occurred within a specific historical context in the German-speaking countries beginning in the early 1800s. Philosophers such as Hegel and Fichte began to question Jesus' Jewish origins. More important for Hitler, however, was perhaps that his idol Richard Wagner, the composer, thought that Jesus was not a Jew but an Aryan. However, the first author to include the idea of Jesus as an Aryan in the title of a book was Max Sebald (1859–?), who published *Jesus der Arier und die jesuanische Weltanschauung* (Jesus the Aryan and the Jesus Worldview) in 1886/87, in which he, among other things, claimed that the authors of the Gospels had, because they were "Orientals," not understood Christ's teachings. Sebald even denied Jesus' divinity and claimed that Joseph, whom he said had been an Aryan too, was Jesus' real father.[112] It would therefore be too simplistic and instrumentalist to assume that Hitler's religious beliefs – including his views on Jesus – were motivated simply by his racism. Such a view cannot explain why the antisemites considered Jesus a person worth salvaging from the wreckage of Christianity in the first place. There also

---

[110] Varshizky, Amit, "The Metaphysics of Race: Revisiting Nazism and Religion," *Central European History*, Vol. 52, No. 2 (2019), pp. 256–257, 259, 276–283.

[111] Fenske, W., *Wie Jesus zum "Arier" wurde . . .* , p. 101.

[112] Ibid., pp. 9–12, 83–85, 92–94. Fenske's book shows just how many thinkers spread this idea.

77 / Christ on the Crooked Cross, Part I

appears to have been a deep and sincere religious belief behind this effort. The reason behind this yearning for an Aryan Jesus is very likely to be found in genuine religious convictions on Hitler's part too.

1.8 Hitler's Understanding of Jesus

The first time the available sources record Hitler speaking about Jesus is on August 31, 1920, when he gave the speech "Why Are We Antisemites?" (for the second time) to an NSDAP crowd in Rosenheim.[113] Hitler then apparently mentioned Jesus again in a speech called "Party Politics and the Jewish Question" delivered on December 8, 1920. The transcription of the speech in the *Völkischer Beobachter* did not mention Jesus, but in the notes to this speech we actually do find a reference to "Christ," and thus it is reasonable to assume that Hitler did indeed mention him.[114] Then, on April 21, 1921, Hitler again spoke at an NSDAP meeting in Rosenheim, where he, according to the *Völkischer Beobachter*, said that all those who did not wish to see Christianity, which today was unfortunately only a token Christianity, be destroyed had to resist the Jews, who had the ambition to rob the Germans of their Christian faith. "I cannot imagine Christ as anything but blond and with blue eyes," Hitler said, and "the Devil, on the other hand, only with the Jewish snout."[115] This was the first time on record that Hitler talked about Jesus as an Aryan.

As we have seen, this was not something that Hitler had dreamed up himself; it was the product of a development within Christian theology from the mid-1800s onward in the works of Ernst Renan, Houston Stewart Chamberlain, and Paul de Lagarde.[116] We know that Hitler was aware of Lagarde, because Alfred Rosenberg records a conversation with Hitler in his diary on December 13, 1941, that mentions

---

[113] *SA*, pp. 220–221 (Document 140); Weikart, R., *Hitler's Religion* . . . , p. 81. Note that the *Völkischer Beobachter* (not yet an NSDAP newspaper) included a shorter summary that does not include these phrases.

[114] *SA*, pp. 276–277 (Documents 172 and 173). Again, the *Völkischer Beobachter* was not yet an NSDAP newspaper. The takeover was announced on December 18, 1920.

[115] *SA*, p. 367 (Document 223).

[116] Heschel, S., *The Aryan Jesus* . . . , pp. 30, 33–37, 41–44, 48–55; Fenske, W., *Wie Jesus zum "Arier" wurde* . . . , pp. 9–88. See also Lorenz, E., *Ein Jesusbild im Horizont des Nationalsozialismus* . . .

78 / Christianity in Hitler's Ideology

Lagarde.[117] As we have seen, several famous and influential German theologians also adhered to this idea.[118] The oppositional Nazi Otto Straßer, too, mentions Lagarde (next to Chamberlain) in his memoir *Hitler und ich* (Hitler and I) and states that it was Eckart who introduced both thinkers to Hitler.[119] Note that none of this should be interpreted as evidence that Hitler read Lagarde in the early 1920s, although he may have. Timothy Ryback has found a well-read 1934 edition of an anthology of Lagarde's antisemitic and nationalist writings, originally published in late 1800s, called *German Essays* that contains almost 100 pages of Hitler's marginal notes.[120] This suggests that Hitler had not read these particular texts before. Hitler therefore most likely initially got his knowledge of Lagarde not from Lagarde directly but from other sources, such as Eckart, whom he celebrated at the end of the second volume of *Mein Kampf*.[121] This would certainly explain how Eckart could be so on point regarding Hitler's views on this topic in his book *Der Bolschewismus von Moses bis Lenin* from 1924.[122]

The Aryan Jesus was a theme that would be raised by Hitler from time to time over the following years. Goebbels recorded a conversation with Hitler in his diary on February 23, 1937, where Hitler said that Christ too had fought against Jewish world domination and for this the Jews had nailed him to the cross and killed him, making it evident that he did not consider Jesus to have been a Jew. Paul (the apostle) had then corrupted the content of Christ's teachings and had thus done to Christianity what Marx had done to Socialism. This fact, however, could not be allowed to stop the NSDAP from being Socialist,

---

[117] Rosenberg, A., *Alfred Rosenberg ...* , pp. 415–416. The table talks record this part of the conversation too, but this version is worded differently and is much less clearly formulated; see Jochmann, W., *Monologe*, pp. 150–151.

[118] Ericksen, R. P., *Theologians under Hitler ...* , passim; Heschel, S., *The Aryan Jesus ...* , pp. 3–6, 26–66, 88–91; Bergen, D. L., *Twisted Cross ...* , pp. 1–8, 98–100, 148–149; Chappel, James, *Catholic Modern: The Challenge of Totalitarianism and the Remaking of the Church* (Cambridge, MA: Harvard University Press, 2018), p. 99.

[119] For this, see Ryback, Timothy W., *Hitler's Private Library: The Books That Shaped His Life* (New York: Alfred A. Knopf, 2008), p. 69.

[120] Ibid., p. 134.   [121] *Hitler, Mein Kampf ...* (Band II), p. 1739 [353].

[122] Eckart, D., *Der Bolschewismus ...* , pp. 18–29. For a critical analysis of Eckart's work, see Plewnia, Margarete, *Auf dem Weg zu Hitler: Der "völkische" Publizist Dietrich Eckart* (Bremen: Schünemann Universitätsverlag, 1970).

79 / Christ on the Crooked Cross, Part I

Hitler said.[123] Richard Steigmann-Gall points out that Hitler here also implies that Paul's corruption of Jesus' teachings should not be allowed to stop the NSDAP from being Christian.[124] The founder of the *Thule Gesellschaft*, the abovementioned Rudolf von Sebottendorff (1875–1945), really Adam Alfred Rudolf Glauer, celebrated the *völkisch* ideologue Jörg Lanz von Lebenfels (1874–1954) as one of the forerunners of National Socialism and noted with approval that Lebenfels had "tried to restore the original text of the New Testament from the books of the church fathers; his books were confiscated and destroyed."[125]

In his memoirs, the former governor-general of the General Government of Occupied Poland, Hans Frank, relates an episode that is said to have happened when Hitler visited Mussolini in Rome in May 1938 (his only visit to the Italian capital). At one point during this visit, Hitler apparently remained standing in front of a very old bust of Jesus (according to Frank, it was the oldest such bust in existence and thought to date back to the second century) and contemplated this work of art. With admiration in his voice, Hitler stated, Frank claims, that this bust could very well have been made by an artist who had had the opportunity to inquire about Jesus' appearance from people who had met him. According to Frank, Mussolini agreed with this view and Hitler then allegedly said that it was the best evidence available for the view that Jesus was not a Jew.[126] This moment thus appears to have had a profound effect, perhaps even a religious one, on Hitler. But can we be sure that Hitler really meant what he said in this instance? No, we cannot. Can we even be certain that this happened and that it is not just a figment of Frank's imagination? The honest answer is that we cannot. The reason is that Frank is not always a reliable witness. However, even if Frank made it all up it still signifies something important, namely the

---

[123] *TBJG*, I/3, p. 55 (February 23, 1937).

[124] Steigmann-Gall, R., *The Holy Reich* . . . , pp. 118–119.

[125] Sebottendorff, R. von, *Bevor Hitler kam* . . . , p. 32.

[126] Frank, Hans, *Im Angesicht des Galgens: Deutung Hitlers und seiner Zeit auf Grund eigener Erlebnisse und Erkenntnisse* (Munich: Friedrich Alfred Beck Verlag, 1953), p. 294. See also Heer, F., *Der Glaube des Adolf Hitler* . . . , p. 343. It is unknown what bust this was because there is no bust portraying Jesus dating to anywhere near the second century in existence. The story may be apocryphal, but it is nonetheless significant since it tells us a lot about how Frank viewed Hitler and his admiration for Jesus.

80 / Christianity in Hitler's Ideology

fact that he obviously did not think that his readers would regard this story as false. The matter-of-fact nature of the story itself as it appears in Frank's memoirs should at least tell us that Hitler's admiration for Jesus was well known within National Socialist circles.

Naturally, Hitler's antisemitism informed his view of Jesus, but the religious aspect must be considered more important here because it is only the religious significance that would make Hitler care about whether Jesus was a Jew or not. There was nothing in the racial antisemitism that demanded that Hitler should shield Jesus from the disdain that he heaped on Paul, for example. In *Monologe im Führerhauptquartier* (the so-called table talks) too, there are several entries that record statements about Jesus as an Aryan and Paul as a Jewish corruptor of Jesus' teachings. This is paralleled in other notes as well.[127] These were the same views that had appeared in Eckart's *Der Bolschewismus von Moses bis Lenin*. The fact that Hitler constantly throughout his life, in several different sources, exempted the figure of Jesus from the vitriolic hostility that he often expressed toward the churches and established Christianity should tell us that he really admired Jesus in a very deep and sincere way.

1.9 The Religious Nature of the Concept of Race in National Socialism

In the introduction to the book *The Aryan Jesus*, Susannah Heschel stresses the importance of understanding that the concept of "race" fundamentally has nothing to do with biology and everything to do with the human soul. The racial hygienists and ideologues were very clear about this fact, and a lot of time was spent on classifying what they

---

[127] *Monologe* ... , pp. 96–99, 150, 412–413; *Bundesarchiv, Berlin-Lichterfelde* (henceforth, BBL), Reichsministerium für die besetzten Ostgebiete, R6/34a fol. 1–82 (henceforth, R6/34a), Aufzeichnungen des persönlichen Referenten Rosenbergs, Dr Koeppen, über Hitlers Tischgespräche 1941 (henceforth, Aufzeichnungen, Koeppen), "Bericht Nr. 48. Führerhauptquartier, Mittwoch, den 22.10.1941. Blatt 2: Mittagstafel 21.10" and "Bericht Nr. 52. Führerhauptquartier, Sonntag, den 26. Oktober 1941. Abendessen 25.10," pp. 60–61, 71. A commented version of Koeppen's notes has been published: Koeppen, Werner, *Herbst 1941 im "Führerhauptquartier": Berichte Werner Koeppens an seinen Minister Alfred Rosenberg. Herausgegeben und kommentiert von Martin Vogt* (Koblenz: Materialen aus dem Bundesarchiv Heft 10, 2002), p. 60.

81 / Christ on the Crooked Cross, Part I

called the spiritual properties in the people they studied. The body was just the physical representation of moral and spiritual qualities, and it was in these latter categories that the threat of miscegenation – that is, mixing with other races – could be found (this was thought to lead to moral and spiritual degeneration). Many of the leading racial ideologues, such as Houston Stewart Chamberlain, even rejected the very idea of science and scientific practice as not worthwhile. It was useless, since knowledge was an intuitive property of the Aryan race. In any case, whether they rejected ostensibly scientific measurements of skulls and bodies or not, the results of these evaluations were the same. Heschel describes the argument that racism is about biology as outdated, because it entirely misses the point that the dangers seen by these racial ideologues concerned what the body (matter) exposed the soul (spirit) to. This essential connection between body and soul is something that the racial ideologues, and later the Nazis, inherited from Christian metaphysics, where focus was on the same problem – the battle between body and spirit, between the material world and the spiritual one. It was a direct reflection of Christian mysticism and the imprint it had left on Western philosophy, according to Heschel. They also got the idea of Judaism and the Jews as a manifestation of the material, and Christianity as a manifestation of the spiritual, from Christian philosophy. Moreover, "blood," which had a central place within the racist discourse, was the link between spirit and body, human and divine, metaphor and reality. This was a Christian view through and through, because blood in Christian theology is the link between body and soul, and ideas about the blood of Jesus and its magical qualities have an equally central place within the Christian faith. Therefore, early National Socialism's explicit connection to Christianity is not at all strange, writes Heschel. Both were in a way naturally attracted to each other.[128]

Samuel Koehne suggests the term "ethnotheism" to describe National Socialism's conception of religion.[129] The higher on the developmental ladder that a people (*Volk*) stood, Hitler explained in a speech on July 12, 1925, the greater spiritual potential it had and the more this

---

[128] Heschel, S., *The Aryan Jesus* ... , pp. 21–23.
[129] Koehne, S., "The Racial Yardstick ... ," pp. 576–577.

82 / Christianity in Hitler's Ideology

spirit came to the foreground. This spirit was the lust for life as it had been manifested in nature, and a righteous God gave the brave peoples their freedom as a reward for their bravery.[130] The historian Gerhard Ritter also noted that the connection between body, mind, and spirit was integral to Hitler's conception of race, even though it remained unclear to him exactly how this relationship looked. Antisemitism appeared to be the most important thing to Hitler, Ritter said, which he thought was a consequence of Hitler's "faith" in the value of the Nordic race.[131] It did apparently not occur to Ritter, a devout Christian and opponent of National Socialism, that Christianity had been preaching anti-Judaism and antisemitism for over 1,000 years prior to Hitler's ascent on the world stage and that this fact could have had something to do with the success of National Socialism.

1.10 Conclusion

In this chapter, I have shown that the ideological roots of National Socialism go back much further than 1919. In fact, National Socialism arose in a conservative religious milieu in Germany in the 1870s, 1880s, and 1890s. By the beginning of the twentieth century, all the constituent elements of Hitler's National Socialism were already well established in German national culture and intellectual tradition. There was therefore nothing new about the National Socialism of the NSDAP per se; what was new was rather the way in which these elements were combined and transformed into the hodgepodge of ideological influences that it was. Yet, this older history is very rarely, and in fact almost never, mentioned when the National Socialism of Hitler and the NSDAP is discussed. This means that we cannot fully make sense of why National Socialism, as an ideology, developed as it did after 1919. The fact that National Socialism had these religious roots already from the start, and long before Hitler became a National Socialist (indeed even long before he was born), is important to know if we wish to understand how and why Jesus came to occupy a place within Nazi ideology and mythology. It was not something that was introduced by Hitler as a cheap propaganda trick. The adoration of Jesus as an Aryan

---

[130] *RSA*, I, p. 107 (Document 55).   [131] Picker, H., *Hitlers Tischgespräche ...*, p. 22.

83 / Christ on the Crooked Cross, Part I

warrior had been rather prevalent in certain Christian theologies for at least half a century by then.

Because of the racial antisemitism that grew stronger and stronger from the mid-1800s onward, more and more Christian theologians started to question the racial status of the central figure in Christianity – Jesus. These theologians, philosophers, and Christian ideologues felt very uneasy with Jesus being a Jew. They therefore began a process of transforming him, first into a Galilean spiritual Aryan of uncertain racial descent, and then into a full-blooded Aryan. This process started already with philosophers such as Hegel and Fichte, moved further via the religious scholar Ernest Renan, and was fulfilled by philologist and theologian Paul de Lagarde and the composer Richard Wagner. Chamberlain followed in his idol Wagner's footsteps. Famous theologians such as Bruno Bauer, Gerhard Kittel, Paul Althaus, Emanuel Hirsch, and Walter Grundmann followed their example and formed the foundations of the forceful movement to eradicate all Jewish influences from the Bible. In Nazi Germany, this project was adopted by the *Deutsche Christen*, the dominant Nazi-sympathizing church movement within German Protestant Christianity.

It was this heritage that Hitler drew upon when he spoke of Jesus as an Aryan warrior who had devoted his life to the struggle against the materialist Jews. It was the Jesus who chased the money-lenders out of the temple grounds that Hitler professed to admire and idolize. Hitler held to his views of Jesus until the very end. He kept insisting that Jesus was not a Jew and kept considering him as a role model for National Socialists everywhere. He did so both in public and, more importantly, in private. Why did he do that if the character of Jesus was not very important for him and his ideological and religious beliefs? There was absolutely no propaganda reason for Hitler to privately state this view at the end of the war if he did not really believe what he said. This is no doubt the strongest evidence that Hitler really did believe what he said about Jesus.

Because of what has been said above, historians have thus far obviously grossly underestimated the role that Hitler's understanding of, and perhaps belief in, Jesus played in the history of his political career and that of the Third Reich. Hitler did not only go from being unpolitical to political, and from an unknown to a political leader of

84 / Christianity in Hitler's Ideology

eventually national fame between 1919 and 1924. At the same time, he also went from being relatively unreligious to a fervent believer in God and Providence. Hitler's talk about God, Providence, and Jesus as an Aryan should not be viewed as mutually exclusive. These were very likely overlapping concepts in his mind. These two developments in his personality were clearly simultaneous and connected. But from whom did Hitler get these ideas and beliefs more directly? The two most important figures for Hitler's religious and ideological development during the early 1920s, the formative period in Hitler's transformation, were Dietrich Eckart and Houston Stewart Chamberlain.

2 HITLER'S RELIGIOUS TEACHERS
Dietrich Eckart and Houston Stewart Chamberlain

2.1 Introduction

When Hitler returned to Munich via Berlin on November 21, 1918, after having been released from the hospital in Pasewalk, he was a man with no real aim or intention in his life. His main fear appears to have been to be forced to go back to the life he had led in Vienna before the war, a life of no steady income and homelessness – in short, a life of misery in the streets. Going back to a life of painting and selling postcards was not an option he seems to have seriously entertained. Instead, he opted for remaining in the military. The profound sense of belonging that he had felt in the army was something that he had never experienced before in his life. He was determined not to give this up, and he was therefore prepared to do whatever it took to hold on to that feeling. That is why he returned to Munich and continued to serve in the army under a Socialist revolutionary regime rather than demobilize and go back to civilian life. This determination to remain in a context that provided him with meaning and belonging – not to mention free housing, free food, and a good monthly salary – is probably an important reason why Hitler's transformation from an unpolitical nobody in November 1918 to a central personality in Munich's *völkisch* and National Socialist underworld by the end of 1919 was so fast. Hitler was of course assisted in this transformation by the rapid pace of events in Munich at this time. History leaped forward during those months,

86 / Christianity in Hitler's Ideology

and once Captain Karl Mayr selected him for an army counterrevolutionary propaganda course in July 1919, in combination with the German government's ratification of the Versailles Treaty on July 9, Hitler's fate was sealed (in a way, Mayr's fate was sealed then too, as he would later be imprisoned in Buchenwald and die on February 9, 1945 during a British air raid on the munitions factory where he was forced to work). Hitler had clearly been a German nationalist even before the war, but it was only in the summer of 1919 that he turned into an extreme right-wing nationalist and genocidal antisemite.[1]

This chapter deals with the influence of two of the most important ideologues on Hitler's religious beliefs during this early period, namely Houston Stewart Chamberlain and Dietrich Eckart. Their impact on Hitler's religious beliefs and interpretation of Christianity as well as the person of Jesus can hardly be overstated. Yet, this intellectual influence on Hitler during the early formative years has not been studied much, and it is almost always glossed over in the major biographies. It is therefore more than justified to take a deeper look at how these two religious racist personalities came to affect Hitler. This chapter will address Chamberlain and Eckart in the chronological order in which their publications appeared; however, it is worth noting that Hitler likely read Chamberlain only *after* he had met Eckart and that *Die Grundlagen* was probably recommended to Hitler by him. This is also most likely the reason why we find a stronger influence from Eckart on Hitler's view of established Christianity and the apostle Paul, among other things.

2.2 Houston Stewart Chamberlain

With the book *Die Grundlagen des neunzehnten Jahrhunderts* (The Foundations of the Nineteenth Century) from 1899, Houston Stewart Chamberlain was propelled to the forefront of the *völkisch* movement and his interpretation of Christianity and Jesus came to be hugely influential, even though he probably never expected this as he

---

[1] The best literature on Hitler's activities in Munich, and his political journey, shortly after the war consists of Joachimsthaler, Anton, Hitlers Weg begann in München 1919–1923 (Munich: Herbig Verlag, 2000), passim; Weber, T., *Becoming Hitler* ... , passim.

87 / Hitler's Religious Teachers

put the final touches on his manuscript in Vienna in the fall of 1898. His marriage to Richard Wagner's daughter Eva in 1908 certainly did not make his reputation any less formidable in those circles. Chamberlain of course benefited from the ideological and theological developments that preceded him during the 1800s and belonged to what Wolfgang Fenske called "the third phase," the period of popularization, of the movement to turn Jesus into an Aryan (roughly 1899–1945). Together with Wagner's widow, Chamberlain is considered to have been the "grey eminence" behind the antisemitic German nationalist scene. What is also notable about Chamberlain is that in 1923 he had already recognized the potential of Hitler as a leader within the *völkisch* movement.[2]

We know that *Die Grundlagen* was one of the many books that Hitler borrowed from the library at Friedrich Krohn's National Socialist Institute in Munich between 1919 and 1921.[3] Hitler eventually met Chamberlain in person in the Wagner family home in Bayreuth in September 1923. Apparently, the admiration did not only go one way, because after this rendezvous Chamberlain wrote a letter to Hitler in which he praised him for having completely transformed his soul and resurrected his belief in Germanness. Perhaps Hitler having told Chamberlain about his plans for a fascist-style revolution in Munich caused the elation? Be that as it may, Chamberlain's feelings reportedly made Hitler beside himself with joy. In connection with this, Chamberlain, who was a deeply believing Christian, also wrote an article in the *Völkischer Beobachter* with the very revealing title "God Wants It! A Deliberation on the Contemporary Condition of Germany." The time was now ready for the natural-born leader who had come forth from the German people waiting for his hour to strike, wrote Chamberlain. Hitler later argued that Bayreuth was the city where the spiritual sword, with which the struggle was now fought, had been made – first by Wagner and then later by Chamberlain.[4]

---

[2] Fenske, W., *Wie Jesus zum "Arier" wurde ...* , pp. 105, 110.
[3] Ryback, T. W., *Hitler's Private Library ...* , p. 50.
[4] Kellog, M., *The Russian Roots of Nazism ...* , pp. 122–123, 206–207. See also Herbst, L., *Hitlers Charisma ...* , pp. 146–147. Hitler's relationship to the Wagner family and Bayreuth is dealt with in detail in Hamann, Brigitte, *Winifred Wagner oder Hitlers Bayreuth* (Munich: Piper Verlag, 2002).

88 / Christianity in Hitler's Ideology

The sword metaphor was a very clear reference to the New Testament and the Gospel of Matthew (10:34), where it says that Jesus had not come to bring peace but a sword. It was precisely this combative Christianity, which portrayed Jesus as a warrior ready to destroy the Jews that Hitler identified with. Significantly, Chamberlain himself quoted this passage in *Die Grundlagen*.[5] In *Mein Kampf*, Hitler openly stated the importance of Chamberlain's work on his ideological development. *Die Grundlagen* was published by a company owned by Hugo Bruckmann, who in turn was the husband of Hitler's benefactor Elsa Bruckmann.[6]

In *Monologe*, in a note dated on the night between January 24 and 25, 1942, Heinrich Heim has Hitler talking about his meeting

---

[5] Chamberlian, Houston Stewart, *Die Grundlagen des neunzehnten Jahrhunderts I. Hälfte* (Munich: Verlagsanstalt F. Brückmann A.–G., 1899), p. 44. See also Sebottendorff, R. von, *Bevor Hitler kam ...* , p. 26.

[6] Weber, T., *Becoming Hitler ...* , pp. 173–174. Hitler met the Bruckmanns already in 1921 via his recent convert, the eccentric but in Munich *salon* society very well-connected American Ernst "Putzi" Hanfstaengl. Elsa Bruckmann became enthralled with Hitler and soon introduced him to several wealthy people that became financers of the NSDAP (Othmar Plöckinger [ed.], *Quellen und Dokumente zur Geschichte von "Mein Kampf" 1924–1945* [Stuttgart: Franz Steiner Verlag, 2016], p. 106). Nonetheless, it was apparently not through the Bruckmanns that Hitler met Chamberlain. This honor has instead been given by most biographers to Helene Bechstein, the wife of the piano manufacturer Carl Bechstein, who like Elsa Bruckmann felt a sort of mother's love for Hitler. Konrad Heiden, however, writes that it was Eckart and Rosenberg that introduced Hitler to the Wagner household. Yet, there is some confusion in the literature regarding exactly when Hitler met Chamberlain. Anton Joachimsthaler dates it to September 30, 1923, which was the date of *Deutsche Tag*, and states (based on the memoirs of the Nazi Ulrich Graf) that Hitler met the Wagners for the first time on that same occasion. Ian Kershaw confusingly gives two different dates. In the text, he says that the visit occurred in October 1923 and only he mentions Hitler meeting the Wagners. However, in the endnote to that very passage he says that Hitler met Chamberlain "on the same occasion, at the end of September 1923." So, which is it? Volker Ullrich writes, based on Chamberlain's letter to Hitler dated October 7, 1923, that Hitler met Chamberlain on September 28 after holding a speech in Bayreuth. The problem is that Hitler held no speech in Bayreuth on September 28. Perhaps this was a mistake on Chamberlain's part: he may have remembered incorrectly. The speech was indeed held on September 30, which we know from Eberhard Jäckel's *Sämtliche Aufzeignungen*. Ullrich then dates Hitler's first visit to the Wagners' family villa "Wahnfried" to October 1, 1923. Hitler thus met Chamberlain, as well as Siegfried and Winifred Wagner, for the first time in late September that year during *Deutsche Tag* in Bayreuth (Ullrich, Volker, *Adolf Hitler: Biographie. Band I: Die Jahre des Aufsteigs* [Frankfurt am Main: S. Fischer Verlag, 2013], pp. 143–144, 873 n160; Heiden, K., *Hitler ...* [Vol. I], p. 114; Joachimsthaler, A., *Hitlers Weg began in München ...* , p. 315; Kershaw, I., *Hitler 1889–1936 ...* , pp. 186–188, 660 n116; *SA*, p. 1020 [Document 576, September 30, 1923]).

with Chamberlain and the visit to the Wagners, and states that Hitler said that "Chamberlain's letter came during my incarceration!"[7] This is incorrect (although it is uncertain if it was Hitler or Heim that made the mistake), as Chamberlain had in fact written to Hitler on October 7, 1923, a letter in which he celebrated Hitler and drew parallels between him and the hero Parsifal in Wagner's opera with the same name. It was instead Hitler who replied to this letter during his time in Landsberg (likely on or around May 5, 1924), although he addressed it to Siegfried Wagner (Richard Wagner's son). Hitler wrote about his visit to the Wagner estate in "the beginning of October" 1923 and also about how he until November 9 had nurtured the hope of being able to thank Chamberlain in person "for his wonderful [and] good letters," saying that Fate (*Schicksal*, i.e. God) should grant him the opportunity to bring the sickly and suffering Chamberlain "the best remedy that the world of today can offer him" but that the failure of the *coup* had crushed this dream.[8] From the way Hitler formulated his letter, it thus seems as if Chamberlain wrote more than one letter to Hitler before November 9, 1923. Be that as it may, there can be absolutely no doubt about the fact that Chamberlain had become completely enchanted by Hitler after only meeting him once.

Chamberlain interpreted the First World War, or the Great War as it was known then, as an anti-German war inspired and controlled by Jewish powers both outside and inside Germany. He was thus also a prominent representative of the "stab in the back" myth according to which Germany had been betrayed from within – and it was all master-minded by the Jews. The parallels between Chamberlain's and Hitler's views of Jesus are many and very significant. In *Die Grundlagen*, Chamberlain claimed that the birth of Jesus signified the introduction into world history of a new race of humans. His Christ was one that celebrated strength and shunned weakness. In this theology, Jesus "was no 'divine voice of compassion for weak humanism'" and Jesus' teachings about turning the other cheek should not be interpreted as such. Instead, Jesus symbolized a rebirth of humanity characterized by

---

[7] *Monologe ...* , p. 224.
[8] *SA*, pp. 1231–1232 (Document 636, probably May 5, 1924); Hesemann, M., *Hitlers Religion ...* , p. 203; Rißmann, M., *Hitlers Gott ...* , pp. 106–107.

90 / Christianity in Hitler's Ideology

heroism – and only true Christians could be truly heroic.[9] This, Rudolf Jung wrote, was the whole purpose of the NSDAP, that is, the spiritual renewal of the German people. The red banner with the black swastika was the symbol of this movement, and "it is our holy conviction" that Hitler and the NSDAP will lead the German people to victory.[10]

There is a very direct line between Chamberlain's and Hitler's views. For example, the latter would often repeat the idea that compassion was "false humanism."[11] To be a true Christian, Hitler told an NSDAP gathering in Augsburg on July 6, 1923, did not mean "to cowardly offer the other cheek, but to be a warrior for righteousness and a combater of every injustice."[12] This was repeated in Sebottendorff's book *Bevor Hitler kam* in 1933, where he wrote that the National Socialists "do not practice the drudgery of humanism" (*Humanitätsdusel*), nor do they "give the other cheek to him who struck us across the opposite one; we strike back and take all our pride in striking hard, to strike so that the opponent remains lying on the ground." He ended this rant by referring to the example of Jesus Christ: "That was also the opinion of our Saviour: he had come to bring the sword."[13] Hitler proclaimed on September 27, 1923, before a congregation of the *Deutschen Kampfbund* (German Combat League) that the NSDAP, as well as the other two organizations making up the *Kampfbund*, rested on "the teaching that Christ had once proclaimed to the world." But he left it up to each individual to decide what being a Christian meant for them.[14] The principle of resisting "false humanity" also formed the foundation of the Nazi eugenics policies, and the leading man in charge of this effort, the deeply religious doctor Walter Groß, motivated these policies and the fight against false humanism in a

[9] Fenske, W., *Wie Jesus zum "Arier" wurde* ... , pp. 105–106; Chamberlain, H. S., *Die Grundlagen* ... , p. 206.

[10] Jung, R., *Der nationale Sozialismus* ... , pp. 63–64.

[11] See e.g. *RSA* II/2, p. 770 (Document 253).

[12] *SA*, p. 947 (Document 544, July 6, 1923). Hans Frank quotes a similar statement made by Hitler in his memoirs; see Frank, H., *Im Angesicht des Galgens* ... , p. 40.

[13] Sebottendorff, R. von, *Bevor Hitler kam* ... , p. 26. It has been stated that Sebottendorff by then "had broken with Christianity" (Weber, T., *Becoming Hitler* ... , p. 133), but the fact that he refers to Jesus as both his own and the movement's savior makes this a lot less likely to be true.

[14] *SA*, p. 1018 (Document 574).

radio speech on July 14, 1933, by saying: "The rose that does not bloom will be pulled up and tossed in the fire, and the gardener will chop down the tree that bears no fruit."[15]

This a close paraphrasing of one of Jesus' parables in the Sermon on the Mount where, according to Matthew 7:19 and 12:33 and Luke 4:43–44, Jesus said that each tree that does not bear fruit will be cut down and tossed into the fire. The same words are also ascribed to John the Baptist in Matthew 3:10. This parable also appears in John 15:1–6, which talks about how "the Father" (i.e. God) is the gardener in the vineyard who breaks off and throws away every branch that does not yield fruit. Jesus then says that he is the wine tree and his followers are the branches and that each of those who do not remain in him will be tossed out like a broken branch and wither and die, and that these branches will then be gathered and thrown into the fire. Groß's, and National Socialism's, message was clear: pity or compassion could not be allowed to interfere with the racial hygiene project.

In the third chapter of the first volume of *Die Grundlagen*, Chamberlain presented his ideas about Jesus under the headline "Die Erscheinung Christi" ("The Appearance of Christ"), and he started by proclaiming that Christ had to be separated from historical Christianity, which was not what Christ had originally taught. Indeed, the concepts of sin, salvation, rebirth, and grace were all old Aryan ideas that the early church had picked up and integrated into its Christianity. The birth of Christ had meant a complete transformation in terms of its "ethical meaning for humanity, [for] the entire 'moral worldview'." He describes Jesus, and the Buddha incidentally, as "moral heroes." Only with Jesus had humanity received "a *moral culture*" [emphasis in original], denoting the great importance that morality and ethics played in Chamberlain's worldview. Jesus had not preached a monastic teaching that was hostile to the world. Instead, Jesus' teaching was characterized by a positive outlook that emphasized the importance of willpower. The enormous focus on willpower was something that characterized Jesus, he claimed. He also stressed that Christ saw "divine

---

[15] Quoted in Koontz, C., *The Nazi Conscience*, pp. 110–111. Translation by Koontz.

92 / Christianity in Hitler's Ideology

Providence" everywhere; nothing happened in the world without God's approval.[16] This view was shared by Hitler to a fault.

This was of course a highly contradictive view, since Chamberlain at the same time stressed the concept and nature of Providence and the omnipotence of God, which really left no place at all for human will to affect the outcome of anything. Racial biologists in Germany, such as Fritz Lenz, were quite preoccupied with this problem since the concept of "will" had been central to German philosophy since Leibniz and was the focus of both Schopenhauer's and Nietzsche's philosophy. The implications for National Socialism were huge, considering the central place of the idea of "willpower" in its *Weltanschauung*. Lenz solved the problem by rejecting rational thinking altogether. He proclaimed that even if it was true that the world was predetermined, it would not deny the existence of free will because the willful act was preconditioned and inevitable.[17] That made absolutely no sense.

But the issue of free will was a classic problem in Christian theology as well. Hitler adopted a view of the problem that was very similar to Lenz's. For example, on June 6, 1937, in Regensburg, Hitler noted how impossible it was to succeed in an undertaking that was "not blessed by this Almighty" and how a mission blessed by God could not be destroyed by man. Just a couple of weeks later, on June 27, he said at a *Gau* party day in Würzburg: "As weak as the individual human is in the end, compared to the almighty Providence and its will, just as strong is he in the moment when he acts according to the intention of this

---

[16] Chamberlain, H. S., *Die Grundlagen* ... , pp. 190–192, 199, 202, 207, 240–241. Later in the book, however, Chamberlain states that it must be admitted that the focus on will is a Jewish influence on Christianity and that in this respect Jesus could not be completely separated from the Jewish context in which he appeared; he indeed *was* a Jew in the moral sense. "I will even say that Christ belongs 'morally' to the Jews," he says in a rather startling passage. Even Jesus' determination and will was to a certain extent Jewish, he proclaimed, since will was the most characterizing trait of the Jews. But he then immediately went on to claim that Jesus the Savior (*Heiland*) broke with this Jewishness in the application of the moral view of God's omnipotence and Providence and in the relation between humanity and God, and in the approach to the human will that followed from it (ibid., p. 248). Hitler obviously never adopted *this* view, and we have no record of him commenting on it.

[17] Varshizky, Amit, "Between Science and Racial Metaphysics: Fritz Lenz and Racial Anthropology in Interwar Germany," *Intellectual History Review*, Vol. 27, No. 2 (2017), pp. 257–259. Quotes from Lenz that follow are cited in this article.

93 / Hitler's Religious Teachers

Providence!" The speech on June 6 was also the first time on record that Hitler used the term "God-belief" (*Gottgläubigkeit*) to describe the religiosity within the NSDAP.[18] This shows how the idea of divine Providence was directly connected to Christian beliefs within this German *völkisch*-inspired tradition. In point 24 of the NSDAP party program, there is a formulation that is strongly reminiscent of Chamberlain's theological ruminations, namely, where it says that positive Christianity "fights against the Jewish-materialist spirit within us and outside of us" and that freedom of religion was the best way to do this as long as the religion in question did not endanger the existence of the state or contradict "the ethical and moral feelings of the Germanic race."[19] This of course per definition excluded Jews and Judaism. While the former was a formulation copied from Eckart, who likely got it from Chamberlain, the latter was directly related to Chamberlain's idea about the importance of the moral and ethical revolution through the advent of Jesus.

As Hitler gathered all the leading generals and officers of the *Wehrmacht* (about 200 people) at noon in the "Great Hall" in the new Reich Chancellery in Berlin on November 23, 1939, to discuss the upcoming *Fall Gelb* (Plan Yellow) – the attack on France, Belgium, and Holland in May 1940 – he stressed the absolute importance of having God on one's side. Hitler started by pointing out that the meeting was meant to give the gathered "insight into the world of ideas" that dominated his thinking. He stressed that he remained strong in his faith, despite many setbacks during the *Kampfzeit* and that "Providence got the last word and granted me success." Because of this, he had the "solid will to make brutal decisions." Hitler then said that it was in 1919 that he "after a long inner struggle decided to become a politician." This was a moment of truthful clarity, since the official story, as told in *Mein Kampf*, was that he had come to this decision while at the hospital in Pasewalk at the end of 1918.

---

[18] *HRP* I/2, pp. 700, 704 (June 6 and 27, 1937).
[19] Point 24 in *Grundsätzliches Programm der Nationalsozialistischen Deutschen Arbeiter-Partei*, http://jgsaufgab.de/intranet2/geschichte/geschichte/natsoz/programm_nsdap_20 .htm. For the same point, see, e.g., Koehne, S. "Religion in the Early Nazi Milieu ... ," p. 675.

94 / Christianity in Hitler's Ideology

Hitler then complained about the lack of "faithful" (*Gläubige*) in the *Wehrmacht* in his foreign policy decisions after 1933, such as the remilitarization of the Rheinland, and noted that many "prophets" had expressed their doubts in him. He ended his speech by once again underlining that the success of *Fall Gelb* was "wholly dependent upon Providence's favour" and the "fanatical determination" of the military leaders. He would destroy the enemy, he said, because "only he who fights on the side of fate can have a favourable Providence. During the previous years I have seen several examples of Providence. Also, in the current development do I see Providence."[20]

It is easy to see why Hitler must have felt this way at that moment because two weeks earlier, on November 8, he had managed to evade an assassination attempt completely unscathed after leaving the *Bürgerbräukeller* in Munich earlier than planned because he had to catch the train to Berlin. The plan had been to fly there, but bad weather made this impossible. The carpenter Georg Elser had placed a bomb under the stage, which was set to explode at 9:20 p.m. That was supposed to have been mid-speech, but Hitler left at 9:07 p.m., which meant that he survived while eight other people died and about sixty more were injured. This was interpreted also by Goebbels as divine intervention and as a confirmation that he would stand under God's protection until he concluded his historic mission. Christa Schroeder, Hitler's long-time secretary, would after the war claim that Hitler shared this conviction. It is indeed very likely that he did, but we do not have any contemporary source that confirms it.[21]

Just like Hitler later would, Chamberlain answered the question of whether Jesus was a Jew negatively. However, he was not mainly talking about Jesus' Jewishness in racial terms – although he considered this to be extremely unlikely considering Jesus' birthplace was Galilee (and not Judea, which also gave no reason to assume that his parents

---

[20] Michalka, Wolfgang (ed.), *Deutsche Geschichte 1933–1945: Dokumente zur Innen- und Außenpolitik* (Frankfurt am Main: Fischer Taschenbuch Verlag, 1996), pp. 180–182 (Document 139). See also Ullrich, Volker, *Adolf Hitler: Biographie. Band II: Die Jahre des Untergangs* (Frankfurt am Main: S. Fischer Verlag, 2018), pp. 101–102.

[21] *TBJG* I/3, pp. 636–637 (November 9, 1939). For Schroeder's version, see Zoller, Albert, Hitler Privat: Erlebnisbericht seiner Geheimsekretärin (Düsseldorf: Droste Verlag, 1949), p. 181.

95 / Hitler's Religious Teachers

were Jews) – but in terms of his upbringing, education, and morality. The latter was more important in Chamberlain's view than the racial issue, which struck him to be a rather constricted way of looking at the problem. But whoever claimed that Jesus was a Jew had to do so against his own better knowledge, he argued, because Jesus did not have a drop of Jewish blood in his veins (thus, Chamberlain *did* lend himself to racial arguments about Jesus after all). Christ embodied, according to Chamberlain, the negation of the Jewish people. In Chamberlain, we also find the view that the Jews were unable to even have a religion.[22] This notion too was shared by Hitler.

Hence, even though there were very clear differences between Chamberlain's and Hitler's views of Christianity and the apostle Paul, it is equally clear that Chamberlain was an important inspiration for Hitler, as their personal interaction and Hitler's later testimony shows. It is likely that Chamberlain became an important figure for Hitler because of his marriage to Richard Wagner's daughter Eva in 1908. Considering Hitler's great interest in Wagner, it is indeed likely that Hitler had heard of Chamberlain at that point. Even though we do not know exactly when Hitler heard of or read *Die Grundlagen* for the first time – in parts or in its entirety, in the original or in secondhand popularized form[23] – we can be very sure that it must have been after 1908, because it is simply extremely unlikely that Hitler had read Chamberlain before he was eighteen/nineteen years old or before his move to Vienna in early 1908. We actually have no direct evidence that he had read Chamberlain even before the First World War. Timothy Ryback notes that Otto Straßer states in his memoir *Hitler und ich* that it was Eckart who introduced the writings of both Chamberlain and Lagarde to Hitler.[24] If this is true, which it very well could be, then that means that Hitler did indeed only read Chamberlain in 1919 at the earliest. Michael Hesemann writes that it was during his time in

---

[22] Fenske, W., *Wie Jesus zum "Arier" wurde . . .* , pp. 106–107; Chamberlain, H. S., *Die Grundlagen . . .* , pp. 18, 211, 214, 218–219, 393, 410.

[23] Brigitte Hamann makes the point that Hitler must not necessarily have gotten all the ideas that paralleled Chamberlain's directly from him, although she still assumes that Hitler read material related to Chamberlain during his Vienna years (Hamann, B., *Hitlers Wien . . .* , p. 334).

[24] Ryback, T. W., *Hitler's Private Library . . .* , p. 69.

96 / Christianity in Hitler's Ideology

Landsberg that Hitler had time to "study Chamberlain's collected works."[25] This sounds reasonable, although we cannot verify it.

That not every prominent Nazi was well-read on Chamberlain is clear. After the war, Rudolf Heß wrote from the Spandau prison in Berlin to his mother, Klara, and told her about how he had finally read Chamberlain's *Man and God: Deliberations on Religion and Christianity (Mensch und Gott: Betrachtungen über Religion und Christentum)*. Through Chamberlain, Heß got a completely new image of Christ, he said, an image that stood in complete contrast to the one that the Christian churches had been spreading. The churches had not even shied away from forging parts of the original text in the New Testament, according to Heß, who had apparently swallowed everything Chamberlain had written hook, line, and sinker. Jesus' religion was the simplest one imaginable, he told his mother, and it demanded no mediators in the form of churches of priests. It was a Christ that was tolerant and simple. His teaching only concerned itself with God's Kingdom and the Heavenly Father. It was a view of the Savior (*Heiland*) that aligned very closely to the one that he had had during his school years as a boy, stated Heß. The Savior's aims did not concern earthly matters but were only concerned with getting the individual into heaven. Only later did Paul enter the picture, and in his wake followed hundreds of church fathers that wished to imprison the free spirit in man. Man only strove upward in his faith, Heß wrote, and God's grace bowed itself toward him. The only thing that was necessary for salvation was faith: "That is how Christ's word is made intelligible: 'Each and every one that believes in God has the life'." Christ had nothing to do with prostrating oneself or forsaking the world, which Heß had previously believed, and he had not spoken about sin; he had not punished the ultimate sinner. The Church had done its best to hide these facts from the believers, Heß said. Heß was obviously arguing on his own behalf here, since he wanted to be forgiven by God for what he had done during his life. It is an interesting fact that several of the letters that Heß wrote while in Spandau had religious content. It seems as if his son was also engaged in religious deliberations and was thinking about joining a Christian congregation. Heß wrote that if his son decided to

[25] Hesemann, M., *Hitlers Religion ...*, p. 214.

97 / Hitler's Religious Teachers

do so, then his father would only be happy, because for him it was of no consequence *how* one found God. The important thing was that it happened in accordance with the personal preferences of the believer.[26]

2.3 Blood Magic, the Theology of Race, and the Spiritual Struggle against the Jews

The studies of the Nazi Christian organizations show very clearly that "Jewishness" most of all was considered a spiritual quality – not a genetic or scientific one. Chamberlain even entirely rejected the idea of a scientific foundation for his beliefs. The Aryan religion, that is, Christianity, and the knowledge of God were given to him through intuition, while the Jewish religion was only a matter of following rules. The Nazi theologians stressed that Judaism was a materialist religion while Christianity was a spiritual religion. The idea of race emphasized this dichotomy that was already embedded within Christianity. Even for the most ardent phrenologists, race was in the end an issue of the spiritual and moral qualities that were housed in the body. That was the real object for their so-called studies. Modern race ideologues viewed the body as the vessel that carried a soul equipped with moral and ethical qualities, Susannah Heschel points out, and this turned race theory into a kind of theology – not a science. Christianity had the very same understanding of the relationship between body and soul. For the Nazis and the race ideologues, it was not the physiques of the Jews that threatened the German people; it was the degenerative effect of the Jewish spirit. That was what threatened the pure Aryan spirit, or soul. It was for this reason that racism was concentrated on the blood because the idea was, just as in many religions, that the blood was

---

[26] Heß, Ilse (ed.), *Gefangener des Friedens: Neue Briefe aus Spandau* (Leoni am Starnberger See: Druffel Verlag, 1955), pp. 169–187, quote on p. 173. It is not without importance that the book contains an afterword from the publisher that questions the validity in the Nuremberg tribunal's life sentence against Heß and expresses the hope that the book would result in Heß's being set free and being allowed to reunite with his wife, Ilse (ibid., pp. 188–195). The letters were thus in a way intended to be "evidence" that Heß was a reformed citizen. Nonetheless, there is no indication that the views expressed about Jesus and his religious faith are untrue.

98 / Christianity in Hitler's Ideology

the link between body and soul, between the human and the divine. Racism, just like religion, attaches moral and spiritual qualities to the blood.[27]

In Nazi mythology, the "essence and character" (*das Wesen und der Karaktär*) of a people was wholly determined by blood because blood (i.e. the spirit) determined race. Cultural matters, such as religion and language, were secondary in this process, according to Hitler.[28] The blood carried spiritual characteristics. Ironically, this was the same view that is to be found in Leviticus 17:14, where it says that "for the life of every creature is its blood: its blood is its life. ... You shall not eat the blood of any creature, for the life of every creature is its blood. Whoever eats it shall be cut off." The same message can be found in Genesis 9:4. These passages become even more ironic when one considers the fact that Hitler abstained (more or less) from eating meat, and therefore blood. The idea that the blood carried moral qualities is also repeated in Matthew 27:4, when Judas says "I have sinned ... for I have betrayed innocent blood." This was a reference to Jesus, who by being divine was entirely free from sin, and to the fact that man's fall from grace and original sin were encapsulated in the blood. In Luke 11:50–51, Jesus curses the Pharisees and says that the blood of all the murdered prophets will be a curse upon them, that is, the Jews. Hitler and National Socialism shared the same basic view of the soul as that which is laid out in the Jewish Torah. It was in essence a biblical worldview.

This was why the battle against the Jews and their purported influence in the world was not first and foremost a material and physical battle but a spiritual one. "We are fighting for a German state," Hitler said on August 1, 1923, "at the forefront of which stands an entity consisting of a social, national, and pure spirit!" It was only because of a lack of such a pure spirit that the German people had perished and were now in dire need of a "fanatical nationalistic attitude" in the people, because only then was man prepared to sacrifice his blood for his fatherland. This state would not be built on "international wisdom," he stressed.[29] Many years later, in January 1941, Hitler spoke about the

---

[27] Heschel, S., *The Aryan Jesus* ... , pp. 18–23.
[28] *SA*, p. 541 (Document 340). See also Hesemann, M., *Hitlers Religion* ... , p. 239.
[29] *SA*, p. 956 (Document 553).

Kampfzeit as "perhaps the greatest battle for the soul that has been fought in our history."[30] When the war was over, he said in October of the same year, then he would return to the German people an even more fanatical National Socialist than ever before.[31] He repeated this idea in May 1942 when he stated in a telegram to Robert Ley that they had gone to war as fanatical National Socialists and that they would return from this battle even more fanatically convinced.[32] The contempt for knowledge shines through here, but the central message is Hitler's understanding of the fight against the Jews, and therefore the fight for Germany, as being a spiritual struggle first and foremost.

When Hitler held his first public speech after being released from the fortress in Landsberg, at an NSDAP meeting in Munich on February 27, 1925, he made certain to underline the spiritual and religious side of the struggle that the party had been founded to wage. With specifically Christian references, he spoke about the "Satanic power" that had thrown Germany down the pit of suffering and about the fight against Marxism and the spiritual carriers of the "world plague" and the "scourge" of humanity: the Jews.[33] Now, was all this religious language really an expression of Hitler's true beliefs, or just a propaganda gimmick with which to woo his audience? It is of course impossible to know for certain what anyone really truly believes. But we are nonetheless all the time trying to establish, in the light of the available evidence, what is most likely to be the case.

First, the question of whether this language reflected Hitler's true beliefs or was just mere propaganda is based on a false premise, namely, that these categories are mutually exclusive. For Hitler, there was no inherent contradiction between propaganda and honestly held views. If he had to use religious language only for propaganda reasons, that was fine by him. If his own religious beliefs could be used as propaganda, that was fine too. After all, historians agree that Hitler and the other National Socialists meant what they said about the Jews in their propaganda. So, what are we to make of these statements above, and in this book as a whole? Hitler likely used the specifically Christian language not only for propagandistic reasons, but for expressing his

---

[30] *HRP* II/4, p. 1658 (January 30, 1941).   [31] Ibid., p. 1766 (October 3, 1941).
[32] Ibid., p. 1881 (May 3, 1942).   [33] *RSA* I, p. 20 (Document 6).

100 / Christianity in Hitler's Ideology

true beliefs as well, because this was how he made sense of the world – as a divine struggle between good and evil. Second, another reason for why we ought to believe that was the case is because the congregation that he was addressing were all ideologically convinced Nazis and members of the NSDAP (although there may have been some nonbelievers in the crowd too). At the very least, Hitler understood that what he said would resonate with his audience because their spiritual beliefs aligned with his own. But there was no real need to put on a show like that for them. Third, a strong argument against the "only propaganda" thesis is also the fact that Hitler used this imagery seldomly. If it was intended to rally supporters to the cause, or make the members even more fanatical, then we should expect to see much more of it. Moreover, we have no evidence at all that indicates that Hitler pandered to a group of believers that he did not agree with. Thus, we ought to take what he said seriously and really consider the possibility that he meant what he said, just like he meant the other things he said about the Jews. Hitler here made the Jews the carriers of a spiritual poison that threatened the German people. Yes, the Jews and their ideological virus in the form of Marxism was a foreign parasite within the body of the German people. Blood and spirit here coalesced into a unified whole – two sides of the same racial coin. Until evidence to the contrary comes to light, we have very good reasons indeed to assume that Hitler was expressing his true beliefs here.

If the so-called body of the people (*Volkskörper*) received foreign blood, Hitler wrote in *Mein Kampf*, then the consequence would subsequently be an "unholy splintering of our inner being." Hitler viewed race mixing as a form of blood poisoning that tore apart the Aryan soul. This mixing of races in the German people had begun in earnest with the Thirty Years' War, he said. This was an idea that Hitler had probably gotten from the American Madison Grant, who had claimed the same thing in his *The Passing of the Great Race* (which had been published in German after the first, but before the second, volume of *Mein Kampf* was available).[34] That was the reason for why Hitler, in the second volume of *Mein Kampf*, argued that the German state should initially turn its attention to strengthening the physical

[34] *Hitler, Mein Kampf* ... (Band II), pp. 1001, 1012–1013 [21, 27].

101 / Hitler's Religious Teachers

fitness and health of the German youth, because with a strong body came the longevity of the soul. The fact that geniuses were often sickly was of no importance, said Hitler. They were only the exceptions that proved the rule. Primarily, the youth would be given a spiritual education, and not a science education, because the important thing was to give the youth willpower and the ability to make decisions. Real knowledge about the world would come second, according to Hitler. The state would proceed from the assumption that it was better that a people was physically fit but uneducated, than a spiritually erudite mass of physically weak individuals. This was surely somewhat contradictory. "A people consisting of learned," Hitler remarked, "will . . . not conquer Heaven." A healthy spirit could in the long run only inhabit a healthy body, he said. Therefore, the schools should devote a massive amount of time to physical activity, since there was no point in burdening the young brain with lots of unnecessary knowledge.[35]

2.4 The Irrational and Anti-scientific Nature of National Socialism

Brigitte Hamann has proposed that Hitler's pseudoscientific racism did not come from reading the primary sources and that he was thus not really inspired directly by, for example, Darwin, Nietzsche, Le Bon, Chamberlain, Dühring, Schopenhauer, or Schiller. Instead, he appears to have read mostly popular versions (and, especially in the case of Darwin, falsified vulgarizations) of these thinkers in newspapers, magazines, pamphlets, and other writings. All these popularized texts had one thing in common: they all stood in clear opposition to the science that was taught and practiced at the universities. According to Hamann, this was in a way a central part of the *Zeitgeist*, one that was filled with suspicion and outright hatred toward established science and knowledge seeking. Chamberlain, for example,

---

[35] Ibid., pp. 1041–1045 [41–43]. See also the rest of the chapter: pp. 1047–1105 [44–73]. Hitler is here alluding to the famous saying "In a sound body lives a sound spirit," which originates with the Roman poet Juvenal's satirical verse "Orandum est, ut sit mens sana in corpore sano" ("It is to be hoped that a sound spirit lives in a sound body"). It was thus originally a satirical phrase, but with time the initial "ordanum est" fell away, and the phrase instead became a truth statement.

102 / Christianity in Hitler's Ideology

declared without a hint of shame that he was an uneducated man; he even bragged about his dilettantism, which he described as a reaction against the "bondage of science." The scientists were "buried" in their particular subjects that made them blind to the world around them. This celebration of dilettantism was supported by Hitler to the last syllable. Even politicians had enormous success among the people if they positioned themselves and dismissed "the Professors," and Karl Lueger, the mayor of Vienna that Hitler held so dear, was precisely such a celebrator of dilettantism. Since Darwin's scientific results came to be misused and to be misinterpreted to such a degree in this culture, we should perhaps not be surprised that the principle of natural selection (which had nothing to do with physical strength or weakness) came to be transformed from simply an evolutionary selection mechanism to a moral imperative that was only concerned with the right of the strong to rule over, and destroy, the weak.[36] For Hitler, this hypothesis became a religious doctrine that neither could nor should be questioned, even when one's own people suffered because of it.

Rosenberg hated scientific rationality too. In fact, he was of the opinion that "the entire liberal-bourgeois order, including its belief in rational thought, scientific positivism and universal progress, reflects an anti-racial system of values, whose roots are found in the 'spiritual dogmatism' of the Church and Jewish law."[37] It should thus be obvious to everyone by now that National Socialism as *Weltanschauung* cannot be said to have contained much in the form of rational scientific thinking. One could of course argue that there was an inherent rationality in Hitler's views if one accepts the premises that National Socialism was based on. That is true. But then we find ourselves in the predicament of having to accept that there are basically no irrational ideologies or people at all, since every system of ideas could be justified on that same basis. More importantly, it is far from evident that Hitler's ideology, or his actions, was rational, even if we accept its basic premises.

---

[36] Hamann, B., *Hitlers Wien* ... , pp. 333–336; Chamberlain, H. S., *Die Grundlagen* ... , p. ix. Note the parallels between Chamberlain's and Hitler's celebration of the unlearned dilettante and today's similar critique of experts and scientific enterprise. The Covid anti-vax movement, Trumpism, flat-earthers, and climate change deniers are only some contemporary examples.

[37] Varshizky, A., "Alfred Rosenberg ... ," p. 320.

Yet, Darwinism, or evolutionary theory as such, was not something that the National Socialists celebrated or built their ideology on. In fact, Darwinism was criticized for being "materialistic," that is, Jewish in spirit. This might seem contradictory at first, but the reason behind this rejection was described by Rudolf Jung in his book *Der nationale Sozialismus* from 1922, in which he approvingly cited Oswald Spengler's judgment: "Darwinism ... makes the condition of the whole soul causally dependent upon the effects of materialistic factors." This was "the especially shallow view of [Georg] Büchner and [Ernst] Haeckel."[38] Rosenberg also proclaimed that the theory of evolution had been used in "the liberal era" in order to falsely defeat "religion as such" through science.[39] Exactly the same point was in fact made by the founder of the *Thule Gesellschaft*, Rudolf von Sebottendorff, in his book *Bevor Hitler kam*, who also mentioned Büchner and Haeckel specifically.[40] Haeckel had explicitly rejected the idea of the soul being independent of the material body.[41]

Even much later, there were many Nazis in leading positions that rejected Darwin for the same reason. One such person was Hans Schemm, who was a *Gauleiter* (regional leader) in Wagner's hometown of Bayreuth as well as the head of the NSDAP Teachers' Association. Schemm was a deeply believing Protestant Christian and known throughout Nazi Germany for his motto: "Our religion is Christ; our politics is the Fatherland!" According to Schemm, Darwin (and Marx) manifested materialism in political form.[42] Erich Ludendorff expressed similar views in 1924 when he said that he could not accept the Darwinist idea that it was not God that drove the development of organisms forward.[43] This is more important than it may seem at first

---

[38] Jung, R., *Der nationale Sozialismus* ... , p. 98.   [39] Rosenberg, A., *Der Mythos*, p. 599.

[40] Sebottendorff, R. von, *Bevor Hitler kam* ... , p. 19.

[41] Kleeberg, Bernhard, *Theophysis: Ernst Haeckels Philosophie des Naturganzen* (Cologne: Böhlau Verlag, 2005), pp. 244–252. Haeckel thought, however, that he could still save the soul's existence by declaring matter to be possessed by a universal spirit. He thought that he in this way had solved the dilemma and overcome the breach between idealism and materialism.

[42] Steigmann-Gall, R., *The Holy Reich* ... , pp. 24–25.

[43] Strohm, Harald, *Die Gnosis und der Nationalsozialismus* (Frankfurt am Main: Suhrkamp Verlag, 1973), pp. 37–38.

104 / Christianity in Hitler's Ideology

because it means that the image of National Socialism as a Darwinist-materialist ideology is completely wrong.

National Socialism was generally skeptical of science, and the *Völkischer Beobachter* often contained articles rejecting the ideals of the Enlightenment and warned against overconfidence in rational thinking. Even Newton was taken to task for being the originator of modern materialism and for being infected by the Jewish mentality and spirit.[44] The Nazi hatred of the Enlightenment was no coincidence. Its leading figures, Voltaire, Rousseau, and Montesquieu, had been instrumental in the emancipation of the Jews in 1791.[45] We have no evidence of Hitler ever mentioning Darwin or Darwinism, much less that he had read or been inspired by Darwin.[46] Darwinism really is a materialist theory that leaves no room for religious spirituality and idealism, which the National Socialist ideologues frequently and fervently claimed was what set the Aryan apart from the Jew. Therefore, Darwinism was suspect from the get-go. Spengler's social Darwinism was acceptable, however, because it emphasized the struggle for survival in human society and culture yet allowed for the spiritual powers of the Aryan and the Jew to have been given by God.

Fritz Lenz, who has been referred to "as an 'archetypal Nazi eugenicist'," has often been cited as saying that "National Socialism is simply applied biology." But what exactly did that mean in the National Socialist and racial anthropology parlance of that age? It in fact had a very different meaning from that which it has today. The National Socialist understanding of biology, writes Amit Varshizky, "transcended mere genetics and biological determinations and consisted of

[44] Dennis, David B., *Inhumanities: Nazi Interpretations of Western Culture* (Cambridge: Cambridge University Press, 2012), pp. 142–147.

[45] Head, P., "The Nazi Quest for an Aryan Jesus," pp. 62–63.

[46] The only exception that I know of is Otto Wagener, who at one point states that Hitler supposedly told him in 1930 that Darwin had been right about natural selection (Wagener, Otto, *Hitler aus nächster Nähe: Aufzeichnungen eines Vertrauten 1929–1932*, ed. H. A. Turner, Jr. [Frankfurt am Main: Verlag Ullstein, 1978], p. 106). However, this is not a reliable source regarding this matter. In an interview from 1964, the former Nazi Hermann Esser also stated that Hitler later in life read Darwin (Weber, Thomas, *Wie Adolf Hitler zum Nazi wurde: Vom unpolitischen Soldaten zum Autor von "Mein Kampf"* [Berlin: Propyläen, 2016], p. 364). Considering the fact that Esser was only a part of Hitler's inner circle during the early 1920s, he was hardly in a position to know what Hitler read or not after that point.

105 / Hitler's Religious Teachers

meta-biological meanings." Lenz was an assistant to, and follower of, Alfred Ploetz, perhaps the most important founder of German racial hygiene and Professor of Racial Hygiene at the University of Munich from 1923 to 1933 (and thereafter Director of the Institute for Racial Hygiene at the University of Berlin). Lenz outright rejected genetics as an explanation for the mental differences the racial hygienists believed they observed between the races. Hans F. K. Günther, another prominent racial theorist in interwar and Nazi Germany, also "criticized all those 'biological' and 'biologistic' worldviews that are especially foregrounded nowadays in current research on race [and] damage the Germanic rebirth." The reason for Lenz's and the other racial anthropologists' and hygienists' rejection of Mendelian genetics and biological science was that it was considered materialist and thereby Jewish.[47] In rejecting "materialistic science," Lenz opted for "vitalistic speculation" instead, and concluded

> that race is an irreducible category that cannot be subjected to any empirical judgement or scientific reasoning, and thus should be ultimately articulated in terms of intuitive and meta-rational experience.[48]

The other racial theorists did so too. For example, in his bestselling *Rassenkunde des deutschen Volkes* (The Racial Science of the German People) from 1922, Günther explained that "any attempt to establish racial science on the principles of naturalistic, positivistic, and value-free methods was doomed to failure, since the racial question was itself a question of value."[49] Lenz also openly admitted in the sixth edition of his book *Grundriß* (Ground Work) from 1936 (first published in 1921) that National Socialism's concept of race did not, and in fact could not, have any scientific basis. Lenz wrote:

---

[47] Varshizky, A., "Between Science and Racial Metaphysics ... ," pp. 247, 253–255, 257.
[48] Ibid., p. 257.
[49] Varshizky, Amit, "Non-Mechanistic Explanatory Styles in Interwar German Racial Theory: A Comparison of Hans F. K. Günther and Ludwig Ferdinand Clauß," in Sabine Hildebrandt, Mirriam Offer, and Michael Grodin (eds.), *Medicine and the Holocaust: New Studies on Victims, Perpetrators and Legacies for the 21st Century* (New York: Berghahn Books, 2019), p. 29.

106 / Christianity in Hitler's Ideology

Following its founder, Adolf Hitler, the National-Socialist state placed race at the center of existence. The National-Socialist world-view is based on faith in race [*im Glauben an die Rasse*]. It is not based upon scientific knowledge [*wissenschaftlicher Erkenntnis*] regarding the essence of race and its life regulations. First and foremost, it is the will for self-realization [*der Wille zur Selbtsbehauptung*] of race itself; this will is previous to any scientific perception and its derivatives. The importance of racial biological knowledge lies therefore in its being an instrument for preserving, recuperating, and improving race.[50]

Günther shared this view and explained that "the Nordic ideal" did not stem from the material but from the spirit. He "acknowledged the supremacy of the spirit, or the will" and was adamant that biology, that is, "empirical and descriptive science," "will never be able to serve as a basis for a *Weltanschauung*."[51] There simply was no way to base Nazi racial policy and ideology on science. The racial biologists therefore willingly opted to leave rational and scientific thinking behind in favor of metaphysical speculation. As Amit Varshizky eloquently puts it:

> Accordingly, the Nazi *Weltanschauung* should be based on "faith" and not on "knowledge"; on a "will for self-realization" instead of "scientific perception." Science thus gains a new meaning here: it is no longer an organized system of principles and regulations directed to achieve meaningful insights about the world. It is an instrument in the service of a meta-rational faith, aimed to push aside any dialectic skepticism and critical judgement in favor of internal conviction and formative will.[52]

Lenz's "faith in race" became the founding principle of National Socialism. The Nazi notion of race was both "irrational and quasimystical," and it was "emptied of its actual biological meaning and invested with idealistic, metaphysical, and even eschatological meanings." This had a long history within the *völkisch* community. It also

---

[50] Varshizky, A., "Between Science and Racial Metaphysics …," p. 260.
[51] Varshizky, A., "Non-Mechanistic …," pp. 29, 31. Translation by Varshizky.   [52] Ibid.

107 / Hitler's Religious Teachers

dominated the interwar *Kulturpessimismus* (cultural pessimism) circles.[53] The racial theorists were worried about "the pressing problem of modern nihilism and the downfall of absolute values" and its influence on science.[54] It was therefore the very opposite of ethical relativism that it has often been made out to be. This is a fundamental insight about racial "science" overall that has not been noticed in much of the scholarship on the issue. The choice to abandon truly scientific methods and values was more or less forced upon the racial anthropologists when the effort to tie their ideology to science failed. But instead of discarding their unscientific racist ideology, they opted for rejecting the scientific method. In short, they had to put the cart before the horse to avoid cognitive dissonance.

2.5   The Apostle Paul: Hitler's Disagreement with Chamberlain

As we have seen, Chamberlain even thought that the materialistic Jews could not be truly religious – they lacked the ability to form a religious community since they came from the wilderness and were equipped with too poor an imagination. Hitler's own views of the Jews in this respect are extremely reminiscent of Chamberlain's, and thus it is very likely that his reading of Chamberlain's opus was of fundamental importance in this instance too. Interestingly, however, Hitler did not share Chamberlain's view of the Apostle Paul, whom Chamberlain considered a heathen who had brought Hellenistic influences into Christianity. On the contrary, Hitler's view of Paul was that he was a Jew who had corrupted Jesus' original teachings by bringing Jewish influences into it. This was an idea that seems to have originated

---

[53] Ibid., p. 261; Varshizky, Amit, "In Search of the 'Whole Man': Soul-Man-World in the National Socialist *Weltanschauung*," *Dapim: Studies on the Holocaust*, Vol. 31, No. 3 (2017), p. 200. This is important since it points to a way out of the debate about whether racial "science" was science or pseudoscience. The racial theorists put *themselves* in more or less complete opposition to the scientific ideals of their time, thereby voluntarily stepping outside the boundaries of scientific values and methods if not the scientific community. For a short discussion of this distinction and debate, see Wetzell, Richard F., "Eugenics, Racial Science, and Nazi Biopolitics: Was There a Genesis of the 'Final Solution' from the Spirit of Science?" in Devin O. Pendas, Mark Roseman, and Richard F. Wetzell (eds.), *Beyond the Racial State: Rethinking Nazi Germany* (Cambridge: Cambridge University Press, 2017), pp. 158–160.

[54] Varshizky, A., "Non-Mechanistic ... ," p. 37.

108 / Christianity in Hitler's Ideology

with Paul de Lagarde. The fact that so many Christian theologians picked up (and developed) this idea during the early 1900s meant that a new Christian ethics, based on racism and with the Aryan Jesus at its core, was used to justify racist violence against, and the murdering and killing of, many other so-called races long before Hitler became chancellor of Germany. Through this lens, the German defeat in The Great War was interpreted as the crucifixion of Germany; a view that Hitler explicitly alluded to in *Mein Kampf* when he spoke of the need for, and his own struggle for, the rebuilding and resurrection of the German nation.[55]

As already mentioned, Rosenberg spoke to Hitler about this theme and about Lagarde on December 13, 1941. The next day, Rosenberg wrote in his diary that he had said to Hitler that he considered Chamberlain's efforts to save Paul's honor unintelligible. Hitler then apparently confirmed that this was indeed the basic error in Chamberlain's thinking.[56] An uncritical attitude toward the sources could lead historians completely down the garden path in this context. For example, in an article from 2015 Johann Chapoutot cites Rauschning's *Gespräche mit Hitler* where Hitler is claimed to have said that Jesus could *absolutely not* have been an Aryan; this was nothing less than pure "nonsense" to Hitler, writes Chapoutot. To try to argue that Jesus was an Aryan, as Houston Stewart Chamberlain had done, was "nonsense" and "just stupid."[57] Peter Head, in an article in the *Journal for the Study of the Historical Jesus* from 2004, also accepts this as a genuine statement from the 1930s and tries to square it with later

---

[55] Heschel, S., *The Aryan Jesus*, pp. 30, 33–37, 41–44, 48–55; Gutteridge, R., *Open Thy Mouth for the Dumb!* ... , pp. 22–23; Hitler, *Mein Kampf* ... (Band I), p. 896 [353]. For more on the background to this theological development, see also Kelley, S., *Racializing Jesus* ...

[56] Rosenberg, A., *Alfred Rosenberg* ... , pp. 415–416. Heinrich Heim wrote down that same conversation in the table talks, but the part about Chamberlain is extremely cryptic, as he wrote that Hitler had said that Chamberlain's mistake was "to believe in Christianity as a spiritual world" (*Monologe* ... , p. 151). Heim thereby gives the reader the impression that Hitler thought that the problem was that Chamberlain was a believing Christian, which is to distort what he said (Rosenberg's notes are here obviously more reliable since they make more sense. Lagarde is not mentioned by Heim, and neither is the fact that this was said as a part of a conversation with Rosenberg).

[57] Chapoutot, Johann, "From Humanism to Nazism: Antiquity in the Work of Houston Stewart Chamberlain," *Miranda*, No. 11 (2015), https://journals.openedition.org/miranda/6680.

pronouncements to the contrary by claiming that Hitler changed his mind on the subject.[58] But this is a view that was diametrically opposed to Hitler's real position on the matter even in the early 1920s. This is yet another nail in the coffin of Rauschning as a reliable source for Hitler's views. Rauschning turned Hitler's real views on Jesus on their head, with the consequence that the latter's admiration for Jesus has completely fallen out of the line of sight for many historians. Rauschning probably did this because he wanted to put as much distance between Hitler and Christianity as possible.

2.6 Dietrich Eckart

Hitler met Eckart at some point in the fall of 1919, perhaps already at Hitler's first DAP meeting on September 12 of that year. Unfortunately, we do not know the details of their first meeting or how their close bond developed. Eckart was already in the DAP at that time and one of the leading ideologues in the party. This means that the antisemitism that Hitler exhibited in the letter to Adolf Gemlich on September 16, 1919, was not a product of Eckart's grooming. That appears to have crystalized during the summer of 1919 during the propaganda course that Hitler attended as part of his education under army captain Karl Mayr. According to contemporaneous sources, in late August 1919 Hitler held a series of talks at Camp Lechfeld, the POW camp outside Munich where he worked, and one of them focused on the issue of capitalism and antisemitism. This is the first known source to mention Hitler's antisemitism.[59] Nonetheless, Hitler was not fully developed ideologically by the time Eckart took him under his wing.

The self-professed Catholic Dietrich Eckart was one of the early National Socialist movement's most important ideologues, not least because of his role as Hitler's personal teacher (and father figure) in Munich. He was the one who introduced Hitler to Alfred Rosenberg, something that Rosenberg wrote about in his diary in October 1936. What Eckart found in Catholicism was the basis for his fanatic

---

[58] Head, P., "The Nazi Quest ... ," pp. 56, 68.
[59] Weber, T., *Becoming Hitler* ... , pp. 109–110, 140–143.

110 / Christianity in Hitler's Ideology

antisemitism. The Christian faith was so important to Eckart, just as it was to many other Nazis at the time, that he considered it impossible to be a true Aryan without it. This was also why the Nazis without hesitating would condemn "sin against the blood" – the religious and the racial categories coexisted and could not be separated without destroying the whole ideology.[60] In *Mein Kampf*, Hitler made the religious connotations even more evident by saying that miscegenation was "to sin against the will of the eternal creator."[61]

Eckart's Catholicism was rather odd compared to what we normally think of when we hear that label. However, his religion was similar to the Catholic Christianity practiced by the so-called *Lorberbewegung* (Lorber Movement), formerly known as the *Neu-Salems-Gesellschaft* (New Salem Society), which was based on the revelational works of Jakob Lorber. The Lorberians were not confessional Christians, that is, they saw themselves as standing above the various confessions and to be a sort of universalist faith. Yet, they remained formally within the Roman Catholic Church since they believed in changing the Church from within rather than from the outside. In June 1937, the authorities banned Lorber's writings and the movement's publishing house, *Neu-Salem-Verlag*, viewing the group as a form of sect that was hostile to the National Socialist state. This caused the head of the publisher *Neu-Salem-Verlag*, Otto Zluhan, to object and to point out that "Dietrich Eckart has cited Neu-Salem's publications and thereby grounded his religious belief" in the movement and referred to Eckart's work *Peer Gynt* from 1912 (even providing a page reference). Zluhan typed his protest on a letter originally written by Eckart in 1912, in which the latter referred not only to Lorber but also to the movement's own monthly publication, *Das Wort* (The Word). The adherents of the movement could not be considered "a sect," Zluhan argued, and "its worldview and religious beliefs cannot

---

[60] Steigmann-Gall, Richard, "Old Wine in New Bottles? Religion and Race in Nazi Antisemitsm," in Kevin P. Spicer (ed.), *Antisemitism, Christian Ambivalence, and the Holocaust* (Bloomington, IN: Indiana University Press, 2007), pp. 289–304; Dietrich, Otto, *12 Jahre mit Hitler* (Munich: Isar Verlag, 1955), p. 178; Rosenberg, A., *Alfred Rosenberg* ... , p. 212.

[61] Hitler, *Mein Kampf* ... (Band I), pp. 743–747 [302–303]. See also Heschel, S., "Being Adolf Hitler ... ," p. 194.

111 / Hitler's Religious Teachers

be considered hostile to the state either, when they come from the same source as the religious beliefs of Dietrich Eckart."[62] Apparently, Zluhan was able to get the ban temporarily lifted, and by changing the name of the publisher he was able to stave off a complete ban until 1941, when it was apparently shut down; it remained so until after the end of the war.[63]

2.6.1 Eckart's *Der Bolschewismus von Moses bis Lenin*: A Religious Pamphlet Featuring Hitler

The idea about the "Jew" as the Antichrist was a central feature of Eckart's religious beliefs. Eckart wrote about this aspect of the faith in his book *Der Bolschewismus von Moses bis Lenin* (Bolshevism from Moses to Lenin) from 1924, a fictitious dialogue between him and Hitler. In this book, Eckart had Hitler condemning the Old Testament and also made him reference the many passages to mass murder and war crimes committed by the old Israelites in the Bible, in order to illustrate that the Jews intended to dominate and eradicate the Christian world if given the chance. The Old Testament is labeled "The Satanic Bible," while the New Testament was described in the opposite way. Jesus was celebrated and sanctified in this work as being an Aryan who had waged war on the evil Jews; but Eckart's Hitler also spent some time on condemning Paul for purportedly having corrupted Jesus' original teachings.[64] We have already seen that it was Eckart who inspired point 24 of the NSDAP program, which spoke of "positive Christianity" as the basis for the party.[65] Everything in the Bible was interpreted through the antisemitic lens. Sebottendorff would later write in 1933 that the Jewish escape from Egypt described in Exodus was not really an escape, but an ousting of the parasitic Jews by the host people, the Egyptians. The Old Testament was used as evidence of the immense

[62] See letter from Eckart, August 27, 1912, from the archives of a private collector in Paris. I thank Thomas Weber for making photographs of these documents available to me.
[63] See information on Lorber Verlag's website: www.lorber-verlag.de/01begruessung/05verlag.htm; August 16, 2021. It seems, however, that the last issue of the *Das Wort* came out in June 1937, because in the online archive there are issues missing from then until 1948 (see https://onedrive.live.com/?id=96DC68F4101B42E2%2I107&cid=96DC68F4101B42E2; August 16, 2021).
[64] Eckart, D., *Der Bolschewismus* …   [65] Tyrell, A., *Vom "Trommler"* … , p. 85.

112 / Christianity in Hitler's Ideology

power and privilege of the Jews. The Bible had been redacted backward from 300 BCE, Sebottendorff claimed. It was "that monstrous deception, from which Christianity still suffers today."[66]

Sebottendorff was not only the founder of the *Thule Gesellschaft*, a cover organization for the Germanic order (a secret society founded in 1912 in Berlin) set up to coordinate *völkisch* propaganda and political activity in Munich. Karl Harrer was also a member of the *Thule Gesellschaft*, and he and Drexler had founded the DAP – or *Deutsche Arbeiterverein* (German Workers' Association) as it was originally called – in a targeted effort to help the upper- and middle-class *Thule Gesellschaft* to reach the working people in Munich as well and to nationalize them. Other members of the society, or that at least frequented its meetings, were Eckart, Drexler, Gottfried Feder, Hans Frank, Alfred Rosenberg, and Rudolf Heß.[67] Sebottendorff also in a way became the founder (and first editor-in-chief) of the *Völkischer Beobachter* when he bought the publishing rights to the newspaper *Münchener Beobachter* in August 1918 from the widow of its original founder, Franz Eher.[68] The paper first became a propaganda organ for the *Thule Gesellschaft*, and then in May 1919 the official outlet for the *Deutsch-Sozialistische Partei* under Hans George Grassinger. The name change occurred on August 9, 1919. The paper was purchased by the NSDAP a little more than a year later on December 17, 1920, a purchase for which Eckart provided the funding.[69]

It is uncertain how much of the dialogue in Eckart's book is complete fiction and how much of it is based on memories of actual conversations between them. Much of it is undoubtedly entirely fictional. The most thorough analysis of *Der Bolschewismus von Moses bis Lenin* can be found in Margarete Plewnia's biography of Eckart entitled *Auf dem Weg zu Hitler* (On the Road to Hitler). Plewnia

---

[66] Sebottendorff, R. von, *Bevor Hitler kam . . .* , pp. 20–21.
[67] Weber, T., *Becoming Hitler . . .* , p. 132. Interestingly, Sebottendorff in fact only mentions Harrer as the founder of the DAP (Sebottendorff, R. von, *Bevor Hitler kam . . .* , p. 8).
[68] Sebottendorff, R. von, *Bevor Hitler kam . . .* , p. 44. The influence of the *Thule Gesellschaft* on National Socialism, especially with regard to esotericism and the occult, is, however, a myth created by postwar Neo-Nazi writers. For this, see François, Stephane, *Nazi Occultism: Between the SS and Esotericism* (London: Routledge, 2023).
[69] See "Münchener Beobachter," in *Historisches Lexikon Bayerns*; www.historisches-lexikon-bayerns.de/Lexikon/Münchener_Beobachter; August 15, 2021.

113 / Hitler's Religious Teachers

concludes that the conversations are entirely fictional and invented by Eckart, and as proof she refers to the fact that Hitler utters statements in the book that Eckart had stated in other contexts. But she also shows that Hitler, in his early speeches between November 1919 and the summer of 1920, evolved and changed the way he spoke about the Jews, and argued that this was due to Hitler's friendship with Eckart.[70] Ernst Nolte, on the other hand, interpreted the agreement between Hitler's views and those that Eckart ascribes to Hitler in his book as evidence that the conversations were authentic.[71] David Redles makes the same argument in a recent book chapter. He cites this source as if it contained Hitler's own words simply because there is a lot of agreement between what Eckart makes Hitler say and what Hitler says in other later sources.[72] However, that reasoning is obviously not logically sound.

Werner Maser did not agree with Plewnia's analysis either, and scoffed at her interpretation: "Mrs. Plewnia refers to so little evidence regarding Hitler that her judgement in the end only has the weight of an opinion."[73] At the same time, however, he accepts the statement that no other person played such an important role for Hitler's ideological development during these years than Eckart.[74] Maser's conclusion is way too harsh, and he does not really give any evidence for his position other than emotional arguments. One suspects that the true reason for his critique in something else, for example the fact that Plewnia as a recent PhD in history had arrived at findings that the more senior historian Maser perhaps thought he should have seen himself, which may have upset him. What also speaks for Plewnia's case is, besides the fact that she convincingly shows how she arrived at her conclusions, is that the Hitler we find in *Der Bolschewismus von Moses bis Lenin* is a much more theoretically laden Hitler than what we find in any other source, including the table talks. Even Maser, who apparently took the

---

[70] Plewnia, M., *Auf dem Weg zu Hitler* ..., pp. 94–112. The conclusion that Eckart inspired Hitler's antisemitism and that the book is literary fiction, rather than a record of actual conversations, is most clearly expressed on pp. 95–96, 105–107.

[71] For this, see Rißmann, M., *Hitlers Gott* ... , pp. 133–134.

[72] Redles, D., "The Apocalypse of Adolf Hitler ...," pp. 222–229.

[73] Maser, Werner, *Adolf Hitler: Legende, Mythos, Wirklichkeit*, 12th ed. (Munich: Bechtle Verlag, 1989), p. 188.

[74] Ibid., p. 193.

114 / Christianity in Hitler's Ideology

book seriously as a record of actual conversations, notes that Hitler displays an amazing knowledge about the Bible and the Talmud. According to Maser, this is corroborated in Hitler's speeches as well as by people who had been close to him, but he gives absolutely no source for this.[75]

I am thus not sure what Maser was referring to here. That Hitler knew, and also referred to, the Bible is of course well known. But the idea that he had read the Talmud does not seem very likely at all; at least we have no such indications in the available sources or newer research in the field. Maser had a tendency to make essentially baseless claims about what Hitler had or had not read (for example, he assumes that Hitler had read Plato because Schopenhauer had said in a preface to one of his works – which he also just assumed Hitler had read – that one should do so in order to understand his own works better).[76] Ironically, Schopenhauer thought that Jesus was indeed a Jew but that his teachings had still been corrupted by the Jews and that is was only though German mysticism that Jesus' message had finally been correctly interpreted.[77] Redles, too, uncritically accepts what Hitler is made to say about the Talmud and writes that while "the words are Eckart's, I will cite 'Hitler' as I believe these words truly reflect ideas, formed under the tutelage of his mentor."[78]

This is flawed reasoning. There is plenty of material in Eckart's pamphlet that Hitler never utters in any other preserved source, which is suspicious, and Hitler is also speaking in a way totally out of character for him (making references to works and authors that clearly must be from Eckart's reading and not Hitler's). As historians, we can therefore not allow ourselves to cite the ideas from Eckart's book as if they reflect Hitler's mind. They are a reflection of Eckart's mind only. Still, it is worth noting that a lot of it – especially the critique of established Christianity, the churches, and the idea that Paul's Christianity was essentially a form of proto-Bolshevism – is the same as that which appears in other independent sources all through Hitler's life. *Der*

---

[75] Ibid., p. 188.   [76] Ibid., p. 190.

[77] Fenske, W., *Wie Jesus zum "Arier" wurde* ... , p. 73.

[78] Redles, D., "The Apocalypse of Adolf Hitler ...," pp. 316–317, n50 and n57. This is kind of like saying that one will cite Rosenberg instead of Hitler simply because they had the same opinion on a matter.

115 / Hitler's Religious Teachers

Bolschewismus von Moses bis Lenin is therefore good evidence of Eckart's influence on Hitler's ideological development, even though it cannot be used as a record of Hitler's thoughts.

This was not a view shared by Chamberlain, although even he notes at one point that the Judaism of the Old Testament had an "explicit *socialistic streak*" that had taken on a rather violent form in the Prophets. Chamberlain based his conclusion on the communal character of Judaism, which according to him completely ignored the individual. The "extreme individualism" of Christ's teachings contained a form of communism (*Kommunismus*) too, he admitted, but this was of a completely different type than "the theological communism of the Prophets," which was Jewish through and through.[79] *Der Bolschewismus von Moses bis Lenin* talks about Bolshevism as being a Jewish creation. This was a view that Hitler would carry with him for the rest of his life, and it is very likely that it was Eckart who implanted it in him. The book argued, in a typically apocalyptic and religious manner, that the final battle between good and evil was close at hand, since the Jews (who were equated with the Devil) were relentlessly pulled toward the destruction of humankind without realizing that this would lead to the destruction of Satan (i.e. the Jews) himself.[80] Note that this is precisely the view expressed by Hitler in his infamous statement in 1939 to the effect that if the Jews managed to drag the world into another war, then it was not the destruction of the world that would follow but the destruction of the Jews.

Eckart often used the book of Revelation to describe the end battle between Christ and the Antichrist that he foresaw in his journal *Auf gut Deutsch* (In Plain German). It was against this ideological background that Hitler just a few years later wrote in *Mein Kampf* that he acted in accordance with the Lord's will, and even *for* the Lord, when he was fighting against the Jews.[81] The fact is that after Hitler, due to some sly tactics, had managed to achieve his dictatorial position within the NSDAP in the summer of 1921, one of the first organizational

---

[79] Chamberlain, H. S., *Die Grundlagen* ... , p. 247.
[80] Here is yet one more parallel, namely, the speech Hitler held in January 1939, in which he warned that a new world war would mean the destruction of the Jewish people.
[81] Kellog, M., *The Russian Roots of Nazism* ... , pp. 238–242.

116 / Christianity in Hitler's Ideology

changes that he made was to install Eckart as editor-in-chief at the party's own newspaper, the *Völkischer Beobachter*. From this central position, Eckart continued his relentless Catholic polemic (which basically consisted of criticizing *political* Catholicism, manifested in its most apparent form in the Catholic *Zentrum* party) until his death. Eckart even signed his first editorial in the *Völkischer Beobachter* with the provocative "Dietrich Eckart, Catholic."[82]

It also seems as if it was Eckart who brought the concept of the "Third Reich" into Nazi ideology. Exactly where Eckart got this idea is unknown, but Klaus-Ekkehard Bärsch believes that it was taken from Ibsen's drama *Emperors and Galileans*, where it was used to describe the kingdom of the Messiah (Jesus as emperor in heaven and as God on earth). In Eckart's mind, the Third Reich would usher in a time of salvation and liberation, one that would see the end of all political conflicts. But the path to eternal peace was war, and not just any war but a religious war, a war between light and darkness, between God and the Devil, where darkness would eventually be destroyed for good – the Final Solution. Evil was of course personified by the Jews. The German people assumed the form of Christ in this cosmic battle, and the Jews the form of the Antichrist. The Third Reich signified a new beginning and a new order, the future world that was once and for all separated from the chaotic and dark contemporary world; it was a world where the German people would find eternal salvation. The idea of a totally destructive end to the current evil world was directly inspired by the book of Revelation in the New Testament. Eckart, naturally, also knew to refer to chapter 8 in the Gospel of John, where it says that the Devil was the father of the Jews. Eckart's conception of God (which was in all essentials identical to that which Hitler would also embrace) clearly shows that his God was a God akin that in Christianity, says Bärsch, and both the Trinity and Jesus played central roles in his Christian mysticism.[83] Note that the latter was *not* something that Hitler adopted;

---

[82] Hastings, D., *Catholicism and the Roots of Nazism ...*, pp. 100–101.

[83] Bärsch, Claus-Ekkehard, *Die politische Religion des Nationalsozialismus: Die religiöse Dimension der NS-Ideologie in den Schriften von Dietrich Eckart, Joseph Goebbels, Alfred Rosenberg und Adolf Hitler* (Munich: Wilhelm Fink Verlag, 1998), pp. 52, 55, 57–92. For the Nazi idea of a cosmic apocalyptic struggle between good and evil, see also Grabner-Haider, Anton, *Hitlers Theologie des Todes* (Kevelaer: Topos, 2009), pp. 32–34, 69–72.

117 / Hitler's Religious Teachers

Hitler never spoke of the Trinity. His religiosity was, on the whole, much less explicitly Christian than Eckart's, even if he kept many central elements of Eckart's teachings.

Nonetheless, Catholicism was, at least initially, very important to Hitler. In *Mein Kampf*, he expressed a profound admiration for the Catholic Church as a bureaucratic organization, as an institution with a strong ideology and core message, and as a propaganda outlet.[84] Eckart had been forced to give up his medical studies and his wish to become a doctor due to his recurrent bouts of morphine addiction. He worked as a publicist and agitator in Munich from 1915 onward, where he preached his apocalyptic message to everyone who was willing to listen (interestingly, he was a bitter critic of none other than Nietzsche).[85] Eckart's Catholicism has, however, apparently been so hard to swallow for some historians that they have tended to ignore it and not recognize that side of Hitler's ideological teacher. For example, Eduard Gugenberger is so busy pushing the hypothesis of Hitler's ideological mentors being occultists that he manages to write no less than fifteen pages about Eckart without mentioning his Catholic faith or his hatred of Nietzsche even once.[86] Eckart's negative sentiments about Nietzsche may also have rubbed off on Hitler, and this could be why we, contrary to popular misconceptions, lack evidence of Hitler having read Nietzsche or having based his ideology on his philosophy.

Eckart got his inspiration for his violent hatred of the Jews from the Old Testament because he thought that it was in this document (which Eckart, and Hitler too, ironically appears to have viewed as a kind of history book) that one could plainly see how bloodthirsty the Jews were and just how much they sought to massacre their opponents. He also used the New Testament to motivate the assumption that Jesus was an Aryan and a rabid antisemite too who had driven the Jewish moneylenders out of the Temple with a whip, calling them the spawns of Satan. From the Old Testament, the Nazis also took the idea that the only way to prevent the destruction of the Aryans at the hands of the

---

[84] Steigmann-Gall, R., *The Holy Reich* ... , pp. 17–18; Rißman, M., *Hitlers Gott* ... , pp. 133–134.

[85] Hastings, D., *Catholicism and the Roots of Nazism* ... , pp. 59–60.

[86] Gugenberger, Eduard, *Hitlers Visionäre: Die okkulten Wegbereiter des Dritten Reichs* (Vienna: Ueberreuter, 2000), pp. 31–44.

118 / Christianity in Hitler's Ideology

Jews was to beat the Jews to it and to destroy them before they could act.[87] Hitler made this view explicit in his notes for a speech on November 2, 1922 (in the speech too, although much less clearly), where he referenced the book of Esther in the Old Testament as a cautionary tale. He pointed to Russia as a repetition of what happened in the book of Esther, where the Jews killed all their enemies. Hitler did not explicitly mention the book of Esther in the speech, but he did use the Bible to prove the evilness and culturally destructive powers of the Jews to his audience.[88] Jung had done the same in his *Der nationale Sozialismus*.[89] This is therefore an interesting case where Hitler used biblical stories as inspiration for his speeches but without explicitly referring to them. This, too, speaks against the idea of his using it only for propaganda purposes.

Eckart's importance for Hitler as a mentor is also evident from the fact that Hitler ended *Mein Kampf* with a dedication to the recently deceased Eckart, who, according to Hitler, was one of National Socialism's greatest heroes:

> And among these I would like to also include the man, one of the best, who dedicated his life to the resurrection of his, our, people in poems and thoughts, to the end, indeed: *Dietrich Eckart*.[90] [emphasis in original]

The fact that these are the last words in *Mein Kampf* testifies to the central place Hitler ascribed to Eckart in his ideological development. Hitler would in fact mention Eckart also in his second unpublished book from 1928. There, he celebrated Eckart, whom he complained had been put into protective custody even though he was sick and lying on his deathbed, as "the greatest poet in Bavaria" and as a true nationalist hero.[91]

---

[87] Redles, David, *Hitler's Millennial Reich: Apocalyptic Belief and the Search for Salvation* (New York: New York University Press, 2005), pp. 59–60.

[88] *SA*, pp. 713–714, 717 (Documents 415 and 416).

[89] Jung, R., *Der nationale Sozialismus* ... , pp. 40–53.

[90] *Hitler, Mein Kampf* ... (Band II), p. 1739 [353]. This chapter was originally intended to end the first volume of *Mein Kampf*, but after the decision to split the book in two volumes had been made the chapter was moved because it was thought that the content could lead to trouble for the newly refounded NSDAP and for Hitler himself (for this, see ibid., p. 1691).

[91] Hitler, Adolf, *Hitlers zweites Buch: Ein Dokument aus dem Jahr 1928. Eingeleitet und kommentiert von Gerhard L. Weinberg. Mit einem Geleitwort von Hans Rothfels* (Stuttgart: Deutsche Verlags-Anstalt, 1961), p. 200.

119 / Hitler's Religious Teachers

Another Catholic who was intimately involved with the early NSDAP was the former priest Bernhard Stempfle (mistakenly said to have been the editor of *Mein Kampf*), one of many "brown" priests documented by Kevin P. Spicer.[92] Stempfle was also a journalist, and he wrote many articles in the *Völkischer Beobachter* during the early 1920s. The topic of these articles was the destructive influence of the Jews on German culture and society (e.g. because they were said to be atheists). The threat they posed warranted the cruellest persecution imaginable, according to Stempfle.[93]

It has been debated whether Hitler knew about, and in that case whether he approved of, the publication of *Der Bolschewismus von Moses bis Lenin*, which occurred during Hitler's time in the Landsberg fortress. The publisher wrote in the preface to the first edition that they hoped that Hitler, after the high treason case against him was over, would continue and complete Eckart's work (Eckart died before he had time to finish the book).[94] That Hitler knew about it seems rather obvious, and it is hard to imagine how he could not have been told about it by someone (even if not by Eckart). One rather solid piece of evidence showing that Hitler at least in some way approved of its content is the fact that he never banned it or tried to destroy it, as he did with so many other things that he found to be an insult to his person or that simply did not fit the propaganda in *Mein Kampf.* On the other hand, as Plewnia points out, the second edition of the book was published without the subtitle *Zweigespräch zwischen Adolf Hitler und mir* (Conversation between Adolf Hitler and Myself), which she explains, with the support of another historian, was due to the fact that Hitler had by then become a published writer in his own right after the first volume of *Mein Kampf* came out, and that the reference to Hitler in Eckart's subtitle then became a minor liability or annoyance. Eckart had given a manuscript to one of the other prominent persons within the NSDAP, his close friend the physician Emil Gansser (an explosives expert at Siemens and NSDAP politician), who, against Eckart's will,

---

[92] Spicer, Kevin P., *Hitler's Priests: Catholic Clergy and National Socialism* (DeKalb, IA: Northern Illinois University Press, 2008), p. 10.
[93] Hastings, D., *Catholicism and the Roots of Nazism* ... , pp. 67–68.
[94] Eckart, D., *Der Bolschewismus* ... , p. 50.

120 / Christianity in Hitler's Ideology

had apparently shown the text to other people. It appears that Eckart did not want Hitler to see, or even know about, the book before it was published, and therefore he was very upset when he heard that Gansser had betrayed his trust by trying to get a copy of the text to Hitler for him to make corrections to the proofs. Eckart argued that it would have been entirely debasing and unworthy to show Hitler a text full of misspellings – the text had to be proofread before it could be given to Hitler, he insisted. Hitler would not appreciate the value of the work if he saw it before it was finished, said Eckart. But Wolfram Pyta refers to a letter from Eckart to Max Amann dated August 28, 1923, in which Eckart wrote that he did not want Hitler to see the manuscript until it was published because he had put words in his mouth that he could not be expected to uncritically approve of. Plewnia does show, however, that the available evidence points to the conclusion that Hitler still tried to prevent the book from being spread to a wider audience, and an academic dissertation from 1940 that dealt with how Judaism was represented in Eckart's works shows that only two copies were available at libraries in Germany at that point in time.[95]

Friedrich Heer has suggested that *Mein Kampf* was Hitler's way of making the wishes of the publisher of Eckart's book come true. Hitler published his own book as a fulfilment of Eckart's work and as one that was intended at least in part to convince the Christian, conservative circles in Germany of the Christian character of his mission.[96] It is an interesting and perhaps even plausible hypothesis. But can it be tested? No, not really. The low-key treatment of Eckart's book by Hitler does not mean that he considered the content to be a misrepresentation of his views. But Hitler may have wanted to control the narrative about him and about National Socialist ideology – he had good reason for wishing his extreme criticism of established Christianity to remain hidden, now that the NSDAP was being reformed and launching itself into mass politics. This was a completely new situation that Eckart could not have foreseen. The same is true for the war years, considering that Hitler was careful about stirring up an open conflict with the churches before Germany had won the war. What Eckart did in his book was similar

[95] Plewnia, M., *Auf dem Weg zu Hitler* ... , pp. 108–109; Pyta, W., *Hitler* ... , p. 172.
[96] Heer, F., *Der Glaube des Adolf Hitler* ... , p. 204.

121 / Hitler's Religious Teachers

to what Plato did in his fictive dialogues with Socrates: the intent was to make a philosophical or moral point. However, *Der Bolschewismus von Moses bis Lenin* simply did not fit well into any political context after 1925. Moreover, it may have been the case, at least initially, that Hitler did not want Eckart's book to outshine his own work *Mein Kampf*, which, if Heer is right in his analysis, was a sort of continuation of Eckart's work. In that case, Hitler's eulogy to Eckart at the end of the last volume of *Mein Kampf* could be seen as an acknowledgment of this fact.[97]

Eckart had withdrawn to Berchtesgaden in April in 1923 to write his book, partly because of a wish to seclude himself and partly because a warrant for his arrest had been issued by the regional court in Leipzig for his having insulted President Hindenburg. He remained there until November 6, when he returned to Munich to take part in the coup attempt, which only got him arrested for that crime instead. He died of the health-related consequences he suffered while being locked up in jail. Wolfram Pyta writes that Eckart expected to make a significant amount of money on his book, which was not an unreasonable expectation considering that there was indeed a demand for a purported programmatic declaration from the now rather famous, but still mysterious and unknown, political star Hitler. Pyta says that this plan nonetheless backfired since Hitler in March 1924 was no longer an up-and-coming political star but instead a criminal being charged with high treason. Still, he points out that the continued lack of a programmatic text gave Hitler the opportunity to fill that void with his own book instead.[98]

But there is something that is off with Pyta's analysis here. First, it was not true that the failed coup meant that Hitler's star was fading; on the contrary, it was shooting upward. The evidence for this is not only the propaganda victory that Hitler turned the trial into, but also his enormous popularity during his time in fortress. The trial made Hitler into a major figure on the extreme right-wing political scene, and his name became known all over Germany and even abroad. The court

---

[97] It was likely also because of the narcissistic desire to appear original that Hitler did not refer to any of his sources in *Mein Kampf*.

[98] Pyta, W., *Hitler: Der Künstler ...* , pp. 171–172.

122 / Christianity in Hitler's Ideology

even broke the law and refrained from deporting Hitler to Austria with the motivation that Hitler was so German in his feelings and thoughts, and when the sentence against him was read on April 1 (ironic considering that the sentence was a really bad joke), the courtroom erupted in a storm of *Heil* screams.[99] These facts are well known, and it was precisely because of this that Hitler decided to write *Mein Kampf*, so it is a bit puzzling why Pyta argues the way that he does. Second, Eckart's book was indeed published, which means that there was not a lack of a programmatic declaration of Hitler's political views when he sat down to write *Mein Kampf*, if it is true that this was the purpose of Eckart's book.

It has even been claimed that Eckart had bitterly withdrawn to the Alps and Berchtesgaden because Hitler had replaced him as editor of the *Völkischer Beobachter* on March 10, 1923 (Alfred Rosenberg had taken over this position).[100] However, Thomas Weber has shown that the purported break between Hitler and Eckart did not happen. Hitler had not replaced Eckart for ideological reasons, but because Eckart's morphine and alcohol abuse problems made him incapable of doing his job. The *Völkischer Beobachter* had large economic problems, and Eckart was not in a condition to deal with the situation and to rectify it. But this did not mean that Hitler and Eckart disavowed each other, writes Weber. They remained ideologically and emotionally close, and Hitler often visited Eckart in his alpine hideout from the end of April 1923 onward. Even by August 1923, Hitler and Eckart remained in close contact, and the two even went to Switzerland together for a fundraising drive with Emil Gansser to raise more money for the newspaper and for the party.[101]

We also know from the memoirs of Hitler's press chief, Otto Dietrich, that Hitler regularly visited Eckart's grave in the small town of Neumarkt in Oberpfalz, Eckart's birthplace. Dietrich states that Hitler repeatedly told him that Eckart had been immensely important for the path his life had taken and for his political career, and that Eckart was

---

[99] Thamer, Hans-Ulrich, *Adolf Hitler: Biographie eines Diktators* (Munich: C.H. Beck, 2018), pp. 94–96.
[100] Reuth, Ralph George, *Hitler: Eine politische Biographie* (Munich: Piper, 2003), p. 143.
[101] Weber, T., *Wie Adolf Hitler zum Nazi wurde . . .* , pp. 386–390.

123 / Hitler's Religious Teachers

"his best friend" and "spiritual father." It was from Eckart that Hitler had come to embrace his "fanatical *völkischer* patriotism and radical antisemitism."[102] Eckart seems to have had this role already by the end of 1919. Eckart was deeply impressed with the young man, and several similarities in their life stories drew them to each other. He even told Hitler during their first meeting of his genocidal desire to load all Jews on a train and drive it into the Red Sea. It was also Eckart who instilled in Hitler the feeling that he was indeed superior to those around him – that he had a mission.[103]

Eckart had in fact been waiting for a character such as Hitler for a long time. He was eager to attach his preexisting Messiah expectation onto someone worthy of it, especially after having been disappointed by the revolutionary Wolfgang Kapp and his failed putsch in Berlin in March 1920. Ludolf Herbst argues that it was after this that he began to see Hitler as the savior of Germany. Eckart took Hitler under his wing and taught him not only how to write but more significantly how to speak, if we can believe Konrad Heiden. The word *Führer* as a designation for Hitler appeared in Eckart's *Völkischer Beobachter* in December 1921 – Eckart was indeed "the spiritual originator of the *Führer* myth," as Heiden put it already in 1936 – but it was only after Mussolini's March on Rome in October 1922 that it became frequently used. His convincing argument is that Hitler's transformation into the *Führer* and a German Messiah figure was not a spontaneous development. This image was consciously crafted by Eckart, Alfred Rosenberg, and a few other of Hitler's closest associates during 1922 and 1923 (and, of course, from 1923 onward not least by Hitler himself).[104] He also introduced Hitler to some wealthy donors from Munich's bourgeois and conservative elite.[105]

To show how successful this propaganda effort was, we can look at the infamous Oberammergau Passion Play of 1934. As the audience watched Jesus being crucified, people gasped as they clearly saw the parallel between the Gospel story and Hitler and the Third

[102] Dietrich, O., *12 Jahre mit Hitler*, p. 168.
[103] Weber, T., *Becoming Hitler* ... , pp. 140–143.
[104] Herbst, L., *Hitlers Charisma* ... , pp. 137–140; Heiden, K., *Adolf Hitler* ... (Vol. I), pp. 58, 85–86.
[105] Dietrich, O., *12 Jahre mit Hitler*, p. 178.

124 / Christianity in Hitler's Ideology

Reich. "There he is. That is our Führer, our Hitler!," they cried. Susannah Heschel notes that this reaction "was ambiguous: was Germany being crucified or was Hitler being identified as the saviour?"[106] Perhaps it was a bit of both. Also, it is worth stressing that this reaction was not the complete creation of Nazi propaganda. No doubt, many Christians in Germany drew these parallels themselves and would probably have done so even without the help of Hitler and his propagandists. Even so, the work of the latter certainly must have made a difference in terms of the number of people who saw Hitler in this play as the savior and the Third Reich as the new promised land.

Thomas Weber has noted that Eckart and Hitler "shared exterminatory rhetoric when referring to the Jews." Eckart had been inspired to become a glowing antisemite from reading the book *Geschlecht und Charakter* (Sex and Character) published in 1903 by the Austrian self-hating Jewish author Otto Weininger. He had in 1902 converted to Protestant Christianity, rejected his Jewish heritage, and ascribed everything he considered evil in the world to the Jews. Unsurprisingly, Weininger suffered from depression and shot himself at the age of twenty-three. But it was precisely Weininger's self-hatred that attracted Eckart and turned him into a rabid antisemite.[107] Eckart never stopped being a hero to the NSDAP. As late as May 5, 1928, the *Völkischer Beobachter* reproduced a poem by Eckart called "The First Antisemite" (*Der erste Antisemit*), in which he argued that the first antisemite in world history was none other than the biblical Cain, who murdered "the Jew," that is, his brother Abel, "the sneaky bastard." According to Eckart, Cain was the first to see through the Jew's efforts to disguise himself and to see him for what he really was.[108] That same year, Rosenberg published a biography of Eckart with the subtitle *A Legacy* (*ein Vermächtnis*) using the NSDAP's own publishing house.[109] Abel thus represented the Jew whose murder Eckart proclaimed to be an action blessed by God.

---

[106] Heschel, S., "Confronting the Past ... ," p. 46.
[107] Weber, T., *Becoming Hitler* ... , pp. 141–142.
[108] Dennis, D. B., *Inhumanities* ... , p. 397.
[109] Hitler, A., *Hitlers zweites Buch* ..., p. 200 n1; Rosenberg, Alfred, *Dietrich Eckart. Ein Vermächtnis. Herausgegeben und eingeleitet von Alfred Rosenberg* (München: Franz Eher Verlag, 1928).

125 / Hitler's Religious Teachers

It is noteworthy that Weininger, just like Chamberlain, argued that the Jewish spirit was present in every person and that everyone therefore had to fight against the Jewishness within themselves.[110] It was thus the same idea that was expressed in point 24 in the NSDAP program regarding how positive Christianity "fights against the Jewish-materialist spirit within us and outside of us." Whether Weininger picked this up from Chamberlain is unknown, but these were ideas that were not uncommon in the late nineteenth and early twentieth centuries. They seem to have been a part of the antisemitic background radiation in Europe at this time; one might even say that they were popular.

All of this means that the history of Eckart's *Der Bolschwismus von Moses bis Lenin* has to be partly rewritten since the earlier interpretations are built on a flawed premise, namely that Hitler and Eckart had distanced themselves from each other. But with the knowledge that Hitler visited Eckart several times during the period when he was writing *Der Bolschewismus von Moses bis Lenin*, it is reasonable to ask whether Hitler did not in fact know about the book after all. Would Eckart really have kept this work secret from his still good friend Hitler? It at least appears much less likely than before.

This remarkable story nevertheless shows two things: (1) that the content of Eckart's book, even though Hitler limited the circulation of it later, cannot have been all that far from the image of Hitler held by other leading members of the NSDAP when it was written, because then Gansser (and also the CEO of the NSDAP's publishing house, Max Amann, who had also read the text) would naturally have recoiled and opined against the false image of the *Führer* that was presented by Eckart and (2) that Eckart clearly still held Hitler in very high regard and that the latter's opinion was important to him. The second point speaks against the assumption that the book gave a misleading picture of Hitler. The same could of course be said with reference to Hitler's dedication of *Mein Kampf* to Eckart several years later.

Historians have noted that Eckart's book seems to make Hitler into a Christian theological antisemite when he in reality during this time had developed a distinctly racial antisemitism.[111] This is true to an

---

[110] Weber, T., *Becoming Hitler* ... , p. 174; Eckart argued the same, see: . S Rosenberg, A., *Dietrich Eckart* ..., pp. 191–230.
[111] Thamer, H.-U., *Adolf Hitler* ... , p. 77; Pyta, W., *Hitler: Der Künstler* ... , p. 172.

126 / Christianity in Hitler's Ideology

extent, that is, Hitler had indeed developed such a race-based antisemit-ism. But the fact that Eckart had put words in Hitler's mouth does not mean that everything included in the text was not true. It is equally obvious from Hitler's speeches and writings of that period that he in addition to the racial antisemitism also often showed clear signs of Christian anti-Judaism and biblically inspired theological antisemitism. Just as it is apparent that Eckart's Hitler is too literarily knowledgeable, it is also clear that the views about Jesus and Paul, and the idea of established Christianity as proto-Bolshevism, are in complete agreement with Hitler's actual views on these topics.

The publication of *Der Bolshevismus von Moses bis Lenin* moreover appears to have been everything but an insignificant chance event, because it came out on March 2, 1924, that is, four months *after* Eckart's death, with the explicit purpose to testify to the Christian values within the *völkisch* movement, writes Friedrich Heer.[112] In addition, Hitler's trial had begun only a few days earlier on February 26, a fact that certainly makes it seem as if the publication was timed to affect the outcome of the trial or at least the popular perception of Hitler. This is perhaps also the reason, although this is indeed speculative, why Hitler did not refer to his religious faith during the trial; and the absence of such references is striking when compared to his writings and speeches both before and after 1924, including *Mein Kampf*. Historians have previously not fully realized the importance of Eckart's book, and therefore they have not tried to explain how it is that the view of established Christianity that Eckart's fictional Hitler expresses was more or less identical to the views that the real Hitler also professed. The likely explanation for this agreement concerning the views on Jesus, Paul, and Christianity in general is of course that Eckart, as Hitler's mentor and close friend, was the original source of Hitler's views and therefore was very well acquainted with them. Eckart could essentially express his own views on these topics and know that Hitler would agree with what he was saying. Although Hitler did not slavishly adopt ideas wholesale from any source, he was not an original thinker or intellectual either. He used what he found in others to create a blend that suited him.

[112] Heer, F., *Der Glaube des Adolf Hitler ...* , p. 204.

2.7 Dressing Antisemitism in Biblical Language and Turning Hitler into a German Messiah

The hateful ideas that Eckart got from Christianity certainly seems a lot more horrible in hindsight, when we know what they eventually resulted in. They also then appear a bit prophetic: there was a war that for Hitler was about defeating the ultimate evil Satan personified in the form of the Jews, whose existence was once and for all to be eradicated in a Final Solution. But the war did not happen by chance. It was Hitler, Eckart's apprentice, who made it happen. Hitler also sprinkled *Mein Kampf* with numerous implicit and explicit references to the New Testament and to the Jews as being in league with the Devil. One example is when he talks about how the Jews produce "eggs of sulfur." Sulfur was connected to the Devil in the book of Revelation, and over time sulfur therefore came to symbolize Hell in Christian culture.[113] The book of Revelation was a source for many more analogies regarding the Jews. For instance, Hitler spoke of them as "our old enemy" (*Widersacher*; a biblical term), which in Christianity was a reference to Satan, as well as "the old serpent"; and in January 1942, he spoke of the Jews as "the *most evil enemy of the world of all time*," who had now played out its role for at least a thousand years. This was a direct reference to Revelation 20:1–3, where it says:

> Then I saw an angel coming down from heaven, having the key to the bottomless pit and a great chain in his hand. He laid hold of the dragon, that serpent of old, who is *the* Devil and Satan, and bound him for a thousand years; and he cast him into the bottomless pit, and shut him up, and set a seal on him, so that he should deceive the nations no more till the thousand years were finished. But after these things he must be released for a little while.[114]

Goebbels also used the same biblical language and the word "enemy" (*Widersacher*) when talking about the Jews, as for instance on

---

[113] *Hitler, Mein Kampf . . .* (Band I), pp. 795–797 [324].

[114] *HRP* I/2, p. 757 (November 8, 1937); *HRP* II/4, p. 1829 (January 30, 1942). See also Reichelt, Werner, *Das braune Evangelium: Hitler und die NS-Liturgie* (Wuppertal: Peter Hammer Verlag, 1990), p. 113; Hesemann, M., *Hitlers Religion . . .* , p. 240.

128 / Christianity in Hitler's Ideology

April 19, 1941, when he spoke about how "our eternal enemy and rival" had declared war on Germany in September 1939.[115] Hitler even explicitly called the Jews the image of the Devil in his speech on May 1, 1923: "The Jew is a race, but not a human. He can not be a human in the sense of being the image of God, the eternal one. The Jew is the image of the Devil. Judaism means the racial Tuberculosis of the people," he said.[116] The Jews were thus certainly a race in Hitler's view, but their spiritual qualities made them unable to be fully human. Hitler was certainly mixing metaphors here, but that does not mean he did not sincerely believe what he said.

David I. Kertzer has detailed the important role of the Catholic Church in the rise of modern antisemitism in his book *The Popes against the Jews*. Even though the Church did not embrace racial antisemitism, it did spread a number of ideas central to modern antisemitism. For instance, it perpetrated the falsehoods that the Jews were seeking to take over the world; that the Jews were evil and wanted to hurt Christians; that Jews were by nature immoral; that the Jews murder Christian children to drink their blood; that they were unpatriotic and cared only for money; and that they controlled the press. Several other such ideas pushed on believers by the Church could be brought up.[117] Also with respect to this fact, it is striking that the biographies of Hitler do not acknowledge Eckart's Christian faith. For example, Fest spent no less than nineteen pages writing about Eckart but does not mention his Catholic faith even once. This is likely because Eckart's religious beliefs did not manifest themselves in a way that corresponds to the traditional idea about what a Catholic is. Fest also claims that Eckart complained about Hitler's Messiah complex to Ernst "Putzi" Hanfstaengl already before the coup attempt in November 1923.[118] It is, however, not likely that this claim is true. The source for this is Hanfstaengl's memoirs, written several decades after the events, and they are simply not credible. But as we shall see, there are more and even better reasons to doubt this claim. Fest is not alone in bringing this matter up though.

[115] *GR* II, p. 57 (April 19, 1941).
[116] *SA*, pp. 918–919 (Document 524). See also Bucher, R., *Hitlers Theologie*, pp. 114–115; Lüdicke, L., *Hitlers Weltanschauung* . . . , p. 73.
[117] Kertzer, D. I., *The Popes against the Jews* . . . , especially pp. 133–236.
[118] Fest, J., *Hitler* . . . , p. 287.

129 / Hitler's Religious Teachers

Thomas Weber also refers to Eckart's purported criticism in his *Becoming Hitler*, and he also uses Hanfstaengl as support – this time based on an interrogation of the latter made by the American OSS intelligence agency in December 1942. This may seem like a better source since it is closer in time to the events described, but it is still two whole decades removed from the events in question. But while Fest, based on the memoirs, states that Eckart had expressed his irritation to Hanfstaengl, Weber writes that Eckart told Hitler as much directly.[119] Hanfstaengl had thus changed his story between the interrogation in 1942 and the time during which he was writing his memoirs. But the idea that Eckart would have been annoyed with Hitler because the latter had compared himself to Jesus is hard to take seriously. There is also something about the chronology that does not make sense here, because how could Eckart have opined against Hitler portraying himself politically as Jesus Christ before November 1923 when Weber himself has just explained to his readers that Hitler in fact did *not* portray himself in this way until the publication of the very first biography of Hitler called *Adolf Hitler: Sein Leben und seine Reden* (Adolf Hitler: His Life and His Speeches), commissioned by Hitler himself and written by Victor von Koerber. The book, which was published in 1923, is among the earliest evidence we have that Hitler saw himself as a Christ figure destined to save Germany and restore its greatness.[120] Until then, he generally preferred to speak about himself as the "drummer" (*Trommler*) who supposedly only prepared the way for the *Führer*.[121]

It should be noted, however, that Hitler had hinted at this theme also prior to November 1923. There are some speeches in which he talks about his role as a leader of the movement that is reminiscent of a Jesus figure. On July 6, 1923, for instance, he told a gathering of NSDAP members in Augsburg that he saw his role as leader as being about assuming the same responsibility for the people as Christ once had. Then, in Munich on September 12, 1923, he said that it was the

---

[119] Weber, T., *Becoming Hitler* ... , p. 264.

[120] Koerber, A.-V. von, *Adolf Hitler: Sein Leben und seine Reden* (Munich: Deutscher Volksverlag, 1923), pp. 6–7; Weber, T., *Becoming Hitler* ... , pp. 285–291.

[121] This psychological, political, and ideological journey was the topic of Albrecht Tyrell's book from 1975. Tyrell in fact uses the Koerber pamphlet as a source: Tyrell, A., *Vom "Trommler"* ... , p. 186 n12.

130 / Christianity in Hitler's Ideology

mission of the leader to awaken the "heroic spirit" (*Heldengeist*) in the German people and to lead them against "death and the Devil" (*Tod und Teufel*). They would not ask God to help them, Hitler proclaimed. They would only ask that he not help their enemies.[122] Nevertheless, Hanfstaengl's story must be a fictional concoction *post facto*. Eckart would certainly not have complained about this, and at the same time write *Der Bolschewismus von Moses bis Lenin*, which was itself a celebration of Hitler that reinforced the image of him as a Messiah figure for the *völkisch* Right.

By glossing over Eckart's Catholicism, these biographies also do not have to explain why Hitler, if he really hated Catholics and Christianity so much, wanted to dedicate *Mein Kampf* to a self-professed Catholic. On the assumption that Hitler hated Christianity in general, and Catholicism especially, it becomes very difficult to understand how Hitler could even stand talking to Eckart, and it makes even less sense for him to have considered Eckart to be his mentor. It was not like Eckart's religiosity was a minor detail; it defined his entire personality and all the hateful articles that he wrote about the Jews. To assume that Eckart put that side of him aside when inspiring and teaching Hitler is simply not reasonable. Considering Hitler's impatient personality, it is very hard to think that he would have put up with Eckart for so long – and even made him editor of the *Völkischer Beobachter* – had his Christian faith been even the slightest problem for him. In addition, Hitler ought to really have distanced himself from Eckart's book *Der Bolschewismus von Moses bis Lenin*, where it is said that Hitler was very influenced by the New Testament and Christianity. Yet, he never did, and he never disowned Eckart. Still, very few scholars would ever question the sincerity of Eckart's Christian faith. Hitler's beliefs, however, will most often be dismissed out of hand. Yet, we really have no more reason to doubt Hitler's purported beliefs than we do Eckart's.

It may be hard to understand and really appreciate the importance of what has been said above if we do not know about the large role that political Catholicism played in the early history of the NSDAP. The significant anti-ultramontanist (ultramontanist means "on the other side

---

[122] *SA*, pp. 946 (Document 544), 1013 (Document 568).

of the mountains") Catholic movement in Bavaria at this time rallied around the NSDAP. The anti-ultramontanists were a sect of ultranationalist Catholics who did not consider the Pope in Rome (on the other side of the Alps) to be the ultimate authority on matters concerning their faith. As German nationalists, they felt that the fate of German Catholics should be decided by Germans, and not a foreign power (i.e. the Vatican). The NSDAP had this bias up until when it was recreated on a parliamentary platform in February 1925. Once the decision to give up the armed revolutionary struggle had been made (effectively by Ludendorff during Hitler's time in the Landsberg fortress and without the latter's permission – Hitler only grudgingly accepted the *fait accompli*), anti-ultramontanist Catholicism became a liability instead of a source of strength. Because while this version of fiercely nationalist Catholicism was well represented in lower Bavaria, it was marginal or even nonexistent in the rest of Germany. To become a true mass movement and to win parliamentary elections, the NSDAP had to change its base. The solution was a thorough reconstitution of the party also in terms of religious grassroots support; while the NSDAP officially remained based on the "positive Christianity" in point 24 of the party program, the party left anti-ultramontanist Catholicism behind and moved over to a Protestant base.[123] Ultramontanism and "clericalism" were explicitly referred to by Rudolf Jung as incompatible with the German nature and spirit.[124] Even though this side to the NSDAP is well-known, it is rarely, if ever, part of the mainstream histories of the party, Hitler, or the Third Reich. But if it is not, then how can we be expected to correctly interpret and understand the movement and Hitler's view of Jesus and his role in National Socialist ideology?

Ian Kershaw claims that although the relationship between Hitler and Eckart was harmonious during the first few years, for Hitler it was mostly a matter of him using Eckart to his advantage. By 1923, this need had become so small that the two had drifted apart, and Eckart allegedly became very hurt and angry when he was replaced as editor of the *Völkischer Beobachter* (Eckart was the main reason for the NSDAP having been able to purchase the newspaper in the first

---

[123] For this, see Hastings, D., *Catholicism and the Roots of Nazism* ...
[124] Jung, R., *Der nationale Sozialismus* ... , p. 78.

132 / Christianity in Hitler's Ideology

place because he had been instrumental in convincing central actors to finance the affair), he writes.[125] Kershaw also states that the dedication to Eckart in *Mein Kampf* was not actually intended for him, but to all those who had known how important Eckart had been to him initially.[126] This account does not sound very plausible at all, and it is not at all clear how Kershaw can know this (he refers to a secondary source here). There are many that would have been deserving of a dedication, according to this criterion, but Hitler chose to ignore the other potential candidates. The natural thing to do if one does not feel a genuine need to express gratitude to someone is of course to keep silent. What also makes Kershaw's argument unconvincing is the fact that Hitler kept speaking of Eckart with warmth and admiration long after having published *Mein Kampf*, and that Eckart returned those feelings for Hitler even after he had lost his position as editor of the NSDAP newspaper.

2.8   Conclusion

Hitler's religious faith was a mixture of influences that he got from a variety of different sources. But he received the foundations for his religious beliefs from two main sources – Dietrich Eckart and Houston Stewart Chamberlain. Of these two, Eckart appears to have been the most important. The reason is most likely very simple, namely the fact that Hitler was very close to Eckart. The affinity between the two is made very evident in Eckart's book *Der Bolschewismus von Moses bis Lenin*, in which he presented fictional religious-philosophical conversations between himself and Hitler. Although the Hitler we meet in this book is a developed fictional character – as if Eckart was writing one of his plays – the religious beliefs that are ascribed to Hitler are still correct. The book is a testimony of the central place religious faith had in the early National Socialism movement.

Chamberlain was clearly also an important religious teacher for Hitler. His views of Jesus as an Aryan warrior became central to Hitler's theology. It is likely that Hitler first learned about Chamberlain's ideas via his spiritual teacher Eckart. He probably read at least parts of

---

[125] Kershaw, I., *Hitler 1889–1936 . . .* , pp. 155–156.   [126] Ibid., p. 651, n119.

133 / Hitler's Religious Teachers

Grundlagen eventually; perhaps during his time in the Landsberg fortress in 1924. There can be no doubt about Chamberlain's importance as an inspiration and spiritual leader for Hitler at the beginning of his political and National Socialist career. Yet, it must be noted that Hitler did not simply graft Chamberlain's ideas onto himself. For example, Chamberlain's views on the apostle Paul were something that Hitler did not accept. While Chamberlain considered Paul to be a man that had de-Judaized Jesus' teachings, Hitler on the contrary regarded Paul as a Jew who had corrupted the original teachings of Christ by Judaizing them. Here Hitler instead followed Eckart's antisemitic line of reasoning.

Eckart's influences on Hitler are much more direct and easier to trace to their source. Historians have generally ignored Eckart's Catholic beliefs, and his role as Hitler's religious mentor, when writing about him and his influence on Hitler in the early 1920s. It is as if this important dimension of their relationship has not been understood to have had the significance that it did to Hitler. Eckart was inspired by Chamberlain too, but also had many other sources for his particular Catholic Christianity. The early 1920s were formative years not only for Hitler's political ideology, but for his religious beliefs as well. It was during this time that his belief in God, or Providence, became an integral part of his political worldview and ideology. His idea about himself as a Messianic figure destined to bring salvation to Germany also began with Eckart. By not paying attention to this aspect of Hitler's worldview, historians have lost sight of a major part of National Socialist ideology as well as a major part of Hitler's personality. We must take Hitler's religious faith seriously to fully understand his motivations.

3 CHRIST ON THE CROOKED CROSS, PART II
Did Hitler Believe That Jesus Was Divine?[1]

3.1 Introduction

What did Hitler really think of Jesus, the central figure in Christianity? Did Hitler ever consider Jesus to have been of divine origin, that is, to have been the Son of God? As we have seen, Hitler had a positive view of Jesus – even though he expressed only contempt for the Christianity of the established churches – and thought Jesus was an Aryan. Hitler considered Jesus a role model for antisemites, and claimed that the National Socialist movement followed in "Christ's footsteps" with the aim of finally realizing the goal that the Nazis thought Jesus had originally had: the eradication of the Jews.[2] While Hitler's religious beliefs and his relationship to Christianity have been the subject of a growing number of studies over the past thirty years, it is still safe to say that Hitler's view of Jesus' divinity has not been fully explored before.[3]

---

[1] A version of this chapter has previously been published as "Christ on the Crooked Cross: The Divinity of Jesus in Hitler's *Weltanschauung*," *Journal of Religious History*, Vol. 45, No. 2 (2021), pp. 233–256.

[2] Tomberg, F., *Das Christentum . . .* , pp. 14, 17.

[3] Heer, F., *Der Glaube des Adolf Hitler . . .*; Strohm, H., *Die Gnosis und der Nationalsozialismus*; Rhodes, J. M., *The Hitler Movement*; Reichelt, W., *Das braune Evangelium . . .*; Bärsch, C.-E., *Die politische Religion des Nationalsozialismus . . .*; Rißmann, M., *Hitlers Gott . . .*; Steigmann-Gall, R., *The Holy Reich . . .*; Hesemann, M., *Hitlers Religion . . .*; Redles, D., *Hitler's Millennial Reich . . .*; Bucher, R., *Hitlers Theologie*; Grabner-Haider, A., *Hitlers Theologie des Todes*; Hastings, D., *Catholicism and the Roots*

135 / Christ on the Crooked Cross, Part II

In his classic study *The Third Reich*, Michael Burleigh laconically concludes: "The Führer talked a lot about God, rarely about the Saviour."[4] As will become evident in the pages below, this is not a fully justified statement. Hitler did in fact speak about Jesus several times as his "Lord and Savior," and he also quite frequently expressed his admiration for "Christ." Yet, Hitler's praise for Jesus is very seldom mentioned in the main biographies, in which his religiosity and his view of Jesus (if mentioned at all) are treated as nothing more than curiosities.[5] In other words, it is safe to say that most historians have thus far not taken Hitler's claim to have been inspired by Jesus seriously. It is only those who have focused specifically on Hitler's religious beliefs that have noticed the importance of the latter for him and for National Socialist ideology. However, the historians writing the broader histories of National Socialism and the Third Reich have been slow or unwilling to pick up on this and to integrate the results of these studies into their works. Apparently, the latter have clearly not recognized the value of the former.

In this chapter, I will detail the role that Jesus played in Hitler's *Weltanschauung* and show that Hitler clearly and repeatedly did speak of Jesus as divine. There is evidence that suggests that Jesus occupied a rather important place in Hitler's worldview and imagination, and that one can find this evidence scattered all over the period from 1920 to 1944. The admiration for Jesus was one of many constant features of Hitler's worldview from the beginning until the end of his National Socialist life. However, at the same time, it is certainly important to acknowledge that the Jesus that Hitler celebrated was a radically different one compared to the figure normally worshipped by the world's Christian population today. It was Jesus as an Aryan and a warrior in constant battle against the Jews, a view with a long tradition within racist religious circles, that had caught Hitler's attention.

---

of Nazism . . .; Herbst, L., *Hitlers Charisma . . .*; Landes, R., *Heaven on Earth . . .*; Kurlander, Eric, *Hitler's Monsters: A Supernatural History of the Third Reich* (New Haven, CT: Yale University Press, 2017).

[4] Burleigh, M., *The Third Reich . . .* , p. 259.

[5] Fest, J., *Hitler . . .*; Kershaw, I., *Hitler: 1889–1936 . . .*; Kershaw, I., *Hitler 1936–45 . . .*; Ullrich, V., *Adolf Hitler: Biographie* (Band I) . . .; Longerich, P., *Hitler . . .*; Pyta, W., *Hitler . . .*; Ullrich, V., *Adolf Hitler: Biographie* (Band II) . . .; Thamer, H.-U., *Adolf Hitler . . .*; McDonough, Frank, *The Hitler Years: Triumph 1933–1939* (London: Head of Zeus, 2019).

136 / Christianity in Hitler's Ideology

While the very idea that Hitler could have been inspired by Jesus may seem contrived, or even hurtful, to Christians today, the purpose of this chapter is simply to present a dispassionate analysis of the evidence. As historians, we cannot refrain from following the evidence and drawing conclusions from it simply because it may be considered offensive to some people. But as Susannah Heschel has remarked, the National Socialist beliefs and statements about Jesus and Christianity must be evaluated within the context in which they were uttered. It is only in their historical context that they can be properly understood.[6]

3.2 Hitler and the Question of Jesus' Divinity

The issue of whether Hitler considered Jesus to be divine is a question that has so far generated surprisingly little interest from historians, considering the consequences for our understanding of Hitler that would follow if it turned out that he did think of Jesus as divine at least at some point during his political career. But it turns out that Hitler spoke of Jesus as divine on several occasions already during the early 1920s. "Our program contains," Hitler said in the speech in Rosenheim on August 31, 1920, "a Gospel for German recovery, moral revival, the principle of human value." But this Gospel was not for the Jews, whom Hitler characterized as unproductive and work-shy money exchangers, "whom our teacher of religion, the carpenter son from Nazareth, drove out *of his father's temple* with his whip" [emphasis added]. According to the report in *Rosenheimer Tageblatt*, Hitler continued by claiming that the NSDAP "stands on the ground of positive Christianity and supports every Christian action as the foundation of authority." It was important to stand united in the struggle against both the Jewish "bloodsucking vampires" and the Freemasons.[7]

---

[6] Heschel, S., "Historiography of Antisemitism ... ," p. 259.

[7] *SA*, pp. 220–221 (Document 140). Note that the *Völkischer Beobachter* (not yet an NSDAP newspaper) included a shorter summary that does not include these phrases. See also *RSA Band III: Zwischen den Reichstagswahlen Juli 1928–September 1930. Teil 3: Januar 1930–September 1930. Herausgegeben und kommentiert von Christian Hartmann*(Munich: K. G. Saur, 1995) [Henceforth: *RSA* III/3], p. 374 (Document 97).

137 / Christ on the Crooked Cross, Part II

One could be led to draw the conclusion that Hitler had denied Jesus' divinity by talking about him as the son of a carpenter; however, by clearly denoting that Christ had driven the Jews out of "his father's temple," he actually did the opposite. No one would seriously suggest that Joseph the carpenter had built and owned the Temple. Nor could we believe that Hitler here used "father's temple" in an allegorical sense, that is, as meaning the temple of Joseph's religion. The Christ that Hitler was talking about here was clearly of divine character, and the idea that Jesus was the son of a carpenter is itself taken directly from the New Testament.[8] Jesus' humanity and the understanding of him as the "Son of Man," which is denoted by the reference to him as the son of a carpenter, is actually the natural counterpart to the "Son of God" in Christian theology.[9]

This of course also begs the question of which "temple" Hitler was referring to here? Obviously, he could not have been speaking of the Jewish Temple that the New Testament refers to, since that would be of absolutely no value to him. This statement must be understood within the context of the idea that the New Testament had been "Judaized" by Paul. Therefore, Hitler probably did not think of the Temple in Jerusalem as a Jewish temple at all, but rather as an originally Aryan religious place of worship, since he was convinced that Jesus was an Aryan leader. But do we have any indications that Hitler held such a belief?

Yes, we do in fact. Hitler did indeed on at least one occasion deny that Jerusalem was the capital of a Jewish state before the reign of King David.[10] Of course, the First Temple in Jerusalem is thought to have been constructed under King Salomon, that is, *after* the reign of King David, but this does not mean that Hitler's statement was not internally consistent. Because there was a mainstream *völkisch* Christian tradition, detailed by the Catholic Bavarian writer Franz Schrönghamer-Heimdal in an article called "Was Jesus a Jew?" in the *Völkischer Beobachter* in March 1920, that said that the Israelites, or

---

[8] Jesus is called a carpenter's son in Matthew 13:55. In Mark 6:3, Jesus is himself called a carpenter.

[9] McGrath, Alister E., *Theology: The Basics*, 2nd ed. (Oxford: Blackwell Publishing, 2008), pp. 67–68.

[10] SA, p. 189 (Document 136).

138 / Christianity in Hitler's Ideology

Arameans, were an Aryan people separate from the Jews.[11] Jesus did, after all, speak Aramaic, and it seems as if Hitler was repeating some of Schrönghamer-Heimdal's views from the article in his speech a few months later. Hitler thus most likely considered the Jewish Temple to be a falsification of history by the Jewish biblical writers. Thus, there would be no contradiction here for either Hitler or his followers, which is proven by the fact that Hitler never considered it necessary to clarify what he meant when referring to "the temple."

When Hitler spoke about Jesus at an NSDAP meeting on January 9, 1921, he said that the National Socialists, along with the rest of the world, celebrated the birth of Christ and remembered how "the Jews had cowardly nailed the World Liberator to the cross." The NSDAP intended to continue Christ's work, Hitler said, according to the police report, and rid the world from its oppressors.[12] Perhaps the most famous occasion, and certainly one of the most frequently quoted, on which Hitler spoke of Jesus was at an NSDAP meeting in the *Bürgerbräukeller* in Munich on April 12, 1922, when he stated that it was precisely his Christian faith that forced him to be a ruthless antisemite. Hitler said: "*My Christian feeling shows me my Lord and Saviour as* [being] *a fighter*" [emphasis in original], a statement that was followed by stormy applause. This feeling:

> shows me the man who once alone, only surrounded by a few followers, saw these Jews for what they really were and who called to arms against them, and who, God's truth [*Wahrhaftiger Gott*], was the greatest not as *victim* but was the greatest as a *warrior*!

He continued:

> With limitless love I read, as a Christian, the part that proclaims to us how the Lord finally pulled himself together and gripped his whip in order to drive out the usurers, these spawns of snakes and vipers, from the temple.[13]

---

[11] Koehne, Samuel, "Were the National Socialists a Völkisch Party? Paganism, Christianity, and the Nazi Christmas," *Central European History*, Vol. 47, No. 4, (2014), pp. 768–769.

[12] *SA*, p. 544 (Document 341). For much more on Schrönghamer-Heimdal, see Hastings, D., *Catholicism and the Roots of Nazism* ... , passim.

[13] *SA*, p. 623 (Document 377). See also Steigmann-Gall, R., *The Holy Reich* ... , p. 37; Bucher, R., *Hitlers Theologie*, p. 116; Rißmann, M., *Hitlers Gott* ... , pp. 29–31, 43–44; Hesemann, M., *Hitlers Religion* ... , p. 207; Gentile, E., *Contro Cesare* ... , pp. 240–241.

139 / Christ on the Crooked Cross, Part II

It is obvious that Hitler here saw a parallel between Jesus and his followers on the one hand and himself and the followers of the NSDAP on the other. Hitler's choice to call the Jews "spawns of snakes and vipers" was hardly accidental. The phrase was taken from the New Testament, where Jesus on several occasions is ascribed these words when speaking about the Pharisees and Sadducees, the learned in Jewish law and tradition.[14] The same phrase (*Schlangen- und Otterngeßücht*) was also used in the National Socialist Artur Dinter's *Die Sünde wider das Blut*, where it was also said that Jesus was the "spiritual counterpart" to the Jews who had scolded the Pharisees, "these archetypes of the Jewish race" (*diese Urbilder des Rassejudentums*).[15]

Hitler also pointed out that as a Christian he too had a duty to be a fighter for truth and right, and thus by implication follow in Jesus' footsteps.[16] It is therefore no accident that this episode was described as "The Conquest of the Temple City" (*Die Eroberung der Tempelstadt*) in a chapter in Hans Hauptmann's book *Jesus der Arier* (Jesus the Aryan) from 1930.[17] This once again stressed the implication that both the Temple and Jerusalem had once been centers of Aryan worship. The military terminology was fitting in the Nazi context, and Chamberlain had stressed in *Grundlagen* that to be a true follower of Christ meant to conduct a "struggle" and that it demanded great courage, a "moral heroism," on the part of the Christian to fight the Jewish slave instinct within him.[18] The battle was after all really taking place in the metaphysical and spiritual realm rather than in the earthly and material one.

3.3 Hitler's Whip: A Signifier of Identification with Jesus?

The story of Jesus chasing the moneylenders out of the Temple square with a whip in hand could be much more important for an understanding of how Hitler viewed himself in the early 1920s than one might think at first. Hitler's photographer, Heinrich Hoffmann, recalled Hitler always carrying a whip with him "like a talisman", from when he first met

---

[14] Matthew 3:7, 12:34, 23:33; Luke 3:7.
[15] Dinter, Arthur, *Die Sünde wider das Blut: Ein Zeitroman* (Leipzig: Verlag Matthes und Thost, 1920), p. 161.
[16] SA, p. 623 (Document 377).   [17] Hauptmann, H., *Jesus der Arier ...*, pp. 132–141.
[18] Chamberlain, H. S., *Die Grundlagen ...*, p. 208.

140 / Christianity in Hitler's Ideology

Hitler in the offices of the *Völkischer Beobachter* in 1922.[19] Biographies of Hitler often mention the fact that Hitler would carry around a whip. He had even been given two dog whips by two of his fanatic elderly women backers, Helene Bechstein and Elisabeth Büchner (his landlady at Obersalzberg), and he also carried a bigger one made from hippopotamus hide. However, no one seems to have been able to make sense of why he carried a whip and have instead simply deemed it to be a "curiosity." Fest thinks it had to do with Hitler wanting to look like the author Karl May (whose books he had enjoyed as a child), and Kershaw speculates that it may have been for protection.[20] None of those explanations seem credible, Kershaw's least of all considering that Hitler also carried a pistol.

As Rudolf Jung had put it in his *Der nationale Sozialismus* in 1922: "One cannot become the master of the beast of mammonism, with the Jewish spirit in its heart and mind, through good admonitions; you have to come [at it] with the whip."[21] What if this statement was much more than simply a metaphor? On November 2 of that year, Hitler said to an NSDAP crowd, at least according to the *Völkischer Beobachter*, that Christ's whip was today represented by the rubber truncheons of the *Sturmabteilung* (SA): "*I will not accept that Christ should be less worthy of love because he gripped the whip!*" [emphasis in original].[22] He thus drew a direct parallel between Jesus whipping the Jewish moneylenders in the first century and the SA beating the Jews in Germany in the 1920s.

Hitler carried whips with him throughout his career, and there are plenty of pictures of him with one even after 1933. Even in the first picture taken of him by Hoffmann, he is dressed in his characteristic trench coat with his hat in one hand and what appears to be his whip, made from hippopotamus skin, in the other. This image was taken in

---

[19] Heydecker, Joe J., *Das Hitler-Bild: Die Erinnerungen des Heinrich Hoffmann* (St. Pölten: Residenz Verlag, 2008), p. 30.

[20] Heiden, K., *Adolf Hitler ...* (Vol. I), p. 197; Fest, J., *Hitler ...* , p. 198; Kershaw, I., *Hitler 1889–1936 ...* , p. 188; Longerich, P., *Hitler ...* , pp. 116–117; Ullrich, V., *Hitler ...* (Band I), pp. 142, 149; Thamer, H.-U., *Adolf Hitler ...* , p. 78. Heiden even has a whole section with the headline "The Hippopotamus Whip" (*Die Nilpferdpeitsche*), although he does not really elaborate on the meaning of this attribute.

[21] Jung, R., *Der nationale Sozialismus ...* , p. 111.

[22] *SA*, pp. 720–721 (Document 416). See also Rißmann, M., *Hitlers Gott ...* , p. 30.

141 / Christ on the Crooked Cross, Part II

the summer of 1923 and used as a postcard to cultivate his image as a *Führer* of the National Socialist and *völkisch* movements. Joachim Fest relates a story, based on Hanfstaengl's memoirs, of how Eckart before the coup attempt in November 1923 had told him that Hitler strutted around with his whip in his hand and spoke about how he had to go to Berlin and like Christ drive the moneylenders out of the Temple.[23] By itself, this information seems rather odd and out of place, and one could certainly be forgiven if one doubted its veracity. But within the context of Hitler's admiration of Jesus and his frequent references to precisely this story in the New Testament, there is a good case to be made for the argument that Hanfstaengl's version of events could have some truth to it. It is at least not a long leap of the imagination to consider this possibility, because there are other episodes that testify to the same phenomenon.

Hitler also made use of the whip during the clearing of his own, "temple," that is, during the so-called Night of Long Knives, a purging of political enemies that lasted from June 30 to July 2, 1934. Hitler's pilot, Hans Baur, testified to having flown an unusually agitated Hitler from Bad Godesberg to Munich, where he was planning on arresting the head of the SA, Ernst Röhm. Baur stated that Hitler was lashing his whip in the air with such a frenzy that he struck his own foot several times. Hitler then went straight from the airport to Bad Weissee, where he burst into Röhm's room with the whip in his hand and shouted that Röhm was now under arrest.[24] The murders carried out during this purge were a cleansing of both the movement and of Hitler's own mind at the same time; grudges that he had held against people for over a decade were done away with. Sure, this is a speculative argument, but it makes a lot of sense considering the central place that the image of Jesus clearing the Temple grounds with his whip in hand played in Hitler's worldview.

What inspired Hitler to carry a whip could therefore very well have been his admiration, and indeed identification with, the Jew-beating Jesus from his favorite Gospel story. This would also explain why Hitler thought the whip enhanced his leadership image. The whip

---

[23] Fest, J., *Hitler* ... , pp. 287, 1070.
[24] Ullrich, V., *Adolf Hitler* ... (Band I), pp. 517–518.

142 / Christianity in Hitler's Ideology

could have been a symbolic nod to the Aryan Jesus that he idolized and whose mission he thought that he himself and the NSDAP had been chosen by God to complete. Rather than being incidental, the whip could therefore very well be a conscious choice and marker on Hitler's part of his identification with Jesus.

3.4   Jesus: Christ and Lord

Ironically, the Nazi remaking of Jesus into a warrior represented a return to the original Jewish idea of the Messiah: a warrior and a revolutionary that would come to defeat the evil powers that be and free the chosen people. It was, however, precisely the downplaying of these traits in the Christian Messiah that the Nazis interpreted as a Judaizing of Jesus, since the Jews were thought of as cowards and pacifists, not brave and warrior-like. At the same time, bringing the interpretation of Jesus as a warrior and revolutionary back meant that it was much easier to make the otherwise rather spurious connection between Hitler and Jesus work, and to argue that the Nazis were indeed continuing and completing the original divine mission of Christ. Hitler was, after all, a revolutionary and had been a soldier too.

The word "Lord," a term that originates with the Greek word *kyrios* (κύριος), denotes Jesus' divinity within the Christian tradition.[25] Thus, Hitler's use of it can absolutely be interpreted as a statement of divinity. Obviously, Hitler's God was not the same God that most Christians were worshipping or adhering to, but the important point here is not the specifics of Hitler's theology. Rather, it is that there was an internal consistency to his religious beliefs.[26] His God was an Aryan God and Jesus was an Aryan savior. The part about how Jesus was greatest not as a victim but as a warrior has been cited also by Richard Steigmann-Gall. However, Steigmann-Gall translates the phrase *Wahrhaftiger Gott*

---

[25]   McGrath, A. E., *Theology* . . . , pp. 64–66.

[26]   If one was to view Hitler's talk about Jesus as only propaganda, one could perhaps argue that the consistency related only to what was communicated outward. However, in that case it was a very carefully thought-out plan. This option appears less probable, especially considering that Hitler upheld this view also in private conversations.

143 / Christ on the Crooked Cross, Part II

incorrectly as "the true God."[27] Richard Weikart has already noted this mistake in his book *Hitler's Religion*.[28]

Still, Weikart argues: "I have never found any evidence that Hitler believed in the deity of Jesus."[29] He does not discuss the fact that Hitler consistently referred to Jesus as "Christ" or as "Lord." The word "Christ" is the religious title given to Jesus, and comes from the Greek word *Christós* (Χριστός) meaning "the anointed one" and indicates nothing less that his divinity.[30] Note that Bormann is the only person who has Hitler using the word "Jesus" instead of "Christ." This happens on two occasions in *Monologe*, that is, on October 21, 1941, and on November 30, 1944.[31] However, we have a parallel note made by Alfred Rosenberg's representative in the *Führerhauptquartier* (FHQ), Werner Koeppen, for October 21, 1941, where the word "Christ" (*Christus*) is used.[32] Heinrich Heim, who made the bulk of the notes in *Monologe*, then has Hitler on December 13, 1941, talking about how "Christ" was an Aryan, and Alfred Rosenberg's diary entry for the same day does so too.[33]

It is certainly true that the use of the term "Christ" does not definitely prove that Hitler considered Jesus to be divine or that it reflects some sort of deeply felt respect for him. It was after all more common than not for both believers and nonbelievers in Germany in the 1920s to refer to Jesus as "Christ." But the use of the term "Christ" by Hitler should not be assessed as evidence in and of itself, but together with all the other evidence put forth in this book. Seen within this context, it is obvious that Hitler's use of the term seems to be a signifier of the admiration that he held for a character that he considered to be the greatest historical example of an antisemite. The fact that Hitler uses

---

[27] Steigmann-Gall, R., *The Holy Reich ...* , pp. 27, 37.
[28] Weikart, R., *Hitler's Religion ...* , pp. 84–85, 322. He mistakenly dates the speech to April 22.
[29] Ibid., p. 84.   [30] McGrath, A. E., *Theology ...* , pp. 62–64, 77–79.
[31] *Monologe ...* , pp. 96, 412.
[32] BBL, R6/34a, Aufzeichnungen, Koeppen, "Bericht Nr. 48, Führerhauptquartier, Mittwoch, den 22.10.1941. Blatt 2: Mittagstafel 21.10," p. 60.
[33] *Monologe ...* , p. 150; Rosenberg, Alfred, *Alfred Rosenberg: Die Tagebücher von 1934 bis 1944. Herausgegeben und kommentiert von Jürgen Matthäus und Frank Bajohr* (Munich: S. Fischer Verlag, 2015), pp. 415–416. Heim is thus recording a conversation between Hitler and Rosenberg.

144 / Christianity in Hitler's Ideology

"Jesus" instead of "Christ" only in Bormann's notes is probably a reflection of Bormann's choice of words and not Hitler's. The hypothesis that all other sources are wrong on this issue is simply not probable. This is significant in the context of whether Hitler considered Jesus to be divine or not. Even if one believes that Hitler used this religious title simply out of convention, one needs to bring this usage up if one makes a statement like Weikart does. Something that makes Weikart's argumentation wholly untenable is that he himself gives several examples of Hitler speaking about Jesus as his "Lord and Savior."[34] It is impossible to argue convincingly that phrases such as "Lord and Savior" do not carry with them the implication that Jesus was divine. The burden of proof is then on the person arguing that this is not significant.

Hitler's Christmas speech in Munich on December 11, 1928, is interesting from this perspective. This time, he did not call Christ the Son of God but instead spoke of him as Christ, our Lord, which was an equally clear reference to Jesus' divinity.[35] Hitler would continue to talk about Jesus in ways that unambiguously pointed to him as being divine. On February 29, 1928, in front of an NSDAP audience in Munich, Hitler referred to Christ as "our uttermost merciful Lord and Savior" (*Herr und Heiland*), and a while later in the same speech he explicitly called Christ the "Son of God" (*der Gottessohn*).[36] Furthermore, Hitler stated sarcastically on July 6, 1929, that for the Catholic *Bayerische Volkpartei* (BVP) the Jew was worth just as much as the Lord Christ.[37] This is also evidence that Hitler made the connection between the expression "Lord and Savior" and Jesus' divinity. Friedrich Tomberg has stated that Hitler did not consider Christ to be divine.[38] But there is no way that Tomberg can know that for sure. Expressions such as these

---

[34] Weikart, R., *Hitler's Religion* . . . , pp. 77, 81.

[35] *RSA* III/1, pp. 349–352 (Document 65). Hitler called Jesus "Christ and Lord" also in a speech held on August 12, 1930: *RSA* III/3, p. 331 (Document 87). See also Tomberg, F., *Das Christentum* . . . , pp. 128–131.

[36] *RSA* II/2, pp. 699, 705 (Document 237). For the theological implications of this concept, see McGrath, A. E., *Theology* . . . , pp. 66–67. This phrase comes from the Greek phrase Θεός ὁ υἱός in the New Testament.

[37] *RSA Band III: Zwischen den Reichstagswahlen Juli 1928–September 1930. Teil 2: März 1929–Dezember 1929. Herausgegeben und kommentiert von Klaus A. Lankheit* (Munich: K. G. Saur, 1994) [Henceforth: *RSA* III/2], p. 285 (Document 48).

[38] Tomberg, F., *Das Christentum* . . . , p. 120.

145 / Christ on the Crooked Cross, Part II

clearly indicate that he did, and there certainly is no evidence of Hitler denying Jesus' divinity. Therefore, the brunt of the available evidence suggests that Hitler saw some kind of divine relationship between God and Jesus, even though it may not have been the type of divinity that most Christians today think of when they make this claim.

In Christian theology, the term "Son of God" has become synonymous with divinity. More importantly, in National Socialist Christian theology the terms "Son of God" and "Christ" were used specifically to distance Jesus from the Jewish concept of the Messiah. Moreover, the term for "Savior" used by Hitler, that is, *Heiland*, was "a central Christological title in the theology of the German Christians" [*Deutsche Christen*], who considered the *Heiland*, that is, Jesus, to be the heavenly guarantor of their struggle in the ranks of Adolf Hitler.[39] They also proclaimed in a programmatic declaration of their faith on April 4, 1939, that "Christian faith is the unbridgeable religious contradiction to Judaism." Theologian Walter Grundmann officially declared the same just a month later.[40] Hitler's terminology was thus not coincidental but tied to specific theological ideas about Jesus. The added statement of Christ being the Son of God was not at all necessary to make, and Hitler had never stated it so clearly before. Furthermore, one could not reasonably argue that this little admission in a speech to NSDAP members in Munich would have any propaganda value worth speaking of. However, if we take this statement seriously, it would go a long way to explaining why we cannot find even one critical word about Jesus in any source for Hitler's statements during his entire political career, as well as why it was so important for him to insist that Jesus was not a Jew but an Aryan.

So, which God was Jesus the son of? Well, once again, the specifics of Hitler's theology are not the topic of study here. But Samuel Koehne has correctly remarked that there was not a clear dichotomy between Christian and pagan ideas in Nazi religiosity but rather that paganism and Christianity existed side by side on "a single continuum" in the Nazi mind. Moreover, some *völkisch* ideologues and

---

[39] Lorenz, E., *Ein Jesusbild im Horizont des Nationalsozialismus* ..., pp. 114–119, 247–253; quote on p. 253.
[40] Head, P., "The Nazi Quest ... ," pp. 76–77.

146 / Christianity in Hitler's Ideology

(later) National Socialists like Theodore Fritsch and Artur Dinter argued that the Aryans had been the true Israelites and that the God of Jesus was a very different God from the God of the Jews (Jahveh), who was considered a "false God."[41] The latter idea was a Gnostic dichotomy and was intimated by Hitler in a speech in Munich on 13 August 1920.[42] Dinter's bestselling *Die Sünde wider das Blut* (The Sins against the Blood) from 1920 was not only dedicated to Chamberlain, but also cited the warning of false prophets in 1 John 4:1 ("Do not believe every spirit, but test the spirits to see whether they are from God") on the title page. Furthermore, it contained a long section about how Jesus could not possibly be Jewish and how Galilee had been colonized by an Indo-Germanic people.[43] In a letter to Fritsch, Hitler later claimed that his work had been important for the National Socialist ideology's success.[44] Suffice it to say that both Hitler and his audience obviously understood what he was talking about.

To argue that it was Hitler's antisemitism that affected his view of Jesus rather than the other way around would be a bit backwards. Nazi religiosity was in fact seen as "a counterresponse to modern secularized culture and its spiritual decay, and as an attempt to carry out a religious renaissance built upon modern and 'secular' foundations." It was motivated by the search for "real authentic spirituality" as "a new ethical and existential fulcrum in the 'Death of God' era, and ... redemption from the vicissitudes of modern nihilism."[45] Of course, there was a causal interplay between the racial-ideological and the religious beliefs, but antisemitism cannot explain the wish to save the figure of Jesus. Rather, then, we should then expect Jesus, who was a

---

[41] Koehne, S., "Were the National Socialists a Völkisch Party? ... ," pp. 761, 764–772.

[42] *SA*, p. 189 (Document 136).

[43] Dinter, A., *Die Sünde wider das Blut* ... , title pages and pp. 153–181. See also Koehne, S., "Religion in the Early Nazi Milieu ... ," pp. 677–678.

[44] *RSA* IV/1, pp. 133–134 (Document 32). See also Ullrich, V., *Adolf Hitler ...* (Band I), pp. 121, 867; Weikart, R., *Hitler's Religion ...* , pp. 153–154. Fritsch has nonetheless not been mentioned often in studies of Hitler's ideological development. Not even Brigitte Hamann mentions Fritsch more than once, and then not even in connection to Hitler (Hamann, B., *Hitlers Wien ...* , p. 367). An exception to this rule is Richard Weikart, who writes about Fritsch in his *From Darwin to Hitler*, although he does not tie Fritsch's ideas directly to Hitler either (Weikart, R., *From Darwin to Hitler ...* , pp. 55–56, 69–123, 142–43, 204–205, 224–225).

[45] Varshizky, A., "The Metaphysics of Race ... ," pp. 287–288.

147 / Christ on the Crooked Cross, Part II

Jew, to be dismissed too. To make sense of this, we simply have to assume that there was a religious belief, and a religious need, underlying this effort to turn Jesus into an Aryan.

When Hitler spoke to NSDAP members on October 27, 1928, in Passau, he revisited the theme of Christ's return to earth and said that the Church could gladly educate the political parties regarding religious services, but it was the task of the NSDAP to educate them to fight for their worldview. It was the conviction of the National Socialists that if Christ returned to earth today, he would not deny his salvation to those who did their best to put Christianity into practice by defending their people and their culture. No harm made to the Christian foundational idea would be tolerated within the party, he said, nor that anyone fought against Christianity or turned themselves in to the archenemy of the Church. "This our movement is really *Christian*," Hitler assured his audience, and he wished for nothing more than that Catholics and Protestants would unite in the fight against the suffering of the German people. The NSDAP never had the intention of degrading Christianity into a tool to be used in the service of politics.[46] Hitler's Christmas speech in Munich on December 11, 1928, is interesting from this perspective. He did not call Jesus the Son of God but spoke of him as Christ, our Lord, which, as we have seen, was an equally clear reference to Jesus' divinity.[47] Once again, speaking of Jesus as "the Lord" makes little sense within any Christian context if Hitler was not referring to him as being divine in some sense of the word, and the idea of Jesus bringing "salvation" also implies a divine connection.

In 1923, he stated that the future National Socialist leader and dictator of Germany would not be responsible to any parliamentary majority but only to "his conscience before God." For this reason, the NSDAP had made no promises in its party program, because they were not seeking a greater mandate in the parliament, that is, the *Reichstag*. The latter institution did not after all possess "the creator activity of a lawgiver like Christ, Solon and so on," as Hitler had pointed out in

---

[46] *RSA* III/1, pp. 191–192 (Document 40).

[47] *RSA* III/1, pp. 349–352 (Document 65). Hitler called Jesus Christ and Lord also in a speech on August 12, 1930: *RSA* III/3, p. 331 (Document 87). See also Tomberg, F., *Das Christentum . . .* , pp. 128–131.

148 / Christianity in Hitler's Ideology

Augsburg already on July 6, 1923.[48] This introduced a clear ambivalence with regard to Jesus' divine status. Hitler here put Jesus (Christ) as a lawgiver and a real person in history in the same category as the ancient Greek philosopher and statesman Solon (640 BCE – 558 BCE). Although we do have proof that Hitler at times equated the term "lawgiver" with God – he expressed this as late as July 4, 1944[49] – Solon was clearly not divine. Jesus, on the other hand, was not a statesman and never issued any secular laws. Thus, Hitler clearly cannot have been speaking of the two men as "lawgivers" in the same sense here, and he was therefore inconsistent in two ways at the same time. Either he contradicted himself, or he may not have intended that these two persons be considered "lawgivers" in the same way: rather, he may have been giving examples of one secular lawgiver (Solon) and one divine lawgiver (Jesus).

All of what has been said above of course does not definitely prove that Hitler believed that Jesus really was divine, since it is impossible to know what someone *truly* believes. But it is impossible to claim (as Weikart does) that there are no indications that Hitler spoke of Jesus as divine. As we have seen, we have a lot of such indications – both implicit and sometimes explicit statements – that attest to such a view. References to Jesus' divinity can in fact be found in almost everything that Hitler said about Jesus, including the fact that he always referred to him as "Christ."

3.5   Did Hitler Pray to God?

But what did Hitler's personal religious practices look like? Did he even have such practices; for example, did he pray to the God he believed in? There is some evidence that he did. First, there is the ample evidence of him publicly offering prayers to the deity both in speeches and in writing. On June 10, 1923, Hitler spoke in Munich to a gathering of members of the *Vaterländische Verbände* (The Associations of the Fatherland). He ended his speech with a statement in the form of a prayer: "Lord God! We promise you that we will sacrifice ourselves to

---

[48] *SA*, p. 946 (Document 544).   [49] *HRP* II/4, p. 2117 (July 4, 1944).

149 / Christ on the Crooked Cross, Part II

the last drop of blood, and pray that you will give us your blessing for this!"[50] It is certainly true that prayers were not common for him, but they do nonetheless occur from time to time in the documentary record. In *Mein Kampf*, too, we find an injunction formulated like a prayer when Hitler is talking about how it was the role of National Socialist propaganda to instill the following prayer in the mind of even the smallest child: "Almighty God, in the days to come bless our weapons; be as righteous as you have always been; judge now if we deserve our freedom; Lord, bless our struggle!"[51]

This same prayer was repeated to NSDAP members in Nuremberg on March 23, 1927.[52] In *Mein Kampf*, we also find the episode where Hitler claimed to have fallen down on his knees and thanked God for the outbreak of war in August 1914.[53] Furthermore, at the end of a speech at an SA rally in Berlin on September 1, 1930, Hitler finished off by asking the almighty God for help in the fight against all the devils. He then, according to the police report, silenced the thundering applause and clasped his hands as if engaged in prayer and contemplating his own words.[54] A few years later, on May 1, 1933, Hitler stated: "Lord, you see that we have changed" and continued by noting that the German people were no longer characterized by shame and a lack of virtue.[55] The moral implication was that the German people had in fact previously deserved to be downtrodden because they had not fought hard enough, but that the moral renewal under National Socialism meant that their fortunes were now about to change. Several more similar examples could be provided, but this should suffice to illustrate that this happened from time to time.

It may once again be tempting to simply write all of this off as just empty words intended as nothing more than propaganda to soothe the Christians (National Socialists or otherwise) in the audience. But before we do that, we should yet again take care to note that the

---

[50] *SA*, p. 935 (Document 534, June 10, 1923).
[51] *Hitler, Mein Kampf* ... (Band II), p. 1605 [**291**]. See also Bucher, R., *Hitlers Theologie*, p. 91.
[52] *RSA* II/1, p. 192 (Document 89, March 23, 1927).
[53] *Hitler, Mein Kampf* ... (Band I), p. 453 [**169**].
[54] *RSA* III/3, p. 379 (Document 100, September 1, 1930).
[55] *HRP* I/1, p. 264 (May 1, 1933).

150 / Christianity in Hitler's Ideology

theology expressed in these prayers align with the theology of Chamberlain and many other National Socialist sincere Christian believers. What I am referring to is the idea that one had to *earn* God's grace through one's actions and faith. It was the focus on will-power and the will to fight for survival that was so central to Nazi ideology. God only rewarded those who deserved to be rewarded. This was how the dilemma embedded in National Socialist theology, how to square the idea of the struggle to be the highest and most sacred principle of the universe with an omnipotent God, was solved. The nonsensical and tautological result was a principle that said: if God did not grant you victory, then you did not deserve it. If Hitler had only intended these words to be for propaganda, then we should expect (1) these prayers to have been offered much more often and (2) for them to have been formulated in a way that better corresponded to mainstream Christian beliefs. The fact that they were not should tell us that Hitler meant what he said. It was of course propaganda as well, but not only.

But why, if these prayers were indeed honest in their intent and content, do they not appear more frequently? Should we not expect Hitler to have sprinkled his public speeches far more often with prayers if his beliefs were genuine? No, that is not at all the most reasonable expectation. We also need to consider the fact that Hitler believed religious practices and theological issues were matters that the individual believer should decide for himself. Religious belief was a private matter. Hitler never had the ambition of becoming a religious figure or leader. In such a context, we should on the contrary expect public displays of religious liturgical practices to be rather infrequent. Once again, Hitler no doubt realized the propagandistic value of public prayers, and yet he did not engage in them. This also corresponds very well with point 24 of the NSDAP party program and its principle of positive Christianity, that is, that all confessions should be able to coexist peacefully side by side within National Socialism.

I have found evidence that Hitler would also on occasion pray in private. This evidence comes from Heinrich Heim, Martin Bormann's adjutant, who wrote down most of the table talk notes, who spent a lot of time with Hitler between mid-1941 and mid-1942, and who in the mid-1970s stated in correspondence with a researcher that Hitler considered his religious beliefs a very personal matter and therefore seldom

151 / Christ on the Crooked Cross, Part II

spoke about them openly. More interestingly, Heim also stated that Hitler would pray to God, although not in front of other people.[56] How did Heim know about this? Unfortunately, he did not reveal this. But considering the amount of time that Heim spent with both Hitler and Bormann, it is not at all unlikely to assume that Bormann or Hitler may have told him.

We do, however, have other indications that Hitler on occasion would enter a prayerlike state. According to Albert Zoller, Hitler's secretary, Christa Schroeder, stated that Hitler "from time to time" remained "standing emerged in thought before a picture of Bismarck, with a dream-like stare, as if in prayer."[57] It may be a provocative thing for many people to think about – Hitler praying to God for advice and direction – but we cannot refrain from considering this scenario simply because we may find it objectionable or even outright offensive. Hitler did, after all, write in *Mein Kampf* that he had fallen to his knees and thanked heaven (God) for the outbreak of war in August 1914.[58] Usually, this has no doubt been interpreted as simply yet another expression of Hitler's characteristic hyperbole and just another piece of political propaganda. But Heim's statement shows that this may have been literally true.

Granted, this evidence is not very strong, and it could very well be argued that Heim was either lying or that he had been told a lie by someone else. Schroeder's testimony does not really claim that Hitler *was* praying, although it suggests that she did not consider such a practice entirely foreign to him. Hitler may also, even if he prayed in private settings, have done so for purely transactional reasons, although it is difficult to see why he would go that far to trick his closest associates. But while this is not strong evidence, it is information that historians have not known about until now and it should not be ignored.

---

[56] University of Arizona Library, Special Collections (UALSC); Papers of Karen Kuykendall (PKK), MS 243; Series II; Box 2, Folder 5; Heim's reply to a question on an undated questionnaire provided to him by Kuykendall, p. 5. From one of Heim's letters in the same folder (dated April 8, 1974), we know that Kuykendall had sent him the questionnaire on March 26, 1973. See also UALSC; PKK, MS 243; Series II; Box 2, Folder 1; undated handwritten interview notes by Kuykendall, pp. 2–4.

[57] Zoller, A., *Hitler privat* ... , p. 16.   [58] *Hitler, Mein Kampf* ... (Band I), p. 453 [169].

152 / Christianity in Hitler's Ideology

3.6 Hitler's Belief in Jesus: Is It Proof That Hitler Was a Christian?

Some readers may think that what has been said thus far reasonably has to be interpreted as evidence that Hitler was not a Christian, because how could someone who thinks that the apostle Paul perverted Christianity be considered a Christian? However, it is not that easy to define who is a Christian and who is not. After all, various denominations and sects of self-proclaimed Christians have been fighting each other for centuries over this exact issue. The fact that we know of no prayer books or crosses (crucifixes) having been in Hitler's possession is perhaps a problem for the thesis of Hitler as an honest Christian believer. However, once again, there are millions of Christian believers that do not use prayer books or crucifixes. The number of Christian denominations is so great, and the individual variations within them even greater, that it is not possible to dismiss the idea that Hitler prayed in private just because we do not have the paraphernalia usually associated with such activity.

There were in fact Christian sects in the early history of Christianity that taught ideas that were very similar to those that Hitler professed. One such sect was the Jewish Christian Ebionites (after the Hebrew word *ebyon* [אֶבְיוֹן, poor]), a group of Christians who did not think that Jesus was divine but an ordinary man who was "adopted" by God when he was baptized. They also rejected Paul, claiming he had perverted Christianity by breaking the Mosaic law prohibiting preaching to gentiles.[59] Opposition against Paul's teaching was not at all uncommon in Christianity's early history, which was filled with sects with widely diverging interpretations of what "true" Christianity was (Paul's epistles in the New Testament also contain evidence of this). A tradition in early Christianity spoke of a serious rift between Paul on the one hand and Jesus' disciple Peter and his purported earthly brother James on the other, which is expressed in the apocryphal *Peter's Letter to James*. This letter refers to Paul as "my [Peter's] enemy" who preached an absurd

---

[59] Erhman, Bart D., *Whose Word Is It? The Story behind Who Changed the Bible and Why* (London: Continuum, 2008), pp. 155–156; Freeman, C., *A New History of Early Christianity*, p. 133.

153 / Christ on the Crooked Cross, Part II

doctrine in direct opposition to Jesus. This critique came from Jewish Christians who thought that Paul's corruption of Jesus' teachings consisted of him having *de*-Judaized Christianity.[60]

Hitler's critique against Paul instead claimed the opposite, that is, that Paul had made Jesus' teachings *more* Jewish. But the point here is that in Christianity's early history there existed groups of Christians who, albeit for entirely different reasons, just as Hitler, argued that Paul had corrupted Jesus' original teachings. The history of Christianity contains so many different expressions of that religion that all arguments that Hitler was not a true Christian become a version of the "no true Scotsman" fallacy. To talk of Nazi Christianity as heresy, writes Susannah Heschel, implies that there is an orthodoxy to compare it to. There is in fact no such thing.[61] The same point has been made by Samuel Koehne, who stresses "that scholars need to consider 'what counts as religion for people in various cultures and at various times and places'."[62] This holds true also today, as there are many Christians who, for example, do not consider the Mormons to be "real" Christians. More importantly, however, Hitler's interpretation fit perfectly into the specific contemporary context of *völkisch* and racist Christian theology.

Heß stated in a letter to the Bavarian Minister President Gustav Ritter von Kahr in 1921 that Hitler was not only religious but also a good Catholic.[63] In a letter from July 15, 1923, Heß wrote about how he went to a Catholic service with Hitler and how the priest, a Father Achtleitner, held a good sermon. Achtleitner had National Socialist sympathies, and he often took part in the NSDAP's meetings, wrote Heß, and on this occasion he also talked to Hitler, who, during the conversation, claimed to think of himself as one of "the good Catholics."[64] This means that Konrad Heiden may in fact have been correct when he wrote, in the first volume of his Hitler biography, that

---

[60] Ehrman, Bart D., *Forged: Writing in the Name of God – Why the Bible Writers Are Not Who We Think They Are* (New York: Harper One, 2011), pp. 60–63. For more on the parallels between early Christianity and National Socialism, see Grabner-Haider, A., *Hitlers Theologie des Todes*, pp. 50–56.

[61] Heschel, S., "Historiography of Antisemitism ... ," p. 271.

[62] Koehne, S. "Religion in the Early Nazi Milieu ... ," p. 669.

[63] Kershaw, I., *Hitler: 1889–1936 ...* , p. 159.

[64] *Rudolf Heß ...* , p. 299 (No. 310). This is obviously not the conversation verbatim, but it probably gives us the gist of the content more or less correctly.

154 / Christianity in Hitler's Ideology

Hitler took communion even during the war, although formal church services seem to have been something he did not usually take part in.[65] Even a receptionist, called Kascha, at the hospital in Pasewalk, where Hitler was treated for battle fatigue symptoms at the end of the war, testified later that Hitler had spoken of himself as a Catholic during his stay at the hospital in the fall of 1918.[66] Moreover, in the handwritten notes on the cover sheet of Hitler's inmate file from Landsberg fortress (and also in another note from the same time), made on November 11, 1923, by fortress warden Otto Leybold, it states that Hitler considered himself a Catholic.[67] Hitler's lawyer, Lorenz Roder, claimed in a letter to the newspaper *Münchener Post* on December 6, 1923, that Hitler "is still to this day a convinced Catholic."[68]

Then, in a letter from the fortress in Landsberg dated August 20, 1924, Rudolf Heß wrote to his beloved Ilse Pröhl that Hitler "is at heart deeply religious." Hitler had said that God lent his support only to those who were brave and who fought for themselves.[69] This was, as we have seen, a belief that Hitler would return to repeatedly during his life. It clearly defined him as a person. He evidently believed in a personal God that could intervene in human history. Now, Hitler was of course not the sort of Catholic who put his faith in the Pope in the Vatican in Rome. But he may have been an anti-ultramontanist Catholic, which was quite common in Bavaria and a powerful force within the NSDAP in the early 1920s.[70] Heß also wrote in a letter dated May 18, 1924, that during his time in the fortress Hitler was often visited by the Protestant priest Gottfried Federschmidt. Hitler also on several occasions drank coffee with a Catholic priest called Fleck.[71]

---

[65] Heiden, K., *Adolf Hitler* ... (Vol. I), p. 351.

[66] Heiden, K., *Adolf Hitler: Ein Mann gegen Europa. Eine Biographie*, Vol. II (Zurich: Europa Verlag, 1937), p. 144.

[67] Fleischmann, P., *Hitler als Häftling* ..., pp. 83, 85.   [68] *SA*, p. 1059 (Document 602).

[69] *Rudolf Heß* ... , p. 351 (No. 353). These letters have been surprisingly ignored by historians. Ian Kershaw, for example, did not use them at all in his two-volume biography of Hitler.

[70] See Hastings, D., *Catholicism and the Roots of Nazism* ... , passim.

[71] Plöckinger, O., *Quellen und Dokumente* ... , pp. 116–117 (Document 31); see especially nn279–280.

155 / Christ on the Crooked Cross, Part II

These sources in fact make it impossible to deny that Hitler, at least in the first half of the 1920s, defined himself, and was defined by others, as some sort of a Catholic. In fact, this may be the single strongest piece of evidence that Hitler really was sincere in his religious beliefs since there was absolutely no propagandistic value to this statement. It was not even Hitler himself who uttered it, but his close confidant Heß. These notes are, as already stated, probably the best evidence we have for how Hitler viewed his own religiosity at the time. While Heß's letter to Kahr could perhaps be argued to have been written for transactional reasons, Hitler's own statement to the warden had very little discernible propaganda value. The same is true for Heß's letter to his fiancée, which had no propagandistic value whatsoever. That was private correspondence between lovers and is thus very strong evidence for Hitler being truly religious – and in a way that corresponded to what he stated in public.

Something that must be addressed in this context is a statement in Alfred Rosenberg's diary from June 28, 1934, where it says that Hitler had said the following: "He stressed, laughing, that he for a long time – now more than ever – had been a pagan."[72] Does this mean that Hitler had changed his religious belief by this time? Possibly, but it is in fact not likely that we should interpret Rosenberg's rendering of Hitler's utterances about being a "pagan" literally. Hitler was always dismissive and disdainful toward the paganist and occult practices within Himmler's *Ahnenerbe* circle.[73] "Pagan" should therefore in this case likely be interpreted as a sarcastic reference to the many charges from the Christian churches regarding Hitler's and the Nazis' paganism. It was, probably, a sort of an inside joke. We know, from one of Goebbels' speeches on December 4, 1935, that the accusation coming from the Church that the Nazis were paganists was sarcastically accepted in this way.[74] Another statement that could be interpreted as

---

[72] Rosenberg, A., *Alfred Rosenberg*, pp. 139–140 (June 28, 1934).

[73] See, for example, Dierker, Wolfgang, *Himmlers Glaubenskrieger: Der Sicherheitsdienst der SS und seine Religionspolitik 1933–1945* (Paderborn: Ferdinand Schöningh, 2003), p. 127; Weikart, R., *Hitler's Religion . . .* , pp. 173–194.

[74] Goebbels, Joseph, *Goebbels Reden 1932–1939, Band I. Herausgegeben von Helmut Heiber* (Munich: Wilhelm Heyne Verlag, 1971), pp. 274–275. See also Steigmann-Gall, R., *The Holy Reich . . .* , p. 125. In fact, even Himmler denied actually being a "pagan." He supposedly told a friend in April 1945 that he was often considered "a heedless pagan,

156 / Christianity in Hitler's Ideology

proof of Hitler having had pagan beliefs is when he said the following at the end of his speech at President Hindenburg's funeral at Tannenberg on August 7, 1934: "Dead Field Marshal, go now into Valhalla!"[75] But according to Hitler's private adjutant, Julius Schaub, this was not an expression of Hitler's religious faith, but instead intended as a spontaneous sarcastic comment to the eulogy that the military chaplain had just held before him.[76] Victor Klemperer also considered this to be a ridiculing statement that desacralized the funeral and not an utterance of Hitler's pagan beliefs.[77]

We know that Hitler throughout his life kept coming back to Christian sites and that he seems to have enjoyed spending time at these places. According to Otto Dietrich, he would often visit the monastery in Banz, and he once observed Hitler having a three-hour conversation about the philosophy of religion and church history with Church Minister Hans Kerrl in the garden of the monastery's church; he often sat and listened to, and very much enjoyed, the famous boy choir *Regensburger Domspatzen* in Regensburg. Whenever he was in Stuttgart, he lived in the Christian hospice there, and he "almost regularly" visited the monastery *Maulbronn* near Pforzheim. After the *Anschluß* in 1938, he took time to visit the monastery school *Lambach*, which he attended as a young boy. Hitler kept a painting by an unknown Italian artist of Jesus' mother, Mary, on the mantelpiece of the open fireplace at the *Berghof*, in front of which he and his entourage would gather in the evenings to converse in the glowing light from the fire. Next to this hung a female nude painting by the deeply religious Italian Renaissance master Sandro Botticelli.[78]

---

but in the depths of my heart I am a believer." This indicates that Himmler interpreted the term "pagan" as being essentially the same as being a nonbeliever, that is, an atheist. "I believe in God and Providence," he allegedly said. For this, see Trevor-Roper, H. R., *The Last Days ...* , pp. 36–37.

[75] *HRP* I/1, p. 438 (August 7, 1934).

[76] Rose, Olaf (ed.), *Julius Schaub – In Hitlers Schatten: Erinnerungen und Aufzeichnungen des persönlichen Adjutanten und Vertrauten Julius Schaub 1925–1945* (Stegen/Ammersee: Druffel & Vowinckel Verlag, 2005), pp. 129–132. See also Longerich, P., *Hitler ...* , p. 420.

[77] Klemperer, V., *Ich will Zeugnis ablegen ...* , p. 137 (August 11, 1934).

[78] Dietrich, O., *12 Jahre mit Hitler*, pp. 168, 177, 180, 194, 229. See also Heer, F., *Der Glaube des Adolf Hitler ...* , p. 319.

157 / Christ on the Crooked Cross, Part II

Another instance that seems to suggest that Hitler's talk about the Nazis being the true Christians was only propaganda comes from Goebbels' diary recording a conversation he had with Hitler about Christianity, and the NSDAP's attitude toward it, on February 23, 1937. Goebbels wrote:

> Not the Party against Christianity, but rather we must declare ourselves to be the only true Christians.[79]

In isolation, this quote may seem to be clear proof of Hitler's insincerity. However, once we look at the context of this statement, as reported by Goebbels, it becomes obvious that this is not how one should understand this quote. Hitler also said that he wished to wage a small war on the churches and priests once the time was ready in the same way as the Marxist leadership had been destroyed by the true Socialism, that is, by National Socialism. Hitler also repeated his view that Christ's true teaching had been corrupted and made unrecognizable by the Jew Paul.[80] This implies that Hitler not only considered the NSDAP to be the only true Socialists, but also the only true Christians. Moreover, the statement seems to make little sense, considering the Nazis had declared themselves the true Christians since at least 1920, with the Christian theological heritage going back much longer to the very origins of National Socialism itself in the mid-1800s.

3.7 Conclusion

The findings presented in this chapter ought to be considered as significant not least because Hitler thought of himself as appointed by God to lead Germany to greatness. Several more examples could have been referred to, although what has been included ought to be enough to be convincing. Hitler consistently throughout his political life kept to his admiration of Jesus and always exempted him from the hatred that he poured over the churches and established Christianity. He referred to Jesus as divine on several occasions, and in a least one instance he

---

[79] *TBJG*, I/3, p. 55 (February 23, 1937). See also Steigmann-Gall, R., *The Holy Reich* ... , p. 118.
[80] *TBJG*, I/3, p. 55 (February 23, 1937).

158 / Christianity in Hitler's Ideology

explicitly called him the Son of God. Then, we have the multiple instances when Hitler talked about Jesus as "Lord," "Savior," "lawgiver," etc. In addition, Hitler several times stated that Jesus used his whip to clear away the Jews from "his father's temple." Obviously, the father that Hitler is talking about here must be God, since it is not reasonable to think that he thought that Mary's husband Joseph owned the Temple. Yet another matter that is likely to be very important here is, as has already been mentioned, the fact that Hitler constantly referred to Jesus as "Christ." Admittedly, this is not one of the strongest indications that Hitler considered Jesus to have been divine. It could certainly be that this was simply a remnant of his Catholic past or an expression of even secular conventional language; however, in the light of all the other evidence presented in this chapter, this seems less likely to be the case.

The explicit references to Jesus are not very frequent, and Jesus can therefore not be said to have been a very common topic of Hitler's public and private statements. Nonetheless, it was not uncommon either. It is evident that most references to Jesus appear during the 1920s and to a lesser extent in the early 1930s. But Hitler made these statements both in public and in private, so it cannot be argued that it was just for outside consumption. During the period 1941–1944, we have a few references to Jesus in, for example, the table talks. However, it also has to be remarked that the evidence is not always crystal clear. For example, Hitler's statements regarding Jesus' divinity were sometimes ambiguous, or even contradictory, and are not always easy to interpret or to square with one another. That said, though, these contradictory statements were drowned out by the statements where he clearly referred to Jesus as "divine."

The idea of Hitler as a follower of Jesus – or rather of Hitler himself, and his Nazi cohorts, looking at him in this way – will surely make a lot of people uncomfortable, but it is not the role of historical science to avoid topics and truths that may be controversial even to most people. Millions of Germans thought of Hitler as being appointed by God to lead Germany to greatness, and many, if not most, of them also considered him a follower of Christ. Instead, it is the task of the historian to explain how this could have been the case even though it contradicts the common-sense idea of who Hitler was

159 / Christ on the Crooked Cross, Part II

and who he was inspired by. Hitler's Christ was not the same figure as the one that the majority of Christians in the world worship today (or even worshipped back then), but it was not a completely alien figure either. Hitler did not create the Aryan Jesus. He inherited it from several generations of European Christian theologians and religious philosophers who had merged their Christian beliefs with their anti-semitic racism and reached the conclusion that Jesus had not been a Jew. This in turn was dependent upon several centuries of Christian theological antisemitism. This view was adhered to by a not so small minority of Christians in Germany and became a fundamental belief among the Nazi leadership as well.

In the end, however, the only person who can judge whether Hitler was sincerely some kind of Christian is Hitler himself. No one can know for sure what goes on inside someone else's head. Some would even argue that we ourselves cannot be certain about who we truly are or what we really believe. People doubt themselves and their convictions all the time and manage to convince themselves about even openly contradictory positions and ideas. Nonetheless, the brunt of the evidence that has been presented here appears to show that Hitler did indeed consider himself a follower of Jesus' original teachings, and that he at least during the 1920s did think of himself as a true Christian, even (initially) a good Catholic. At least regarding Jesus, he continued, even in private, to consider him to be an Aryan until the very end. This shows that this was a very deeply and honestly held belief.

HITLER'S DAMASCUS ROAD EXPERIENCE

4 *How Hitler Modeled His Political Conversion Narrative in* Mein Kampf *on the Apostle Paul's Religious Conversion in Acts 9*

4.1 Introduction

This chapter presents and addresses something that has so far gone unnoticed by those who have previously studied Hitler's religiosity, namely, the parallels between Hitler's narrative of how he came to dedicate his life to politics as told in *Mein Kampf* and elsewhere, and Paul's Damascus Road experience as told in Acts 9.[1] It argues that they are not likely to be accidental, considering Hitler's good knowledge of the Bible. Given what we have already learned about Hitler's admiration for Jesus in the previous chapters, in this chapter I argue that the parallels are hardly incidental but actual allusions and that Hitler purposefully constructed his conversion narrative in *Mein Kampf* based on the story of Paul's Damascus Road experience in Acts 9. Note that I am only arguing that what has gone unnoticed by other scholars is specifically the modeling of Hitler's conversion narrative in *Mein Kampf* on Acts 9. Others, not least Thomas Weber, have already noted that

---

[1] Interestingly, the story of Paul's conversion in Acts 9 is itself a rewrite of the Emmaus narrative in Luke 24:13–35; for this point, see Carrier, Richard, *On the Historicity of Jesus: Why We Might Have Reason for Doubt* (Sheffield, UK: Phoenix Press 2014), pp. 365–366.

161 / Hitler's Damascus Road Experience

Hitler often used the Bible to stage himself in several other contexts.[2] In this case, however, the staging is not explicit.

This fits well with the fact that *Mein Kampf* was much more a work of fiction than a real attempt at autobiography. Weber has aptly referred to it as Hitler's *Bildungsroman* in which he claimed that the war "had provided him with prophet-like revelations."[3] The *Bildungsroman* is a literary genre that focuses on the coming-of-age of the protagonist and that places an extremely important emphasis on fundamental changes in the hero's moral and psychological character. In *Mein Kampf*, Hitler constructed a new life history for himself, one that was intended to appeal to his followers and cement his position as the charismatic genius and *Führer* of the NSDAP.[4] The same argument has poignantly been made by Susannah Heschel and other scholars.[5]

Wolfram Pyta has remarked that *Mein Kampf* was written in a context, and we have already seen many examples of this, where objective knowledge and academic science were looked down upon, distrusted, and even despised. In this setting, the individual autodidact genius could be made into an epistemic example, that is, Hitler could thus use his subjective experience in order to lend his *Weltanschauung* plausibility and authenticity. In fact, the "genius of action" (*Genie der Tat*) concept was a genre in its own right, in which an individual was ascribed powers and talents induced by the divine, and it had been used by theologians about Jesus, and it came to be used both by Hitler and his followers as a complement (*Ergänzung*) to the charisma concept.[6] Indeed, the Gospels and Acts contain basically the same elements as the *Bildungsroman* and can be read as such.[7] It would therefore make perfect sense for Hitler to model parts of his political conversion narrative upon a text from a similar tradition.

---

[2] Weber even divided his book *Becoming Hitler* into three sections called "Genesis," "New Testaments," and "Messiah."

[3] Weber, Thomas, *Hitler's First War: Adolf Hitler, the Men of the List Regiment, and the First World War* (Oxford: Oxford University Press, 2010), pp. 269, 271.

[4] Hans-Ulrich Thamer calls it an *Entwicklungsroman*, which essentially means the same thing but with lesser focus on personal development. See Thamer, H.-U., *Adolf Hitler ...*, p. 17.

[5] Heschel, S., "Being Adolf Hitler ...," pp. 185–196.

[6] Pyta, W., *Hitler ...*, pp. 221–222, 241–260.

[7] Summerfield, Giovanna and Downward, Lisa, *New Perspectives on the European Bildungsroman* (London: Continuum, 2010), p. 38.

162 / Christianity in Hitler's Ideology

I should also be perfectly clear with what I am *not* doing here. In this chapter, I am not arguing that Hitler, by using images and expressions from Paul's conversion in Acts 9, was idolizing Paul. He most certainly was not; in fact, as I have already pointed out, he despised Paul and considered him the corruptor of Jesus' original teachings. This might make some readers question the validity of the argument of this chapter already at the outset. But this would be a mistake. Acts was not written by Paul, so Hitler was not actually referring to Paul's own writings in this case, but rather to a story about him written by somebody else that would have been very familiar to every Christian in Germany. Using such a well-known story as a model does not imply any ideological affinity with the writer of that original story or with any of the characters in it. In this chapter, therefore, in contrast to what has thus far been argued in this book, I am suggesting that we look at these similarities as a purposefully and skillfully crafted piece of propaganda. Some of the parallels are entirely fictional; but many of them contained grains of truth in that they were based on real events that were made to fit an allegorical narrative.

Michael Rißmann has remarked that Hitler's rendition of his own life bears clear parallels to that which the New Testament gives of Jesus' life. Just like Jesus, Hitler is said to have been born under very simple circumstances, which is a very common theme in the salvation literature.[8] Hitler made this comparison explicitly in a speech to an NSDAP crowd in Dingolfing on December 12, 1925. Christmas was celebrated in memory of Christ and his struggle against Jewish materialism, Hitler said. Then, just like now, salvation had come from a salvation teaching (*Heilslehre*) whose preacher had been born under the most impoverished of circumstances.[9] In *Mein Kampf*, Hitler began the first book by stating that it was due to divine "fate" (*Schicksal*) that he had been born in Braunau am Inn of all places, a city on the border between the two German nations that he would later strive to bring together into a Greater Germany during his whole political career. Rißmann also notes that Hitler, just as the New Testament writers did regarding Jesus, introduced the first calling, that is, the first divine mission, to a point in time about thirty years later.[10]

---

[8] Rißmann, M., *Hitlers Gott* ... , p. 43. [9] *RSA* I, p. 237 (Document 92).
[10] Rißmann, M., *Hitlers Gott* ... , p. 43.

163 / Hitler's Damascus Road Experience

Hitler makes this point in *Mein Kampf*, when he starts chapter 3 by saying that he had become convinced that a man, unless he had not been blessed with remarkable talent, should not begin his public political career before the age of thirty. It was of course true that even thirty year olds had a lot to learn during their life, Hitler states, but this would only be a filling up of the already established frames because "his learnedness will no longer be a principal re-learnedness, but rather a continued learning, and his supporters will not have to suppress the depressing feeling that they have previously been wrongfully educated by him, ... since his learnedness only means a deepening of their own teaching."[11] It is clear that Hitler is here alluding to the Gospel of Luke and the claim that "Jesus himself was about thirty years old when he began his ministry."[12] The parallel between Hitler and Jesus was also the main theme of Victor von Koerber's *Adolf Hitler: Sein Leben und seine Reden*.[13] As we have seen, Hitler did not consider his mission to be simply a secular one; on the contrary, the mission to save the German nation and the German people was always also seen as a divine task filled with religious meaning.

4.2   A Stint of Temporary Blindness

The first similarity to be addressed here is the fact that both Hitler's and Paul's conversion narratives include a stint of temporary blindness. Paul experiences this for three days.[14] Hitler does not specify how many days he suffered from his blindness, ostensibly caused by a British mustard gas attack, but he writes that he was on his way toward recovery when the news about the revolution in Germany reached him on November 8, 1918, and that this caused the receding blindness to return.[15] Hitler experienced the gas attack, in which he was "lightly" wounded, on October 13/14, 1918, and was hospitalized first in a field hospital by La Montange between October 15 and 16, after which he was transferred to a hospital in the town Oudenaarde. Only after

---

[11] *Hitler, Mein Kampf* ... (Band I), pp. 235–237 [67–68].
[12] Luke 3:23 (NIV). For this point, see also Reichelt, W., *Das braune Evangelium* ... , p. 15.
[13] Koerber, A.-V. von, *Adolf Hitler* ... , pp. 6–7; Weber, T., *Becoming Hitler* ..., pp. 285–291.
[14] Acts 9:8–9.   [15] *Hitler, Mein Kampf* ... (Band I), pp. 547–553 [212–215].

164 / Christianity in Hitler's Ideology

having spent three or four days there was he transferred, via Ghent, to Pasewalk, where he arrived on October 21, and he remained there until November 19.[16] Now, this would certainly not be worth mentioning here if Hitler was really blinded in a gas attack.

However, Thomas Weber has questioned whether Hitler was ever blinded at all. The small quantity of gas that Hitler was exposed to did not warrant such a long stay at the hospital, and he has instead described Hitler's reaction as psychosomatic. This is not at all an implausible view. According to a US intelligence report, based on an interview with one of the doctors from the psychiatric department at the hospital, Hitler was admitted to the hospital's psychiatric ward, writes Weber.[17] In fact, Friedrich Heer suggested already in 1968 that Hitler's blindness was a consequence of hysteria.[18] This may also explain why Hitler's hospital file is missing.[19] Hitler probably saw to it that this file was destroyed. Most likely, Hitler was anyway no longer suffering from the gas attack once he was transferred to Pasewalk. His main problems were thus likely mental, probably the result of battle fatigue (he had after all been on active duty for most of the time since November 1914) or shell shock syndrome.

Why is this fact important for the argument made in this chapter? Well, it is important because it makes it very likely that Hitler was indeed inventing, or at least greatly exaggerating, his stint of blindness. Hitler was not still suffering from blindness when the war ended several weeks after he had arrived at Pasewalk. This means that he was consciously constructing a false narrative about blindness using this piece of information, and it is this that makes the story about Paul's blindness in Acts 9 potentially so significant. Why did Hitler choose to emphasize blindness rather than, say, blisters on the skin or lungs, and the pain associated with these injuries, which are also caused by mustard gas? Reasonably, he chose blindness because blindness has a symbolic meaning in Christian belief. Symbolic statements are only

[16] Joachimsthaler, A., *Hitlers Weg ...* , pp. 174–175; Plöckinger, Othmar, *Unter Soldaten und Agitatoren: Hitlers prägende Jahre im deutschen Militär 1918–1920* (Paderborn: Ferdinand Schöningh, 2013), p. 27.

[17] Weber, T., *Hitler's First War ...* , pp. 220–222.

[18] Heer, F., *Der Glaube des Adolf Hitler ...* , p. 343.

[19] Joachimsthaler, A., *Hitlers Weg ...* , p. 184.

165 / Hitler's Damascus Road Experience

meaningful to an audience if there is a shared cultural and ideological context within which they can be interpreted and understood as such. The New Testament provided precisely such a context for Hitler's readers. If Hitler was in fact suffering from shell shock (or war-related fatigue) and was treated for this at Pasewalk's psychiatric department, then the significance of the blindness is greatly enhanced. It is then more or less an entirely fictional element introduced into *Mein Kampf* much later.

Friedrich Heer has suggested that it may have suited the hysterical Hitler very well to interpret the regaining of his eyesight as a miraculous sign of his having been appointed by God.[20] I agree with Heer, although I argue that this was a narrative created by Hitler after the fact, and that it was inserted at a point in time *after* the temporary blindness caused by the mustard gas had gone away. However, this assumes that Hitler really experienced blindness at all and that he really interpreted it as divine intervention. We have no way to assess Hitler's true feelings on this matter, however. What we can do, though, is determine whether Hitler made this narrative a part of his public persona even before he wrote *Mein Kampf*. We do have proof that Hitler tied the story of blindness to an experience of the divine. In fact, such stories were circulating in both German and American newspapers already in 1923, that is, even before *Mein Kampf* was published, in which the blindness was given a religious dimension and tied to a divine message. The evidence comes in the form of two newspaper articles from 1923, one in *Frankfurter Zeitung* and one in *The Nation*, which reported that Hitler had received a divine revelation during his state of blindness. In an editorial in January in the *Frankfurter Zeitung*, it was claimed that "Hitler was 'delivered by an inner rapture that set him the task of becoming his people's deliverer'." The article in *The Nation* even stated that Hitler's eyesight was restored in direct connection to "seizures" during which he had "ecstatic visions" of Germany's future victory.[21]

It is not known where this information originated, but it is hard to imagine that the NSDAP's political opponents would have had an

---

[20] Heer, F., *Der Glaube des Adolf Hitler* ... , p. 343.
[21] Quoted in Redles, D., *Hitler's Millennial Reich* ... , p. 113.

166 / Christianity in Hitler's Ideology

interest in spreading this idea. It must have come from within the Nazi Party, perhaps even from Hitler himself, as a favorable piece of propaganda that was then allowed to circulate in the press. Hitler also brought this topic up, although without the overt religious connotations, during the attempted coup on November 8, 1923, when he, according to a report by the NSDAP, referred to how he, at the time when he "was laying in the hospital as a blind cripple," had sworn never to rest until the November criminals had been defeated.[22] He then returned to this theme later during the trial, saying that he had feared that he would never be able to see again, and that he lay "broken and with great pains" in his hospital bed, but that he nonetheless decided, during the night of November 9, 1918, "that I, if I regained the light, would turn to politics."[23]

The fact is that the same story was included in the first biography of Hitler, *Adolf Hitler: Sein Leben und seine Reden*, published in 1923, which also portrayed Hitler as a new Jesus. It is possible that the story in *The Nation* came from this biography because it too says that his eyesight was restored, his dead eyes were given new light, in a state of ecstasy. The painful struggle that Hitler went through in his hospital bed is referred to as his "Golgotha" and as a "spiritual and bodily crucifixion."[24] Hitler had gone through a passion, died, and risen again. This text was ostensibly written by Victor von Koerber, but Weber has found evidence that shows that Hitler was most likely the real author.[25] Thus, here Hitler's story about his stint of blindness was turned into a transposition of Hitler into Jesus' place in the Gospel stories. Perhaps Hitler later decided that this comparison was a bit too much for it to be included in *Mein Kampf* and toned it down a bit, drawing on parallels to Paul instead of Jesus. The important point here is that Hitler used the blindness episode to create a symbolic religious narrative – the connection to the Bible and Christian myths thus seemed obvious to him.

---

[22] *SA*, p. 1055 (Document 596, November 8, 1923).

[23] *SA*, pp. 1062–1064 (Document 605, February 24, 1924).

[24] Koeber, A.-V. von, *Adolf Hitler* ..., pp. 6–7.

[25] "Wer schreib 'Sein Leben und seine Reden'?," *Die Welt*, October 8, 2016, www.welt.de/geschichte/article160311381/Wer-schrieb-Sein-Leben-und-seine-Reden.html.

167 / Hitler's Damascus Road Experience

Hitler's choice of words here – that is, if he "regained the light" (*das Licht wiederbekäme*) – is obviously full of religious symbolism and not at all likely to be coincidental. From having been covered in darkness, a common metaphor for evil and ignorance, this appears to be a promise to God that if he was given the light back – a symbol of goodness, knowledge, and insight – he would dedicate himself to fighting what he construed as the ultimate evil in this world, that is, the Jews. This is exactly what we find also in Acts, where it says that, after Paul had been touched by Ananias, "there fell from his eyes something like scales, and he received sight forthwith." He then got up, got baptized, and started preaching the Gospel.[26] Paul was thus born again through baptism and became the founder of a religious faith movement. Hitler was born again too, in the sense that he became a new person, a politician, after having undergone a baptism of fire during the war he became the leader of a political faith movement. Paul also went from being an opponent of the followers of Jesus to a supporter. This was also something that Hitler could relate to in his own life since he had been working for the Socialist revolutionary authorities in Munich prior to May 1919.

Perhaps the idea that Hitler had been born again after undergoing a baptism of fire seems far-fetched? In fact, Hitler would make precisely this claim himself in a speech in Pasewalk of all places held on October 25, 1932 (published also in the *Völkischer Beobachter*). Hitler said that he just as likely might have died on the battlefield like so many millions of his comrades, and he therefore interpreted the fact that he had not died there in the following manner: "I have taken my life back as a gift from Providence and sworn to dedicate this life to the people."[27] In order to take one's life back, one must first have lost it at some point. Of course, Hitler did not mean literal death here. He was talking about a spiritual death. He was saying that he had lost his life spiritually, but that God had blown new spiritual life into him. What is important here is of course not whether Hitler really meant what he said, that is, whether he was convinced that he was telling the truth or not, although he certainly may have been, but simply that he chose to

---

[26] Acts 9:18–20 (KJ21).
[27] *HRP* I/1, p. 141 (October 25, 1932); Bucher, R., *Hitlers Theologie*, p. 84.

168 / Christianity in Hitler's Ideology

narrate his decision to dedicate himself to politics in this overtly religious manner and with these clear allusions to Paul's experience as portrayed in Acts 9.

That these remarks were made in Pasewalk specifically, the place where it all supposedly had happened, is of course even more significant. It shows that Hitler kept this myth alive for a very long time, and it is a good indication of him having internalized this narrative to a degree where he probably had begun to believe it himself. After Hitler came to power in January 1933, Pasewalk was declared a national shrine of sorts, and together with Hitler's birthplace, Braunau am Inn, it became a pilgrimage site for faithful National Socialists. Hitler would never let go of the blindness narrative, and referred to it even as late as 1944, as he celebrated his appointment to Chancellor, when he stated that the road between him as a half-blind soldier in November 1918 and the realities facing Germany in 1944 was longer and more difficult than that which now lay between Germany in 1944 and victory in the war.[28]

This is further supported by Hans Frank, who also cites Hitler in his memoirs and says that Hitler had told him that, as he was lying in his hospital bed, he had promised God that if he was to be made well again then he would dedicate his life to politics. As he then got his eyesight back a little later, he had been "completely shaken and took it as a calling from heaven for me."[29] First, we know that this cannot be a true story because Hitler did not decide to become a politician while in Pasewalk, but it may still be that it is true in the sense that Hitler really told Frank a story like this. Second, while these sources cannot be trusted to provide verbatim records, they probably reflect the spirit of what Hitler had said. It could be that by then Hitler believed that what he said was true. Perhaps he really did interpret his inner voice as being of divine origin, and in hindsight really did consider the Pasewalk experience as a calling from God. Perhaps he had internalized his own narrative to such a degree that he had convinced himself that what he said was true.

---

[28] *HRP* II/4, p. 2086 (January 30, 1944).
[29] Frank, H., *Im Angesicht des Galgens …*, p. 315. See also Heer, F., *Der Glaube des Adolf Hitler …*, p. 343.

169 / Hitler's Damascus Road Experience

4.3 Conversations with the Divine: God Speaks to Hitler

The second similarity between the stories in *Mein Kampf* and Acts 9 is the conversations with God that both of them entail. In Acts 9, Paul has a conversation with Jesus in a vision in which the latter told him that he was the one that Paul was persecuting. Jesus then told Paul to stand up and go into Damascus, where he was going to be told what to do next. Obviously, the God that Paul was speaking to did not want him to dwell on the past but to move forward and focus on the future. Through the similar conversation that Jesus had with Ananias in the following verses, this was made perfectly clear: God did not want them to focus on the past, that is, on Paul's work against God and the followers of Christ, but instead to turn their attention to the future.[30] This, too, is closely mirrored in *Mein Kampf*.

Hitler writes that as he was lying in the hospital filled with self-pity, worrying about being blinded forever, his own conscience spoke to him. But the way in which this is described makes it quite obvious that it was not simply an internal conversation at all. Hitler wrote "Then thundered the voice of conscience to me: miserable squealer, you may well howl," but, said the voice, his suffering was nothing compared to that which all the fallen German heroes had had to withstand. These young men had died in vain, now that the war was over, after having been betrayed by the Jews in Germany. Then, in a passage that reminds us also about the story in Matthew 27:52–53 in which the graves in Jerusalem opened up after the injustice of Jesus' death, Hitler asks rhetorically if the graves of the dead soldiers will not open up and if they will not wander off back to Germany and exact revenge for this betrayal and injustice.[31] Hitler would return to this particular image in his speech at the *Berliner Sportpalast* on February 10, 1933, when he stated that if the graves of the fallen soldiers were to open up today, then the spirits of the past, of those who had once fought and died for Germany, would fall in behind the government and support it.[32]

It is true that Hitler does not explicitly say in *Mein Kampf* that it was God who spoke to him, but that would on the other hand have been

---

[30] Acts 9:4–16.   [31] *Hitler, Mein Kampf ...* (Band I), p. 553 [215].
[32] *HRP* I/1, p. 207 (February 10, 1933).

170 / Christianity in Hitler's Ideology

very uncharacteristic of him, since he never ever claimed to have had any such direct conversations with God. Such was not the nature of Hitler's relationship to his God and his religion. Hitler's God never spoke directly to people, but he intervened in history in other ways. Instead, Hitler ascribes this voice to his own conscience. Note how Hitler talks about this inner voice in the third person singular, as if it was something removed from him and not belonging to him. The same effect is achieved by the fact that this inner voice addresses Hitler in the second person singular with the pronoun "you" (*du*). Furthermore, the use of the word "thundered" is reminiscent of how God addresses wrongdoers in the Bible.

Nonetheless, the idea that Hitler's inner voice was intended to mean the voice of God may still not seem entirely convincing. Is there any actual explicit evidence that Hitler thought of his inner voice of conscience in this way, or is this simply a contrived parallel? As it turns out, there is indeed such evidence available. The proof is provided by the former SA leader Otto Wagener,[33] who claimed in his memoirs, written in captivity in Wales in 1946, that Hitler once said to him that the *Führer* was responsible only "to the people and to his conscience, and this is given to him by God, it is the divine voice within him."[34] According to Wagener, then, Hitler thought that his own inner voice of conscience was in fact of divine nature, that is, God's guiding voice inside him.

But it turns out that Hitler seems to have told another story to his close companions during the 1920s that also referred to this inner voice having spoken to him and having saved his life. In this case, it is quite obvious that the inner voice is actually of divine origin and coming from a source outside Hitler. The event in question was said to have occurred during the First World War and is retold in Konrad Heiden's Hitler biography from 1936 – Heiden even calls this section in the book

---

[33] Between 1929 and 1932, Wagener belonged to Hitler's closest circle, being a leader in the SA, and after that he was in charge of the economic-political department in the NSDAP in Munich until July 1933, after which he fell out of favor with Hitler even though he remained a lower-level SA *Gruppenführer* until 1938.

[34] Wagener, O., *Hitler aus nächster Nähe* ..., p. 191. See also Redles, D., *Hitler's Millennial Reich* ..., pp. i, viii, x, 132–133.

171 / Hitler's Damascus Road Experience

"The Inner Voice" (*Die innere Stimme*). According to a witness, whom Heiden regarded as trustworthy and who had personally heard Hitler tell this story, Hitler claimed:

> I was sitting in the field and eating with several comrades. Suddenly, the inner voice ordered me: Stand up and sit down on the spot over there! I obeyed; the spot was about twenty meters away. Just as I had arrived the grenade hit my comrades; no one survived.[35]

The story itself is, of course, most likely entirely fictional. Interestingly though, Hitler told different variants of this story to various people over the years. John Toland, for example, cites this story from the British journalist Ward Price's book *I Know These Dictators* from 1937, although some of the details are different and the story is a bit more elaborated in Price's version than the one Heiden reports.[36] Apparently, Hitler developed the narrative over time and tried it out for effect. The implication that it was God who told him to move and who saved his life is obvious.

The story is, as already mentioned, most likely a fantasy based on a few real experiences that Hitler had. One occurred on November 17, 1914, in connection with Hitler having been recommended for the Iron Cross for the first time. As the list of suggested recipients was being discussed at the improvised regimental command post, Hitler and some of his comrades had to leave to make room for four company commanders. Five minutes later, a grenade struck the post, killing and wounding all of those inside, and one of the wounded was Hitler's Regiment Commander Phillipp Engelhardt – whom Hitler idolized – who had recommended Hitler for the award because Hitler had apparently helped save his life two days earlier. Hitler told his acquaintances Joseph Popp and Ernst Hepp about this episode in letters on December 3, 1914, and February 5, 1915, which is why we can be rather certain that it actually

---

[35] Quoted in Heiden, K., *Adolf Hitler* ... (Vol. I), p. 352.

[36] Toland, J., *Adolf Hitler*, p. 64. Toland actually seems to take this story seriously (but refers to the wrong page in Price's book, i.e. p. 40 instead of p. 38). Ian Kershaw notes also Price's version and remarks that Hitler added things to this (Kershaw, I., *Hitler: 1889–1936* ... , p. 634, n111). See Price, Ward, *I Know These Dictators* (London: Harrap, 1937), p. 38.

172 / Christianity in Hitler's Ideology

happened, describing it as the worst moment of his life.[37] The second incident happened on October 5, 1916, in the village of Le Barqué during the Battle of the Somme, when the entrance to the dugout where Hitler and two of his fellow dispatch runners sat was hit by a British shell. Hitler was wounded by a shell fragment in his left upper thigh. As Thomas Weber has noted, none of the others present were killed, contrary to what Nazi propaganda would later claim.[38] But it seems as if Hitler really did tell this story to his followers during the so-called *Kampfzeit*. The reason seems obvious, that is, to portray himself as a man who had always been guided and protected by God. This case makes the argument that Hitler considered his inner voice to be God speaking to him even more credible.

Apparently, others understood Hitler in this way as well, seemingly without having been told this by Hitler himself. In his book *Das braune Evangelium*, Werner Reichelt cites "an evangelical state commissar" who in 1933 said: "We trust in the Führer, sent to us by God, who at the time as an almost blinded received God's command: You shall save Germany!"[39] This is proof of the fact that Hitler's Damascus Road experience narrative had indeed generated the same kind of religious response among his Nazi followers as the story in Acts 9 had among Christians (many National Socialists were also believing Christians, which means their faiths overlapped in this case).

Note that I am not the first to draw a parallel between Hitler and the Damascus Road conversion story. Other scholars, for example Thomas Weber, have used the term "Damascus Road experience" with regard to Hitler's political conversion before, but then only as a well-known and established cultural metaphor and *not* in the direct sense of Hitler actually modeling his own conversion story on Acts 9.[40] Hitler's inner voice was explicitly interpreted, both by Hitler himself and his followers, as being the voice of God purveying a message to him. If Hitler had not intended for people to interpret his narrative in *Mein Kampf* in this way, this is surely an extraordinary coincidence.

[37] *SA*, pp. 60–61, 68 (Documents 26 and 30). See also Joachimsthaler, Anton, *Korrektur einer Biographie: Adolf Hitler 1908–1920* (Munich: Herbig, 1989), pp. 130–131; Weber, T., *Hitler's First War . . .* , pp. 53–54.
[38] Weber, T., *Hitler's First War . . .* , p. 154.
[39] Quoted in Reichelt, W., *Das braune Evangelium . . .* , p. 79.
[40] Weber, T., *Becoming Hitler . . .* , p. 81.

173 / Hitler's Damascus Road Experience

Obviously, this was how Hitler wanted people to interpret this passage, since he himself told his followers this. Hitler was thus, just like Paul, on the road to his personal "Damascus," claiming that he had been told what to do next by this inner divine voice, that is, by God, namely, he was to go into politics and save Germany and its people by leading it to greatness again.

4.4   Cursing the Ruling Criminal Classes

The third parallel is a bit less direct but nonetheless very interesting and relevant. The conversion narratives in both *Mein Kampf* and Acts 9 include scathing critique against the perceived ruling groups of the age. In Acts 9, it is the Jews and rabbis in Jerusalem that are attacked for being the enemies of the church and for persecuting Christians, and in *Mein Kampf* it is the Jews and politicians in Berlin that are attacked for being the enemies of the Fatherland. Hitler curses those he considered to be "criminals" and tells his readers how, during the nights after the news of Germany's surrender had reached him, his hatred for those he considered responsible for this catastrophe grew and increased in strength. In Acts 9, the Jews are said to have conspired against Paul, on several occasions, to try to capture and kill him. Thus, in Acts, too, the enemies of the hero are portrayed as criminals.[41]

The fact that Hitler's narrative in *Mein Kampf* differs considerably in the details from that in Acts 9, to which I argue that Hitler was alluding, cannot be used as an argument against the proposition made in this chapter, because we should not expect them to be exactly the same. On the contrary, we should expect them to differ quite a bit since the story would not have been believable had he copied Acts 9 too closely. Hitler used his *licentia poetica* to rewrite the story about Paul in Acts 9 and adapt it to plausibly fit into his own quasi-factual/semifictional autobiography. Making the parallels too evident would defeat the purpose of the whole endeavor. It is the nature of every allusion that it cannot be too obvious.

---

[41] *Hitler, Mein Kampf* ... (Band I), pp. 555–557 [216–217]; Acts 9:1, 14, 20–23, 29.

174 / Christianity in Hitler's Ideology

4.5   From Anonymity to Greatness

If we step outside of Acts and *Mein Kampf* for a moment, we will discover yet other similarities between Paul and Hitler, this being our fourth example. In the letter to the Galatians, Paul tells his readers that he had initially been completely unknown to the Christians in the whole of Judea.[42] Hitler too often spoke of his initial anonymity. In fact, this was an important part of his outwardly projected self-image. Thus, anonymity before ascending to prominence is another parallel between Paul's and Hitler's official autobiographies. In Hitler's case, this idea was presented as the theme of the unknown soldier who had created a large movement from extremely humble beginnings. Hitler used it publicly on several occasions during his life.

For example, on August 18, 1930, Hitler stated that twelve years ago nobody knew who he was or what he wanted. To the question of who he was, he could then have answered: "I have no name. ... I have only a number ... 'the Bavarian Reserve Infantry Regiment No. 16, No. 167.' That was me; nothing else."[43] Hitler is essentially reducing himself to the barest minimum, to almost nothing. He was saying that he had started from as humble a position as possible only to rise to fame and lead a great movement. This is in fact also extremely reminiscent of what the apostle Peter says of Jesus in Acts, namely, that Jesus was "the stone which was set at nought by you builders and which has become the head of the corner."[44] The meaning of the two stories is exactly the same: the least important man had become the most important one – the chosen one – the last had indeed become the first.

Hitler would come to repeat this image of himself many times over the years. On September 14, 1936, Hitler stated the following in a speech that ended the NSDAP congress:

> Woe to the one who does not believe [in Adolf Hitler]. This one sins against the whole meaning of life. ... What would have become of Germany if not in the year 1919 an unknown soldier had had the faith to save the German nation from its decay through the will to defend it, and through courage and the spirit

---

[42] Galatians 1:22.   [43] *RSA* III/3, p. 358 (Document 90, August 18, 1930).
[44] Acts 4:8–12 (KJ21).

175 / Hitler's Damascus Road Experience

of self-sacrifice? ... It was a miracle of faith that saved Germany. Today, after all these historically unique successes, it is the Party's duty, now more than ever, to recall this National Socialist creed and yet again put it forth as the holy sign of our struggle and our certain victory.[45]

This is truly the language of a religious zealot. Besides presenting the idea of the unknown soldier, Hitler here also made sure to base his statements on rhetoric that was thoroughly religious. Two-and-a-half years later, he said:

I can only express my deepest feelings in the form of a humble thank toward Providence that has called me, and that has let me succeed, as a once unknown soldier in the war, to rise up as the leader of my sincerely beloved people. It let me find the way so as to liberate our people from its deepest suffering without bloodshed and to continue to lead it forward. It has let me fulfil my life's only task: to lift my German people out of its defeat and liberate it from the shackles of the most shameful dictate of all time.[46]

Once again, the "unknown soldier" theme is used in a heavily religious-laden rhetoric. This makes it clear that Hitler wished his audience to connect the two. There was no way that this simple soldier would have been able to become the leader of a great revolutionary movement unless God had had a hand in this development and wanted him to succeed.

Goebbels also underlined Hitler's humble beginnings in a speech in November 1942, as he declared that the *Führer* was a gift from God to the German people.[47] A few months later, in February 1943, Hitler also claimed the right to believe that Providence had appointed him to fulfil the task of exterminating the Jews, because without God's blessings he would never, completely unknown as he was, have stepped onto the stage on February 24, 1920, nor could he have come to power and won all those victories for Germany.

[45] *HRP* I/2, p. 647 (September 14, 1936).   [46] *HRP* II/3, p. 1148 (April 28, 1939).
[47] *GR* II, p. 157 (November 17, 1942).

176 / Christianity in Hitler's Ideology

Moreover, he had been lucky enough to have a community of faithful and sworn believers that had dared to tie their destinies to his and to regard him as their leader in this struggle.[48] This was how Hitler always interpreted what he considered to be his mission: as a task given to him by God that he was chosen to fulfil. This theme was used by Hitler in more private settings as well. Heinrich Heim reported in 1942 that Hitler told his entourage in one of his wartime headquarters how he had been totally incognito within the *völkisch* community during the early 1920s simply because no one knew what he looked like, and that he could sit and listen to people talk about him without them knowing that he was present among them.[49]

It is of course true that Hitler *did* go from being an unknown to being well-known in the whole of Germany (and eventually the rest of the world). But at the same time, we also do know that Hitler used this for his propaganda purposes. His unwillingness to have pictures taken of him is an example of this. In interviews from the 1950s, Hitler's photographer Heinrich Hoffmann claimed that Dietrich Eckart told him that this was a conscious "propagandistic chess move made by him." People read about him, and heard about him, but no one could find a picture of him. This created a demand and a desire in people to come and see him speak: "They came out of curiosity and left as enrolled party members," Hoffmann is quoted as saying.[50] This is probably not the whole truth, however. Peter Longerich casts doubt on the whole idea and states that the real reason was that Hitler wished to remain unknown outside of Bavaria so that he could avoid being arrested by the police due to the warrants for his arrest that were from time to time issued, as well as avoiding being targeted by political opponents.[51]

---

[48] *HRP* II/4, pp. 1990–1993 (February 24, 1943).

[49] *Monologe* ... , pp. 204–205 (January 16/17, 1942). This note is quite suggestive and engaging, but one should not make the mistake of assuming that Heim wrote down Hitler's words verbatim. His notes were carefully proofread, corrected, and rewritten after the fact. This particular note happens to be among the few proof pages that still exist; see BBL, NS 6; Vol. 819; "16/17.1.1942, nachts," p. 5 (Document 17). The truth is that we do not know exactly what Hitler said during this nightly conversation. For more on the source-critical issue regarding the table talks, see Nilsson, M., *Hitler Redux* ... , passim.

[50] Heydecker, J. J., *Das Hitler-Bild* ... , pp. 28–29.

[51] Longerich, P., *Hitler* ... , pp. 117–118.

177 / Hitler's Damascus Road Experience

I do not think that we must choose between these two scenarios, because both can easily be true at the same time. Longerich also points out that Hitler suffered from a fear of looking ridiculous in images, a fear that remained with him all his life.[52] Hitler's almost obsessive secrecy is, as Ian Kershaw has pointed out, one of main reasons why we know so little about him and why Churchill's words (albeit uttered in another context) about him were so fitting: "a riddle wrapped in a mystery inside an enigma." Kershaw called it "the emptiness of the private person," a situation that is a consequence of "the fact that Hitler was highly secretive – not least about his personal life, his background, and his family." Kershaw agrees that although these were elements of his personal character Hitler also exploited this for propaganda purposes.[53] At the same time, Hitler also did his best to change the historical record of his past – an effort that not least *Mein Kampf* is a clear testament to. Just how successful Hitler and his sympathizers were at forging his past has been proven in many books that have corrected the official histories.[54]

4.6 Conclusion

In this chapter, I have suggested that Hitler's narrative of his decision to dedicate his life to politics, as laid out in *Mein Kampf*, is a conscious allusion to Paul's conversion story in Acts 9. The parallels between *Mein Kampf* and Acts 9 are indeed very clear and obvious. What is debatable is *why* they are there – that is, because of coincidence or because of choice? Taken separately, each of these parallels can certainly be thought of as being coincidental. However, to assume that all these parallels are simply coincidental does not seem at all plausible. We are therefore justified in assuming that the similarities are purposeful.

In *Mein Kampf*, Hitler presented his Damascus Road experience, and in doing so he put himself on a par with the real founder of Christianity, Paul of Tarsus. Both narratives include a period of temporary blindness, a highly symbolic theme in the Christian tradition. Both

---

[52] Ibid., p. 118.   [53] Kershaw, I., *Hitler 1889–1936* ... , p. xxv.
[54] See, e.g., Weber, T., *Hitler's First War* ...; Jetzinger, Franz, *Hitlers Jugend: Phantasien, Lügen – und die Wahrheit* (Vienna: Europa Verlag, 1956); Weber, T., *Becoming Hitler* ...

178 / Christianity in Hitler's Ideology

stories contain a conversation with some divine entity. In Paul's case, God speaks to him from the outside in the form of a vision. In Hitler's case, God, in the form of his own conscience, thunders his commands from the inside. In *Mein Kampf*, it is not explicitly said that this was a vision per se, but several newspaper reports from 1923 stated exactly that. It is very likely that these reports were based on interviews with Hitler himself or someone close to him and therefore represented the view that Hitler wished to give of himself. This obviously served as a propaganda tool as well. Both in the case of Paul and in the case of Hitler, these voices are said to have urged them to let go of the past and present, and instead focus their energy on the future and the tasks that lay ahead.

In both Hitler's and Paul's cases, a point is made of them having been unknown to the world prior to the foundation of their movements. Hitler would return to this point many times in several speeches during his lifetime, and it did indeed form a rather central part of his narrative of the NSDAP's origins. This was quite natural since it made the NSDAP's and his own success seem all the more miraculous. Both Acts 9 and the end of chapter 7 in *Mein Kampf* relate a spiritual journey from ignorance to knowledge, from uncertainty to certainty, and from falsehood to truth. Yet another thing that they both have in common is of course the overarching idea that both Paul and Hitler were appointed and guided by God to fulfil a historic mission.

Hitler had good reason to model his narrative on Acts 9, because the Damascus Road experience was a well-known narrative in Germany at this time, since an overwhelming majority of the population consisted of believing Christians. He may in fact have looked up to Paul in the latter's role as a founder of a hugely successful worldview because we know that Hitler admired the Catholic Church's organization and propaganda work even though he hated its politics and theological dogmas. Thus, even though Hitler had nothing but scorn for Paul because of his perceived role in corrupting the true message of Jesus, whom Hitler consistently called Christ, this does not mean that Hitler did not wish to use the Acts 9 story. Certainly, on some occasions the analogy may have been too subtle for people to notice, at least consciously, but it may still have piggybacked on the familiarity of these stories within a thoroughly Christian culture.

Furthermore, the Damascus Road experience provided a convenient and readily available analogy for Hitler when he wished to model his own narrative of his political conversion in *Mein Kampf*. Hitler's conversion did contain elements that he himself interpreted through a religious lens as a sign that he had been appointed by God to lead Germany to future greatness. He was careful enough not to make the parallels between his narrative and that in Acts 9 too obvious by making them too similar, as this would have been hard for the readers to take seriously. As any good storyteller knows to do when borrowing a story from another piece of fiction, he made use of a *licentia poetica* to rewrite it and fit it in to his own semifictional biography. The basic structure is the same, but the specific details are different. It is the same way that Hitler used the Catholic Church as a model for the NSDAP, that is, by cherry-picking what he considered to be useful and discarding the rest. It is within this religious and literary framework that the idea that Hitler modeled his conversion narrative in *Mein Kampf* on Acts 9 not only makes sense but is actually highly likely.

5 JESUS AS AN IDEOLOGICAL INSPIRATION FOR HITLER AND THE NSDAP

5.1 Introduction

In this chapter, I intend to show that Hitler in fact looked upon Jesus as an ideological inspiration not only for himself, but for the NSDAP and the *völkisch* movement overall. This is a subject that has not received much attention by historians thus far. While this may sound very provocative and perhaps even unbelievable to many readers, if you have not yet been convinced that this is the case, then by the end of this chapter it will be clear that this must be the necessary conclusion to be drawn from an analysis of the documentary evidence. Although it is not my intention to be offensive, some readers may indeed find themselves to be offended by much of what they will learn below; however, bear in mind that Hitler's religious beliefs do not in any way reflect negatively on any Christian, or otherwise religious person, who does not ascribe to the same ideas and beliefs as Hitler and the Nazis.

Hitler, and many other Nazis on every level in the party, considered the NSDAP as the only true followers of Jesus' original teachings, that is, before they had been ostensibly corrupted by Paul, the Jew. As we have seen previously, Jesus was thought of as an Aryan warrior who had given his life in the struggle against the Jewish "menace." It was because of this that the Jews, not the Romans, had had him killed on the cross. The NSDAP simply picked up where Jesus left off. In Chapter 2, we saw that Hitler mentioned Jesus in speeches from

181 / Jesus as an Ideological Inspiration for Hitler and the NSDAP

1920 onward. The fact that he spoke about Jesus from the very beginning of his political career is very significant, because it shows that this was not a theme that he added later in order to make National Socialism more palatable to larger groups of people. The fact that he did not speak about Jesus all that frequently may seem to indicate that the topic was not important for Hitler. But I believe that it would be a mistake to draw such a conclusion from this fact. On the contrary, I think that this fact is a clear indication that this was not a topic that Hitler used for propaganda purposes only. If that had been the case, then surely Jesus would have been brought up far more often in his speeches.

5.2 Following in the Footsteps of Jesus Christ

There can be no doubt about the fact that Hitler considered his own struggle to be a divine mission.[1] Albrecht Tyrell has stated that the realization that he was chosen to lead a divine mission against the Jews and against Bolshevism/Communism/Marxism had been a gradual process for Hitler from mid-1921 to early 1924, whose endpoint was encapsulated in the following infamous and oft-quoted passage in *Mein Kampf*: "Today I hence believe that I am acting in accordance with the Almighty Creator's intention: *when I defend myself against the Jews, I am fighting for the Lord's work*" [emphasis in original].[2] Although formulated in a for Hitler characteristically pompous way, we as historians should take his words seriously. But as we have seen above, there is good reason to believe that Hitler started this process even earlier, already in 1920. Perhaps Hitler's identification with Jesus was also part of the reason why he always expected that he would not live a long life.

There are several good indications that Jesus was an important character in Hitler's life. One such example is when he stressed that

---

[1] This has been noted by most historians who study Hitler, and it has also been the topic of the previous chapters in this book. Still, a great overview of the evidence for this belief is given in Rißmann, M., *Hitlers Gott ...* , pp. 56–76, 174–206; Bucher, R., *Hitlers Theologie*, pp. 77–124.

[2] Tyrell, A., *Vom "Trommler" ...* , pp. 132–174; Hitler, *Mein Kampf...* (Band I), p. 231 [66]. The German word *Werk* has a number of possible meanings, and could also be translated as "creation," "handiwork," "deed," or "oeuvre."

182 / Christianity in Hitler's Ideology

Christ's message was of central importance to the movement; that the National Socialists were the ones who had brought Christ's teachings back to life, that the NSDAP was the carrier of the "true message" of Christianity, and that the aim of the party was to resurrect the treasures of the living Christ. Where the churches had failed – that is, to install objective ethics into secular society – the National Socialist movement would be successful. It is obvious, says Richard Steigmann-Gall, that Hitler not only read the New Testament, but that he also stated that he was inspired by it in both his public and private life.[3] Goebbels did not shy away from quoting the Gospels either, as when he ended his note of despair in his diary in 1925 by stating that what was given to others fate did not grant him. Goebbels even used the phrase "My Lord, My Lord, why have You forsaken me?," that is, Jesus' last words on the cross according to the Gospel of Matthew, to finish his lament off.[4]

On November 2, 1922, Hitler said, according to the *Völkischer Beobachter*, that the Jews should be combatted just as Christ had battled against them. "Either our struggle is holy, or it's unjust," Hitler said. Everything was allowed when the existence of a people was at stake, he exclaimed, and pointed out that if Christ had walked through the world today, he would have been extremely critical of the fact that the Germans were now learning from the Jews, the people that he had branded as the spawn of vipers.[5] Clearly, Hitler was inspired by Jesus and considered the NSDAP's members to be the true followers of his teachings.

But was not all this simply a convenient way of spreading his antisemitic propaganda to a largely Christian population? I argue that this is not a plausible explanation for what the evidence shows. If the aim were to rally large amounts of Christians to the NSDAP, then surely Hitler would have tailored his message to fit the prevalent image of Jesus among Christians in Bavaria at the time. The fact that Hitler never compromised on this point should tell us that the argument that his statements about Jesus were only propaganda appears rather dubious. That does not mean that they were not *also* propaganda. They certainly

[3] Steigmann-Gall, R., *The Holy Reich* ... , pp. 27–28.
[4] Kershaw, I., *Hitler: 1889–1936* ... , p. 271.
[5] *SA*, pp. 720–721 (Document 416). See also Rißmann, M., *Hitlers Gott* ... , p. 30.

183 / Jesus as an Ideological Inspiration for Hitler and the NSDAP

were – there was, as already mentioned, no contradiction between the two. But there are, as we have already seen in the previous chapters in this book, very good reasons to assume that they were much more than that, namely, that they were honestly felt opinions and beliefs. The evidence clearly indicates that Hitler really did look up to Jesus as a role model for himself and his movement. It was Christ the warrior and not the pacifist that stood as a model for Hitler. If this theme was a simple propaganda ruse, we should also expect it to have been brought up much more often. Moreover, the fact that the NSDAP was not a mass movement from 1919 to the mid-1920s, combined with the relatively fewer public mentions of Jesus post-1925, seems to clearly negate the "only propaganda" thesis. Because if it was only propaganda, we would expect the usage of this theme in the propaganda to increase as the NSDAP tried to enrol ever-larger sections of the German public. All the reasons listed above strongly support the interpretation that these were honestly held opinions.

On April 6, 1923, Hitler said, according to the *Völkischer Beobachter*, that one of the movement's main objectives was to elevate Christianity once again in society. But it was a very specific interpretation of Christianity that Hitler was referring to, namely, a "Warrior-Christianity":[6]

> Christianity is not the teaching of silent suffering … , but of battle. We have a duty as Christians to combat injustice with every means that Christ has given us, and now the time has come to fight with fist and sword.[7]

This was the same message as that which Hitler had stressed on April 12, 1922: Jesus was greatest *not* as a victim but as a fighter.[8]

A few days later, on April 10, 1923, Hitler built upon a passage from Revelation 3:16, which says: "So, because you are lukewarm – neither hot nor cold – I am about to spit you out of my mouth." He argued that a middle-of-the-road approach would never achieve

---

[6] *SA*, p. 867 (Document 505). See also Weikart, R., *Hitler's Religion …* , p. 75.
[7] *SA*, p. 867 (Document 505). See also Weikart, R., *Hitler's Religion …* , p. 75; Hastings, D., *Catholicism and the Roots of Nazism …* , p. 113. For the same, see: Sebottendorff, Rudolf von, *Bevor Hitler kam …* , p. 26.
[8] *SA*, p. 623 (Document 377).

184 / Christianity in Hitler's Ideology

the movement's goals. One had to incite hatred against the Jews in the people. The book of Revelation purports to purvey Jesus' words in this instance, and in the *Völkischer Beobachter*'s report the statement was subsequently ascribed to "the great Nazarene."[9] Hitler returned to the Revelation passage on January 1, 1932, when he drew attention to "the Bible word" that "indeed condemns the lukewarm to get spit out" and claimed that it was the Almighty himself, through his grace, who had created the conditions for the extermination of "the lukewarm middle," that is, the Conservative and Liberal parties, and thereby guaranteed the victory of the NSDAP.[10] Hitler used the Bible to argue for his celebration of ideological fanaticism.

Shortly before October 1923, Hitler was interviewed by George Sylvester Viereck, at which time he again quoted Jesus and the Sermon on the Mount:

> The Bible tells us, "If thy right eye offend [sic] thee, pluck it out, and cast it from thee: for it is profitable for thee that one of thy members should perish, and not that thy whole body should be cast into hell. And if thy right hand offend [sic] thee, cut it off and cast it from thee: for it is profitable for thee that one of thy members should perish, and not that thy whole body should be cast into hell."[11] [English in original]

Of course, such an interview had great propaganda value and cannot be taken at face value. However, in combination with all the other similar evidence it does illustrate that Hitler did not shy away from using quotes from the Bible and that he knew the book rather well. He of course always took care to quote only those passages that agreed with, or that made sense within the context of, National Socialist ideology.

It is therefore not true, as Lars Lüdicke argues in *Hitlers Weltanschauung*, that the principles that Jesus taught, for example, those presented in the Sermon on the Mount, were impossible to square with Hitler's worldview. The message was reinterpreted so that the

---

[9] *SA*, pp. 873, 877–878 (Document 508).
[10] HRP I/I, p. 61 (January 1, 1932). See also Reichelt, W., *Das braune Evangelium ...*, pp. 36–37.
[11] *SA*, p. 1026 (Document 578).

religious and political beliefs were harmonized. The reason why Lüdicke cannot see this even though he goes on to describe Hitler's views of Jesus and Christianity is likely because he does not take Hitler's religiosity and admiration for Jesus seriously.[12]

We do know that Hitler had a beautiful calfskin edition of Houston Stewart Chamberlain's *Worte Christi* (The Words of Christ), the title printed in gold lettering on the cover, on his bookshelf.[13] This book was hugely popular in Germany and went through ten editions between 1901 and 1941. It consisted of 160 sayings by Jesus presented to the reader in six chapters with one saying on each page. It contained no commentary, references, or historical or biblical context to them. The sayings were of a very generic kind that emphasized a "general and internal sort of piety" such as "Believe in God" and "Fear not, only believe!" Notably, it also contained a section that scolded Jesus' Jewish enemies.[14] There are good indications that Hitler had read and pondered this work, because in the margin he has marked certain passages. One of these is to be found in the Gospel of Mark (12:30–31) and says:

> Love the Lord your God with all your heart and with all your soul and with all your mind and with all your strength. The second is this: "Love your neighbour as yourself." There is no commandment greater than these.[15]

Hitler owned several similar books, among them *Das Leben Jesu, Unseres Heilands*; Max Erich Winkels' *Der Sohn: Die evangelischen Quellen und die Verkündigung Jesu von Nazareth in ihrer ursprünglichen Gestalt und ihre Vermischung mit jüdischem Geist* from 1935; Josias Tillenius' *Rassenseele und Christentum* from 1926; Georg Lomer's *Die Evangelien als Himmelsbotschaft* from 1930; Hermann Karwehl's *Deutschland für Christus* from 1933; and Jörg Lanz von Liebensfels' *Buch der Psalmen teutsch: Das Gebetbuch der*

---

[12] Lüdicke, L., *Hitlers Weltanschauung* ... , pp. 148–154. Another problem is that Lüdicke bases all of this on *Monologe* and *Tischgespräche*, i.e., the table talk notes.

[13] Ryback, T. W., *Hitler's Private Library* ... , pp. xv–xvi.

[14] Head, P., "The Nazi Quest ... ," p. 66.   [15] Hesemann, M., *Hitlers Religion* ... , p. 29.

186 / Christianity in Hitler's Ideology

Ariosophen, Rassenmystiker und Antisemiten from 1926.[16] The fact that he owned these titles does not mean, of course, that he ever read them, or that he was inspired by them. They were most likely sent to Hitler as gifts from the authors or the publishers. Therefore, the fact that Hitler owned these books, or that he got them from his admirers, is not in isolation evidence of him using them or sympathizing with their message. But taken together with all the other evidence that shows him espousing religious and other ideological views that clearly align with the topics of these books, they ought to at least be added to the rather large mass of evidence of Hitler's preoccupation with, and admiration for, Jesus.

On December 18, 1926, Hitler spoke at an NSDAP meeting in Munich, and the police report described Hitler's views of Jesus in a very illuminating way. The Christmas celebration had a heightened significance for National Socialists, Hitler said, "because Christ was the greatest fighter in the struggle against the Jewish world enemy." Christ was not the Apostle of peace that the Church had turned him into, according to Hitler, but instead the greatest fighter that had ever lived. The fundamental teaching of Christ was the battle against the Jews, and "this mission that Christ had begun, but not been able to finish, he [Hitler] would end." "National Socialism," said Hitler, according to the police report, "was nothing less than a follower of Christ's teachings in practice."[17] Here, we see the idea of the Jews as the enemies of the world, which comes from the First Letter to the Thessalonians in the New Testament.[18]

Already the next day, Jesus was once again the theme in Hitler's speech at a party gathering in Augsburg. He reminded the audience that the Christmas celebration now even more than before ought to be a time to remember the great man (Jesus) who over 1,000 years ago had entered the world stage in the moral chaos of the time with his holy and pure idea. One should remember how he, with his whip in hand,

---

[16] Ibid. Hesemann here refers to Ryback but also indirectly to an article in *Frankfurter Allgemeine Sonntagszeitung* from April 13, 2003. Oddly enough, Ryback leaves out the fact that Hitler underlined these passages from Mark. It is not possible to say what source Hesemann is basing this on.

[17] *RSA* II/1, pp. 105–106 (Document 59). See also Rißmann, M., *Hitlers Gott ...*, p. 44.

[18] 1 Thessalonians 2:15.

187 / Jesus as an Ideological Inspiration for Hitler and the NSDAP

cleared the Temple grounds of the moneylenders and usurers. The same powers (i.e. the Jews) that Christ had fought against back then were today about to enslave the German people and threaten their very existence with moral poisoning. Christ's work had not been completed, Hitler once again remarked, but it was the task of National Socialism to finish the struggle for which the great martyr had died on the cross.[19] The idea that the Jews lacked morality was a point often stressed also by Gottfried Feder.[20]

An interesting fact in this context is that Rudolf Heß's uncle, Adolf Heß, founded a local group of the *Deutsche Christen* in Hamburg in 1929. This congregation was frequently visited by many National Socialists in Brown Shirts.[21] The Catholic Church was indeed not completely immunized against the ideas spread by the Nazi Christians even after 1924. As late as 1939, Archbishop Gröber announced that even if Jesus was not an Aryan – a statement that echoed the Catholic Church's uneasiness with the Aryan Christ – he did stand in complete contrast to the Jews, who had crucified him and who had continued their murderous activities into the present. Bishop Hilfrich of Limburg wrote in his pastoral letter for Easter that same year that Christianity had outgrown its Jewish nature, and could therefore not be considered a Jewish product, that is, it was not an anti-German doctrine.[22]

There were indeed plenty of Catholic clergy that were members of the NSDAP and even more that sympathized with the regime and idolized Hitler even if they remained uneasy about official party membership. Germany's most prolific and influential Catholic theologian from 1933 to 1945, Karl Adam (1876–1966), used the Catholic dogma of the Virgin Mary's sanctification in her mother's womb, that is, the immaculate conception (not to be confused with Jesus' conception), to justify why the Church, during the height of the Holocaust in 1943, had no reason or responsibility to consider the Jews of Europe as belonging

---

[19] *RSA* II/1, p. 106 (Document 60). See also Tomberg, F., *Das Christentum...*, p. 125.

[20] See, e.g., Sebottendorff, R., von, *Bevor Hitler kam...*, pp. 79–81.

[21] *Rudolf Heß...*, p. 398 (No. 391).

[22] Cited in Voegelin, Eric, "Descent into the Ecclesiastical Abyss: The Catholic Church," in *The Collected Works of Eric Voegelin, Vol. XXXI: Hitler and the Germans,* tr. and ed. *Detlev Clemens and Brendan Purcell* with an introduction (Columbia, MI: University of Missouri Press, 1999), p. 191.

188 / Christianity in Hitler's Ideology

to the same race or ethnicity as Jesus. Adam never went as far as to claim that Jesus was not a Jew, but he did argue that due to his mother's immaculate state *she* had not been Jewish either in body or spirit. Since the Jews as a race were by their very nature sinful, Mary could not be a Jew in the same sense, since that would mean that she was sinful and thus that she would have transferred this sinfulness to her son, Jesus. In this way, Adam "could build a bridge between Catholic theology and Nazi teaching."[23]

Adam explained it in the following way in a public lecture in 1943, a lecture that was a defence against both the Nazi critique of the Church for basing its teachings on Jewish myths, and the claim that Jesus was not Jewish. Adam could not go as far as accepting Chamberlain's idea of an Aryan Jesus, but he could not get himself to condemn the Nazi view either. Instead, he tried to both have his cake and eat it too by claiming that this distinction was nonsensical. He said:

> This view is based on the truth of faith that Mary was conceived without original sin, in other words in perfect purity and beauty, i.e. with the noblest dispositions and powers. It is this dogma of the immaculate conception of Mary that in the Catholic view makes all those malicious questions and complaints so completely senseless, as if we had to recognize Jesus as a "descendant of the Jews" despite his finer qualities. For it testifies to us that Jesus' mother Mary, had no physical or moral connection with those ugly dispositions and forces that we condemn in full-blooded Jews. Through the miracle of the grace of God she is beyond these Jewish hereditary traits, a figure that transcends Judaism.[24]

Another contextualizing fact that is important to understand here is that Adam had been a fierce German nationalist since the end of the First World War and shared a lot of views with Hitler. He too considered the Versailles Treaty a great injustice, and in his 1928 book *Christ and the*

---

[23] Blüger, Thomas, "Following the Virgin Mary through Auschwitz: Marian Dogmatic Theology at the Time of the Shoah," *Holocaust Studies: A Journal of Culture and History*, Vol. 14, No. 3 (2008), pp. 1–24. For a detailed history of the Catholic Nazi priests, see Spicer, K., *Hitler's Priests* . . . , passim.

[24] Cited in Blüger, T., "Following the Virgin Mary . . . ," p. 6.

189 / Jesus as an Ideological Inspiration for Hitler and the NSDAP

Spirit of the Western World he pondered "the German 'mission' to the Kingdom of God." Adam believed Germany could only be healed by a great leader, and he discovered this character in Hitler. He was convinced that Hitler was the savior that would lead Germany to greatness once again. Adam was not alone among Catholic theologians to believe this. Other prominent people in this group were Karl Eschweiler, Michael Schmaus, and Joseph Lortz. In 1933, Adam wrote in his article "Volkstum and Catholic Christianity":

> And he came, Adolph Hitler. From the south he came. From the Catholic south he came, but we knew him not. For he has gone through suffering and terror and had fought for Germany's salvation against those who had called themselves our leaders up to then ... But the hour came and we saw him and recognized him ... He now stands before us as the one who has been prophesied by our poets and our wise men, who is the liberator of German genius, who has taken the blindfold from our eyes, and has led us through all political, economic, societal, and confessional traumas to see the one essential moment: our unity in blood, our German self, the homo Germanus.[25]

Note that the phrases and language used by Adam are indistinguishable from those used by Hitler and the Nazis. This shows that even by late summer 1933, when the Nazi dictatorship had a full grip on Germany, leading Catholic minds were still arguing that the Catholic faith could be perfectly harmonized with National Socialism, and they were using National Socialist language to do it. The Messianic language is almost explicit here: Hitler's journey from an unknown to world fame, discussed in Chapter 4, is present here; Adam has Hitler going through a passion (he could have added a trial to his narrative) and even a figurative resurrection; like Jesus, the coming of Hitler had been foreseen by the prophets. This sounded very similar to what the Nazi pastor, and member of the *Deutsche Christen*, Julius Leutheuser had stated in

---

[25] Cited in Ibid., p. 4. See also: Scholder, Klaus, *The Churches and the Third Reich,* Vol. I: *Preliminary History and the Time of Illusions 1918–1934* (Eugene, OR: Wipf & Stock, 1988), pp. 426–427.

190 / Christianity in Hitler's Ideology

the *Peniger Tageblatt* already in 1931, although Leutheuser was much more explicit:

> In Adolf Hitler we see the powers again awakening which were once given to the Savior. For the National Socialists there is the experience of joy that finally one can sacrifice his life for something that will remain. ... Our way is rough, but one thing we know, that we shall as a result maintain a pure soul. Golgotha is followed by the resurrection. We are still standing on the way to Golgotha. Some will remain on it, but the soul, it cannot be stolen. Into your hands we commend our spirit, for Adolf Hitler we will gladly die.[26]

Here, Hitler was literally portrayed as the Messiah empowered by God, just as Jesus had been, that the faithful would lay down their lives for, so that Germany could be resurrected after this greatest of sacrifices. God was guiding Hitler on his way to Golgotha. It is no wonder that the audience at the Obergammau Passion Play in 1934 thought of Hitler and Germany as Jesus was being hoisted onto the cross.

The Protestant *Deutsche Christen* theologians tied their interpretation of the New Testament to Martin Luther and his theological, but most of all antisemitic, works. Luther was made into a direct predecessor to Hitler as well as the other way around: without Hitler, no Luther. It would not have been possible to conclude Luther's work without Hitler (note the parallel to the argument about Jesus), it was argued. Walter Grundmann argued in 1936 that the *Deutsche Christen* fought for Luther's work to be fulfilled in the National Socialist German nation. Luther was nothing less than the prototype of a *Deutsche Christen*, writes Elisabeth Lorenz. Luther, too, had been searching for the fundamental meaning in the New Testament, argued the theologian Erich Fromm, who stressed that Luther's greatness had not been as a translator of the Bible but in reinterpreting the text. This was a way for the *Deutsche Christen* to justify the often very large changes to the text of the Gospels that they initiated. They also produced a pamphlet called *God's Message*, which went through several editions. The number of copies and the dissemination of it appear to have been quite substantial. Already during

---

[26] Cited in Heschel, S., "Confronting the Past ... ," p. 47.

191 / Jesus as an Ideological Inspiration for Hitler and the NSDAP

the first six months after its publication in 1940, it was said to have reached about 200,000 (this figure is according to the publisher, which means it could be an exaggeration, and it is not possible to corroborate it).[27] This publication was also called *The People's Testament* and consisted of carefully edited and selected parts of the New Testament.[28]

Othmar Plöckinger says that these do indeed seem to have been Hitler's honestly held beliefs, at least during the early 1920s. It was the same Christian National Socialism that had been preached by the cofounder of the DAP, Anton Drexler.[29] In his grossly antisemitic "memoir" from 1919 called *Mein politisches Erwachen* (My Political Awakening), Drexler, a devoted Catholic, brought up Christ as well. Derek Hastings has claimed that Drexler wrote that he was directly inspired by the heroic political career of Jesus Christ when he founded the party in January of 1919. That is not an entirely accurate description. What Drexler said was that the fight against the Jews would be conducted based on "Socialism and communalism in the spirit of Christ, the outstanding character in world history." Note here the similarity to the words that Otto Wagener puts in Hitler's mouth in his memoirs (see below). Drexler added that "only Christian Socialism can give you the power to remain victorious in the fight against the materialistic-Talmudic world hegemony." He also wrote about his view of the Aryan Jesus in the *Völkischer Beobachter* on June 12, 1921. Hitler, in turn, claimed to have been attracted to the party by Drexler.[30] Heiden was the first historian to write about how Drexler put his pamphlet in Hitler's hand at the very first DAP meeting that Hitler attended on September 12, 1919.[31] This is also what Hitler states

---

[27] Lorenz, E., *Ein Jesusbild im Horizont des Nationalsozialismus . . .* , pp. 5–6. See also Carter, Guy C., "Martin Luther in the Third Reich: Recent Research on Luther as Iconic Force in Hitler's Germany," *Seminary Ridge Review*, Vol. 12, No. 1 (2009), pp. 42–62.

[28] Lorenz, E., *Ein Jesusbild im Horizont des Nationalsozialismus . . .* , pp. 29–30. Lorenz's book offers a detailed analysis and textual comparison of the Institute's People's Testament and the texts in the New Testament.

[29] Plöckinger, O., *Unter Soldaten und Agitatoren . . .* , p. 340.

[30] Hastings, D., *Catholicism and the Roots of Nazism . . .* , pp. 64, 209 n88; Drexler, Anton, *Mein politisches Erwachen: Aus dem tagebuch eines deutschen sozialistischen Arbeiters* (Munich: Deutscher Volksverlag, 1937, originally published in 1919), p. 48.

[31] Heiden, K., *Hitler . . .* (Vol. I), pp. 81–82. See also Weber, T., *Becoming Hitler . . .* , pp. 111–115. John Toland mistakenly claimed that Hitler had attended one DAP before that on September 12 but that it made such little impression on him that he did not even

192 / Christianity in Hitler's Ideology

in *Mein Kampf*, where he claimed to have read it "with interest" and that he saw his own political journey and awakening in Drexler's memoir.[32]

We cannot know if this story is entirely true, although Drexler very likely did provide Hitler with a copy of his pamphlet, since it was intended to sway people to join the National Socialist cause. Exactly when he did so is another question.[33] But considering the fact that the first written evidence of Hitler's antisemitism – i.e. the letter to Adolf Gemlich, in which he pointed to the connection between the Jews and international capitalism, and said that disorderly pogroms were not the right way to get rid of the Jews – is dated September 16, 1919, we can be absolutely certain that Hitler was already a radical, eliminationist

---

mention it in *Mein Kampf* (Toland, J., *Adolf Hitler*, p. 85). He gives no source for this claim.

[32] *Hitler, Mein Kampf ...* (Band I), pp. 587, 589 [230–231]. Weber notes that this was perhaps a *faux pas* by Hitler, who with this latter statement implicitly "admitted to his left-wing past," and that he too had dabbled in Social Democracy before becoming a National Socialist (Weber, T., *Becoming Hitler ...* , p. 114). A lot has been made from Hitler's service under first the Socialist (November 8, 1918–April 5, 1919) and then the Communist (April 6–May 3, 1919) revolutionary regimes in Munich during the spring of 1919. The leader of the Bavarian SPD (*Sozialdemokratische Partei Deutschlands*), Erhard Auer, claimed already in 1923 that Hitler had been a sympathizer of the Social Democratic Party in the spring of 1919. His source of information was likely Captain Karl Mayr, Hitler's (by 1923) former mentor in the army and head of the propaganda unit that trained Hitler during the summer of 1919. Hitler then appears to have been "on the moderate left," Weber writes (ibid., pp. 65–67). However, we should remember that serving under the revolutionary regimes does not necessarily say much about a soldier's political ideology; many other soldiers who did not demobilize or leave the army after the revolution did so too. That is true also for Mayr himself, who continued serving the revolutionary regimes. The fact that Hitler did not leave the army could just as well be seen as a sign that he was not yet ready to act based on a political conviction, or even that he did not yet have one. Having an income and a purpose was more important to him at this point. After all, he formally served the Weimar Republic too, even after the ratification of the Versailles Treaty, and he certainly did not have any affinities for the Weimar state. Moreover, far from every soldier that served in the *Wehrmacht* during the Hitler years was a Nazi sympathizer.

[33] Sven-Felix Kellerhoff has shown that Hitler lied in *Mein Kampf* about many other things that supposedly happened at this first meeting. For instance, the confrontational debate between Hitler and "a professor," who allegedly got so mangled by Hitler's rhetorical skills that he left the meeting, did not happen. Kellerhoff proves this by referring to the meeting attendance list – there was no professor there. It may be that something like this occurred during the *second* DAP meeting that Hitler attended on October 16, 1919, where *Gymnasialprofessor* (i.e. secondary school teacher) Adalbert Baumann was present. Kellerhoff still thinks that Drexler may have given Hitler his pamphlet at the meeting in September (Kellerhoff, S. F., *Die NSDAP ...* , pp. 37–38; Weber, T., *Becoming Hitler ...* , pp. 112, 363 n31).

193 / Jesus as an Ideological Inspiration for Hitler and the NSDAP

antisemite when he attended the DAP meeting. Hitler even referred to the Bible and the Jews dancing around the golden calf in the letter.[34]

Antisemitism was a position Hitler had adopted already during the summer of 1919 during his participation in Mayr's propaganda classes. We have already seen that the first witness report of Hitler uttering antisemitic propaganda came from a speech he held at Camp Lechfeld not even a month earlier (the report is dated August 25). It was a speech on the intimate connection between international capitalism and the Jews, a view that was shared by broad layers of the Bavarian population – whether in political Catholic circles or among farmers – in the summer of 1919. It was common knowledge, as Wolfram Pyta notes, "that anyone who speaks about capitalism should not be silent about the Jews."[35] So deplorable was the culture of the time.

The young Bavarian nobleman Count Anton Arco-Valley, who had murdered the Jewish Democratic Socialist minister president of Bavaria, Kurt Eisner, on February 21, 1919, stated during his trial in January 1920 that he had done it because he hated Jews and Bolshevists. At the same time, he announced that he loved "the real people of Bavaria" and that he was "a true Catholic." Even the prosecutor, who had seen to it that he received the death sentence, admired the "glowing enthusiasm" of Arco-Valley and considered it an inspiration for all German youth.[36] Valley was never executed, however. He served less than five years in the fortress in Landsberg and was released in 1925 and eventually pardoned in 1927 (he survived the war but was killed in a traffic accident in June 1945). As a final ironic twist to this story, it appears that Arco-Valley was evicted from his cell in Landsberg to make room for a new prisoner – none other than

---

[34] For the letter, see *SA*, pp. 88–90 (Document 61, September 16, 1919).

[35] Weber, T., *Becoming Hitler* . . . , pp. 109–110, 362 n23; Pyta, W., *Hitler: Der Künstler* . . . , pp. 141–146. The report on Hitler's speech was written by the leader of the propaganda (*Aufklärung*) team at Lechfeld, Rudolf Beyschlag.

[36] Taylor, Cory, *How Hitler Was Made: Germany and the Rise of the Perfect Nazi* (Amherst, NY: Prometheus Books, 2018), p. 130. The tragic irony about all of this was that Arco-Valley's mother was Jewish. Sebottendorff claimed in his book *Bevor Hitler kam* in 1933 that the murder was a way for Arco-Valley who had "Jew blood in his veins" to show that even a half-Jew could commit such an act and thereby to try and prove himself worthy of membership in the *Thule Gesellschaft*, which had rejected him due to his Jewish heritage (Sebottendorff, R. von, *Bevor Hitler kam* . . . , p. 82).

194 / Christianity in Hitler's Ideology

Hitler.[37] Note also the similarity to how Hitler was treated during his trial after the failed coup. This kind of extremism and fanaticism was thus part of everyday life and the culture of Bavaria at the time. It was a very violent and turbulent age. All of this means that Hitler was already primed to accept what he heard at the DAP meeting, as well as what Drexler wrote in his pamphlet. These were views that he was familiar with and felt well at home with.

The views that Hitler espoused were common goods (one could even consider them politically correct) within right-wing nationalist-conservative and *völkisch* circles at the time. In 1920, for example, Rudolf John Gorsleben published a book with the title *Die Überwindung des Judentums in uns und außer uns* (Overcoming the Jewishness within and outside Us), in which he argued in the same way as Hitler did in his letter to Gemlich. The Jews had neither ethos nor idealism; only money and profit was important to them. The title of Gorsleben's book expressed Chamberlain's idea that the Jewish spirit had infected everyone and that the task now was to overcome it through hard inner work on one's soul and character. The year before, in 1919, Wilhelm Meister had also condemned the corrupting Jewish material-ism in the book *Judas Schuldbuch: Eine deutsche Abrechnung* (The Debt Register of Judas: A German Accounting). He also brought up the Jews dancing around the golden calf and their incapacity for honor and virtue. Both these books were published by the *Deutscher Volksverlag* in Munich. Meister's book was in addition published under the auspices of the extremely nationalistic and antisemitic *Deutschen Schutz- und Trutzbund* (The German Protection and Defense League) founded in 1919, whose roster included many future leading Nazis such as Eckart, Gottfried Feder, Reinhard Heydrich, Fritz Sauckel, and Julius Streicher.[38]

Was Hitler at this point, in September 1919, convinced ideo-logically, that is, did he really mean what he said about the Jews, or was

---

[37] Robb, David, "Count Anton Graf von Arco auf Valley: The Assassin Who Sparked the Rise of the Nazi Party," *Crime Magazine*, October 24, 2013; www.crimemagazine.com/count-anton-graf-von-arco-auf-valley-assassin-who-sparked-rise-nazi-party.

[38] Plöckinger, O., *Unter Soldaten . . .* , pp. 338–339. The word *Abrechnung* is a bit difficult to translate, and it seems to be a play on words in this case. In addition, it can mean "invoice" or "deduction" but also "revenge." The latter meaning was no doubt intended.

195 / Jesus as an Ideological Inspiration for Hitler and the NSDAP

he simply regurgitating talking points? That we can never know for sure. Perhaps it does not even matter, since the result was the same in the end, and he certainly was convinced that what he said was true by the time he became the leading force in the NSDAP. It may be that Hitler's search for a new home meant that he simply soaked up from the diverse right-wing ideological sects around him that which he felt could advance his position in the National Socialist/*völkisch* community in Munich. He internalized this new ideological good, discarded what he felt he could not use, and eventually made it his own.

5.3   Otto Wagener, Hitler, and Jesus

The former NSDAP/SA leader Otto Wagener's memoirs, *Hitler aus nächster Nähe* (Hitler Up Close), are, after *Tischgespräche*, probably the most frequently cited source for Hitler's views of Jesus and Christianity.[39] Wagener is nonetheless a relatively unknown Nazi leader even though he was part of Hitler's inner circle from 1929 and 1932, was Chief of Staff for the SA (from early September 1930 to January 1931 the de facto Head of the SA), and was in charge of the Economy Department within NSDAP's National Secretariat in Munich. From September 1932, he was in Berlin on Hitler's staff, and until July 1933 he was *Reichskommissar* for the Economy. The reasons for his being almost entirely unknown to everyone but experts on Hitler are that (1) Nazi economic policy is not something that is a common theme in popular histories on National Socialism and (2) Wagener fell out of favor with Hitler in July 1933 and spent the period until 1938 as an unremarkable SA *Gruppenführer*. Nonetheless, he remained a Hitler loyalist and a great admirer of Hitler and National Socialism as an ideology even after the war. During his time in the circle of power, he met and interacted with Hitler hundreds of times, and on many of these occasions he was alone with Hitler and therefore had lots of opportunities to speak to

---

[39] It is an interesting fact that while historians often use Wagener's memoirs, basically all biographies have ignored what Wagener writes about Hitler's religiosity. If this is because they have not found these particular parts trustworthy, that should be mentioned in a source-critical discussion. That such discussions are absent instead implies that historians have had trouble squaring these parts with the generally accepted image of Hitler, even though there are no cogent reasons for leaving them out.

196 / Christianity in Hitler's Ideology

him.[40] However, just how close he really was to Hitler is impossible to know. It must be assumed that Wagener took the opportunity to aggrandize himself when he wrote his memoirs after the war.

Wagener has written the following about Hitler's view of what the term "Socialism" in National Socialism really meant:

> Socialism is a worldview! But this worldview is not really something new. I am always surprised when I read the New Testament, and the revelations of the prophets ... how much has been accomplished by these men blessed by God, especially Jesus Christ's, clear, and in its nature so unique, doctrine and religious and spiritual teachings. *They* created, launched, taught, and lived this new worldview that we now call Socialism![41] [emphasis in original]

This should not be interpreted as a verbatim record of what Hitler said to Wagener; his memoirs are not that kind of source. They certainly purvey Wagener's *own* views. However, his rendition and testimony are still interesting in and of themselves and because of the seemingly odd connection they draw between Jesus' teachings and Hitler and National Socialism. Overall, these views match what we know from other, more reliable sources about Hitler's ideas. Wagener then has Hitler throwing a curse on the organized churches that had transformed Jesus' teachings into something that was unrecognizable:

> But these communities that then called themselves Christian churches did not understand them! Or if they did, they have lied about, and betrayed, Christ! For they have turned the holy idea of Christian Socialism into its opposite! They killed it, just like the Jews then nailed Christ to the cross; they buried it, like when Christ's body was buried. But they let Christ return to life in order to make it appear as if his teaching had been resurrected too.[42]

---

[40] Wagener, O., *Hitler aus nächster Nähe ...* , pp. i, viii, x.   [41] Ibid., p. 257.   [42] Ibid.

197 / Jesus as an Ideological Inspiration for Hitler and the NSDAP

Hitler also solemnly, according to Wagener, declared that it was the National Socialists who would be the first to unearth Christ's true teachings:

> *We are the first to unearth this teaching!* Only *through us* does this teaching celebrate its resurrection![43] [emphasis in original]

Once again, the exact words are not Hitler's, but their spirit seems plausible, even if they are somewhat exaggerated. We see a similar idea in Rudolf Jung's *Der nationale Sozialismus* when he points out that one central aim of the NSDAP was the "spiritual renewal of our people, [and the] development of its religious life in a German spirit."[44]

After this, Wagener's Hitler complains about how the Church's forging of Jesus' original message had led this institution to supress freedom of religion and to persecute the true Christians; it had led to the mass murders of the inquisition, burnings of witches, and armed campaigns against the free and true Christian faith (it is uncertain what Wagener is implying here; obviously, he must be referring to historical groups such as the Hussites, Albigensians, Cathars, and other heretical groups – e.g. Rosenberg thought very fondly of them).[45] It must then be the task of National Socialism, Wagener says, to see to it that especially the youth get to experience every word of Christ in their soul, which would tell them to love each other, to look after their neighbor, and to know that they were all brothers created by God. But this youth would then turn with hatred against every hypocrite who came at them with Christ in his mouth but the Devil in his heart.[46]

Even though this is not a source that gives us Hitler's words as they were possibly once spoken to Wagener, and even though what we have in front of us is more Wagener's words than Hitler's, it is still significant and highly interesting that Wagener chose to portray Hitler in this way. The gist of the message Wagener purveys here can nonetheless be assumed to be correct (even if slightly embellished), because most of it is supported by independent and reliable sources – not least Hitler's

---

[43] Ibid., p. 258. [44] Jung, R., *Der nationale Sozialismus* ... , p. 72.
[45] For Rosenberg's admiration of the heretical sects of medieval Europe, see Varshizky, A., "Alfred Rosenberg ... ," pp. 322–323.
[46] Wagener, O., *Hitler aus nächster Nähe* ... , p. 258.

198 / Christianity in Hitler's Ideology

own speeches and writings. This could of course be because Wagener based his memoirs on those very speeches and writings, but it is hard to see that he would have had access to such texts while in British captivity after the war. It is therefore more plausible to assume that he was working from memory and his personal knowledge of the kind of religiosity that Hitler was known to express.

It is thus clearly a religious, and in a way even Christian, Hitler that we encounter on the pages of Wagener's memoirs. His testimony appears to show that Hitler adhered to some sort of proto-church, or Gnostic, Christianity. This was indeed the kind of Christianity that Chamberlain, Eckart, and Rosenberg (who had been deeply inspired by the former two) adhered to as well, which has been described as a National Socialist form of modern gnosis.[47] Amit Varshizky has succinctly summarized Rosenberg's worldview in the following way:

> Rosenberg regarded himself as part of a German intellectual tradition that understood Germany's distress in terms of a theological crisis, which requires a spiritual reawakening through the adaption of Christian religion to particular, national needs. ... For Rosenberg, the Nazi *Weltanschauung* presupposes a religious attitude. Rosenberg considered atheism as the greatest threat to the strength of the German people, and claimed that it rendered Germans exposed to "Jewish materialism."[48]

This might as well be a description of Hitler's *Weltanschauung* as well, and it is indeed striking that it was precisely these ideas that Hitler presented to those who listened to his speeches – yet another indication that Hitler really meant what he said. It is the same view that we find in Wagener's memoirs too.

To be sure, it is reasonable to question how well Wagener's memories, or at least his portrayal of them (written down several decades after the conversations had taken place), reflect the details of what Hitler and Wagener spoke about. But at the same time, there is little reason for us to doubt the gist of the text. H. A. Turner, Jr., Professor of History at Yale University, who edited and wrote the

---

[47] For a detailed study of this, see Varshizky, A., "Alfred Rosenberg ... ," pp. 311–331.
[48] Ibid., p. 319.

199 / Jesus as an Ideological Inspiration for Hitler and the NSDAP

introduction to Wagener's memoirs, also discusses how historians should approach the Hitler that we encounter in these pages. He stresses that the memoirs are a valuable source for *the types* of conversations that Hitler and Wagener used to have, and perhaps also of their overall content. This is because the words placed in Hitler's mouth are in no way simply taken or fabricated out of thin air. Wagener claimed that he had in fact made notes of the conversations directly afterward and that he regularly wrote a diary during the period that the memoirs cover. However, he did not have access to these much more reliable sources when he wrote his memoirs as a POW in Britain in 1946; this was thus an effort to recreate these earlier notes long after the conversations that he records took place, that is, in the late 1920s and early 1930s. Turner, Jr. writes that if one assumes that Wagener read these notes anew during his time in political exile in Germany between 1934 and 1939, then Wagener can be considered a good source regarding the views of Hitler during these years. He does add, though, that Wagener's text must be scrutinized in the same critical manner that we scrutinize similar texts.[49] Turner, Jr. may be a bit too optimistic here. Considering that Wagener was a devout Hitler admirer even after the war, he may have had reason to portray Hitler in this way to make him appear less evil and as a man with only the best of intentions.

Michael Rißmann has claimed that Hitler's religious beliefs, such as they are presented by Wagener, in several cases directly contradict the ideas that we find in other sources. However, his examples are not all that convincing; and sometimes they are even incorrect. An example of the latter is when Rißmann cites a, according to him, clear contradiction between Wagener and Hitler. It is a passage from a speech on April 6, 1922, where Hitler said that Christianity prescribed faith, hope, and love, but that "love and hope cannot help us; only faith," while Wagener claims that Hitler had said that the primary task of the NSDAP was to "evoke faith, love, and hope."[50] At first, this does seem to prove that Wagener gives an incorrect view of Hitler's idea, if it were not for the, for Rißmann, somewhat bothersome fact that Hitler

---

[49] Wagener, O., *Hitler aus nächster Nähe* . . . , pp. vi–vii.
[50] Rißmann, M., *Hitlers Gott* . . . , pp. 166–168. See also Wagener, O., *Hitler aus nächster Nähe* . . . , p. 331. Wagener repeats this several times on this page.

200 / Christianity in Hitler's Ideology

on January 3, 1923, said that the most striking feature of the German people was "hope" (*die Hoffnung*).[51] Then, a little later, on May 1, 1923, in Munich, he told, according to the *Völkischer Beobachter*, the gathered NSDAP members that "the three words that many utter completely thoughtlessly, are for us more than just catch-words: the words love, faith, and hope." Hitler then explained in detail what that meant.[52] The fact is that he repeated the same statement in a speech on August 5, 1923.[53]

It is therefore, after all, not Wagener that presents a contradiction here. If one exists at all, then it is Hitler himself that bears responsibility for it. The explanation is probably that Hitler meant that from a certain perspective Christianity's talk of hope and love was not to the benefit of the movement or the *Volk*. This does not mean that Hitler really told Wagener this; it could be that Wagener is getting this from another source (however, this then needs to be proven), but it cannot be used to argue that Wagener's version of events contradicts independent records. Moreover, since the May 1 speech came *after* the one that Rißmann refers to, it is not possible to argue that Hitler later changed his mind either.

Faith, hope, and love were Christian cardinal virtues.[54] Does this mean that Hitler cynically used these concepts in his National Socialist propaganda? One could certainly interpret his use of them in that way, but that would require that we disregard Hitler's reinterpretation of them. Of course, Hitler thought there was a propaganda value to them, or otherwise he would not have used them. But if it were purely a matter of cynical propaganda, with no honest intent at all, then a redefinition would not really be necessary. Hitler might then just as well have used these concepts in the traditional way. But he did not do that. He even saw to it to explicitly define what he meant by them in his speeches. In the May 1, 1923, speech, he makes it perfectly evident that

---

[51] *SA*, p. 778 (Document 454).   [52] Ibid., p. 920 (Document 524).
[53] Ibid., p. 963 (Document 554).
[54] This point is made in Reichelt, W., *Das braune Evangelium* ... , pp. 41–42. Reichelt, however, argues that these were then pushed to the background and that they were eventually replaced by other virtues. This is only true if one gives these words the meaning they have within orthodox Christian theology and philosophy. But Hitler defined them in another way, which can hardly have escaped his followers.

201 / Jesus as an Ideological Inspiration for Hitler and the NSDAP

these words had a different meaning to him by contrasting the way the National Socialists used them to the way they were normally used. This was why Hitler, in the April 6 speech, specifically points out that out of the traditional Christian interpretations of these words it was only one, namely hope, that could be of any use in the battle the National Socialists were conducting. Hitler must necessarily have used a different interpretation of the concepts of love and faith in that speech than he used in the May 1 speech in the previous year.

A possible explanation is offered by something that Hitler said in a speech on January 30, 1940, when he claimed that the National Socialist movement had arisen out of the realization "that one cannot disrespect oneself on this earth by hoping, praying, and protesting; but that one had first and foremost been put on this earth to help oneself."[55] What is apparent here is thus the tension that existed between Hitler's clamoring for hope, love, and faith as a motivation for struggle, on the one hand, and his conviction that God would only support, and give victory to, the one who did what he could to aid himself, on the other. Hitler always and endlessly repeated the mantra that it was not enough to ask for God's support; God would only give his blessings to the one that fought the most and the hardest – it was only in such a context that hope and faith were worth anything. We therefore do not see the negation of faith and hope in God here, but a confirmation of the validity of these concepts in Hitler's worldview.

The fact is that Hitler further developed his thoughts concerning these concepts on January 25, 1923. Hitler remarked that the faith in the eternal right and saving power in one's own people had been dislocated in Germany. This had "been replaced by a *stupid* hope in love and reconciliation, as a basis for the coming world order."[56] At the same time, he underlined that the National Socialists possessed a glowing love for the fatherland, and that anyone who still had a glimmer of hope of a coming age of German greatness should put their hopes with the NSDAP.[57] Here, we find all three elements – faith, hope, and love – explained in all of their, to Hitler, positive and negative meanings. On May 1, 1938, Hitler stressed that "we Germans want to

---

[55] *HRP* II/3, p. 1454 (January 30, 1940). [56] *SA*, p. 800 (Document 463).
[57] Ibid., pp. 800–801.

202 / Christianity in Hitler's Ideology

settle with the people's love for one another." This was essentially the same message of love that we find ascribed to Jesus in John 13:35: "By this all people will know that you are my disciples, if you have love for one another."[58] Other historians, such as David Redles and Friedrich Tomberg, have made a completely different judgment and consider Wagener's memoirs as a completely reliable source for Hitler's verbatim statements.[59] However, this is not a viable argument.

In a speech in Rosenheim on May 2, 1920, Hitler claimed, according to the newspaper report from the meeting, that the party wished "freedom of religion for everyone, [and] to fight against Jewish mammonism."[60] Hitler here used a rhetorical figure that he once again got from Jesus, from the Sermon on the Mount in Matthew 6:24 no less, which said: "No one can serve two masters. . . . . You cannot serve both God and mammon."[61] We find the same words in Luke 16:13, but then not in the Sermon on the Mount but instead in connection to the Pharisees, "who were lovers of money."[62] We have already seen that Jung stressed the same theme in his *Der nationale Sozialismus*. Chamberlain brought this theme up too in *Die Grundlagen* and stated that the appearance of Christ meant the appearance of a new species of human that opposed the Jewish spirit in the world, he claimed, and Jesus had proclaimed the choice between either God or mammon.[63] The idea of the Jews as lovers of money, mammon, is thus as old as the New Testament, and this was a fundamental theme in National Socialism and its conspiratorial thinking about the Jews, who were thought to control both international finance capitalism *and* Bolshevism. Jung wrote that although mammonism (i.e. finance capitalism) and Bolshevism appeared to be opposites, both were in fact in reality the result of the Jewish spirit and the Jewish effort to make all other peoples into slaves both physically and spiritually. "The Jew knows only one form of reign: dictatorship!," Jung wrote. It was of no importance whether this was expressed in the form of capitalism or Bolshevism since the goal was still to undercut all other peoples and to rule them. As proof of this outlandish claim, Jung

---

[58] Reichelt, W., *Das braune Evangelium* . . . , p. 47.

[59] Redles, D., *Hitler's Millennial Reich* . . . , pp. 196–197; Tomberg, F., *Das Christentum* . . . , pp. 132–148.

[60] *SA*, p. 129 (Document 97).   [61] Matthew 6:24.   [62] Luke 16:13.

[63] Chamberlain, H. S., *Die Grundlagen* . . . , p. 204.

brought up *The Protocols of the Elders of Zion*. International democracy too was nothing but an attempt for Jewish world hegemony in disguise, according to him.[64] The cursing of the purported Jewish materialistic love of money was a foundational feature of Hitler's ethics and morality, and it was in the end a complete moral condemnation of the Jewish collective spiritual character.

The importance that Hitler gave his religious faith is over and over again attested to by Wagener, who returns to this theme repeatedly throughout his memoirs. According to Wagener, Hitler portrayed National Socialism's primary task as being the creation of a racial community for the German people, and that one should preach like Christ and love one's Aryan brothers. Wagener states that Hitler once made it clear that he did not view God as a person in human form with a long white beard, but as the God described in the Gospel of John (a Gospel that Hitler often cited): God as *Logos* (the Word) become flesh and who had lived in the world.[65] In the spring of 1932, Hitler supposedly asked Wagener to guard what he had told him as if he were the "guardian of the Holy Grail." This was also how Wagener felt, even after he and Hitler had become estranged – he felt obliged by a promise to his *Führer* to keep this knowledge alive for the coming generations.[66] It is, once again, not very likely that Hitler told Wagener this in those exact words, but there can be little doubt that Wagener thought he gave an honest portrayal of Hitler.

5.4 Nazi Christmas: Celebrating the Birth of Christ in the Third Reich

In an article in *Die Welt*, Sven Felix Kellerhoff writes about the fact that Hitler absolutely observed Christmas traditions. But Kellerhoff simultaneously says that these celebrations had precious little to do with Christianity. This is obvious, he says, from an analysis of all twenty-four Christmas celebrations that Hitler and the NSDAP organized between 1920 and 1944. He goes on to catalogue some of these occasions. In 1935, Hitler celebrated Christmas with about 1,200 so-called

[64] Jung, R., *Der nationale Sozialismus ...*, pp. 50–53.
[65] Wagener, O., *Hitler aus nächster Nähe ...*, pp. 349, 359.   [66] Ibid., pp. 480–481.

204 / Christianity in Hitler's Ideology

old fighters in a salon at Hotel Wagner in Munich. During the celebration at the Reich Chancellery on December 18, 1937, Hitler received gifts from no less than two Santa Clauses – all of it caught on camera – and the next year, Goebbels let himself be photographed together with one of his young daughters, a Santa, and a young woman dressed as an angel. From this perspective, their celebration appears to have been rather conventional after all. We do not have any information about the Christmas celebrations during the period 1941–1943, that is, the time when Hitler spent this part of the year in his wartime FHQs on the Eastern Front. This does not mean that there were no celebrations though. In Hitler's work calendar on December 24, 1944, when Hitler was in his FHQ *Adlerhorst* near the town of Bad Nauheim in Hessen on the Western Front, the notation only says "private" for the hours between 8 p.m. and 11 p.m. (between 6 p.m. and 8 p.m. his generals had briefed him about the situation at the front), that is, during the time when the Christmas celebration usually took place.[67]

Hitler held two Christmas speeches to NSDAP members in Munich (in *Bürgerbräukeller* and *Münchner-Kindl-Keller*) on December 17, 1922. The theme for the first speech was (according to the unfortunately very short police report) the birth, life, and death of Christ. One ought to follow this man's example, Hitler said. Christ had been born in a hut, but despite this fact he was a man who followed great ideals and who the Jews had crucified for precisely that reason. Christ was an idealist, Hitler claimed, and lived not for gold or material things. According to the *Völkischer Beobachter*, Hitler also said that Christ had dedicated his life to a bitter and relentless struggle against the primacy of evil, which was manifested by the Jews. The National Socialists were not to be Christians in word alone, but also in action.[68]

In the second speech of the evening, Hitler continued along these lines, and according to the police report Hitler once again held up Christ as a role model for the National Socialists. Even though the world had been drenched in the material spirit of the Jews for 1,900

---

[67] Kellerhoff, Sven Felix, "So feierte Adolf Hitler Weihnachten," *Die Welt*, December 25, 2018, www.welt.de/geschichte/zweiter-weltkrieg/article185955824/Nationalsozialismus-So-feierte-Adolf-Hitler-Weihnachten.htm.

[68] *SA*, pp. 769–770 (Document 450).

years, idealism – which Hitler here equated with true Christianity – persisted still. Just as Christ had let himself get crucified by the Jews, so too each National Socialist had to be prepared to sacrifice himself for the Fatherland, Hitler preached.[69] "The character of the German people is idealistic," he said, "its defining feature is hope. The Jew's character is materialistic. His motto is called: money." Against the usurers, one should not put the love of one's neighbor, Hitler said on January 3, 1923, but instead "the scourge of Christ, the gallows."[70] It is worth noting that at this point in time when the NSDAP was still a small and insignificant revolutionary, nonparliamentary party, the focus was on Jesus' death and sacrifice.

Hitler's Christmas speech in Munich on December 11, 1928, is interesting from this perspective. Hitler began by making it clear that to the National Socialists the "Christ Festival" (*Christfest*) had a very special meaning. Two thousand years ago the world looked about the same as it did today, he claimed. Materialism ruled people's lives: gold, egotism, and nonidealism. These outer desires sold out the inner life of a human to purely an outer material existence. The Christ Festival was celebrated in honor of "the birthday of the man who had performed the most violent struggle" against this very same Jewish materialism that the National Socialists were fighting today. Hitler stated that he knew that during this time of year a lot of people would feel the need to love one's neighbor. The National Socialists also wished to keep the peace with other people, he said, but qualified this statement immediately by adding that this went only for the people who had a good will. Against those of bad faith and ill will, one could only fight. When some said that it was un-Christian to fight against other people, then one should retort that one did not wish to do anything but what this bringer of peace had done. Like Christ, they would clear out the German temples that the Jews had turned into their robbery chests. Christ was a fighter in the eyes of the National Socialists, and one who had been persecuted by the enemies of this world until his death. A people that did not have the desire to fight for its existence were not a Christian people, Hitler said. Christ was a symbol of limitless faith and assurance to the National Socialists, and as Christians they viewed this gigantic struggle that had

---

[69] *SA*, p. 770 (Document 451).   [70] Ibid., p. 779 (Document 454).

206 / Christianity in Hitler's Ideology

begun 2,000 years ago as a source of faith, in that a great ideal really could be victorious if the battle was waged in a truly heroic manner. This heroism meant that one, just like Christ, was prepared to sacrifice one's own life in the fight against the Satanic power. As Christ had once told the people to render unto the emperor what belonged to him and to God what belonged to him, now one could say today: give to the people what belongs to them. Therefore, the Christ Festival was more than simply a time for sentimental reminiscing – it was a call to arms. Even if the German people were still chained on the outside, they were free on the inside, Hitler preached and ended his speech by wishing peace to those with a good will.[71]

Note that while the topic of Jesus' self-sacrifice was still present, by 1928 the NSDAP had expanded its operations and support greatly. It was now represented all across Germany and had even entered the *Reichstag* (having received 2.6 percent of the popular vote, which meant twelve seats) in the elections in May 1928. Now the idea of Jesus as a fighter who never gave up had moved to the forefront, no doubt to inspire the NSDAP members to keep fighting the "good" fight against Germany's purported enemies.

It has been argued by Samuel Koehne that it is "significant" that the *Völkischer Beobachter* did not speak of the Nazi Christmas celebration "as the *Christfest* (celebration of Christ)" in 1920/21 and 1921/22 and also that the term *Julfest* (Yule Festival) showed how infused Nazi ideology was with pagan ideas at the time.[72] However, what has already been said above shows that Christ as an example of a warrior against the Jews and his deep admiration for him were still the topics of Hitler's speeches at these celebrations in the early 1920s. Also, one should perhaps not make too much out of the term *Julfest*, considering that in Scandinavia Christmas is called *Jul* even though there is nothing pagan about the celebration at all. Context and content matters more than the terms used to describe the tradition.

---

[71] *RSA* III/1, pp. 349–352 (Document 65). Hitler called Jesus "Christ and Lord" also in a speech on August 12, 1930: *RSA* III/3, p. 331 (Document 87). See also Tomberg, F., *Das Christentum* ... , pp. 128–131.

[72] Koehne, S., "Were the National Socialists a Völkisch Party? ... ," pp. 777, 784.

Moreover, the term *Christfest* was used several times by Hitler, both at the time and later. For example, on January 9, 1922, the Munich police reported Hitler as having used the term. The *Christfest* was the time when the whole world celebrated in honor of the "Liberator of the World," who was crucified by the Jews. He ended the speech with the words: "May God watch over us! Amen!"[73] The *Völkischer Beobachter* did not report these words, and Koehne does not mention the police report when he states that "the second Nazi Christmas was a celebration of Germany rather than a commemoration of the birth of Christ."[74] So perhaps the fact that the *Völkischer Beobachter* did not mention it is not that significant after all? What Koehne presents in his article seems to be a careful selection of quotes intended to prove his argument regarding pagan influences in early Nazi Christmas celebrations. Furthermore, Koehne does not comment on the fact that the NSDAP Christmas 1921 celebration occurred on January 6, 1922, that is, on the Feast of The Three Kings (*Heliger Dreikönigstag*) or The Lord's Epiphany (*Erscheinung des Herrn*), which commemorated the three so-called wise men, or sages, based on the Gospel of Matthew, and it was during this special date that Jesus' divinity was celebrated. This was a clear sign of the Catholic influences on the NSDAP prior to the failed coup attempt.

We can already see that Kellerhoff's claim that the NSDAP Christmas celebrations had very little to do with Christianity cannot be upheld. The evidence says something else, and the celebrations of Jesus' birth continued within the NSDAP. On Christmas Eve 1925 (the Germans, like the Swedes, celebrate Christmas on December 24), however, Hitler appears to have left for the Alps in order to get away from the Christmas celebrations, according to one informant (it is unclear how correct this memory is), but already next year he was celebrating as usual again.[75] It is likely that this was in order to get away from the infighting within the NSDAP and the *völkisch* movement that was going

---

[73] *SA*, p. 544 (Document 341).
[74] Koehne, S., "Were the National Socialists a Völkisch Party? … ," p. 783. One could perhaps argue that the police report does not give us Hitler's exact words; however, that claim can easily be made about the account in the *Völkischer Beobachter* too. The two accounts do not contradict each other, but rather complement each other.
[75] Kellerhoff, S. F., "So feierte … ".

208 / Christianity in Hitler's Ideology

on at the time, and to work on the second volume of *Mein Kampf*. Hitler had in fact gone to Berchtesgaden for four months in August 1925 for the purpose of working on his book.[76] This of course does not mean that Hitler did not celebrate Christmas.

The focus on celebrating the birth of Christ is clear. In his Christmas speech to NSDAP members in Munich in 1928 and to the *Schutzstaffel* (SS) in 1930, Hitler said that the celebration of Christ was a call to arms. To the SS, Hitler stated that the celebration of Christ was a reminder of "the immortal example" of how even the smallest thing could grow big and that the National Socialists serve religion "more than the politicized servants of religion serve religion, in that we do not confuse it with politics but in our political actions promote principles for which Christ was once born and for which [he] was persecuted and nailed to the cross by the Jews." This drew down thunderous applause from the gathered SS men, according to the *Völkische Beobachter*.[77] We can here see clear traces of the NSDAP's election success in September 1930 when the party received a whopping 18.3 percent of the vote. The NSDAP was now suddenly the second-largest party in the *Reichstag* and had gone from insignificant to a potent power player in Germany, and Hitler saw the parallel to the growth of Jesus' movement.

Why stress the importance of religion to the SS if it was only a matter of ideology? The reaction also shows that the SS men too understood and embraced Jesus as an example for them. All of this clearly illustrates that Hitler drew political and ideological lessons from his faith in Jesus. At around the same time, Rosenberg had declared in *Der Mythos* that if Jesus' teaching of giving to God what belongs to God and to the state what belongs to the state was respected by the churches, then no intrusions into churchly life by the state would ever be necessary.[78] He also celebrated the "thoroughly un-Jewish" nature of Jesus' "teachings of the 'kingdom of heaven within us'."[79] This underlined the principle that religious belief was a personal matter that did

---

[76] *Hitler, Mein Kampf* ... (Band I), p. 17.

[77] *RSA* III/1, pp. 349–352 (Document 65). Hitler called Jesus "Christ" and "Lord" also in a speech on August 12, 1930, see *RSA* III/3, p. 331 (Document 87). For the speech to the SS, see *RSA* IV/1, pp. 148–149 (Document 38).

[78] Rosenberg, A., *Der Mythos* ..., p. 609.   [79] Head, P., "The Nazi Quest ... ," p. 69.

209 / Jesus as an Ideological Inspiration for Hitler and the NSDAP

not need to be mediated by either the state or the church (unless the faith in question was considered hostile to the *Volk* of course).

Thus, with regard to Koehne's conclusions, it is obvious that what the *Völkischer Beobachter* wrote in the early 1920s is not always a good indicator of Hitler's views during his life. Nazi ideology was still much more eclectic during those years than it would eventually become once Hitler had taken firm ideological control of the movement.

Hitler also expressed his admiration for Jesus in *Mein Kampf* in the following way:

> [The Jew's] life is truly only of this world, and his soul is for example just as intimately alien to the true Christianity as his essence was to the high founder [Christ] of the new teaching two thousand years ago. For a fact he did not keep his feelings for the Jewish people a secret; even gripped the whip, when it was necessary, in order to drive out these enemies of humanity, who also back then viewed religion as only a business-like means to its own existence, out of the Lord's temple. For that reason, Christ was then later nailed to the cross.[80]

This was almost an verbatim repetition of what Hitler had said in his speech in Munich on April 12, 1922. Christ had fought against the Jewish poison and because of this he had bled to death on the cross.[81] It is likely that Hitler at this point considered such an ending for himself and every fanatical Nazi to be very likely. The inclusion of this expression of admiration for Jesus in *Mein Kampf*, and the fact that this passage appeared in the editions printed after 1933, also contradicts the argument that Hitler did not refer to Jesus in public after he had become chancellor. Hitler could easily have taken this passage out of his book if he did not think that it represented his views in a satisfactory way.

Hitler's Christmases during the years right after his niece Geli Raubal's suicide had apparently been spent in great misery. He wrote to Winifred Wagner at the end of December 1932 that for the last two years Christmas had only meant sorrow for him and that he was unable

---

[80] *Hitler, Mein Kampf* ... (Band I), p. 799 [325].
[81] *SA*, p. 623 (Document 377). See also Rißmann, M., *Hitlers Gott* ... , p. 30.

210 / Christianity in Hitler's Ideology

to find his old self.[82] Hitler also had his own tradition, which consisted of him always, a few days before Christmas, visiting the elderly couple Elsa and Hugo Bruckmann, who had been such important economic supporters of his during the years after the First World War, in Munich. Christmas of 1939 was then for propaganda purposes spent among the soldiers on the Western Wall on the Western Front.[83] Hitler visited one contingent of troops near Aachen, as well as Sepp Dietrich's *SS Leibstandarte Adolf Hitler* in Bad Ems.[84] Hitler does appear to have preferred to celebrate Christmas in private, but sometimes for publicity reasons he was forced to participate in spectacles like these.

This means that we unfortunately do not know how Hitler spent his last Christmas, but the fact that he withdrew does suggest that he preferred some sort of private celebration. It is likely that Hitler spent this time with Eva Braun, who had probably accompanied him when he left Berlin on December 10, 1944. There is reason to believe that Hitler may have assumed that this would in fact be the last Christmas of his life. On precisely Christmas Eve, the weather cleared up and the German positions were targeted for ferocious bombings by about 5,000 Allied bombers, and already on Boxing Day it was evident that *Operation Herbstnebel* (Operation Autumn Fog, better known as the Ardennes Campaign) had failed after only ten days. Nicolaus von Below states in his memoirs (written after the war) that Hitler had told him (sometime after Boxing Day) that he realized that the war was lost and that he most of all preferred to put a bullet in his head.[85] It may well have been the case that Hitler's insight had struck him already on Christmas Eve after his generals had finished the military briefing.

As already mentioned, the exception in 1925 was most likely related to his work on *Mein Kampf*. The expectation appears to have been that Hitler would finish the second volume so that it could be published before Christmas of 1925, and in October that year he was

---

[82] Simms, Brendan, *Hitler: Only the World Was Enough* (London: Allen Lane, 2019), p. 182.

[83] Ullrich, V., *Adolf Hitler* ... (Band II), pp. 103–104.

[84] Eberle, Henrik and Uhl, Matthias (eds.), *Das Buch Hitler: Geheimdossier des NKWD für Josef W. Stalin, zusammengestellt aufgrund der Verhörprotokolle des Persönlichen Adjutanten Hitlers, Otto Günsche, und des Kammerdieners Heinz Linge, Moskau 1948/49* (Bergisch Gladbach: Gustav Lübbe Verlag, 2005), pp. 114–117.

[85] Görtemaker, Heike B., *Eva Braun: Leben mit Hitler* (Munich: C. H. Beck, 2010), pp. 263–265; Kershaw, I., *Hitler: 1936–1945*, pp. 743–747.

211 / Jesus as an Ideological Inspiration for Hitler and the NSDAP

deeply engaged in this work. He even cancelled a whole series of speeches in November with explicit reference to the work on the book. Contemporary political problems and ideological conflicts within the NSDAP did, however, intervene, and at some point around October/ November 1925, Hitler changed his plans. This was not a good time to be writing books, Othmar Plöckinger concludes in his history of *Mein Kampf*. Nonetheless, Plöckinger insinuates that Hitler perhaps did complete the second volume "at the end of 1925" after all.[86] However, in the introduction to the critical edition of *Mein Kampf* it says, with reference to Plöckinger, that the work on the book "stopped almost completely."[87]

At the Christmas celebration on January 9, 1921, Hitler spoke about Jesus and how the National Socialists, together with the whole world, celebrated this day in remembrance of how the Jews "had cowardly nailed the Liberator of the World to the cross." This was of course a bit odd, since Christmas celebrates the *birth* of Jesus, not his death and resurrection (which would be Easter); however, Hitler never missed an opportunity to harp on the Jews. The NSDAP had as its aim to continue Christ's work, said Hitler according to the police report from the meeting, by ridding the world of its oppressor. As unified as the world stood in the celebration of Christ, it would also stand when the power of the Jews (symbolized as international finance capital) had been crushed. "May God reign," Hitler concluded. The *Völkischer Beobachter*'s report from the same meeting contains more details and makes it clear that Hitler also spoke about Jesus' birth. According to the newspaper, Hitler said that the birth of Christ was the beginning of the battle between two worldviews that could never ever reach a compromise: on the one hand, the mammonistic-materialistic worldview, and on the other hand, the idealistic one. The *Yule* celebration, the German celebration, proved that idealism, despite the dominance of Jewish materialism, was not yet dead.[88]

As we have seen, Jesus condemned the worship of mammon in the Sermon of the Mount in Matthew 6:24. The anti-materialistic theme is of course something that is frequent in the New Testament. In John

---

[86] Plöckinger, O., *Geschichte eines Buches ...* , pp. 90–94.
[87] *Hitler, Mein Kampf ...* (Band I), p. 17.   [88] SA, p. 544 (Document 341).

212 / Christianity in Hitler's Ideology

18:36, Jesus declares that "my Kingdom is not of this world," a phrase that Chamberlain contrasted to the Jewish materialist expectation for a kingdom of this earth,[89] and in John 15:19 he says: "If you belonged to the world, it would love you as its own. As it is, you do not belong to the world, but I have chosen you out of the world. That is why the world hates you." Here, it is once again worth bringing up how Chamberlain influenced Hitler in interpreting some of Jesus' statements as they are portrayed in the Gospels. Hitler used Jesus' words about his kingdom not being of this world to criticize the Catholic Church for meddling in politics both directly and via Catholic parties such as *Zentrum*.[90]

On December 12, 1925, Hitler had told the NSDAP members that had gathered for the Christmas celebration in Dingolfing the same thing. The National Socialists were driven by the most ardent Christian faith when they fought for a movement that had as its goal to liberate the Aryans, and the entire world, from Jewish materialism and to give the German people eternal peace, Hitler proclaimed. In Christ's life's work, the National Socialists saw the opportunity to achieve the impossible through fanatical faith, he continued. Christ, too, had arisen in a fallen world, he had preached the faith and been ridiculed, and despite this a worldwide movement had grown out of this faith. National Socialism wanted to do the same in the world of politics, Hitler said, and if every member carried the conviction that this was possible in their hearts, then no earthly power would be able to stop this ideology from reigning victorious. This battle had to be fought in such a way that coming generations could look back and be able to say that the struggle had been carried out in a proper way, not only by Germans, but by real Christians.[91]

On November 5, 1930, Hitler replied to the question of why the NSDAP used a hedonistic sign (the swastika) while claiming to speak for Christianity. The reason for this, he said, was that the Christian cross had been emptied of meaning and content through the explicitly Christian political parties' collaboration with the Marxist atheists. He explained, accompanied by storming approval from the crowd, that

---

[89] Chamberlain, H. S., *Die Grundlagen . . .* , p. 240.
[90] Letter from Hitler to Magnus Gött, March 2, 1927; *RSA* VI, p. 332 (Document 10).
[91] *RSA* I, pp. 237–238 (Document 92).

one would do best to keep away from this symbol until such time that the Christian cross was no longer used in such politicized contexts. He also stated that he was convinced that if the Lord Christ would return to the unfortunate German people of today, he would not join the *Zentrum* faction in the *Reichstag*, whereupon the audience replied with yet more storming approval.[92] The swastika was, he said, "the cross of revival and of freedom!"[93] Granted, Hitler was preaching to the choir here, but it must still have been the case that the audience agreed with him for them to give him this reaction.

5.5 Hitler's Theology in the Gött Letters

On February 4 and March 2, 1927, Hitler wrote two very interesting letters to Magnus Gött, a Catholic priest in Augsburg who, since 1922, had supported the NSDAP (and who had been slapped with a publication injunction by the Bishop's Ordinate in 1924 because of this). The first letter was a reply to one that Gött had written in December the year before complaining about an article in the *Völkischer Beobachter* that had expressed hostility toward the Catholic Church. Hitler asked Gött to not judge the NSDAP too hard and pointed out that it was after all not the NSDAP's fault that people were walking away from the churches. It was never the intention of the NSDAP to function as a gathering point for the piously faithful Christians, Hitler said, but for all Germans in order to achieve their spiritual and moral revival. With an allegory from the four Gospels, he then remarked that Peter had renounced Christ three times before the cock cried twice, but Peter had even so become the rock upon which the Church was built. With Peter in mind, Hitler assured Gött that he would realize that the battle that the National Socialist movement was fighting, that which he was now critical of, nonetheless "is today a true crusade for the Christianity of the Lord," one that was taken very seriously, and that if there in this movement perhaps was a Peter, then he should let mercy go before judgment in this case.[94] Once again,

---

[92] *RSA* IV/1, p. 33 (Document 14).   [93] Ibid., p. 62 (Document 21).

[94] *RSA* VI, pp. 327–329 (Document 9); Matthew 26:69–75; Mark. 14:66–72; Luke 22:54–62; John 18:25–27. See also: Rißmann, M., *Hitlers Gott ...*, p. 27.

214 / Christianity in Hitler's Ideology

Hitler exhibited his good knowledge of the Bible, and even if he is here trying to repair damage done, it is clear that he did not resort to just any lies in order to achieve his goal. His qualifications should make us consider the possibility that Hitler really did look at the NSDAP as a champion of the type of Christianity that he had confessed to so many times.

Gött replied that even though he supported the NSDAP program both politically and socially, he did not do so in a religious way. In his reply on March 2, Hitler deplored that Gött found the program too meager to form a religious point of view, but, he explained, this was a consequence of the fact that he thought that the contemporary political parties meddled too much in religious affairs. The secular liberal state that Gött complained about was supported by parties, such as the Catholic *Zentrum*, that were explicitly religious and in their party programs advocated a specific confession. This politicization of religion was pernicious, said Hitler, and Christ's teachings had not gained any followers because of it, but rather lost millions who did not wish to see their religious ideals serve as political fulcrums. It was always a great tragedy when religion, no matter which confession, entered politics, just as it was a tragedy when religion ventured into areas where it risked coming into collision with science. "I am deeply and sincerely convinced that this was neither Christ's own wish nor will," Hitler wrote. The greater the distance between politics and religion, the less damage religion risked suffering because of the liberal freedom in politics, science, and the arts. Hitler remarked that even the Church and the Pope in Rome had repeatedly been guilty of the sin of meddling in contemporary politics. But Christ's struggle had not been for a kingdom of this world, Hitler pointed out in a reference to John 18:36, but one above it. While Christianity had conducted its crusades against the heathens, National Socialism conducted its political crusade against the states of today, against the poisoning of the race, the splintering of the people, and the destruction of the Fatherland. This was a political struggle, and the cross under which it was fought was the swastika. Just as the German people could not reach happiness in any other way than through Christ, the nation could not achieve purification and power other than through the swastika. Hitler then stated that he could picture how the German people would one day stand united with the swastika

215 / Jesus as an Ideological Inspiration for Hitler and the NSDAP

on the left side of the sword and the Lord's cross on the right side. The Catholic *Zentrum* betrayed religion when it created alliances with the Marxist atheists – the NSDAP had never concluded an alliance with these God liars, he remarked. When the NSDAP in its program simply stated that it stood for a positive Christianity, a position that held both Christian confessions to be holy and untouchable, then that was all that needed to be said. More than that could only hurt religion. The NSDAP would be a party where the most convinced Protestant could sit beside the most ardent Catholic without a conflict of conscience, he concluded.[95]

Gött's motivation for why he could not fully support the NSDAP is highly reminiscent of theologian Karl Adam's stated reasons for why he could not do so either (although uttered in 1941). In correspondence with a fellow priest who was an NSDAP member, Adam stated that "no matter how highly I regard Hitler's heroic figure and no matter how much I believe in the providential nature of his activity," he could not honestly call himself a National Socialist and become a party member. The reason was not Hitler's brutal antisemitism or the war that he had begun. No, instead it was because he would then "be obliged to follow [Hitler's] decision totally and submit completely to his program. Most severe conflicts of conscience will then be inevitable." He was nonetheless prepared to "serve the National Socialist spirit, deeply though I experience it, in my own way, without a precise 'National Socialist' brand." He said this on June 24, 1941, only days after Hitler's invasion of the Soviet Union had begun.[96] It is also worth noticing that Hitler did not bend over backward to assure Gött, or others, that the NSDAP stood for their type of Christian belief. He kept insisting that the party would be able to gather together all Christian confessions – the only thing that he consistently clearly distanced himself from was atheism.

Hitler repeated his and the party's view that politics and religion ought to stay separate, as well as the view that criticism of political priests was not the same as critique of Christianity, on February 29, 1928. The party did not want to encourage any Wotan cults, Hitler

---

[95] *RSA* VI, pp. 329–335 (Document 10).
[96] Cited in Blüger, T., "Following the Virgin Mary through Auschwitz...," p. 7.

216 / Christianity in Hitler's Ideology

said, because this cult was just too stupid. The only thing it wished to do was to prevent a conflict between Protestants and Catholics. He also took the opportunity to criticize the Social Democrats and the Marxists once again for their godless attitudes, as well as *Zentrum* for its collaboration with these parties. If Christ had risen today and seen the situation in the Bavarian Parliament (the *Landtag*), then he would once again have grabbed his whip, he said. The Bible's advice to look out for false prophets was truer today than ever before.[97] Then he called Christ "our most merciful Lord and Saviour," who had driven the Jews, these "serpents" and spawns of Satan, out of the Temple. But Christ, he sarcastically remarked, probably did not know best what Christianity was; surely, the *Bayerische Volkspartei* (BVP) must know better. The point he wished to make was that antisemitism was often considered un-Christian.[98] But how could antisemitism by un-Christian, when the great mayor of Vienna, Karl Lueger, who was a deeply faithful Catholic and leader of the Christian Social Party, was a fanatical anti-semite? Was it really un-Christian to defend oneself, he asked rhetorically?[99]

Friedrich Tomberg nonetheless claims that Hitler never intended to strengthen his audiences in their Christian faith,[100] and that is of course a correct conclusion if one with "Christian faith" refers to a modern-day Christian. But as we have seen, our understanding of what Christianity could mean has to be expanded in the case of Hitler and the National Socialists. Many of the Nazis, including Hitler himself, considered themselves to be faithful Christians, and in *that* sense it is entirely plausible to assume that Hitler indeed wished to strengthen the audiences in their Christian faith – that he even wanted them to be fanatical in their faith. If Tomberg's conclusion were true, then Hitler's propaganda strategy would have been very irrational indeed, since there would have been a considerable risk that the audience would have

---

[97] *RSA* II/2, pp. 694–699, 705–707 (Document 237).   [98] Ibid., p. 699 (Document 237).
[99] Ibid., p. 754 (Document 242).
[100] Tomberg, F., *Das Christentum* ... , p. 127. Tomberg gets himself into trouble with this interpretation and claims that there was something very paradoxical about Hitler, who, in an effort to save Germany from the damaging effects of Christianity, was forced to portray himself as a true Christian and as a follower of Christ (ibid., p. 131). But with the interpretation presented in this book, there is no paradox to explain. It makes perfect sense.

217 / Jesus as an Ideological Inspiration for Hitler and the NSDAP

believed his lies and become even more firmly entrenched in their Christian faith, and thereby become even more difficult to recruit for the purposes of National Socialism. Hitler was not stupid enough to risk all his and the NSDAP's propaganda success by spreading a false message to the party members and the voters that might be misinterpreted and used against him. It would have been like propagating a nonantisemitic message while wanting to pursue an antisemitic policy; such rhetoric would draw the wrong crowd and the wrong kind of supporters. Once again, Hitler's actions are most easily explained if we simply take him at his word.

He clearly knew when to bring up religion and when not to do so. For example, he did not bring up religion at all when he spoke to members of the political, military, and economic elite in the *National-Klub von 1919* (National Club of 1919) in Hamburg on December 1, 1930, but, as we have already seen (see page 208), he did do so when he spoke to the SS in Munich four days later. As we remember, he stated to the SS men that Christmas was a reminder of the immortal example of how even the smallest thing could grow big, "and today we may perhaps to us National Socialists with good reason confess that we serve religion more than the politicized servants of religion serve religion in that we do not mix it with politics, but in our political action promote principles for which Christ was once born and for which [*he*] was persecuted and nailed to the cross by the Jews" [emphasis added]. The gathered SS men then drenched Hitler in storming applause for his words. The battle was for the freedom of the German people's soul, he proclaimed.[101] On December 7, he expressed the hope to an NSDAP gathering that "the Almighty and merciful God" would finally let the great moment arrive when the Germans would once again be elevated to honor and dignity.[102] It is really interesting that Hitler would stress Christ's teachings to members of the SS of all people. The SS was, after all, the organization that was the most hostile toward the Christian churches after the Nazi revolution.[103] Hitler could not benefit from

---

[101] *RSA* IV/1, pp. 141–144, 148–149 (Documents 36 and 38). See also Tomberg, F., *Das Christentum* ... , p. 125.

[102] *RSA* IV/1, p. 159 (Document 39).

[103] See, e.g., Dierker, W., *Himmlers Glaubenskrieger* ...

218 / Christianity in Hitler's Ideology

portraying the movement as a direct heir to Christ unless the SS men who were listening to him sympathized with the message and understood what he meant by that. Hitler appears to have refrained from emphasizing his religious faith in precisely the contexts where it would have served him extra well propagandistically, such as in interviews with foreign journalists.

In preparation for the election in July 1932, an appeal was published in the *Völkischer Beobachter* on June 22, in which Hitler stated his conviction that "God willing" the NSDAP would be able to form a government on August 1.[104] Hitler thus ascribed to God an active role in German history in making him the savior of Germany. Hitler did not get to form his government in August, however. But he was not far off.

5.6 Jesus as Inspiration for the Ultimate Evil: Did Hitler Plan the Holocaust from the Outset?

Let us take Hitler's admiration of Jesus seriously, as well as his declared faith in a God and his view of himself as a tool of divine Providence. The events of July 1921, when Hitler exited the NSDAP and demanded dictatorial powers (which he got) as a condition to reenter, may have been the defining moment. In his classic study, Albrecht Tyrell stresses that it was after this point in time that Hitler developed his self-image as *Führer*; a transformation that was completed after his arrest and stint in the Landsberg fortress after the failed coup attempt. Tyrell argues that Hitler's decision to leave the party was not a result of a calculated plan, but instead the desperate act of a hysterical man; it was a reaction to a situation where his place in the NSDAP (and perhaps even life itself) was threatened and where he saw no other solution than to play *va banque* – to put everything on the line and either win it all or lose everything, as he would so often do later in life as well.[105] Most historians have accepted this general timeline and development.[106]

---

[104] *HRP* I/1, p. 114 (June 22, 1932).   [105] Tyrell, A., *Vom "Trommler"* ... , pp. 150–174.
[106] Reuth, R. G., *Hitler* ... , p. 129; Kershaw, I., *Hitler: 1889–1936*, p. 163; Longerich, P., *Hitler* ... , pp. 98–99; Thamer, H.-U., *Adolf Hitler* ... , pp. 81–82.

219 / Jesus as an Ideological Inspiration for Hitler and the NSDAP

However, Thomas Weber has remarked that Eckart and Rosenberg, as well as other Hitler followers, had already started to portray Hitler as a Messiah around this time. Hitler accepted this view of him, and Bavarian newspapers even began to refer to him as the "Bavarian Mussolini" already in 1922. It is therefore not possible to argue that Hitler saw himself as simply "the drummer" (*Trommler*) up until the coup attempt, Weber argues.[107] It is equally clear that Hitler already in July 1921 was well aware of the fact that he was an enormous asset to the NSDAP, in that he was a speaker that could draw rather large crowds.[108] Hitler must therefore reasonably have begun the journey to see himself as the one who was meant to lead the party already before July 11, 1921, or else his actions would have made absolutely no sense. He did, after all, demand dictatorial powers, and he would hardly have done that unless he thought he deserved them and that there was a sizable chunk of the party that would support him.

Perhaps it was precisely the development within the NSDAP to look at him as a German Messiah that made Hitler think that his *va banque* action had a chance of succeeding. The success of this strategy in this case may also have been a factor in his decision to act in this way in so many major decisions in his political career after that. It was certainly not a character trait that had been visible in his life up to that point. The fact that his strategy paid off is also likely to have assured him even further that he indeed was protected and appointed by God to do great things. That it was a formative experience is unquestionable, and it reasonably made him even more confident that he would prevail as he encountered difficulties along his way. His lack of compromise would pay off in the end – because God wanted it. God, however, had nothing to do with the decision of the NSDAP to accept him back into the fold; instead, it was Eckart, the person who had inculcated this belief in Hitler and who also saw him this way himself, that had pressured the chairman Anton Drexler to accept Hitler's ultimatum.[109]

---

[107] Weber, T., *Wie Adolf Hitler zum Nazi wurde* ..., p. 353. Hans-Ulrich Thamer generally follows Weber's view but adds nuance by remarking that Hitler referred to himself as the "drummer" also in 1922 on several occasions (Thamer, H.-U., *Adolf Hitler* ..., pp. 82–87).

[108] Joachimsthaler, A., *Hitlers Weg* ..., p. 286.

[109] Ibid., pp. 286–287; Reuth, R. G., *Hitler* ..., pp. 129–130.

220 / Christianity in Hitler's Ideology

Hitler's status as a Messiah figure only grew from there. Walter Buch, one of the most powerful Nazis in the Third Reich, compared the NSDAP's members to the disciples of Christ and the early Christians, and argued that just as fanatical faith had been absolutely vital for the survival of Christianity the same was true of the spiritual National Socialist movement.[110] The editor of *Der Stürmer*, Julius Streicher, explicitly compared Hitler to Jesus in a speech he held during a course at the National Socialist Student Union's Reich School in Bernau in July 1935. Even though the Catholic Church was attacked by the movement, the NSDAP did not reject Christianity, Streicher explained to the audience, and continued by saying that Hitler spoke plainly and simply just as Christ had done. Christ could not speak as openly as he would have liked to, Streicher said, and had to resort to parables. For example, Christ spoke of the flower and the weed, the latter symbolizing the Jews, Streicher said. He then explained to the students that the Bible was a great work seen from a racial perspective, because Christ had been an Aryan and the greatest antisemite of all time.[111]

It may come as a surprise that the editor of the crude antisemitic hate and propaganda vessel *Der Stürmer* would say such things. However, Victor Klemperer noted in his diary in August 1936 that *Der Stürmer* did in fact have the following as its watchword: "He who fights against the Jews wrestles with the Devil."[112] As a matter of fact, religious imagery, parallels, and themes were quite common in the pages of *Der Stürmer*. Previously, it had recurrently had the epigraph "Love is the devotion before God in – man" in the paper.[113] The lies that Streicher spread in *Der Stürmer* were of course not seen as lies by the Nazis themselves. On the contrary, they considered that the propaganda "informed" the reader of the actual state of the world. The fact is that on the front page, below the name of the paper, it said: "A German weekly for the fight for the truth."[114] The parallels to the

[110] Steigmann-Gall, R., "Old Wine in New Bottles? ... ," p. 296.
[111] Cited in Steigmann-Gall, R., *The Holy Reich* ... , pp. 125–126.
[112] Klemperer, V., *Ich will Zeugnis* ... (Band I), p. 300 (August 29, 1936).
[113] Roos, Daniel, *Julius Streicher und "Der Stürmer" 1923–1945* (Paderborn: Ferdinand Schöningh, 2014), p. 422.
[114] See a facsimile of *Der Stürmer*'s frontpage in McDonough, F., *The Hitler Years ...* , p. 125.

221 / Jesus as an Ideological Inspiration for Hitler and the NSDAP

Internet outlets that spread false information, fake news, and propaganda online today is striking.

This means that we should also take Streicher's testimony after the war, about when he had heard Hitler speak for the very first time, seriously. In his memoirs, written while awaiting trial in Nuremburg, he described how he had attended a meeting in the *Bürgerbräukeller* in Munich in 1922 and had seen a man that, to him, appeared to have been obviously appointed by God to accomplish a divine mission. Streicher wrote that Hitler's message that night

> was a revelation of a deep faith in God ... Everyone [who was there] felt it: This man speaks because of a divine calling, he speaks as someone appointed by Heaven.[115]

Note that even though Streicher is not a particularly reliable source (for instance, he wrote two versions of his memoirs that differ quite substantially from one another), his description of his experience in this case is very similar to how many other Nazis described their first Hitler speech. But the fact that Streicher spoke of Hitler in this way even after the war had ended shows, if nothing else, that it appeared reasonable to him to describe Hitler, and the feeling he had gotten the first time he saw and heard him, in this manner.

There is a broad consensus among those that study Hitler that the Holocaust was not planned or thought-out from the outset, but that it was the result of a gradual process of radicalization over time that resulted in increasingly brutal "solutions" to the "Jewish problem." Yet, there are pieces of evidence that should perhaps make historians reconsider this consensus, at least in the sense that Hitler may well have had a wish to murder the Jews from very early on. In *Mein Kampf,* for instance, there are passages that express murderous motives against Jews. The most infamous example is when Hitler in the second volume talks about gas warfare during the First World War and writes:

> Had one at the start of the war, and during the war, put twelve to fifteen thousand of these Hebrew destructors of the people under poison gas, in the same way that hundreds of thousands

[115] Roos, D., *Julius Streicher ... ,* p. 66.

222 / Christianity in Hitler's Ideology

> of our best German workers from all layers and professions had to endure in the battlefield, then the sacrifice of millions at the front would not have been in vain.[116]

Historians have stressed that it is not possible to draw a straight line between this statement and the Holocaust. However, Ian Kershaw argues that this does show that the connection between the extermination of the Jews, war, and the rescue of the German nation had already been made in Hitler's mind. The use of terms such as "extermination" and "destruction" had been very frequent in Hitler's speeches long before that.[117] At the same time, as there is a lot of merit in Kershaw's judgment, it is worth noticing that Hitler only seems to be speaking of a smaller number of very influential Jews that he thought were responsible for Germany having lost the war, that is, he must have been thinking of representatives of "international Jewish capital." Oddly enough, Hitler does not seem to have thought that the war could have been avoided, or perhaps not even that Germany would have been able to win if this mass murder had been undertaken. If he had, why point out that the millions of dead at the front would then not have been in vain?

But there are letters in Rudolf Heß's correspondence that point to another conclusion regarding this matter. Heß's letters were published already in 1987, but oddly enough Kershaw did not use them when writing his two-volume biography, which must reasonably mean that he did not know about them. It is two of these letters that are of considerable interest to us in this case. The first was written on June 11, 1924 (while he and Hitler were still in fortress in Landsberg) and the second was on March 8, 1928. The first is the one that is most packed with content, and Heß describes that it was only once they were locked up together in the Landsberg fortress that he really got to know Hitler, and he also notes the difference this made compared to his previous experiences of him from his speeches or brief meetings. The relevant part reads:

---

[116] *Hitler, Mein Kampf* ... (Band II), p. 1719 [**344**]. See also Longerich, P., *Hitler* ... , p. 150; Kershaw, I., *Hitler 1889–1936* ... , p. 244.

[117] Longerich, P., *Hitler* ... , p. 150; Kershaw, I., *Hitler 1889–1936* ... , p. 244.

223 / Jesus as an Ideological Inspiration for Hitler and the NSDAP

> For instance, I had also never imagined that he only after a great inner struggle had reached the position on the Jewish question that he has today. Constant returning doubts if he is not actually committing an injustice. And still today he speaks in a different manner in a small circle of initiated than how he must in front of the masses; only in front of these [the initiated] can he present the most radical standpoint.[118]

There are several interesting things in this passage. One of them is for sure that Heß says that Hitler had suffered moral qualms over his solution to the "Jewish problem." This is in and of itself new information. Yet, Heß remains silent on what this radical solution entailed, and this surely implies that we are dealing with something very radical, brutal, and controversial. His real solution was something that he could only share with his most intimate followers, according to Heß. This fits well with Thomas Weber's point that Hitler and Eckart shared a genocidal rhetoric concerning the Jews from very early on.[119] But in a newspaper interview made by a Catalonian journalist shortly before

---

[118] *Rudolf Heß ...* , pp. 334–335 (No. 339).

[119] Martin Menke claims in a recent anthology chapter that Hitler in "a letter written in 1919 ... identified 'overnight murder' of the Jews as 'the best solution, but short of that, mass expulsion'" (Menke, Martin, "Catholic Authority and the Holocaust," in John J. Michalczyk et al. (eds.), *Hitler's* Mein Kampf *and the Holocaust: A Prelude to Genocide* [London: Bloomsbury Academic, 2022], p. 197). This piqued my interest, since I was aware of no such letter and I thought that maybe Menke had discovered a previously unknown primary letter from Hitler's hand (that would be no small matter). Menke's source is a footnote in the expertly annotated IfZ edition of *Mein Kampf*. However, it turns out that not only is Menke mistaken in referring to a letter from 1919, but his quotes are also not to be found in the footnote he references. The footnote contains quotes from *two different* sources, one being the infamous letter to Adolf Gemlich of September 16, 1919, and the other being an interview with Hitler by a Catalonian journalist shortly before the coup attempt on November 8–9, 1923. The Gemlich letter does not contain anything even remotely like what Menke cites, but in the 1923 interview, in which Hitler argues *against* the effectiveness of medieval-style pogroms as a solution to the "Jewish question," we find Hitler asking what good it would do to force all the Jews out of Munich when the rest of the country's money and political power were still in the hands of the Jews. There were over a million Jews in Germany, he added. Then he said (clearly addressing those who argued for such pogroms): "What do you want to do? Kill them all over night? That would of course be the best solution, and if one could get away with it then Germany would be saved. But that is not possible. I have investigated the problem from all sides: it is not possible. The world would attack us, instead of thanking us, which they ought to do. ... We have already seen that it can't be done by pogroms. Hence, only expulsion remains: a mass expulsion" (*Hitler, Mein Kampf ...* [Band I], p. 206, n172. It is

224 / Christianity in Hitler's Ideology

the putsch attempt in November 1923, Hitler candidly intimated that the mass expulsion of Germany's one million Jewish citizens was the only realistic and possible solution to the "Jewish problem." Killing them all would certainly be the best solution of all, Hitler said, but he stressed that he had pondered the issue from all perspectives, and arrived at the conclusion that this was simply not possible.[120] While this is not a statement of intent and is not evidence of a genocidal plan against the Jews, it does show that Hitler had certainly entertained the idea of killing all the Jews in Germany by this point in time.

Hitler supposedly said something similar to the Bohemian NSDAP member N. Kugler from Vienna, who visited him on July 29, 1924. Hitler told the newspaper *Der Nationalsozialist* about this conversation, and this report was published on August 17. Apparently, Hitler believed this issue to be of such importance that it deserved to be spread to a larger audience. Hitler said that he had come to change his attitude on the issue regarding the fight against the Jews. When he was working on his book, he had come to realize that he had previous been "too mild" and that the "sharpest weapon" (*schärfsten Kampfmittel*) ought to be used if one were to be successful. It was not simply a matter of a fateful question for the German people, Hitler said, but for all peoples in the world since "Juda" was the "world plague" (*Weltpest*).[121]

In his letter from 1928 (the same year as Eckart's Cain article was published in the *Völkischer Beobachter*, see Chapter 2), Heß writes simply that Hitler had held a private lecture for him about the solution to the Jewish problem *"which I was deeply stunned by"* [emphasis in original].[122] Is it really reasonable to believe that this "sharpest weapon" and the "most radical standpoint" that would be used to rid the world of the Jewish "world plague" did *not* include massive violence against the Jews? Heß was a battle-hardened soldier who had experienced lots of killing both during and after the war as a member of

---

clear that Hitler was not stating his own genocidal plans in this interview. The citations Menke offers are thus bogus.

[120] *Hitler, Mein Kampf* ... (Band I), p. 206, n172.

[121] *SA*, p. 1242 (Document 654); Lüdicke, L., *Hitlers Weltanschauung* ... , p. 72; Fleischmann, P., *Hitler als Häftling* ... , p. 362.

[122] *Rudolf Heß* ... , p. 391 (No. 384).

Freikorps Epp. If *he* was stunned, then we have good reason to assume that what he was told was something very radical indeed.

It is therefore not completely unrealistic to assume that Hitler already in 1924 had arrived at the conclusion that the Jews had to be physically exterminated if Germany was to be saved. Did this mean that he envisioned a mass murder of all the Jews in Europe, or just a policy that would be so extreme that it would, after a frenzy of violence against them, drive every Jew out of Germany through forced emigration and deportations? We do not know the answer to this question. But is it likely that Hitler would have moral qualms about simply driving all the Jews out of Germany? Was this really such a radical idea that he could not speak openly about it in his speeches, but only to his close faithful partners in crime? Would Heß have found such a proposal so astonishing as late as 1928? No, it is difficult to imagine that Hitler's idea did not include much more radical acts and measures than forced emigration and deportation. Hitler was also a hardened criminal and a soldier, and was used to extreme violence and death. The fact that it appeared so foreign to Heß must at least mean that it had to do with the fact that Hitler was still far from being in power in Germany, and that there was no historical parallel to what he wanted to do.

Wolfram Pyta, too, has given cogent reasons for why we should assume that Hitler had come to take an extremely radical position with regard to the Jews and actually argued for mass murder, already in the early 1920s. First, Pyta refers to a letter written by Heinrich Heim (the main author of the table talk notes) to Fritz von Trützschler on August 12, 1920. Heim wrote that Hitler had said that one had to eradicate the Jewish *bacillus* from the body of the German people. When it came to the existence or nonexistence of the people, one could not allow oneself to shy away from taking the lives of "citizens" (*Staatsangehörige*), and even less so when it came to threatening and hostile foreign tribes. In addition, the former Protestant priest Georg Schott wrote to Houston Stewart Chamberlain on April 13, 1924, and told him that he had heard Hitler mention that the end point was the brutal physical destruction of the Jews. Pogroms were not enough, Hitler supposedly said, because this would not cut this "evil" (*Übel*) off at the root once and for all. Schott even used the expression "the final solution to the Jewish question." This proves that Hitler already at

226 / Christianity in Hitler's Ideology

this early stage – even before he had finished *Mein Kampf* – had formulated a gigantic plan to murder the Jews, Pyta concludes, and points out that it is surprising that historians have so far so unanimously ignored these statements when they so clearly point to a continuity between Hitler's genocidal antisemitism from the 1920s and the Holocaust in the 1940s.[123]

It is worth drawing attention to the fact that Schott's letter was written just a few months before Heß wrote about Hitler's difficult decision and moral doubts on this matter, as well as the conversation with Kugler in the Landsberg fortress. The two documents are independent of, and support, one another. Considering that Heim's statements from 1920 are almost identical to those that were published in *Der Nationalsozialist* in August 1924, we are forced to draw the conclusion that Hitler's utterance to Kugler was not completely truthful. Hitler did *not* come to this conclusion during the work on *Mein Kampf*; he in fact had had the same view regarding the Jews at least since the summer of 1920. Instead, what we encounter here is just yet another one of Hitler's many autobiographical lies. It is not at all implausible that Hitler played the same game in front of Heß, and that Heß bought it all hook, line, and sinker and therefore may have honestly believed that Hitler had suffered under an ethical dilemma. But whether he actually did, we can never know.

It is perhaps significant that Heß's phrase "the most radical" solution to the so-called Jewish question was used also by Goebbels almost twenty years later on October 7, 1943. Goebbels, who by then was well aware of the mass murder of the Jews, commented on Himmler's speech in Posen the day before (he had also held a similar speech on October 4) during which Himmler talked about how it was easy enough to utter the statement the Jews must be exterminated but that for those who had to actually do it this was the most difficult thing imaginable. Himmler was nonetheless committed to killing them all – men, women, and children.[124] Himmler held his speech just after the

---

[123] Pyta, W., *Hitler . . .* , pp. 172–173.

[124] There is some confusion in the literature and sources regarding the exact wording of Himmler's second Posen speech. Speer cites it in his book *Der Sklavenstaat: Meine Auseinandersetzungen mit der SS* (Stuttgart: Deutsche Verlags-Anstalt, 1981), p. 376, but when Kershaw and Matthias Schmidt cite the same passage, they give it a slightly different

227 / Jesus as an Ideological Inspiration for Hitler and the NSDAP

largest killing frenzies during the Holocaust. In the spring of 1942 no less than 75 percent of all victims in the Holocaust were still alive; a year later, the opposite was true: by then, 75 percent of all those who would be murdered were already dead. The so-called *Operation Reinhard* (and its ending *Operation Erntefest* – Operation Autumn Festival) had not only seen about 1.3 million Jews gassed to death in the gas chambers in Treblinka, Auschwitz, Sobibor, Belzec, and Majdanek. In addition, around 1.5 million were shot in close-up executions during the same period. In total, almost half of the about 6 million victims of the Holocaust were murdered in such close-range killings.[125] Himmler was touching upon the very personal nature of the murders in his speech, when he spoke of the difficulty for the murderers. So make no mistake. The Holocaust was very personal for both victims and executioners. It was this that Goebbels approvingly commented on by saying that "the most radical" solution was absolutely necessary.[126] This similar choice of words could of course be a coincidence. However, the Nazis from very early on developed a "groupspeak," forming a dictionary of morbid euphemisms that basically remained the same over the years.

Alon Confino addresses the same paradox in his book *A World without Jews*, when he writes that Hitler (and Himmler and Goebbels) did not have any moral qualms about the mass murder of the Jews, but that at the same time their actions indicate a certain awareness that a line had been crossed and that a taboo had been violated. Because

---

wording than Speer (see Kershaw, I., *Hitler 1936–1945 ...*, p. 605; Schmidt, Matthias, *Albert Speer: Das Ende eines Mythos. Die Aufdeckung seiner Geschichtsverfälschung. Speers wahre Rolle im Dritten Reich* [Bern: Schertz, 1982], p. 231). Their versions agree, even though they seem to have different sources. Schmidt, however, begins his quote differently, while Kershaw starts his quote a bit later in the text. Instead of the first two sentences in Speer's version, Schmidt has another wording. Moreover, both Kershaw and Schmidt have a different wording in the part about the children, compared to Speer. Their version sounds more complete, and it may be that Speer forgot to include some words. Speer also appears to have excluded a whole sentence following this passage. Goebbels' diary, on the other hand, states that Himmler said that he expected this issue to be solved by the end of 1943. This is included by Speer too, but not in the version cited by Kershaw and Schmidt (see *TBJG* II/10, p. 72 [October 7, 1943]).

[125] Confino, Alon, *A World without Jews: The Nazi Imagination from Persecution to Genocide* (New Haven, CT: Yale University Press, 2014), p. 190.

[126] *TBJG* II/10, p. 72 (October 7, 1943). See also Brechtken, M., *Albert Speer ...* , pp. 220–226.

228 / Christianity in Hitler's Ideology

despite having spent years screaming from the rooftops about the destruction of the Jews, they could not bring themselves to talk openly about this extermination once it had been started and was going on. Goebbels wrote about three million words every year, Confino remarks, but still could not bring himself – with one single exception – to mention any details about the Holocaust with even one syllable.[127] The exception mentioned by Confino is a passage from Goebbels' diary on March 27, 1942, where he describes how the Jews, starting in Lublin, were now being sent eastward from the General Government to become slave laborers and to be murdered.[128]

After the war, Hans Frank remembered how Hitler in the *Reichskanzlei* in 1938 had told him that in the Gospels the Jews had cried out to Pilate, after he had refused to crucify Christ, that Christ's blood would now be upon the Jews and their children (a reference to Matthew 27:25). According to Frank, Hitler then stated that he may have to make this curse come true.[129] If Frank's memory is reasonably correct, and if we assume that he was not making this episode up as he was awaiting his death in Nuremberg prison (Frank had rediscovered his Catholic faith while in captivity), then it is safe to say that Hitler's admiration for Jesus had a very grim and ominous side, one that may directly have influenced his decision to launch the Holocaust. But even if this story is a figment of Frank's imagination, it is still instructive that he expected his readers to believe that Hitler could have made such a statement.

Another particularly grim aspect of Hitler's religiosity we find in the concept of "Christian productivism" described in Chapter 1. This was an integral part of National Socialist ideology, and it was expressed particularly well in the following phrase: "The one who is unwilling to work shall not eat." This moral principle was *not* taken from Oswald Spengler or some secular social Darwinist ethos. It came straight out of the New Testament, namely 2 Thessalonians, where it says:

[127] Confino, A., *A World without Jews* ... , p. 197.
[128] *TBJG*, II/3, p. 561 (March 27, 1942).
[129] Frank, H., *Im Angesicht des Galgens* ... , p. 315. See also Heer, F., *Der Glaube des Adolf Hitler* ... , p. 350.

229 / Jesus as an Ideological Inspiration for Hitler and the NSDAP

> nor did we eat anyone's food without paying for it. On the contrary, we worked night and day, laboring and toiling so that we would not be a burden to any of you. We did this, not because we do not have the right to such help, but in order to offer ourselves as a model for you to imitate. For even when we were with you, we gave you this rule: "The one who is unwilling to work shall not eat."[130]

In a speech held on October 28, 1925, Hitler cited this passage and called it "an eternal and highest right on earth … : he who does not work shall not eat." He did this in a religious rant about how God had created peoples (*Völker*), not classes, and that the Aryan had been created by God to be a "culture-bearer" (*Kulturträger*) and a creator of civilizations.[131]

It appears that this passage was much more important for National Socialist ideology than these two occasions suggest; indeed, it was one of the most fundamental aspects of the ideology. He later quoted the same passage again in a speech on March 23, 1927. Life was a struggle, and he who did not work should not eat. Here we see how productivist ideology and theology combined into a forceful reinterpretation of the Bible's message. Hitler referred to Genesis 3:19, and God's judgment over humankind after the fall from grace, where it states that humans were from then on to eat their bread in the sweat from their brows. This might seem grim, but it was actually a blessing. Only the workshy Jews could consider it a curse, Hitler reasoned with characteristic antisemitic spite. He therefore reinterpreted it as being a blessing – it was in fact the source of all life on earth.[132]

This was not something that Hitler had made up on the fly either. It was an established moral principle within the National Socialist movement from very early on. Rudolf Jung talked about it in his *Der nationale Sozialismus* in 1922, where he lamented the fact that the principle of "he who does not work should also not eat" was no

---

[130] 2 Thessalonians 3:8–10 (NIV).
[131] *RSA* I, p. 202 (Document 78, October 25, 1925). For the point about God having created peoples and not classes, see also Lüdicke, L., *Hitlers Weltanschauung …*, p. 56.
[132] *RSA* II/1, p. 192 (Document 89, March 23, 1927). See also Bucher, R., *Hitlers Theologie*, p. 121.

230 / Christianity in Hitler's Ideology

longer applied in society. He did this in the context of explaining precisely the distinction between "productive" (*schaffender*) and "unproductive," or rather [money-] "grubbing" (*raffender*), work. The latter, that is, "workless income," was synonymous with the Jewish "capitalistic mammonistic" economy of the day, and indeed its greatest and most severe feature.[133] The term "mammonism" was of course also taken from the Bible.

Jung referred to the "grubbers" as the "sons of the desert" (*Wüstensöhne*) (a reference to the story in the Old Testament about the Israelites wandering in the desert for forty years after the escape from Egyptian captivity) who were now firmly "planted in the ocean of houses [*Häusermeer*] in the big city, this desert of the present." As prime examples of money-grubbing capitalists and representatives of the despised "interest" (*Zins*) in the modern economy, Jung mentioned "the Rothschilds and company," who he referred to as "the uncrowned King Judas." These people were only interested in "workless income," and, remarked Jung, "workless income prepares for them a punishment from God."[134] Jung mixed his metaphors here and displayed the National Socialist romanticism about the farmer and life outside the urban milieu. He also made clear the religious significance of the National Socialist political ideology and message when he spoke of God's punishment for the supposedly idle Jews, a punishment that the National Socialists were to dole out on his behalf.

Those who could not contribute "productively" by performing slave labor were thus considered "useless eaters" (*unnütze Esser*) or "harmful eaters" (*schädliche Fresser*). Giving such people food was considered a waste of precious resources. Hans Frank used these expressions when he talked about how the Jews in Poland had to be exterminated, as did the murderous death camp inspector Christian Wirth and the commander of Treblinka Franz Stangl.[135] I believe that David

---

[133] Jung, R., *Der nationale Sozialismus* ... , pp. 92–94.   [134] Ibid., pp. 91–92, 100–101.
[135] Gerlach, Christian, *Der Mord an den europäischen Juden: Ursachen, Ereignisse, Dimensionen* (Munich: C. H. Beck, 2017), pp. 79–85, 89–90, 238; Piotrowski, Stanislaw (ed.), *Hans Franks Tagebuch* (Warsaw: Polnischer Verlag der Wissenschaften, 1963), p. 347; Pauer-Studer, Herlinde and Velleman, J. David, *"Weil ich nun mal ein Gerechtigkeitsfanatiker bin": Der Fall des SS-Richters Konrad Morgen* (Berlin: Suhrkamp Verlag, 2017), pp. 189–190.

231 / Jesus as an Ideological Inspiration for Hitler and the NSDAP

Redles is correct in stressing the eschatological and religious aspects in the origins of the Holocaust. Hitler and the other leading Nazis viewed the struggle against the Jews as a holy war between good and evil, a war that the Aryan Germans had to win no matter what the cost.[136]

This was thus a perfect fit with, and no doubt caused by, the productivist ideology that had been preached by the pioneering National Socialists Naumann, Fritsch, and Marr (that we also encountered in Chapter 1) in the late 1800s and early 1900s. The idea that those who did not work should not eat was the foundation for the NSDAP party program's obsession with, and hatred of, workless income. Hard work, on the other hand, was liberating and would set you free because it meant liberation from the "idle" and "parasitic" Jewish spirit that had infested all people to a lesser or larger extent. What we find here is nothing less than the philosophy and moral theology behind the taunting phrase on the gates to the Dachau, Groß-Rosen, Sachsenhausen, Theresienstadt, and – perhaps most infamously – Auschwitz labor camps: *Arbeit macht frei*.[137] It was *not* a phrase intended to imply that the slave labor that the Jews were forced to perform in these camps would lead to their release from the camps if they only "served their sentence" and did enough of it. The message that these signs were conveying was a spiritual one since the purported problem with "the Jew" was his very nature and his soul. The labor the Jews were forced to do in these, and the other, camps would thus liberate their *spirit* – God was handing down their punishment and the forced labor was, seen through the twisted logic of Nazi theology, a way for the Jews to make amends to God for their idleness. This aspect only adds to the limitless cruelty of the Nazi camps and of these signs.

---

[136] Redles, D., "The Apocalypse of Adolf Hitler ... ," pp. 213–233.
Chamberlain, H. S., *Die Grundlagen* ... , p. 247.

[137] The Buchenwald camp instead had the similar phrase *Jedem das seine* (To each his own), which also meant that you would get what you deserved. Although the origin of this phrase is a translation of Cicero's *suum cuique*, the concept as such has deep roots in Christianity too, since the idea is that each will get their just punishment or reward in the end. The phrase *Arbeit macht frei* had a longer intellectual history in Germany. It was even the title of a book by the nationalist author Lorenz Diefenbach from 1872. It had also been used in Weimar Germany from 1928 onward in the context of large-scale publicly funded programs to deal with mass unemployment. There were thus many layers that interacted in the Nazis' choice of words.

232 / Christianity in Hitler's Ideology

5.7 Conclusion

In this chapter, we have seen that there can be no doubt that Hitler and the National Socialists considered Jesus to be an important inspiration for them. Hitler considered Jesus to have been the greatest Aryan fighter against the Jews that had ever lived. But Christ had been killed by the Jews before he could bring his holy mission to an end. Therefore, the NSDAP intended to finish Jesus' divine mission, that is, to rid the world of the Jewish people. It is hard to find a more central ideological goal of National Socialism than that. This means that the idolizing of Jesus is at the very center of Nazi ideology. How come we have not learned this before? The reason is that historians have thus far not taken Hitler's, and the other leading Nazi ideologues' claims seriously.

Could it be that Hitler was inspired by Jesus to murder the Jews? The question itself might initially seem as offensive as it appears absurd. But this book should leave no doubt that we must take Hitler's admiration for the central character of Christianity – Jesus of Nazareth – seriously. Hitler repeatedly, both in public and private settings, expressed that Jesus was the greatest Aryan warrior, that Jesus had fought against the Jews and was killed by them before he had time to finish his work, that is, the physical destruction of the Jewish people, and that the NSDAP was going to pick up where he left off and this time his work would be brought to completion. In *Mein Kampf*, Hitler stated that when he was fighting against the Jews he was fighting for the Lord. This passage has usually been treated simply as a curiosity by historians. I argue that we should really take Hitler at his word. The Jesus that inspired Hitler – the Aryan warrior Christ – was thus not a Jesus that Christians of today would recognize. It was not a Christ of compassion and love, but of vengeance and hatred. But it is important to remember that Hitler and the Nazis did not invent this antisemitic Aryan Jesus. They simply latched on to theological ideas and developments that predated National Socialism by several decades. This battle later evolved to include mass murder. The answer to the seemingly offensive and absurd question put above can therefore absolutely be a terrible and chilling "yes."

From the New Testament, Hitler and National Socialism got the ethical principle that "he who does not work shall not eat." This

233 / Jesus as an Ideological Inspiration for Hitler and the NSDAP

principle was implemented with absolutely no regard for the consequences for those at the sharp end of it. It was used relentlessly on Soviet POWs as well as Jewish slave laborers, and it became the guiding ethos within Himmler's camp system. The fact that it was a self-fulfilling prophesy – a prisoner weakened by too small rations of food cannot work as hard – did not bother the Nazis and their henchmen. The prisoners had value only to the extent that they could perform work for the Reich. Once this capacity had been lost, they were killed. Killing them was of course also simultaneously a way to save food, which meant even more food could be sent back to Germany to feed the *Volk*. It was a criminal enterprise of staggering proportions.

With the phrase *Arbeit macht frei*, National Socialist theology received one of its ugliest and most horrendous forms. It expressed the Nazi understanding of the Jews as a people who were characterized by idleness and "workless income." It was in their nature and in their very soul. Thus, the phrase on the gates to so many concentration camps must be understood as a reference to this view of the Jews. Within these camps, the Jews would be forced to work, and through this process their soul would be cleansed before God. The liberation was therefore not physical or of this world but spiritual and of another world. It was a horribly cruel way of taunting the camp prisoners – as if the SS personnel were doing the captives a favor by working them to death.

CONCLUSION

"The 'Hitler Case' remains as a cautionary example for all time," writes Volker Ullrich in the second (and last) part of his extensive Hitler biography. He continues to correctly point out that perhaps the foremost lesson that we can learn from this terrible part of history is how fast democracy can be dismantled and done away with if the political institutions and civil society are too weak to oppose the authoritarian forces. We will never "be done" with Hitler, he says, because we are forever linked to him and the legacy he left behind.[1] Today's political developments in both the United States and Europe show us beyond a reasonable doubt that this judgment is correct. Authoritarian tendencies, mostly on the right, are growing stronger in nation after nation. The ideals of democracy and humanism are yet again under attack, and nationalism and xenophobic hatred, even antisemitism, are growing in scope and strength. There is even an increasing lack of respect for expertise, knowledge, research, and science – something that is apparent in above all the staggering spread and belief in, and concomitant popularity of, all kinds of unscientific conspiracy theories. Hopefully, this book can serve as at least a partial remedy to this sickness of our times.

Furthermore, it is my hope that this book has enlightened, inspired, but also provoked, and that it will lead to more research and

---

[1] Ullrich, V., *Adolf Hitler* ... (Band II), p. 694.

235 / Conclusion

more scholarship on this and similar topics in the future. There is still much to be done: for instance, the relationship between Nazi ethics and morality and the religious beliefs of leading National Socialist ideologues still needs to be investigated more fully. Perhaps this will become the topic of a coming book. Nazi moral philosophy is a subject that has thus far generally not received enough attention from scholars. To be sure, the very idea that National Socialism had an ethos may seem counterintuitive, offensive, and rebel against our deepest moral sentiments. However, there can be no doubt that the old but widespread idea that National Socialism was nihilistic is thoroughly and absolutely mistaken. It is an outdated view that contributes no understanding to why the Nazis did what they did and how they were so successful.

In this book, I have investigated an issue that has thus far been overlooked: the question of what role the figure of Jesus played in National Socialist ideology in general and for Adolf Hitler in particular. I have argued that Hitler's religious beliefs, and particularly his admiration for and belief in Jesus, the central figure of Christianity, are essential for understanding his ideological positioning from late 1919 onward. On many occasions throughout his career, Hitler referred to Jesus as an inspiration both for him personally and for the National Socialist movement. Hitler clearly understood himself as having been appointed by God for a divine mission and to complete the task that Jesus had been unable to fulfil before being crucified, namely, to rid the earth of "the scourge of the Jews." Hitler took his mission extremely seriously, and the Holocaust was the terrible result of this religious and fanatical conviction of being morally in the right when exterminating the Jewish people in Europe.

The National Socialist admiration of Jesus went much further back in time than Hitler. Compared to that prehistory, Hitler's love for Christ was a newfound one. Christ had been at the forefront of National Socialism from the very beginning in the mid-1800s, at least since Naumann's Christian National Socialism, and most definitely since Chamberlain's ruminations in his epos *Die Grundlagen*. Even Drexler gave Christ his due in his quasi-autobiography *Mein politisches Erwachen*, in which he stated that the fight against the Jews should be conducted in the spirit of Jesus Christ, the National Socialist savior.

236 / Christianity in Hitler's Ideology

This has not been picked up on by most historians. In fact, as far as I know, Derek Hastings is the only one to mention it at all. Granted, this may be because very few seem to have read Drexler's pamphlet first-hand. This is not a small matter. In fact, this was the very pamphlet that Drexler put in Hitler's hand at one of the first meetings (perhaps even the very first) of the DAP that he attended. It was a vital part of the process that recruited Hitler to the party. In *Mein Kampf*, Hitler claimed to have lain awake that night reading Drexler's political memoir.

We do not know whether Hitler had already come to adopt Jesus as his savior figure and considered him the foremost inspiration for all antisemites before reading Drexler's *Mein politisches Erwachen*. But it is obvious that this was the role that Jesus played in the ideology of the very recently established DAP, and it must at the very least have strengthened Hitler in his faith in this imaginary Aryan Jesus. No doubt, too, it was Eckart who came to really cement this belief in Hitler's mind over the course of the following three years. Once Eckart died in late 1923, Hitler had emerged from his ideological cocoon and transformed himself into a full-fledged horrendous moth: a rabidly racist and anti-semitic Messiah figure that National Socialism as a movement, and the NSDAP as a party, had sought and longed for. Jesus had led by example, according to the National Socialist mythology that Hitler believed in with all his heart. Jesus had given his life and died on the cross, not for the sins of humankind but for having fought the Jews and, consequently, for having been murdered by them before he had a chance to finish his divine mission. It was now up to the NSDAP and Hitler himself to pick up where Jesus had left off and to complete his divinely ordained struggle to rid the world of the Jews.

Drexler was far from alone among DAP/NSDAP ideologues in referring to Jesus as their role model or savior. So did Rosenberg in *Der Mythos des 20 Jahrhunderts* and Sebottendorff in his *Bevor Hitler kam* from 1933. Rudolf Jung held Jesus in very high regard, as is obvious in his *Der nationale Sozialismus* from 1922, where he portrayed him as an example for National Socialists to follow, and even compared Hitler to Jesus – as if Hitler was a reincarnation of Christ – after having visited Hitler in the fortress at Landsberg am Lech. It is immediately apparent in all the writings of the early Nazi ideologues that religiosity and belief in God were of central importance to their worldview. It was through

237 / Conclusion

the spiritual renewal of the German people that Germany would be saved. The Germans had become weak in spirit and needed to be made strong again. To achieve greatness, the people would have to rid themselves of the Jewish materialistic spirit that held sway over them and that had enslaved them to do the Jews' biddings. This was a spiritual and a moral struggle as much as a physical one. The blood had to be made pure not in a biological sense first and foremost, but in a moral, spiritual, and religious sense. The soul of Germany's *Volkskörper* – the body of the people – had to be cleansed from the contaminating and paralyzing influence of the Jews. A healthy people could not nurture parasites in their very hearts and souls.

It is indeed striking how absent these early National Socialist texts are of racial arguments of even a pseudoscientific kind. Biology was not the main focus for these writers. The real struggle was in the spiritual domain, and the National Socialists were convinced that they had God on their side and that they were on the side of good in a battle against an overwhelming enemy, an enemy that was everywhere, in everything, and in everybody. The Jews were truly a force to be respected and perhaps even feared. Yet, the image of Jesus and how this purported Aryan warrior had stood up to the Jews, chased them out of the most sacred of places with his whip in hand, and almost defeated them was a source of great inspiration and hope for the National Socialists in general and for Hitler in particular. This was the guiding light that would lead the fight.

I have argued that Hitler may have been so inspired by the example of Jesus, as retold in the Gospels in the New Testament, chasing the Jewish money changers out of the Temple while beating them with his whip, that this could be the explanation for why Hitler carried a whip himself. This has been judged to be a curiosity by previous scholarship, but I suggest that it might be much more significant than that. Hitler made use of this biblical story on so many occasions that we simply cannot ignore the rather obvious symbolic identification with Jesus that Hitler's whip constitutes. Hitler, too, had the ambitions to drive the "money changers," that is, the Jews, out of the "Temple," which in his case was Germany, and to clear the holiest of holy places from what he considered to be a great evil and an abomination.

238 / Christianity in Hitler's Ideology

Hitler was deeply inspired by the religious philosophy and beliefs of foremost Houston Stewart Chamberlain and Dietrich Eckart. Of these two, Eckart was the most important not least because he became an ideological mentor for Hitler once he had joined the DAP. It was Eckart who groomed the young veteran soldier as he developed into a fervent and fanatical National Socialist and the unquestionable leader of the NSDAP after mid-1921. Both Eckart and Chamberlain immediately understood that Hitler was the one they had been waiting for to lead the National Socialist cause and to lead Germany to greatness once again, but it was Eckart who convinced Hitler himself of his divine mission that led to him beginning to consider himself a Messiah figure that should finish what Jesus had started.

Hitler's religious conviction was to follow in the footsteps of Jesus, who in the National Socialist *Weltanschauung* was the greatest Aryan fighter against the Jews that had ever lived. To battle the Jews was, according to this interpretation, not only a moral duty for every National Socialist, but it was also to fulfil Jesus' original divine mission to exterminate the Jews and the Jewish spirit from the face of the earth. It was a clearly genocidal framework from the start, and it is no wonder that Hitler already from the early 1920s seems to have developed a violent and radical solution to the "Jewish problem." There are multiple, independent, and corroborative witnesses from this period that show that Hitler was most likely planning some sort of genocide of the Jews. The details of this plan are unknown, however, since these witnesses never spelled out what Hitler had suggested to them. That is how radical and horrible they must have been to these witnesses – they could not dare to repeat this message even in private. Yet, the very fact that these battle-hardened criminals, killers, and thugs, several of whom were veterans of the First World War and of the interwar era *Freikorps*, thought that his solution was so radical should tell us that it must indeed have been. There is thus good reason for historians to adjust the thesis that the Holocaust was something that occurred to Hitler only much later. Rather, it seems as if Hitler was only searching for the right moment to unleash his planned orgy of mass murder of the Jews. The war, which was also planned from very early on, provided him and the Nazis with the perfect opportunity. In the lawless "bloodlands" (to use Timothy Snyder's phrase) of Central and Eastern Europe,

239 / Conclusion

one could organize the greatest crime in human history and (at least before 1945, and in far too many cases much longer than that or even indefinitely) literally get away with murder.[2]

I have shown that the religious moral principle that guided the productivist thinking within National Socialism, that is, the division of the world between "productive" (characterized by the Aryan) and "unproductive" work (characterized by the Jew), where only the former was worth anything, was founded on interpretations of the Bible. In Hitler's case, this was expressed as the principle taken from 2 Thessalonians 3:10 that those who did not work should not eat. Hitler called this the highest moral right on earth. It was this very same moral theology that formed the basis behind the words *Arbeit macht frei*, which ordained the gates to the Dachau, Groß-Rosen, Theresienstadt, Sachsenhausen, and Auschwitz slave labor camps. This principle was brutally enforced by the SS camp authorities and millions of people lost their lives because of it. Only if the prisoners could perform productive work did they have any value. Once they were too weak to work, they were either starved or gassed to death. Since "idleness" was considered by the Nazis to be the natural characteristic of the Jewish spirit, that is, their soul, and factoring in that forced labor was intended to "cure" the Jews of this spiritual "disease," we could (or perhaps even should) view the slave labor system in the Nazi concentration camps as an effort to eradicate the Jewish spirit per se – to commit a spiritual genocide of the Jews to match the physical one.

The many examples of Hitler's use of the Bible clearly show that he was using it as a source of religious and ideological inspiration rather than as a source of facts, that is, Hitler was not using the Bible foremost as a history book. Hitler was indeed fond of making use of history to solve the contemporary problems that he saw, but this was thus not how he approached the Bible, and the parts that he cited cannot be understood simply as historical examples. It may of course be troubling or even outright offensive to believing Christians today (and to many at the time) to even consider the possibility that Jesus could have inspired Hitler to launch the Holocaust on the Jews of Europe. Yet, we already

---

[2] See Snyder, Timothy, *Bloodlands: Europe between Hitler and Stalin* (New York: Basic Books, 2010).

240 / Christianity in Hitler's Ideology

know for a fact that Christian mainstream theological antisemitism played a vital part in making the Holocaust possible through centuries of preaching about the evil of the Jews. The Jews had always been considered collectively guilty for the killing of Christ. Even the Gospels claimed that his blood was upon them and their children. For centuries, Christian Europe had systematically discriminated, spread hatred, and launched violent pogroms against the Jews. The mass violence against Europe's Jews during the Second World War, but also during the 1930s, did not simply come into existence *ex nihilo*.

The churches clearly understood this too, which is why they, after the war, hurried to do damage control by claiming that the Nazis were either atheists or pagans, and that Christians had been almost as persecuted by the Nazis as the Jews. The main "sin" of the Hitler regime had not been the mass murder of the Jews but the placing of nationalism, the NSDAP, and Hitler higher in the hierarchy than Christianity. If the churches had collaborated with the Nazis, it was because they had been forced to at gunpoint. The defensive turnaround was often macabre, as when theology professor Wolf Mayer-Erlach, "a notorious Nazi propagandist and leader of the German Christian movement" that before and during the war had worked tirelessly to expunge the Hebrew Bible from the Christian Bible, in 1947 compared the German people to the biblical Israelites who after captivity in Babylon had to do slave labor in Egypt.[3] This of course ignored all those heroes of the churches that really did oppose Hitler and the NSDAP. But this was not how the regime itself understood its mission in the world. Instead, it considered its role to be to finish what Jesus had begun and to eradicate the Jews from the face of the earth.

From this perspective, the idea that Hitler's idolizing of Jesus contributed to making him into a genocidal madman is not so hard to comprehend after all. We must remember that Hitler was not alone in orchestrating the Holocaust and that this way of dealing with the perceived "Jewish problem" therefore must have seemed reasonable to a huge number of people. This is the power of ideology and religion. Ideas matter and have material consequences because they form the

---

[3] For a good overview of this, see Heschel, S., "Confronting the Past ... ," pp. 46–70, quote on p. 48.

241 / Conclusion

foundations for our interpretation of the world, and they consequently influence our actions in the world. The idea sows the seed, and our actions are the ripe fruit of the tree that grows from that seed. In Hitler's case, the seeds had been sown already during the summer of 1919 as he took part in captain Karl Mayr's propaganda courses. His attendance at the DAP meeting on September 12, 1919, made the seed grow roots, and from it grew a trunk and branches that eventually bore the most horrible fruit imaginable. No one could have seen it coming in 1920, and yet given the nature of the causal, physical reality that we all inhabit, the result was inevitable.

I have argued that Hitler modeled his mythic transformation into a National Socialist and a politician on the story about Paul's conversion on the road to Damascus in Acts 9. The many parallels between the two tales are too many for them to be purely accidental. Hitler knew the New Testament stories very well, as he often displayed in his speeches during the 1920s, and it would not at all be beyond him to borrow from a saga that would be well familiar to every Bavarian in the early 1920s. By keeping silent about the fact that he was treated for battle-fatigue-related symptoms at the hospital at Pasewalk, and instead focusing on the stint of temporary blindness from the mustard gas attack, the parallel was obvious. The blindness, both a literal and metaphorical one, was lifted once the truth, it too both literal and metaphorical, had been revealed to him. The corrupt nature of the world that he had served so faithfully for so long was revealed to him, just as it had been to Paul. Hitler had served the useless, cowardly, and treasonous politicians in Berlin; Paul had served the decadent and corrupt Jewish authorities and persecuted Christians. Hitler was through the looking glass – former enemies became allies and former allies became his mortal enemies. Hitler even engineered an inner dialogue with his conscience that mirrored Paul's conversation with Jesus. The self-doubt and the wrestling with the new reality that he claimed he was faced with all had their counterparts in the story about Paul in Acts 9. At the same time, he portrayed himself as the great founder of a new movement, a new faith.

It is a troubling fact that mainstream scholarship and the main biographies on Hitler and National Socialism have been very slow, or even outright unwilling, to pick up on the exciting and enlightening

242 / Christianity in Hitler's Ideology

research that has been done on the religiosity of the NSDAP leadership for several decades now. This means that an important and central aspect to the ideological development of National Socialism was put to the side when the major syntheses of the history of Nazi Germany were being written. It is about time to put an end to this neglect. Hitler's religious beliefs should be given the attention they deserve. At the very least, those historians who wish to treat them as nothing more than a meaningless curiosity should have to justify their decision to do so.

The conclusion that Hitler was genuinely inspired by Jesus in his antisemitic struggle against the Jews thus cannot be avoided. Hitler viewed Jesus as the original Aryan warrior who had begun an apocalyptic battle against the Jews, but who had been killed before he had had a chance to finish the job. Historians must start taking Hitler's (and the other leading Nazis') religious beliefs seriously if we wish to fully understand how Hitler and his followers could be so morally convinced that what they were doing was the right thing – indeed, the "good" thing – to do. It adds significantly to our understanding not only of how Hitler could sway so many Germans to do what he wanted, but also of how the Nazis' ultimate crime – the Holocaust – was possible to undertake in one of Europe's most "civilized" and culturally and economically developed nations. Hitler thought he was following in the footsteps of Jesus – an alleged Aryan warrior who had dedicated his life to fighting the Jews – and that the National Socialists had a duty to finish what he was convinced Jesus had started: the eradication of the Jewish people from the face of the earth.

BIBLIOGRAPHY

Archives

Bundesarchiv, Berlin-Lichterfelde
NS 6
R6/34a
University of Arizona Library Special Collections
Papers of Karen Kuykendall, MS 243.

Literature and Printed Primary Sources

Adolf Hitler: Sein Leben und seine Reden. Herausgegeben von Adolf-Victor von Koerber (Munich: Deutscher Volksverlag, Dr. E. Boepple, 1923).

Aly, Götz, *Europa gegen die Juden 1880–1945* (Frankfurt am Main: S. Fischer, 2017).

Arendt, Hannah, *The Origins of Totalitarianism.* New ed. with added prefaces (New York: Harcourt Brace Jovanovich, 1973, originally published in 1951).

Baranowski, Shelley, *The Sanctity of Rural Life: Nobility, Protestantism, and Nazism in Weimar Prussia* (Oxford: Oxford University Press, 1995).

Bärsch, Claus-Ekkehard, *Die politische Religion des Nationalsozialismus: Die religiöse Dimension der NS-Ideologie in den Schriften von Dietrich Eckart, Joseph Goebbels, Alfred Rosenberg und Adolf Hitler* (Munich: Wilhelm Fink Verlag, 1998).

Bel, Germà, "Against the Mainstream: Nazi Privatization in 1930s Germany," *Economic History Review*, Vol. 63, No. 1 (2010), pp. 34–55.

Bembridge, Steven, "Jesus as a Cultural Weapon in the Work of Jack London," *Studies in American Naturalism*, Vol. 10, No. 1 (2015), pp. 22–40.

244 / Bibliography

Bergen, Doris L., *Twisted Cross: The German Christian Movement in the Third Reich* (Chapel Hill, NC: University of North Carolina Press, 1996).

Besier, Gerhard, "The Churches and National Socialism between Hitler's Religious Equivocation and Rosenberg's Myth: Ambiguities, Fascination and Self-Assertion," in Martin Nykvist, David Gudmundsson, and Alexander Maurits (eds.), *Classics in Northern European Church History over 500 Years: Essays in Honour of Anders Jarlert* (Frankfurt am Main: Peter Lang, 2017), pp. 153–198.

Bialas, Wolfgang, "The Eternal Voice of the Blood: Racial Science and Nazi Ethics," in Anton Weiss-Wendt and Rory Yeomans (eds.), *Racial Science in Hitler's New Europe 1938–1945* (Lincoln, NE: University of Nebraska Press, 2013).

Bialas, Wolfgang and Fritze, Lothar, *Nazi Ideology and Ethics* (Newcastle upon Tyne: Cambridge Scholars Publishing, 2014).

Blüger, Thomas, "Following the Virgin Mary through Auschwitz: Marian Dogmatic Theology at the Time of the Shoah," *Holocaust Studies: A Journal of Culture and History*, Vol. 14, No. 3 (2008), pp. 1–24.

Brechtken, Magnus, *Albert Speer: Eine deutsche Karriere* (Munich: Siedler, 2017).

Brechtken, Magnus and Becker, Maximilian, "Die Edition der Reden Adolf Hitlers von 1933 bis 1945," *Vierteljahrshefte für Zeitgeschichte*, Vol. 67, No. 1 (2019), pp. 147–163.

Browning, Christopher R., *The Origins of the Final Solution: The Evolution of Nazi Jewish Policy, September 1939–March 1942*. With contributions by Jürgen Matthäus (Lincoln, NE: University of Nebraska Press, 2004).

Bucher, Rainer, "Hitlers Theologie? Einige Voraussetzungen," in Lucia Scherzberg (ed.), *Theologie und Vergangenheitsbewältigung: Eine kritische Bestandsaufnahme im interdiziplinären Vergleich* (Munich: Ferdinand Schöningh, 2005).

Bucher, R., *Hitlers Theologie* (Würzburg: Echter Verlag, 2008).

Bucher, R., *Hitler's Theology: A Study in Political Religion*. Translated by Rebecca Pohl (London: Continuum, 2011).

Bullock, Alan, *Hitler: A Study in Tyranny* (London: Odhams Press, 1952).

Burleigh, Michael, *The Third Reich: A New History* (New York: Hill and Wang, 2000).

Carrier, Richard, "Hitler's Table Talk: Troubling Finds," *German Studies Review*, Vol. 26, No. 3 (2003), pp. 561–576.

Carrier, R., *On the Historicity of Jesus: Why We Might Have Reason for Doubt* (Sheffield, UK: Phoenix Press, 2014).

245 / Bibliography

Carroll, James, *Constantine's Sword: The Church and the Jews. A History* (Boston, MA: Houghton Mifflin Company, 2001).

Carter, Guy C., "Martin Luther in the Third Reich: Recent Research on Luther as Iconic Force in Hitler's Germany," *Seminary Ridge Review*, Vol. 12, No. 1 (2009), pp. 42–62.

Chamberlain, Houston Stewart, *Die Grundlagen des neunzehnten Jahrhunderts I. Hälfte* (Munich: Verlagsanstalt F. Brückmann A.–G., 1899).

Chapoutot, Johann, "From Humanism to Nazism: Antiquity in the Work of Houston Stewart Chamberlain," *Miranda*, No. 11 (2015), https://journals .openedition.org/miranda/6680.

Chapoutot, J., *La révolution culturelle nazie* (Paris: Gallimard, 2017).

Chappel, James, *Catholic Modern: The Challenge of Totalitarianism and the Remaking of the Church* (Cambridge, MA: Harvard University Press, 2018).

Clemens, Detlev and Purcell, Brendan (eds.) and (trans.), *The Collected Works of Erich Voegelin. Vol. XXXI: Hitler and the Germans* (Columbia, MI: University of Missouri Press, 1999).

Confino, Alon, "Why Did the Nazis Burn the Hebrew Bible? Nazi Germany, Representations of the Past, and the Holocaust," *The Journal of Modern History*, Vol. 84, No. 2 (2012), pp. 369–400.

Confino, A., *A World Without Jews: The Nazi Imagination from Persecution to Genocide* (New Haven, CT: Yale University Press, 2014).

Deines, Roland, "Jesus der Galiläer: Traditionsgeschichte und Genese eines antisemitischen Konstrukts bei Walter Grundmann," in Roland Deines, Volker Leppin, and Karl-Wilhelm Niebuhr (eds.), *Walter Grundmann: Ein Neutestamentler in Dritten Reich* (Leipzig: Evangelische Verlagsanstalt, 2007), pp. 43–131.

Dennis, David B., *Inhumanities: Nazi Interpretations of Western Culture* (Cambridge: Cambridge University Press, 2012).

Dierker, Wolfgang, *Himmlers Glaubenskrieger: Der Sicherheitsdienst der SS und seine Religionspolitik 1933–1945* (Paderborn: Ferdinand Schöningh, 2003).

Dietrich, Otto, *12 Jahre mit Hitler* (Munich: Isar Verlag, 1955).

Dinter, Arthur, *Die Sünde wider das Blut: Ein Zeitroman* (Leipzig: Verlag Matthes und Thost, 1920).

Domarus, Max (ed.), *Hitler: Reden und Proklamationen 1932–1945. Kommentiert von einem deutschen Zeitgenossen. Band I–IV, 1932–1945* (Munich: Süddeutscher Verlag, 1965).

Drexler, Anton, *Mein politisches Erwachen: Aus dem tagebuch eines deutschen sozialistischen Arbeiters* (Munich: Deutscher Volksverlag, 1937, originally published in 1919).

246 / Bibliography

Eberle, Henrik and Uhl, Matthias (eds.), *Das Buch Hitler: Geheimdossier des NKWD für Josef W. Stalin, zusammengestellt aufgrund der Verhörprotokolle des Persönlichen Adjutanten Hitlers, Otto Günsche, und des Kammerdieners Heinz Linge, Moskau 1948/49* (Bergisch Gladbach: Gustav Lübbe Verlag, 2005).

Eckart, Dietrich, *Der Bolschewismus von Moses bis Lenin: Zweigespräch zwischen Adolf Hitler und mir* (Munich: Franz Eher Verlag, 1924).

Erhman, Bart D., *Whose Word Is It? The Story behind Who Changed the Bible and Why* (London: Continuum, 2008).

Ehrman, B. D., *Forged: Writing in the Name of God – Why the Bible Writers Are Not Who We Think They Are* (New York: Harper One, 2011).

Ericksen, Robert P., *Theologians under Hitler: Gerhard Kittel, Paul Althaus, and Emanuel Hirsch* (New Haven, CT: Yale University Press, 1985).

Ericksen, Robert P. and Heschel, Susannah, "The German Churches and the Holocaust," in Dan Stone (ed.), *Historiography of the Holocaust* (London: Palgrave Macmillan, 2004), pp. 296–318.

Evans, Richard J., *The Third Reich in Power 1933–1939* (London: Allen Lane, 2005).

Fenske, Wolfgang, *Wie Jesus zum "Arier" wurde: Auswirkungen der Entjudaisierung Christi im 19. und zu Beginn des 20. Jahrhunderts* (Darmstadt: Wissenschaftliche Buchgesellschaft, 2005).

Fest, Joachim, *Hitler: Eine Biographie* (Berlin: Propyläen, 1973).

Fest, J., *Hitler: Eine Biographie* (Berlin: Propyläen, 2008).

Fischer, Klaus P., *Nazi Germany: A New History* (London: Constable, 1995).

Fleischmann, Peter, *Hitler als Häftling in Landsberg am Lech 1923/24: Der Gefangenen-Personalakt Hitler nebst weiteren Quellen aus der Schutzhaft-, Untersuchungshaft-, und Festungshaftanstalt* (Neustadt: Verlag PH. C. W. Schmidt, 2015).

François, Stephane, *Nazi Occultism: Between the SS and Esotericism* (London: Routledge, 2023).

Frank, Hans, *Im Angesicht des Galgens: Deutung Hitlers und seiner Zeit auf Grund eigener Erlebnisse und Erkenntnisse* (Munich: Friedrich Alfred Beck Verlag, 1953).

Freeman, Charles, *A New History of Early Christianity* (New Haven, CT: Yale University Press, 2009).

Friedländer, Saul, *Nazi Germany and the Jews*. Vol. I: *The Years of Persecution, 1933–1939* (New York: Harper Perennial, 1997).

Gärtner, Sandro, *Die Synthese des Nationalen und des Sozialen bei Friedrich Naumann* (Studienarbeit GRIN, 2001).

247 / Bibliography

Genoud, François, *Libres propos sur la Guerre et la Paix: Recueillis sur l'ordre de Martin Bormann. Préface de Robert d'Harcourt de l'Academie française. Version française de François Genoud.* Vol. I (Paris: Flammarion, 1952).

Genoud, F., *Libres propos sur la Guerre et la Paix. Recueillis sur l'ordre de Martin Bormann. Préface de Robert d'Harcourt de l'Academie française. Version française de François Genoud.* Vol. II (Paris: Flammarion, 1954).

Gentile, Emilio, *Contro Cesare: Cristianesimo e totalitarismo nell'epoca dei fascism* (Milan: Feltrinelli Editori, 2010).

Gerdmar, Anders, *Roots of Theological Anti-Semitism: German Biblical Interpretation and the Jews, from Herder and Semler to Kittel and Bultmann* (Leiden: Brill, 2009).

Gerlach, Christian, *Der Mord an den europäischen Juden: Ursachen, Ereignisse, Dimensionen* (Munich: C. H. Beck, 2017).

Glover, Jonathan, *Humanity: A Moral History of the Twentieth Century* (London: Jonathan Cape, 1999).

Goebbels, Joseph, *Goebbels Reden 1932–1939. Band I & II. Herausgegeben von Helmut Heiber* (Munich: Wilhelm Heyne Verlag, 1971).

Goebbels, J., *Die Tagebücher von Joseph Goebbels 1924–1945. Im Auftrag des Instituts für Zeitgeschichte und mit Unterstützung des Staatlichen Archivdienstes Rußlands. Herausgegeben von Elke Frölich. Band I–IV & Band I–XV* (Munich: K. G. Saur, 1987–1995).

Goeschel, Christian, *Mussolini and Hitler: The Forging of the Fascist Alliance* (New Haven, CT: Yale University Press, 2018).

Goldhagen, Daniel Jonah, *Hitler's Willing Executioners: Ordinary Germans and the Holocaust* (New York: Alfred A. Knopf, 1996).

Görtemaker, Heike B., *Eva Braun: Leben mit Hitler* (Munich: C. H. Beck, 2010).

Grabner-Haider, Anton, *Hitlers Theologie des Todes* (Kevelaer: Topos, 2009).

Grundsätzliches Programm der Nationalsozialistischen Deutschen Arbeiter-Partei, http://jgsaufgab.de/intranet2/geschichte/geschichte/natsoz/programm_nsdap_20.htm.

Gugenberger, Eduard, *Hitlers Visionäre: Die okkulten Wegbereiter des Dritten Reichs* (Vienna: Ueberreuter, 2000).

Gutteridge, Richard, *Open Thy Mouth for the Dumb! The German Evangelical Church and the Jews, 1879–1950* (Oxford: Basil Blackwell, 1976).

Hamann, Brigitte, *Hitlers Wien: Lehrjahre eines Diktators* (Munich: Piper, 1996).

Hamann, B., *Winifred Wagner oder Hitlers Bayreuth* (Munich: Piper Verlag, 2002).

Hastings, Derek, *Catholicism and the Roots of Nazism: Religious Identity and National Socialism* (Oxford: Oxford University Press, 2010).

248 / Bibliography

Hauptmann, Hans, *Jesus der Arier: Ein Heldenleben* (Munich: Deutscher Volksverlag Dr. E. Boepple, 1930).

Head, Peter, "The Nazi Quest for an Aryan Jesus," *Journal for the Study of the Historical Jesus*, Vol. 2, No. 1 (2004), pp. 55–89.

Head, P., "Susannah Heschel's *The Aryan Jesus*: A Response," *Journal for the Study of the New Testament*, Vol. 32, No. 4 (2010), pp. 421–430.

Heer, Friedrich, *Der Glaube des Adolf Hitler: Anatomie einer politischen Religiosität* (Munich: Bechtle Verlag, 1968).

Heiden, Konrad, *Adolf Hitler: Das Zeitalter der Verantwortungslosigkeit. Eine Biographie.* Vol. I (Zurich: Europa Verlag, 1936).

Heiden, K., *Adolf Hitler: Ein Mann gegen Europa. Eine Biographie.* Vol. II (Zurich: Europa Verlag, 1937).

Herbst, Ludolf, *Hitlers Charisma: Die Erfindung eines deutschen Messias* (Frankfurt am Main: S. Fischer Verlag, 2010).

Herf, Jeffrey, *The Jewish Enemy: Nazi Propaganda during World War II and the Holocaust* (Cambridge, MA: The Belknap Press of Harvard University Press, 2006).

Hermle, Siegfried, "Die antijudische NS-Politik als Herausforderung des Protestantismus," in Thomas Brechenmacher and Harry Oelke (eds.), *Die Kirchen und die Verbrechen im nationalsozialistischen Staat* (Göttingen: Wallstein Verlag, 2011), pp. 175–200.

Heschel, Susannah, "Reading Jesus as a Nazi," in Tod Linafelt (ed.), *A Shadow of Glory: Reading the New Testament after the Holocaust* (New York: Routledge, 2002), pp. 27–41.

Heschel, S., *The Aryan Jesus: Christian Theologians and the Bible in Nazi Germany* (Princeton, NJ: Princeton University Press, 2008).

Heschel, S., "Confronting the Past: Post-1945 German Protestant Theology and the Fate of the Jews," in Jonathan Frankel and Ezra Mendelsohn (eds.), *The Protestant-Jewish Conundrum: Studies in Contemporary Jewry*, Vol. XXIV (Oxford: Oxford University Press, 2010), pp. 46–70.

Heschel, S., "Jewish Studies in the Third Reich: A Brief Glance at Viktor Christian and Kurt Schubert," *Review of Rabbinic Judaism*, Vol. 13 No. 2 (2010), pp. 236–249.

Heschel, S., "Historiography of Antisemitism versus Anti-Judaism: A Response to Robert Morgan," *Journal for the Study of the New Testament*, Vol. 33, No. 3 (2011), pp. 257–279.

Heschel, S., "Being Adolf Hitler: *Mein Kampf* as Anti-Semitic Bildungsroman," in John J. Michalczyk, Michael S. Bryant, and Susan A. Michalczyk (eds.), *Hitler's Mein Kampf and the Holocaust: A Prelude to Genocide* (London: Bloomsbury Academic, 2022), pp. 185–196.

249 / Bibliography

Hesemann, Michael, *Hitlers Religion: Die fatale Heilslehre des Nationalsozialismus* (Munich: Pattloch Verlag, 2004).

Heß, Ilse (ed.), *Gefangener des Friedens: Neue Briefe aus Spandau* (Leoni am Starnberger See: Druffel Verlag, 1955).

Heydecker, Joe J., *Das Hitler-Bild: Die Erinnerungen des Heinrich Hoffmann* (St. Pölten: Residenz Verlag, 2008).

Hitler, Adolf, *Hitlers zweites Buch: Ein Dokument aus dem Jahr 1928. Eingeleitet und kommentiert von Gerhard L. Weinberg. Mit einem Geleitwort von Hans Rothfels* (Stuttgart: Deutsche Verlags-Anstalt, 1961).

Hitler, A., *Hitler, Mein Kampf: Eine kritische Edition. Band I & II. Herausgegeben von Christian Hartmann, Thomas Vordermayer, Othmar Plöckinger, und Roman Töppel* (Munich: Institut für Zeitgeschichte, 2016).

Hitler, A., *Hitler: Reden, Schriften, Anordnungen. Februar 1925 bis Januar 1933 Band I: Die Wiedergründung der NSDAP Februar 1925–Juni 1926. Herausgegeben und kommentiert von Clemens Vollnhals* (Munich: K. G. Saur, 1992).

Hitler, A., *Hitler. Reden, Schriften, Anordnungen. Februar 1925 bis Januar 1933. Band II: Vom Weimarer Parteitag bis zur Reichstagswahl Juli 1926–Mai 1928. Teil 1: Juli 1926–Juli 1927. Herausgegeben und kommentiert von Bärbel Dusik* (Munich: K. G. Saur, 1992).

Hitler, A., *Hitler: Reden, Schriften, Anordnungen. Februar 1925 bis Januar 1933. Band II: Vom Weimarer Parteitag bis zur Reichstagswahl Juli 1926–Mai 1928. Teil 2: August 1927–Mai 1928. Herausgegeben und kommentiert von Bärbel Dusik* (Munich: K. G. Saur, 1992).

Hitler, A., *Hitler: Reden, Schriften, Anordnungen. Februar 1925 bis Januar 1933. Herausgegeben vom Institut für Zeitgeschichte. Band III: Zwischen den Reichstagswahlen Juli 1928–September 1930. Teil 1: Juli 1928–Februar 1929. Herausgegeben und kommentiert von Bärbel Dusik und Klaus A. Lankheit unter Mitwirkung von Christian Hartmann* (Munich: K. G. Saur, 1994).

Hitler, A., *Hitler: Reden, Schriften, Anordnungen. Februar 1925 bis Januar 1933. Herausgegeben vom Institut für Zeitgeschichte. Band III: Zwischen den Reichstagswahlen Juli 1928–September 1930. Teil 2: März 1929–Dezember 1929. Herausgegeben und kommentiert von Klaus A. Lankheit* (Munich: K. G. Saur, 1994).

Hitler, A., *Hitler: Reden, Schriften, Anordnungen. Februar 1925 bis Januar 1933. Herausgegeben vom Institut für Zeitgeschichte. Band III. Zwischen den Reichstagswahlen Juli 1928–September 1930. Teil 3: Januar 1930–September 1930. Herausgegeben und kommentiert von Christian Hartmann* (Munich: K. G. Saur, 1995).

250 / Bibliography

Hitler's Table Talk 1941–1944: His Private Conversations. With an introductory essay on the mind of Adolf Hitler by H. R. Trevor-Roper) (London: Weidenfeld & Nicolson, 1953).

Jäckel, Eberhard (ed.), *Hitler: Sämtliche Aufzeichnungen 1905–1924* (Stuttgart: Deutsche Verlags-Anstalt, 1980).

Jäckel, E., *Hitlers Weltanschauung: Entwurf einer Herrschaft*. New revised ed. (Stuttgart: Deutsche Verlags-Anstalt, 1991).

Jetzinger, Franz, *Hitlers Jugend: Phantasien, Lügen – und die Wahrheit* (Vienna: Europa Verlag, 1956).

Joachimsthaler, Anton, *Korrektur einer Biographie: Adolf Hitler 1908–1920* (Munich: Herbig, 1989).

Joachimsthaler, A., *Hitlers Weg begann in München 1919–1923* (Munich: Herbig Verlag, 2000).

Jung, Rudolf, *Der nationale Sozialismus: seine Grundlagen, sein Werdegang und seine Ziele*, 3rd ed. (Munich: Deutscher Volksverlag, Dr. E. Boepple, 1922).

Junginger, Horst, "From Buddha to Adolf Hitler: Walther Wüst and the Aryan Tradition," in Horst Junginger (ed.), *The Study of Religion under the Impact of Fascism* (Leiden: Brill, 2008), pp. 107–177.

Kedar, Asaf, "National Socialism before Nazism: Friedrich Naumann and Theodor Fritsch, 1890–1914," PhD diss. (University of California, Berkeley, 2010).

Kellerhoff, Sven Felix, *Die NSDAP: Eine Partei und ihre Mitglieder* (Stuttgart: Klett-Cotta, 2017).

Kellerhoff, S. F., "So feierte Adolf Hitler Weihnachten," *Die Welt*, December 25, 2018, www.welt.de/geschichte/zweiter-weltkrieg/article185955824/ Nationalsozialismus-So-feierte-Adolf-Hitler-Weihnachten.htm.

Kelley, Shawn, *Racializing Jesus: Race, Ideology and the Formation of Modern Biblical Scholarship* (London: Routledge, 2002).

Kellogg, Michael, *The Russian Roots of Nazism: White Émigrés and the Making of National Socialism 1917–1945* (Cambridge: Cambridge University Press, 2005).

Kershaw, Ian, *Hitler 1889–1936: Hubris* (New York: W. W. Norton & Company, 1998).

Kershaw, I., *Hitler 1936–45: Nemesis* (London: Allen Lane, 2000).

Kershaw, I., *Hitler, the Germans, and the Final Solution* (New Haven, CT: Yale University Press, 2008).

Kertzer, David I., *The Popes against the Jews: The Vatican's Role in the Rise of Modern Anti-Semitism* (New York: Alfred A. Knopf, 2001).

Klee, Ernst, *"Die SA Jesu Christi": Die Kirche im Banne Hitlers* (Frankfurt am Main: Fischer, 1989).

251 / Bibliography

Kleeberg, Bernhard, *Theophysis: Ernst Haeckels Philosophie des Naturganzen* (Cologne: Böhlau Verlag, 2005).

Klemperer, Victor, *Ich will Zeugnis ablegen bis zum letzten: Tagebücher 1933–1941. Herausgegeben von Walter Nowojski unter Mitarbeit von Hadwig Klemperer Band I–II* (Berlin: Aufbau Verlag, 1995).

Koehne, Samuel, "The Racial Yardstick: 'Ethnotheism' and Official Nazi Views on Religion," *German Studies Review*, Vol. 37, No. 3 (2014), pp. 575–596.

Koehne, S., "Were the National Socialists a Völkisch Party? Paganism, Christianity, and the Nazi Christmas," *Central European History*, Vol. 47, No. 4 (2014), pp. 760–790.

Koehne, S., "Religion in the Early Nazi Milieu: Towards a Greater Understanding of 'Racist Culture'," *Journal of Contemporary History*, Vol. 53, No. 4 (2018), pp. 667–691.

Koerber, Adolf-Victor von (ed.), *Adolf Hitler: Sein Leben und seine Reden* (Munich: Deutscher Volksverlag, 1923).

Koonz, Claudia, *The Nazi Conscience* (Cambridge, MA: The Belknap Press of Harvard University Press, 2003).

Kuehnelt-Leddin, Erik R. von, "The Bohemian Background of German National Socialism: The D.A.P., D.N.S.A.P., and N.S.D.A.P.," *Journal of the History of Ideas*, Vol. 9, No. 3 (1948), pp. 339–371.

Kurlander, Eric, *Hitler's Monsters: A Supernatural History of the Third Reich* (New Haven, CT: Yale University Press, 2017).

Landes, Richard, *Heaven on Earth: The Varieties of the Millennial Experience* (Oxford: Oxford University Press, 2011).

Longerich, Peter, *Hitler: Biographie* (Munich: Siedler, 2015).

Longo, James, *Hitler and the Habsburgs: The Vendetta against the Austrian Royals* (New York: Diversion Books, 2018).

Lorenz, Elisabeth, *Ein Jesusbild im Horizont des Nationalsozialismus: Studien zum Neuen Testament des "Instituts zur Erforschung und Beseitigung des jüdischen Einflusses auf das deutsche kirchliche Leben'"* (Tübingen: Mohr Siebeck, 2017).

Lüdicke, Lars, *Hitlers Weltanschauung: Von "Mein Kampf" bis zum "Nero-Befehl"* (Paderborn: Ferdinand Schöningh, 2016).

Maser, Werner, *Adolf Hitler: Legende, Mythos, Wirklichkeit*, 12th ed. (Munich: Bechtle Verlag, 1989).

McDonough, Frank, *The Hitler Years: Triumph 1933–1939* (London: Head of Zeus, 2019).

McGrath, Alister E., *Theology: The Basics*, 2nd ed. (Oxford: Blackwell Publishing, 2008).

252 / Bibliography

Menke, Martin, "Catholic Authority and the Holocaust," in John J. Michalczyk, Michael S. Bryant, and Susan A. Michalczyk (eds.), *Hitler's Mein Kampf and the Holocaust: A Prelude to Genocide* (London: Bloomsbury Academic, 2022), pp. 197–212.

Michalka, Wolfgang (ed.), *Deutsche Geschichte 1933–1945: Dokumente zur Innen- und Außenpolitik* (Frankfurt am Main: Fischer Taschenbuch Verlag, 1996).

Monologe im Führerhauptquartier 1941–1944. Die Aufzeichnungen Heinrich Heims herausgegeben von Werner Jochmann (Hamburg: Albrecht Knaus, 1980).

Nilsson, Mikael, "Hugh Trevor-Roper and the English Editions of *Hitler's Table Talk* and *Testament*," *Journal of Contemporary History*, Vol. 51, No. 4 (2015), pp. 788–812.

Nilsson, M., "Constructing a Pseudo-Hitler? The Question of the Authenticity of *Hitlers politisches Testament*," *European Review of History–Revue Européenne d'histoire*, Vol. 26, No. 5 (2018), pp. 871–891.

Nilsson, M., "Pinsamt: Förfalskade dokument om Führern tas för sanna i Svante Nordins bok'Hitlers München'," *Dagens Nyheter*, June 4, 2018.

Nilsson, M., "Hitler Redivivus: 'Hitlers Tischgespräche' and 'Monologe im Führerhauptquartier': eine kritische Untersuchung," *Vierteljahrshefte für Zeitgeschichte*, Vol. 67, No. 1 (2019), pp. 105–146.

Nilsson, M., *Hitler Redux: The Incredible History of Hitler's So-Called Table Talks* (London: Routledge, 2021).

Pauer-Studer, Herlinde and Velleman, J. David, *"Weil ich nun mal ein Gerechtigkeitsfanatiker bin": Der Fall des SS-Richters Konrad Morgen* (Berlin: Suhrkamp Verlag, 2017).

Petropoulos, Jonathan, *Artists under Hitler: Collaboration and Survival in Nazi Germany* (New Haven, CT: Yale University Press, 2014).

Picker, Henry, *Hitlers Tischgespräche im Führerhauptquartier 1941–42. Im Auftrage des Deutschen Instituts für Geschichte der nationalsozialistischen Zeit geordnet, eingeleitet und veröffentlicht von Gerhard Ritter* (Bonn: Athenäum Verlag, 1951).

Pinker, Steven, *The Better Angels of Our Nature: The Decline of Violence in History and Its Causes* (London: Allen Lane, 2011).

Piotrowski, Stanislaw (ed.), *Hans Franks Tagebuch* (Warsaw: Polnischer Verlag der Wissenschaften, 1963).

Piper, Ernst, "Steigmann-Gall, *The Holy Reich*," *Journal of Contemporary History*, Vol. 42, No. 1 (2007), pp. 47–57.

Plewnia, Margarete, *Auf dem Weg zu Hitler: Der "völkische" Publizist Dietrich Eckart* (Bremen: Schünemann Universitätsverlag, 1970).

253 / Bibliography

Plöckinger, Othmar, *Geschichte eines Buches: Adolf Hitlers "Mein Kampf" 1922–1945. Eine Veröffentlichung des Instituts für Zeitgeschichte.* 2nd updated ed. (Munich: Oldenburg Verlag, 2011).

Plöckinger, O., *Unter Soldaten und Agitatoren: Hitlers prägende Jahre im deutschen Militär 1918–1920* (Paderborn: Ferdinand Schöningh, 2013).

Plöckinger, O. (ed.), *Quellen und Dokumente zur Geschichte von "Mein Kampf" 1924–1945* (Stuttgart: Franz Steiner Verlag, 2016).

Pois, Robert A., *National Socialism and the Religion of Nature* (New York: St. Martin's, 1986).

Price, Ward, *I Know These Dictators* (London: Harrap, 1937).

Pyta, Wolfram, *Hitler: Der Künstler als Politiker und Feldherr. Eine Herrschaftanalyse* (Munich: Siedler Verlag, 2015).

Rauschning, Hermann, *Die Revolution des Nihilismus: Kulisse und Werklichkeit im Dritten Reich* (Zurich: Europa Verlag, 1938).

Redles, David, *Hitler's Millennial Reich: Apocalyptic Belief and the Search for Salvation* (New York: New York University Press, 2005).

Redles, D., "The Apocalypse of Adolf Hitler: *Mein Kampf* and the Eschatological Origins of the Holocaust," in John J. Michalczyk, Michael S. Bryant, and Susan A. Michalczyk (eds.), *Hitler's Mein Kampf and the Holocaust: A Prelude to Genocide* (London: Bloomsbury Academic, 2022), pp. 213–233.

Reichelt, Werner, *Das braune Evangelium: Hitler und die NS-Liturgie* (Wuppertal: Peter Hammer Verlag, 1990).

Reuth, Ralph George, *Hitler: Eine politische Biographie* (Munich: Piper, 2003).

Rhodes, James M., *The Hitler Movement: A Modern Millenarian Revolution* (Stanford, CA: Stanford University Press, 1980).

Rißmann, Michael, *Hitlers Gott: Vorsehungsglaube und Sendungsbewusstsein des deutschen Diktators* (Zurich: Pendo, 2001).

Robb, David, "Count Anton Graf von Arco auf Valley: The Assassin who Sparked the Rise of the Nazi Party," *Crime Magazine*, October 24, 2013, www.crimemagazine.com/count-anton-graf-von-arco-auf-valley-assassin-who-sparked-rise-nazi-party.

Roos, Daniel, *Julius Streicher und "Der Stürmer" 1923–1945* (Paderborn: Ferdinand Schöningh, 2014).

Rose, Olaf (ed.), *Julius Schaub – In Hitlers Schatten: Erinnerungen und Aufzeichnungen des persönlichen Adjutanten und Vertrauten Julius Schaub 1925–1945* (Stegen/Ammersee: Druffel & Vowinckel Verlag, 2005).

Rosenbaum, Ron, *Explaining Hitler: The Search for the Origins of His Evil* (London: Papermac, 1999).

254 / Bibliography

Rosenberg, Alfred, *Dietrich Eckart. Ein Vermächtnis. Herausgegeben und eingeleitet von Alfred Rosenberg* (München: Franz Eher Verlag, 1928).

Rosenberg, A., *Der Mythos des 20 Jahrhunderts: Eine Wertung der seelichgeistigen Gestaltenkämpfe unserer Zeit,* 3rd ed. (Munich: Hoheneichen-Verlag, 1934).

Rosenberg, A., *Alfred Rosenberg: Die Tagebücher von 1934 bis 1944. Herausgegeben und kommentiert von Jürgen Matthäus und Frank Bajohr* (Frankfurt am Main: S. Fischer, 2015).

Rubenstein, Richard L., *The Cunning of History: Mass Death and the American Future* (Baltimore, MD: Johns Hopkins University Press, 1992).

Rudolf Heß: Briefe 1908–1933. Herausgegeben von Wolf Rüdiger Heß. Mit einer Einführung und Kommentaren von Dirk Bavendamm (Munich: Langen Müller, 1987).

Ruppert, Wolfgang (ed.), *Künstler im Nationalsozialismus: Die "deutsche Kunst," die Kunstpolitik und die Berliner Kunsthochschule* (Cologne: Böhlau Verlag, 2015).

Ruppert, W., "Künstler im Nationalsozialismus: Künstlerindividuum, Kunstpolitik und die Berliner Kunsthochschule," in Wolfgang Ruppert (ed.), *Künstler im Nationalsozialismus: Die "deutsche Kunst," die Kunstpolitik und die Berliner Kunsthochschule* (Cologne: Böhlau Verlag, 2015).

Ryback, Timothy W., *Hitler's Private Library: The Books That Shaped His Life* (New York: Alfred A. Knopf, 2008).

Sarkowicz, Hans, *Hitlers Künstler: Die Kultur im Dienst des Nationalsozialismus* (Frankfurt am Main: Insel Verlag, 2004).

Schmidt, Matthias, *Albert Speer: Das Ende eines Mythos. Die Aufdeckung seiner Geschichtsverfälschung. Speers wahre Rolle im Dritten Reich* (Bern: Schertz, 1982).

Schneider, Wolfgang, *Adolf Hitler: Politischer Zauberlehrling Mussolinis* (Oldenburg: De Gruyter, 2017).

Scholder, Klaus, *The Churches and the Third Reich. Vol. I: Preliminary History and the Time of Illusions 1918–1934* (Eugene, OR: Wipf & Stock, 1988).

Schreiber, Gerhard, *Hitler Interpretationen 1923–1983: Ergebnisse, Methoden und Probleme der Forschung* (Darmstadt: Wissenschaftliche Buchgesellschaft, 1984).

Sebottendorff, Rudolf von, *Bevor Hitler kam: Urkundliches aus der Frühzeit der nationalsozialistischen Bewegung* (Munich: Deukula-Verlag Graffinger & Co., 1933).

Simms, Brendan, *Hitler: Only the World Was Enough* (London: Allen Lane, 2019).

Snyder, Timothy, *Bloodlands: Europe between Hitler and Stalin* (New York: Basic Books, 2010).

255 / Bibliography

Speer, Albert, *Erinnerungen* (Berlin: Propyläen, 1969).

Speer, A., *Inside the Third Reich: Memoirs by Albert Speer* (London: Weidenfeld and Nicolson, 1970).

Speer, A., *Spandauer Tagebücher* (Berlin: Propyläen, 1975).

Speer, A., *Der Sklavenstaat: Meine Auseinandersetzungen mit der SS* (Stuttgart: Deutsche Verlags-Anstalt, 1981).

Spicer, Kevin P., *Hitler's Priests: Catholic Clergy and National Socialism* (DeKalb, IA: Northern Illinois University Press, 2008).

Steigmann-Gall, Richard, *The Holy Reich: Nazi Conceptions of Christianity, 1919–1945* (Cambridge: Cambridge University Press, 2003).

Steigmann-Gall, R., "Was National Socialism a Political Religion or a Religious Politics?" in Michael Geyer and Hartmut Lehmann (eds.), *Religion und Nation, Nation und Religion: Beiträge zu einer unbewältigten Geschichte* (Göttingen: Wallstein Verlag, 2004), pp. 387–408.

Steigmann-Gall, R., "Christianity and the Nazi Movement: A Response," *Journal of Contemporary History*, Vol. 42, No. 2 (2007), pp. 185–211.

Steigmann-Gall, R., "Old Wine in New Bottles? Religion and Race in Nazi Antisemitsm," in Kevin P. Spicer (ed.), *Antisemitism, Christian Ambivalence, and the Holocaust* (Bloomington, IN: Indiana University Press, 2007), pp. 289–304.

Strohm, Harald, *Die Gnosis und der Nationalsozialismus* (Frankfurt am Main: Suhrkamp Verlag, 1973).

Summerfield, Giovanna and Downward, Lisa, *New Perspectives on the European Bildungsroman* (London: Continuum, 2010).

Taylor, Cory, *How Hitler was Made: Germany and the Rise of the Perfect Nazi* (Amherst, NY: Prometheus Books, 2018).

Thamer, Hans-Ulrich, *Adolf Hitler: Biographie eines Diktators* (Munich: C. H. Beck, 2018).

Toland, John, *Adolf Hitler* (New York: Doubleday & Company, 1976).

Tomberg, Friedrich, *Das Christentum in Hitlers Weltanschauung* (Munich: Wilhelm Fink Verlag, 2012).

Trevor-Roper, Hugh, *The Last Days of Hitler* (London: Macmillan & Co., 1947).

Trommer, Isabell, *Rechtfertigung und Entlassung: Albert Speer in der Bundesrepublik* (Frankfurt: Campus Verlag, 2016).

Tyrell, Albrecht, *Vom "Trommler" zum "Führer": Der Wandel von Hitlers Selbstverständnis zwischen 1919 und 1924 und die Entwicklung der NSDAP* (Munich: Wilhelm Fink Verlag, 1975).

Ullrich, Volker, *Adolf Hitler: Biographie. Band I: Die Jahre des Aufstiegs* (Frankfurt am Main: S. Fischer Verlag, 2013).

256 / Bibliography

Ullrich, V., *Adolf Hitler: Biographie. Band II: Die Jahre des Untergangs* (Frankfurt am Main: S. Fischer Verlag, 2018).

Varshizky, Amit, "Alfred Rosenberg: The Nazi *Weltanschauung* as Modern Gnosis," *Politics, Religion & Ideology*, Vol. 13, No. 3, (2012), pp. 311–331.

Varshizky, A., "Between Science and Racial Metaphysics: Fritz Lenz and Racial Anthropology in Interwar Germany," *Intellectual History Review*, Vol. 27, No. 2 (2017), pp. 247–272.

Varshizky, A., "In Search of the 'Whole Man': Soul-Man-World in the National Socialist *Weltanschauung*," *Dapim: Studies on the Holocaust*, Vol. 31, No. 3 (2017), pp. 200–226.

Varshizky, A., "The Metaphysics of Race: Revisiting Nazism and Religion," *Central European History*, Vol. 52, No. 2 (2019), pp. 252–288.

Varshizky, A., "Non-Mechanistic Explanatory Styles in Interwar German Racial Theory: A Comparison of Hans F. K. Günther and Ludwig Ferdinand Clauß," in Sabine Hildebrandt, Mirriam Offer, and Michael Grodin (eds.), *Medicine and the Holocaust: New Studies on Victims, Perpetrators and Legacies for the 21st Century* (New York: Berghahn Books, 2019), pp. 21–43.

Voegelin, Eric, "Descent into the Ecclesiastical Abyss: The Catholic Church," in *The Collected Works of Eric Voegelin*. Vol. XXXI: *Hitler and the Germans*. Translated, edited, and with an introduction by Detlev Clemens and Brendan Purcell (Columbia, MI: University of Missouri Press, 1999).

Wagener, Otto, *Hitler aus nächster Nähe: Aufzeichnungen eines Vertrauten 1929–1932*. Edited by H. A. Turner, Jr. (Frankfurt am Main: Verlag Ullstein, 1978).

Weber, Thomas, *Hitler's First War: Adolf Hitler, the Men of the List Regiment, and the First World War* (Oxford: Oxford University Press, 2010).

Weber, T., *Wie Adolf Hitler zum Nazi wurde: Vom unpolitischen Soldaten zum Autor von "Mein Kampf"* (Berlin: Propyläen, 2016).

Weber, T., *Becoming Hitler: The Making of a Nazi* (Oxford: Oxford University Press, 2017).

Weikart, Richard, *From Darwin to Hitler: Evolutionary Ethics, Eugenics and Racism in Germany* (Houndmills, UK: Palgrave Macmillan, 2004).

Weikart, R., *Hitler's Religion: The Twisted Beliefs that Drove the Third Reich* (Washington, DC: Regnery History, 2016).

"Wer schreib 'Sein Leben und Seine Reden'?," *Die Welt*, October 8, 2016, www.welt.de/geschichte/article160311381/Wer-schrieb-Sein-Leben-und-seine-Reden.html.

Werner, Koeppen, *Herbst 1941 im "Führerhauptquartier": Berichte Werner Koeppens an seinen Minister Alfred Rosenberg. Herausgegeben und kommentiert von Martin Vogt* (Koblenz: Materialen aus dem Bundesarchiv Heft 10, 2002).

Wetzell, Richard F., "Eugenics, Racial Science, and Nazi Biopolitics: Was There a Genesis of the 'Final Solution' from the Spirit of Science?" in Devin O. Pendas, Mark Roseman, and Richard F. Wetzell (eds.), *Beyond the Racial State: Rethinking Nazi Germany* (Cambridge: Cambridge University Press, 2017), pp. 147–175.

Wiskemann, Elizabeth, *Rome-Berlin Axis: A History of the Relations between Hitler and Mussolini* (Oxford: Oxford University Press, 1949).

Wladika, Michael, *Hitlers Vätergeneration: Die Ursprünge des Nationalsozialismus in der k.u.k. Monarchie* (Vienna: Böhlau Verlag, 2005).

Zoller, Albert, *Hitler Privat: Erlebnisbericht seiner Geheimsekretärin* (Düsseldorf: Droste Verlag, 1949).

Websites

www.diewelt.de
www.historisches-lexikon-bayerns.de
www.lorber-verlag.de
https://onedrive.live.com

INDEX

1 John (book in the New Testament), 146
2 Thessalonians, 239

Abel (biblical character)
  as representative of the Jew, 124
Achtleitner (priest), 153
Acts 9, 6, 160, 162, 164, 168–169,
  172–173, 177–179, 241
Adam, Karl, 188–189, 215
Adolf Hitler: Sein Leben und seine Reden
  (first Hitler biography, by Victor
  von Koerber), 129, 163, 166
Ahnenerbe, 63
Albigensians, 197
Althaus, Paul, 65, 83
Aly, Götz, 21–23, 29
Amann, Max, 120, 125
Anschluß, 156
Antichrist, 59, 111, 115
  Jews being, 59, 116
Anti-Judaism, 22–23, 72, 74, 82,
  126
Antisemitische Volkspartei (People's
  Party), 40
Antisemitism, 5, 21–24, 32, 39–40, 43,
  45–52, 54, 56, 59, 64, 66, 68,

70–72, 74, 76, 78, 80, 82–83,
  86–87, 109–111, 117, 123–126,
  128, 134, 143, 146, 159, 182,
  190–194, 215–217, 220, 226, 229,
  232, 234, 236, 240, 242
Anti-ultramontanism, 130–131, 154
Aquinas, Thomas, 50
Arbeit macht frei, 231, 233, 239
Arco-Valley, Anton, 193
Arendt, Hannah, 19–20
Aryanization, 45
Atheism, 57, 63, 119, 156, 198, 212,
  215–216, 240
Auf gut Deutsch (Dietrich Eckart's
  journal), 115
Augsburg, 62, 90, 129, 148, 186, 213
Auschwitz (slave labor and death camp),
  227, 231, 239
Austria, 4, 122

Battle of the Somme, 172
Bauer, Bruno, 38, 83
Bauer, Walter, 65–66
Baur, Hans, 141
Bavaria, 118, 131, 153–154, 176, 182,
  193, 216, 219, 241

259 / Index

violent extremism in, 194
Bavarian Reserve Infantry Regiment
No. 16, 174
Bayerische Volkspartei (German political
party), 57, 144, 216
Bayreuth, 87–88, 103
Bechstein, Carl, 88
Bechstein, Helene, 88, 140
Beethoven, Ludwig van, 58
Bekennende Kirche (Confessing Church),
71–72
Belgium, 93
Below, Nicolaus von, 210
Belzec (death camp), 227
Berchtesgaden, 121–122, 208
Bergen, Doris L., 18, 74–75
Berghof, 156
Berlin, 7, 12, 52, 58, 75, 85, 93–94, 96,
105, 112, 123, 141, 149, 173, 195,
210, 241
Berliner Sportpalast, 169
Bevor Hitler kam (book by Rudolf von
Sebottendorff), 40, 90, 103, 236
Bible, 37, 64, 68, 83, 98, 111, 114, 118,
161, 166, 170, 184, 190, 193, 214,
216, 220, 229–230, 237, 239–240
Hitler's good knowledge of, 160
Jewish contamination of, 68
purging of all Jewish influences from,
65
Blutsünde, 17
Bolshevism, 114, 181, 193
as Jewish creation, 26, 59, 115, 126,
202
Book of Esther (book in the Old
Testament), 118
Book of Revelation (book in the New
Testament), 115, 127, 183–184
Bormann, Martin, 33, 72–74, 143–144,
150–151
Bottichelli, Sandro, 156
Bousset, Wilhelm, 65
Braun, Eva, 210

Braunau am Inn, 162
British National Socialist Party, 4
Browning, Christopher R., 22
Bruckmann, Elsa, 88, 210
Bruckmann, Hugo, 88, 210
Brunner, Alfred, 45
Buch, Walter, 220
Buchenwald (concentration camp), 231
Bucher, Rainer, 25
Bullock, Alan, 8, 26, 29–30
Burleigh, Michael, 17, 31, 135
BVP. *See Bayerische Volkspartei*
Büchner, Elisabeth, 140
Büchner, Georg, 103
Bürgerbräukeller, 94, 138, 204, 221
Bärsch, Claus-Ekkehard, 116

Cain (biblical character)
as the first antisemite, 124, 224
Capitalism, 40, 42, 44, 50–51, 109,
192–193, 202
Cathars, 197
Catholic Church, 3, 60, 110, 128,
178–179, 187, 212–213, 220
Hitler's admiration of, 117
Catholicism, 18, 23, 55, 57, 60, 64–65,
67, 74, 109–110, 116–117, 119,
128, 130–131, 133, 137, 144, 147,
153–155, 158–159, 178–179,
187–189, 191, 193, 207, 212–216,
220, 228
Centralverein für Sozialreform (Central
Association for Social Reform), 39
Chamberlain, Houston Stewart, 5, 59, 64,
68–69, 78, 84, 86–87, 89–90, 95, 97,
101, 107, 125, 132–133, 139, 146,
185, 194, 198, 225, 235, 238
Christian faith, 64, 67–69, 77, 86–88,
92–93, 150
meeting Hitler, 87–89
rejecting science, 81
views of apostle Paul, 6, 107–108,
115, 133

260 / Index

Chamberlain, Houston Stewart (cont.)
views of Jesus, 6, 38, 64, 83, 86, 89, 91–94, 96, 108, 132, 188, 202, 212
Chapoutot, Johann
citing Rauschning, 108
claiming Hitler rejected the idea of an Aryan Jesus, 108
Christ. *See* Jesus of Nazareth
Christian antisemitism, 138
Christian National Socialism, 47
Christian productivism, 47–48, 50, 52, 228–229, 239
Christian Socialism, 50, 54, 191, 196, 235
Christianity, 1, 3, 5, 18, 24, 27, 32–34, 37–38, 42, 49–51, 55–57, 60, 62–67, 69–70, 72–78, 80–83, 86, 88, 91, 93, 95, 97, 107, 109–110, 112, 114, 116, 120, 124, 126–127, 130, 133–134, 136, 145, 147, 152–153, 157, 177, 182–183, 185, 187, 195, 198–200, 203, 205, 207, 209, 212–216, 220, 232, 235, 240
as proto-Bolshevism, 114, 126
Christianity of deeds, 63
Christianity of words, 63
Christlich-Soziale Arbeiterpartei (Christian-Social Workers' Party), 34
Christmas, 144, 147, 162, 186, 203–212, 217
call to arms against the Jews, 206
Church of England, 56
Civiltà Cattolica, 38
Communism, 42, 181
Confino, Alon, 57, 227–228
Conservative Socialism, 34, 39, 42
Croatia, 75
Czech National Socialist Party, 4
Czechoslovakia, 35

Dachau (concentration camp), 71, 231, 239
Damascus Road experience, 160, 172, 177–179, 241

DAP (*Deutsche Arbeiterpartei*), 35–36, 41, 45, 109, 112, 191, 193–194, 236, 238, 241
Darwin, Charles, 101–104
no evidence Hitler ever read, 104
no evidence Hitler reading or mentioning, 104
Darwinism. *See* Theory of evolution
Delff, Hugo, 76
Democracy, 23
causing antisemitism, 21
Jewish world domination in disguise, 203
under attack, 234
volatility of, 234
Der Bolschewismus von Moses bis Lenin (book by Dietrich Eckart), 6, 34, 78, 80, 111–113, 115, 119, 121, 125–126, 130, 132
Der Mythos des 20 Jahrhunderts: Eine Wertung der seelich-geistigen Gestaltenkämpfe unserer Zeit (book by Alfred Rosenberg), 52, 60–61, 63, 69, 208, 236
Der nationale Sozialismus (book by Rudolf Jung), 35, 37, 43, 59, 69, 103, 118, 140, 197, 202, 229, 236
Der Nationalsozialist (newspaper), 224, 226
Der Sieg des Judentums über das Germanenthum (book by Wilhelm Marr), 47
Der Staatssozialist (journal), 39
Der Stürmer, 220
Deutsch-Soziale Partei (German-Social Party), 40, 49
Deutschsozialistische Partei (German Socialist Party), 45
Deutsche Arbeiterpartei German. *See* DAP
Deutsche Arbeiterpartei (German Workers' Party), Austrian, 4, 35

261 / Index

Deutsche Arbeiterverein (German Workers' Association). *See* DAP
Deutsche Christen, 5, 65, 67, 70–72, 83, 145, 187, 189–190
Deutsche Nationalsozialistische Arbeiterpartei. *See* DNSAP
Deutsche Reformpartei (German Reform Party), 40
Deutschen Schutz- und Trutzbund, 194
Deutscher Volksverlag (publisher of antisemitic literature), 194
Devil. *See* Satan
Die Grundlagen des neunzehnten Jahrhunderts (book by Houston Stewart Chamberlain), 64, 86–89, 91, 95, 133, 139, 202, 235
Die Revolution des Nihilismus (book by Hermann Rauschning), 30
Die Spur des Juden im Wandel der Zeiten (book by Alfred Rosenberg), 59, 69
Die Sünde wider das Blut (book by Artur Dinter), 139, 146
Die Überwindung des Judentums in uns und außer uns (book by Rudolf John Gorsleben), 194
Die Welt (newspaper), 203
Dietrich, Otto, 122, 156
Dinter, Artur, 139, 146
DNSAP (*Deutsche Nationalsozialistische Arbeiterpartei*), 4, 35–37
Domarus, Max, 11–12
Drexler, Anton, 35, 41, 45–46, 112, 191–192, 194, 219, 236
  Catholic faith, 191
  celebrating Jesus, 191, 235–236
  DAP based on Socialism and communalism in the spirit of Christ, 191
DSP (*Deutschsozialistische Partei*), 45–46, 49, 112, 190
Dühring, Eugen, 47, 51–52, 101
  rejecting Jesus, 52

Ebionites, 152
Eckart, Dietrich, 5–6, 34, 37, 45–46, 55, 78, 80, 84, 86, 93, 95, 109–114, 116–133, 141, 176, 194, 198, 219, 223–224, 236, 238
  Catholic faith, 109–111, 115–117, 127–128, 130, 132–133
  death of, 121
  dedication in Mein Kampf, 118, 121, 125
  funding the NSDAP purchase of the *Völkischer Beobachter*, 112
  morphine addiction, 117, 122
Eisner, Kurt, 193
Elser, Georg, 94
Emperors and Galileans (drama by Henrik Ibsen), 116
Engelhardt, Phillipp, 171
Enlightenment
  Nazi rejection of, 104
Erinnerungen (book by Albert Speer), 9
Eschweiler, Karl, 189
Esterwegen (concentration camp), 71
Ethnotheism, 81
Eugenics, 90, 104
Europe, 5, 19, 21, 23–24, 61, 125, 159, 187, 225, 234–235, 238–240, 242
Evangelical Christianity, 71
Evans, Richard J., 27
Exodus (second book of the Old Testament), 111

Fall Gelb (Plan Yellow), 93
Fascism, 5, 43, 87
Feder, Gottfried, 44–47, 112, 187, 194
Federschmidt, Gottfried, 154
Fest, Joachim, 8–9, 27–29, 128, 140–141
Fichte, Johann Gottlieb, 38, 76, 83
Fiebig, Paul, 65
The Final Solution. *See* Holocaust
First World War, 4, 35, 89, 95, 149, 170, 188, 210, 221, 238

262 / Index

France, 93
Frank, Hans, 79, 112, 168, 228, 230
Frankfurter Zeitung (newspaper), 165
Freikorps, 238
Freikorps Epp, 225
Frey, Thomas. *See* Fritsch, Theodor
Friedländer, Saul, 22
Friedrich II (the Great), 63
Fritsch, Theodor, 4, 38–39, 47–48,
    50–52, 146, 231
Fromm, Erich, 190

Galatians (book in the New Testament),
    174
Galilee, 94, 146
Gansser, Emil, 119, 122, 125
Gemlich, Adolf, 51, 192, 194, 223
    first written evidence of Hitler's
        antisemitism, 109
General Government, 79, 228
Genesis (first book in the Old
    Testament), 49, 98, 229
Genoud, François, 2
German National Socialist Workers'
    Party. *See* DNSAP
German Socialist Party. *See* DSP
Germany, 3–9, 19–23, 29, 38–39,
    41–43, 45, 47, 54, 58–59, 65–75,
    82–83, 87, 89, 92, 99, 103, 105,
    108, 120–121, 123–124, 128–129,
    131, 133, 140, 143, 147, 157–159,
    162–163, 165, 168–169, 172–175,
    178–179, 185, 187, 189–190,
    198–199, 201, 206–208, 218, 222,
    224–225, 233, 237–238, 242
Geschlecht und Charakter (book by Otto
    Weininger), 124
Gespräche mit Hitler (book by Hermann
    Rauschning), 33, 108
Glauer, Adam Alfred Rudolf. *See*
    Sebottendorff, Rudolf von
Glover, Jonathan, 2
Gnosticism, 67–68, 146, 198

God, 3, 6–7, 16–17, 20, 25, 28, 31,
    37–38, 40–41, 52, 54, 57–58, 62,
    65, 67–70, 82, 84, 87, 89, 91–94,
    96, 103–104, 116, 128, 130,
    133–135, 137–138, 142–152, 154,
    156–158, 165, 167–173, 175–176,
    178–179, 181, 185, 188, 190,
    196–197, 201–203, 206–208, 211,
    215, 217–221, 229–233, 235–237,
    blessing the murder of Jewish Abel,
        124
    punishing the idle Jews, 230
Goebbels, Joseph Paul, 10, 12, 57–58,
    78, 155, 157, 175, 182, 204,
    226–227
    knowledge of the Holocaust, 226–228
    NSDAP as the true Christians, 157
    religious beliefs, 27, 57–58, 94, 127,
        182
Goldhagen, Daniel Jonah, 24
Golgotha, 166, 190
Gorsleben, Rudolf John, 194
Gospel of John, 37, 59, 62, 116, 203,
    211, 214
Gospel of Luke, 67, 91, 98, 163, 202
Gospel of Mark, 62, 185
Gospel of Matthew, 62, 88, 91, 98, 169,
    182, 202, 207, 211, 228
Gospels (four books of the New
    Testament), 54, 60–61, 67, 76, 123,
    141, 161, 166, 182, 190, 212–213,
    228, 237, 240
Gött, Magnus, 213–215
Grant, Madison, 100
Grassinger, Hans George, 112
Great Britain, 4, 199
Great War. *See* First World War
Groß, Walter, 90
    rejecting humanism, 91
Groß-Rosen (concentration camp), 231,
    239
Grundmann, Walter, 65–66, 71–73, 145,
    190

263 / Index

Grundriß (book by Fritz Lenz), 105
Günther, Hans F. K., 105–106
  rejecting scienctific method, 105

Haeckel, Ernst Heinrich, 38, 103
Hamann, Brigitte, 95, 101
Hamburg, 71, 187, 217
Hanfstaengl, Ernst "Putzi," 128, 130, 141
Harmful eaters, 230
Harnack, Adolf von, 68
Hastings, Derek, 18, 63, 191, 236
Hauptmann, Hans, 59, 139
Head, Peter, 72–73, 108
Heer, Friedrich, 18, 120–121, 126, 164–165
Hegel, Georg Wilhelm Friedrich, 38, 76, 83
Heiden, Konrad, 13, 35, 46, 88, 123, 153, 170, 191
Heim, Heinrich, 89, 108, 143, 150–151, 176, 225–226
  Hitler praying in private, 151
Hepp, Ernst, 171
Herbst, Ludolf, 16, 123
Heschel, Susanna, 18, 23, 52, 61, 64, 71–73, 80–81, 97, 124, 136, 153, 161
Heß, Adolf (uncle of Rudolf), 187
Heß, Rudolf, 13, 96, 112, 153–155, 187, 222–226
  views of Jesus, 96
Heß, Wolf Rüdiger (son of Rudolf), 13
Heydrich, Reinhard, 194
Himmler, Heinrich, 226, 233
  speech in Posen, 226
Hindenburg, Paul von, 121
  funeral of, 156
Hirsch, Emanuel, 65, 83
Hitler, Adolf, 1, 3–4, 7–8, 11, 14, 30–32, 35, 38, 51, 54, 66, 77–79, 82, 86, 90, 94–95, 98, 106, 108–109, 114, 121, 124–125, 128, 131, 133, 135,

144, 160, 168, 194, 196, 209, 215, 218, 234, 240
  "When I defend myself against the Jews, I am fighting for the Lord's work," 181
  achieving dictatorial powers in the party, 115, 218–219
  admiration for Catholic Church, 117
  admiration for Dietrich Eckart, 132
  admiration for Jesus, 5, 7, 20, 31–32, 53–54, 60–61, 77, 79–80, 83, 109, 135–136, 146, 157–158, 160, 186, 204
  admiration for Jesus, sincerity of, 158
  admiration for Jesus not just propaganda, 33
  admiration for Karl Lueger, 53
  admiration for Mussolini, 43
  admiring bust of Jesus in Rome, 79
  aim to destroy the Jews, 118
  Alan Bullock changing his mind about, 30
  Albert Speer's phony Hitler quotes, 9
  in Alfred Rosenberg's diaries, 13
  alleged designer of party emblem, 36
  alleged occult influences on, 117
  alleged powers of persuasion, 8
  allegedly on the moderate left in 1919, 192
  allegedly reading Plato, 114
  allegedly rejecting an Aryan Jesus, 108–109
  allegedly using Dietrich Eckart, 131
  animated by ideas and ideology, 24
  anonymity as propaganda tool, 176–177
  from anonymity to greatness, 174, 176, 178
  anti-conservatism of, 42
  antisemite and a Christian, 27
  and antisemitism, 47, 194
  antisemitism in early speeches, 113

264 / Index

Hitler, Adolf (cont.)
  antisemitism in *Mein Kampf*, 47–48, 51
  antisemitism influencing view of Jesus, 80
  antisemitism of, 82, 99
  and apostle Paul, 6, 153
  on the apostle Paul, 107
  and apostle Paul, corrupting Jesus' teachings, 79
  approving of *Der Bolschewismus von Moses bis Lenin*, 119
  the Aryan Jesus, 107
  attending army propaganda course, 86, 109, 192–193, 241
  attending his first DAP meeting, 191
  as the Bavarian Mussolini, 219
  Bayreuth as the place where the spiritual sword was made, 87
  becoming famous during trial, 121
  being a pagan, 155
  being suggested party name by Rudolf Jung, 35
  belief in being sent by Providence, 30
  belief in God in the NSDAP, 93
  biographies not mentioning Eckart's Catholicism, 130
  biographies not mentioning Eckart's Christian faith, 128
  birthplace becomes pilgrimage site, 168
  on blood and spirit, 98
  Bolshevism as Jewish creation, 115
  borrowing Chamberlain's *Die Grundlagen* from the library, 87
  both creator and product of the Third Reich, 24
  calling Jesus Lord and Savior, 135
  and Captain Karl Mayr, 86, 193
  and Carl and Helene Bechstein, 88
  carrying a whip like Jesus, 139–141
  Catholic faith of, 153–155, 159

  Catholic faith of, taking communion, 154
  celebrated by Goebbels, 57
  celebration of dilettantism, 102
  celebration of Karl Lueger in *Mein Kampf*, 53
  Chamberlain draws parallel between Parsifal and, 89
  Chamberlain enchanted by, 89
  Chamberlain writing to, 89
  Chamberlain's influence on, 90, 92, 95
  on Chamberlain's view of the apostle Paul, 108
  changing his personal history, 177
  as charismatic leader, 19
  as Christ-like leader, 37
  Christ fighting against the Jews, 57
  and Christian National Socialism, 47
  and Christian productivism, 48, 196, 228–229, 239
  Christianity as proto-Bolshevism, 126
  Christianity of deeds, 63
  and Christmas celebration, 181, 203–208, 210, 212
  citing the Gospel of John, 203
  claim that Rudolf Jung made him an antisemite, 37
  combining traits of early Christian National Socialists, 42
  commissions first biography of himself, 129, 166
  compared to Jesus, 220
  compared to Jesus by Rudolf Jung, 37
  concept of race, 82
  conception of God, 116
  on confessional conflicts, 56
  constantly exepting Jesus from critique, 80
  constructing political conversion narrative on Acts 9, 160–170, 172–179, 241
  as convinced ideologue, 27

265 / Index

as convinced National Socialist, 29–30
court transcripts from trial, 11
criticizing the Catholic Zentrum party,
55
critique of atheism, 216
as cynic only interested in power, 30
Damascus Road experience, 172–173,
177, 179
on deciding to become a politician, 93
deciding to write *Mein Kampf*, 122
dedication to Eckart in *Mein Kampf*,
118, 121, 125, 132
and *Der Bolschewismus von Moses bis
Lenin*, 55, 78, 111, 113–114,
119–120, 125–126, 130, 132
in *Der Bolschewismus von Moses bis
Lenin*, 6, 34
designation *Führer* used for first time,
123
development into extreme right-wing
nationalist and antisemite, 86
dictations for speeches, 10
Dietrich Eckart as father figure for,
109
Dietrich Eckart as mentor of, 130
Dietrich Eckart as spiritual father of, 123
Dietrich Eckart introducing
Chamberlain and Lagarde to, 95
Dietrich Eckart most important
influence for, 132
Dietrich Eckart not wanting to show
*Der Bolschewismus von Moses bis
Lenin* to, 120
Dietrich Eckart teaching how to write
and speak, 123
Dietrich Eckart's admiration for, 132
Dietrich Eckart's Catholic beliefs,
133
and Dietrich Eckart's Catholicism, 117
Dietrich Eckart's influence on, 113,
115, 118, 122, 132–133, 238
differences compared to early National
Socialists, 41

discovering Chamberlain, 95
dismissive of/toward paganism in the
SS, 155
on a divine mission, 6, 163, 176,
178–179, 181, 219, 221, 235, 238
divine mission of, 157
divinity of Jesus, 6, 135–137,
142–145, 147–148, 157–158
doing God's work when fighting the
Jews, 115
early 1920s as formative years, 133
ecstatic by Chamberlain's praise, 87
editions of speeches and writings as
sources, 10
effort to create a state church, 69
and Elsa Bruckmann, 88
entering prayer-like state, 151
equating the Jews with Satan, 115,
127–128
established Christianity as Jewish in
spirit, 51
ethics and morality, 20
the evil of the Jews, 118
experiences in First World War,
171–172
exposed to mustard gas, 163–164
expressing genocidal intent toward the
Jews to Dietrich Eckart, 123
exterminatory rhetoric toward the
Jews, 124
on false humanism, 90
false statements in the table talks, 15
the Final Solution, 127
first public antisemitic statements, 88
first time speaking about Jesus, 77
first time speaking about Jesus as an
Aryan, 77
forged diaries of, 11
on free will, 92
frequency of public appearances over
time, 10
fundraising in Switzerland with
Dietrich Eckart, 122

266 / Index

Hitler, Adolf (cont.)
 gas-induced blindness questioned, 164
 as genius of action, 161
 as Germany's Messiah, 123, 129–130,
  158, 166, 172, 175, 189–190,
  219–220, 236
 giving up on creating a state church,
  56
 God gave right to exterminate the Jews
  to, 175
 God intervening in human history, 17
 God speaks through inner voice, 170,
  172–173, 178
 in Goebbels' diaries, 13
 Gospel not for the Jews, 136
 grudgingly accepting parliamentary
  platform of NSDAP, 131
 hatred of Hohenzollern family, 42
 hatred of the Habsburg family, 42
 in Heß private letters, 13
 hinting at his resemblance to Jesus,
  129
 historians dismissing religious beliefs
  of, 130
 history of party name, 35
 hostility to materialism, 26
 hostility to science, reason, and
  rationality, 17
 hostility toward Christianity, 2
 hostility toward conservatives, 42
 hostility toward education, 101
 hostility toward organized
  Christianity, 31–32, 130
 hostility toward the Catholic Church,
  213–214
 Houston Stewart Chamberlain
  important religious teacher of, 132
 Houston Stewart Chamberlain
  praising of, 87
 Houston Stewart Chamberlain
  recognizing potential of, 87
 Houston Stewart Chamberlain's
  influence on, 133

 ideological and religious development,
  5
 ideological development of, 5
 ideological formation, 6
 ideological influences on, 82
 ideology central for understanding of,
  29
 idolized by Catholic clergy, 187–189,
  215
 IfZ new edition of speeches and
  writings, 12
 illogical view of Jesus, 52
 impatient personality of, 130
 as imperialist and expansionist, 58
 importance of analyzing ideology, 24
 importance of having God on one's
  side, 93
 on the importance of Houston Stewart
  Chamberlain, 88
 importance of physical fitness, 100
 on importance of religious tolerance,
  56
 importance of support from the
  Deutsche Christen, 72
 importance of Wagner for his views on
  Jesus, 76
 inaccuracies in transcribed speeches,
  12
 influenced by Madison Grant, 100
 influenced by Theodor Fritsch, 48
 influences on early religious beliefs, 86
 inspired by Jesus, 7
 inspired by the New Testament,
  182–185, 203, 241
 inspired to revolutionary action by
  Mussolini, 43
 as intellectual force in National
  Socialism, 24
 internal consistency of National
  Socialism, 102
 introduced to social elite, 123
 introduction of swastika, 36
 invasion of the Soviet Union, 215

irrationality of, 102
and Jesus, 131–132, 134–135, 138
Jesus as a warrior, 59
Jesus as an Aryan, 146
Jesus as an Aryan warrior, 34, 83,
    135–138, 143, 145, 183, 186, 209,
    232
Jesus as inspiration for the Holocaust,
    228, 231–232, 235, 238–240, 242
Jesus as lawgiver, 147–148
Jesus as Lord and Savior, 144–145,
    158
Jesus as Son of God, 145
Jesus being called Son of God by, 144
Jesus chasing the moneylenders out of
    the Temple with his whip, 55, 83,
    139–140, 158, 186, 216, 237
Jesus not being Jewish, 138
Jewish God as false God, 146
Jews a race but not fully human, 128
Jews and religion, 107
Jews as carriers of spiritual poison,
    100
on Jews as parasites in the body of
    other people, 48
Jews as spawns of snakes and vipers,
    139
Jews unable to have a religion, 95
Jews workshy money exchangers, 136
keeping books about Jesus, 185–186
knowledge of Paul de Lagarde, 77–78
knowledge of publication of *Der
    Bolschewismus von Moses bis
    Lenin*, 119
knowledge of the Bible, 114
Konrad Heiden's misjudgement of, 46
lack of faithful in the *Wehrmacht*, 94
laws of race as revealed by God, 31
leaving the NSDAP, 218
letter to Adolf Gemlich, 51, 109, 192,
    194
lies about debate during first DAP
    meeting, 192

lies in *Mein Kampf*, 36
life as struggle, 55
long history of Christian antisemitism,
    82
making efforts to hide the Holocaust,
    227
and Martin Luther, 190
Marxism as a Jewish ideological virus,
    100
meeting Alfred Rosenberg, 109
meeting Dietrich Eckart, 109
meeting Houston Stewart
    Chamberlain in Bayreuth, 87–89
meeting the Wagner family, 88
and *Mein Kampf*, 118, 120–121
Mein Kampf as a source, 14
Mein Kampf as *Bildungsroman*, 161
mentioning Eckart in second book,
    118
Messianic expectations on, 28–29
missing statements on religion, 12
moral imperative to destroy the weak,
    102
morality and ethics ordained by God,
    17
as narcissistic and stubborn, 36
National Socialism as religious
    politics, 31
National Socialism as true
    Christianity, 3, 62, 147, 157–158,
    183
National Socialism as true Socialism,
    196
National Socialism based on Christ's
    teachings, 90
National Socialists, followers of Jesus,
    158
National Socialists as true Christians
    and true Socialists, 79
never mentioning Darwin, 104
never mentioning the Trinity, 116
and Nietzsche, 117
Night of Long Knives, 141

268 / Index

Hitler, Adolf (cont.)
as nihilist, 30
no ambition to become religious
leader, 150
no break between Dietrich Eckart and,
122, 125
no religious statements during trial,
126
no true Scotsman fallacy, 153
as nonbeliever and anti-Christian, 2
not an original thinker or intellectual,
126
not deported to Austria, 122
not lacking moral principles, 27
not quasi-religious, 29
not speaking from a manuscript, 10
not the inventor of National Socialism,
4
not the originator of the Aryan Jesus,
77
NSDAP continuing Christ's work,
138–139, 142, 147
and NSDAP the true followers of
Jesus, 180–184, 186–187, 191,
195–205, 208–209, 211–218, 232,
235–238
and Obergammau Passion Play, 123,
190
obsessive secrecy of, 177
opposing hedonism in the NSDAP, 27
opposing struggle against the
churches, 27
originator of the Holocaust, 24
and Otto Wagener, 195, 198–200, 203
parallels between biblical stories about
the life of Jesus and, 162–163, 166,
169
on parties *Zentrum* and BVP, 57
at Pasewalk, 164, 166, 168–169
Pasewalk declared national shrine, 168
at Pasewalk, hospital file missing, 164
physically unfit geniuses exceptions to
the rule, 101

pioneering privatization of economy,
41
planning war against the churches,
157
plotting extermination of Jews from
the start, 221–226, 238
political beginnings, 85
political conversion narrative, 6
and positive Christianity, 136
praying to God, 149, 151–152
praying to God falling on his knees,
149
praying to God in private, 150–151
and previous scholarship, 1, 3, 7–9,
15, 17–19, 25, 29, 31, 33, 35, 73,
83, 113–114, 133, 135, 199, 202,
216, 234, 241
professed belief in God, 31
promises God to dedicate life to
politics, 168
as prophet, 57
on Providence, 94
pseudoscientific racism of, 101
race laws revealed by God, 17
on race mixing, 100, 110
racial and theological antisemitism,
126
as radical anti-Christian, 18
as rational materialist, 26
Rauschning forging statements of,
109
reading Chamberlain, 95
receives calling from God, 168
receives Iron Cross, 171
reception of his antisemitism in
Germany, 71
recruited by Anton Drexler, 191–192,
194, 236
reference to Bible in speeches, 118
referencing the New Testament, 88
referring to Jesus as divine, 6
as reincarnation of Jesus, 236
as reincarnation of the Messiah, 72

269 / Index

reinterpreting Jesus, 61
relationship to Christianity debated, 1
relationship to Jesus, 1, 3, 5–6
reliability of notes from speeches, 10
religious belief, Christian aspects of, 156
religious belief, sincerity of, 159
religious beliefs, 3, 5–6, 16–17, 25–27, 34, 68, 84, 132–135, 153, 180, 201
religious beliefs and the Holocaust, 24
religious beliefs not just propaganda, 74, 82–83, 99, 150–151, 155, 181–182, 200, 216–218, 242
religious beliefs not motivated by racism, 76
religious fatalism of, 92
religious practice, 148, 150
religious practice as a private matter, 150–151
religious views in *Mein Kampf*, 55
replacing Eckart as editor of *Völkischer Beobachter*, 122
resentment toward organized Christianity, 26
resonating with his audience's spiritual beliefs, 100
return to Berlin after First World War, 85
right-wing but not a conservative, 42
risen spiritually by Providence, 167
role of Theodor Fritsch for, 146
Rudolf Jung dedicates book to, 36
in same cell as Count Anton Arco-Valley, 194
as the savior, 37
as savior-leader appointed by God, 16
second book, 11
as secular phenomenon, 26
self-image as genius, 49
serving under revolutionary Socialist and Communist regimes in Munich, 192
shifting religious base of NSDAP, 131

similarities between his and Chamberlain's view of Jesus, 89
similarities to Ebionite faith, 152
source for anti-Christian statements, 7
speaking about Jesus in *Der Bolschewismus von Moses bis Lenin*, 55
speaking about the Aryan Jesus, 78
speaking at Camp Lechfeld in August 1919, 109, 193
speaking at Hindenburg's funeral, 156
speaking of Valhalla, 156
speaking to Goebbels about the Aryan Jesus, 78
speaking to his generals, 93
spiritual battle against the Jews, 98–99
spiritual education instead of science, 101
spiritual potential of various peoples, 81
starting to compare himself to Jesus, 129
suffering from Messiah complex, 128
suffering hysteria in First World War, 164–165
suggesting Social Revolutionary Party as party name, 35
surviving assassination attempt, 94
swastika as symbol of true Christianity, 212
in the table talks, 15
takes part in formulation of NSDAP program, 46
and Temple in Jerusalem, 137–138
temporary blindness, 6
thanking God for survival of assassination attempt, 94
theology of, 6, 25, 84, 142, 145–146, 154, 170, 178, 201, 213, 218
told he had a divine mission by Dietrich Eckart, 123
transformation into Führer, 123
trial of, 126

270 / Index

Hitler, Adolf (cont.)
from unreligious to fervent believer, 83
unwillingness to spread pictures of
himself, 176
use of Acts 9, 6
using his trial as propaganda platform,
121
using the Bible as history book,
117
using the Bible to stage himself, 161
value of Albert Speer's books as
historical sources on, 9
value of contemporary eyewitnesses
as sources about Hitler's religious
beliefs, 8
value of the Nordic race, 82
value to the NSDAP, 219
view of the soul, 91
viewing himself as Jesus figure, 130
views on the apostle Paul, 133
visit to Rome in May 1938, 79
visited by priest in Landsberg fortress,
154
visited in jail before trial by Rudolf
Jung, 37
visited in Landsberg fortress by Rudolf
Jung, 36
visiting Dietrich Eckart in hiding,
122
visiting Dietrich Eckart when writing
*Der Bolschewismus von Moses bis
Lenin*, 125
visiting Dietrich Eckart's grave, 122
and Wagner's operas, 68
Walter Riehl of DNSAP as ideological
inspiration, 37
wish to avoid open conflict with the
churches, 120
wish to control the narrative about
himself, 120
working for Socialist revolutionaries in
Munich in 1919, 167
wounded in First World War, 172

writing to Houston Stewart
Chamberlain, 89
zero tolerance of confessional
infighting in NSDAP, 56
Hitler: A Study of Tyranny (book by
Alan Bullock), 8, 30
Hitler aus nächster Nähe (book by Otto
Wagener), 195
Hitler's table talk, 2, 7–8, 15, 80, 113
Hitler und ich (book by Otto Straßer),
78, 95
*Hitlers Tischgespräche im
Führerhauptquartier 1941–1942*,
15, 33, 195
Hoffmann, Heinrich, 139–140, 176
Holland, 93
Holocaust, 4–5, 20–23, 25, 28, 38, 116,
127, 187, 221–222, 225, 227–228,
231, 235, 238–240, 242
number of victims, 227
Hussites, 197

I Know These Dictators (book by Ward
Price), 171
Ibsen, Henrik, 116
Institut für Zeitgeschichte (IfZ), 11–12,
14, 223
*Institut zur Erforschung und Beseitigung
des jüdischen Einflusses auf das
deutsche kirchliche Leben* (The
Institute for the Study and
Eradication of Jewish Influence in
German Church Life), 71–73

Jäckel, Eberhard, 30
Jerusalem, 137, 139, 169, 173
Jesus als Volksman (book by Friedrich
Naumann), 53
Jesus der Arier (book by Hans
Hauptmann), 59, 139
*Jesus der Arier und die jesuanische
Weltanschauung* (book by Max
Sebald), 76

271 / Index

Jesus der Galiläer und das Judentum
(book by Walter Grundmann), 66
Jesus of Nazareth, 1, 3, 5–7, 20, 25, 29,
31–34, 37–38, 49, 53–57, 59–67,
69, 71, 73, 75–84, 86, 88–91,
93–94, 96, 98, 107–108, 111,
114–116, 123, 126, 129, 131,
133–136, 138–139, 141–146, 148,
152–153, 156–159, 161–163,
166–167, 169, 174, 181–182,
184–191, 195–197, 202, 204–209,
211–214, 216–218, 220, 232,
235–238, 241
Alfred Rosenberg's celebration of, 69
apostle Paul corrupting teaching of,
78, 80, 157
as an Aryan warrior, 59–61, 63–67,
73, 76–78, 80, 82, 88–89, 108, 117,
132, 134–135, 137–138, 141–143,
145, 159, 180, 183, 186–187, 191,
204–206, 208–209, 211, 232, 235,
237, 242
as not divine, 65
being Judaized, 142
called an Aryan for the first time by
Hitler, 77
called lawgiver by Hitler, 147
called Son of God by Hitler, 144–145,
158
chasing the moneylenders out of the
temple, 59, 117, 136–137, 139–140,
216
coming to bring the sword, 90
considered divine by Hitler, 135–137,
143–145, 147–148, 157–158
dedicating his life to fighting the Jews,
204
fighting to eradicate the Jews, 134
first mentioned by Hitler, 77
his blood was upon the Jews, 228
Hitler admiring bust of, 79
Hitler and NSAD continuing the work
of, 142

Hitler and NSDAP as the true
followers of, 138–139, 158, 180,
183, 196–197, 218, 220, 238
Hitler borrowing biographical details
from, 163
Hitler compared to, 220
Hitler identifying with, 181
Hitler imagining return of, 147
Hitler inspired by, 135–136, 141,
159–160, 178, 180, 185–186, 204,
208, 212, 235–237, 240
Hitler praising, 135, 145, 181, 209,
232, 235
Hitler's deep admiration of, 80
as Hitler's Lord and Savior, 135,
144–145, 147
inspiration for killing Jews, 205
inspiration for the Holocaust, 228,
232, 235, 238–240, 242
inspiring sacrifice for the Fatherland,
205
king of the Jews, 73
leader of a movement just like Hitler,
129
moral alibi to kill Jews, 70
Nazis clearing the German temples of
Jews, 205
need to love one's Aryan brothers, 203
need to sacrifice one's life fighting evil
(Jews), 206
no Jewish blood, 95
not member of any race, 66
not the king of the Jews, 73
persecuted by the Jews, 73
and Pilate, 228
pure idealism of, 76
raised from the dead by God, 196
shielded from critique by Hitler, 80
strong and without weak humanism,
89
teaching as communist, 115
teaching importance of willpower, 91
the greatest antisemite of all time, 220

272 / Index

Jesus of Nazareth (cont.)
  transcending his Jewishness, 64
  un-Jewish nature of, 208
Jewish Question, 22, 51, 225–226
Jews, 5, 21, 23, 95, 104, 113, 173, 194,
    204, 211, 232, 242
  allegedly impossible to assimilate, 39
  as the Antichrist, 59, 116
  Aryanization, 45
  atheist nature of, 57
  blood libel, 128
  as bloodsucking vampires, 136
  Christian antisemitism, 22, 27, 37–39,
    59, 72–74, 76, 81, 93, 112, 117,
    119, 130, 139, 188, 193, 240
  Christians claiming they had been just
    as persecuted as, 240
  Church had no responsibility to care
    about, 187
  conspiring against the apostle Paul,
    173
  corruptors of Christ's teachings, 114
  cosmopolitan and nomadic nature of,
    51
  cowards and pacifists, 142
  dancing around the golden calf,
    193–194
  disorderly pogroms could not
    exterminate the Jews, 192
  divine moral duty to exterminate the,
    238
  enemies of the Fatherland, 173
  enslaving all other peoples, 237
  as evil incarnate, 23, 51–52, 73,
    115–116, 118, 124, 127–128, 167,
    204, 220, 231, 240
  Goebbels writing about the mass
    murder of, 228
  Goebbels writing about the need to
    exterminate, 226
  hatred of, 23
  Hitler doing God's work when fighting
    against, 115, 181–182, 232

Hitler fighting against, 7
Hitler inciting hatred against, 184
Hitler planning to murder, 221–226
Hitler proclaiming the destruction of,
    115, 175
Hitler stating he wanted to kill all,
    123–124, 238
immoral by nature, 37, 56, 187–188,
    194
and international capitalism, 192–193,
    202, 211
Jahveh as false God, 146
Jesus fighting against, 31, 38, 49, 61,
    83, 88, 118, 134–135, 137–138,
    140, 158, 186–187, 191, 205–206,
    216, 232, 235–238, 242
as killers of Christ, 23, 60, 67, 73, 78,
    98, 138, 180, 187, 196, 204–205,
    207–208, 211, 217, 228, 232, 236,
    240
lovers of money, 202
mass murder of, 7, 24, 51, 227, 230,
    232, 235, 239–240, 242
materialistic by nature, 205, 211–212
and miscegenation, 22
as murderers, 111, 117
Nazi hatred of, 70
Nazi moral obligation to kill, 70
Nazi propaganda against, 21
Nazi spiritual struggle against, 97–99
Nazi struggle against, 5
Nazis' hatred of, 21
not human, 128
and NSDAP party program, 44–47
number murdered in the Holocaust,
    227
only a race, not a religion, 51, 75, 95,
    107, 128
oppression of, 21–22, 40, 72
originators of both Communism and
    capitalism, 42
as parasites, 48, 52, 100, 111, 237
racial hatred of, 22, 43

273 / Index

source of all misery, 50
spawns of Satan, 59
as spawns of Satan, 77, 116
as spawns of snakes and vipers, 139, 182
stab in the back myth, 89, 169
as "a state within a state", 47
to be respected and feared, 237
used as slave labor, 51, 231, 233, 239
as usurers, 47
wearing religion as a cloak, 76
as workshy, 47, 50, 136, 229–231, 233
John the Baptist, 37, 91
Jones, John Joseph "Jack" (leader of British National Socialist Party), 4
Judaism, 22–23, 64, 66, 72–74, 81–82, 93, 97, 115, 120, 126, 128, 145, 188
Judas Schuldbuch: Eine deutsche Abrechnung (book by Wilhelm Meister), 194
Judea, 94, 174
Judeo-Bolshevism, 26, 59
Jung, Rudolf 34, 59, 90, 103, 131, 140, 197, 229, 236
celebrating Jesus, 37, 59–60, 90, 236
comparing Hitler to Jesus, 37
mistake to reject Jesus, 69
suggesting NSDAP name to Hitler, 35
visiting Hitler in Landsberg fortress, 36

Kahr, Gustav Ritter von, 153, 155
Kampfzeit, 93, 99, 172
Kapp, Wolfgang, 123
Kapp, putsch, 123
Katedersozialisten (Socialists of the lectern), 39
Kedar, Asaf, 4, 52
Kellerhoff, Sven Felix, 35, 192, 203, 207
Kerrl, Hans, 156
Kershaw, Ian (Sir), 19, 36, 88, 131–132, 140, 154, 171, 177, 222, 227

Kittel, Gerhard, 65, 83
Klee, Ernst, 18, 71
Klemperer, Victor, 75, 156, 220
Koehne, Samuel, 47, 81, 145, 153, 206–207, 209
Koeppen, Werner, 143
Koerber, Victor von, 129, 163, 166
Koonz, Claudia, 28
Kuhlen (concentration camp), 71
Kujau, Konrad, 10–11

Lagarde, Paul de, 38, 77–78, 83, 95, 108
Hitler's knowledge of, 77
masculine Jesus, 38
Lambach (Hitler's monestary school), 156
Landes, Richard, 26
Landesverein für Innere Mission (Country Association for the Inner Mission), 71
The Last Days of Hitler (book by Hugh R. Trevor-Roper), 8, 29
Landsberg am Lech, 36, 89, 96, 99, 119, 154, 193, 222, 226, 236
Leben Jesu (book by Ernest Renan), 38
Lebenfels, Jörg Lanz von, 79
Leffler, Siegfried, 66, 70
theological obligation to kill Jews, 70
Leibniz, Gottfried Wilhelm, 92
Lenz, Fritz, 92, 104–105
admitting race concept was unscientific, 105
faith in race instead of science, 106
rejecting genetics, 105
rejecting materialist science, 105
Leutheuser, Julius, 189
Leviticus (third book in the Old Testament), 98
Ley, Robert, 99
Leybold, Otto, 154
Limpezia de sangre (purity of blood), 23
Longerich, Peter, 18, 176
Lorber, Jakob, 110

274 / Index

Lorberbewegung (Lorber Movement), 110
Lorenz, Elisabeth, 66, 190–191
Lortz, Joseph, 189
Ludendorff, Erich, 103, 131
Lüdicke, Lars, 184
Lueger, Karl, 48, 53, 102, 216
Luther, Martin, 69
  antisemitism of, 190
  as predecessor to National Socialism, 190

Majdanek (death camp), 227
Mammonism, 44, 53, 140, 202, 211, 230
Manichean Christianity, 68
March on Rome, 43, 123
Marcion: Das Evangelium vom fremden
  Gott (book by Adolf von Harnack),
  68
Marcion of Sinope (early church father),
  67–68
Marr, Wilhelm, 21, 47, 50–51, 53, 231
Marx, Karl, 40, 42, 57, 78, 103
Marxism, 4, 34, 39–40, 42, 44, 46, 51, 57,
  59, 99–100, 157, 181, 212, 215–216
Maser, Werner, 113
May, Karl, 140
Mayr, Karl, 86, 109, 192–193, 241
Mein Kampf, 6, 14, 16, 36, 47–48, 51,
  53, 55, 64, 66, 78, 88, 93, 100, 108,
  110, 115, 117–122, 125–127, 130,
  132, 149, 151, 160–163, 165–166,
  169, 172–173, 177–179, 181, 192,
  208–211, 221, 223, 226, 232, 236
Mein politisches Erwachen (memoir by
  Anton Drexler), 191, 235–236
Meister, Wilhelm, 194
Mendelian genetics
  rejected as Jewish and materialist, 105
Mensch und Gott: Betrachtungen über
  Religion und Christentum (book by
  Houston Stewart Chamberlain), 96
Messiah, 60, 62, 65, 72, 116, 123, 128,
  130, 142, 145, 190, 219–220, 236,
  238

Meyer-Erlach, Wolf, 66, 240
Miscegenation, 17, 22, 51
  sin against God, 110
Monologe im Führerhauptquartier
  1941–1944, 15, 80, 88, 143
Montesquieu, Charles-Louis de
  Secondat, 104
Moral reform, 42, 136, 149, 213
Morality and ethics, 5, 17, 20, 27–28,
  37, 42, 47–48, 53, 56, 67, 70–72,
  81, 91–93, 95, 97–98, 102, 121,
  128, 136, 148–149, 161, 186–188,
  203, 213, 223, 225–229, 231, 235,
  237–239, 242
  He who does not work shall not eat,
  232
Mormonism, 153
Munich, 35, 43, 56, 64, 85, 87, 94, 99,
  105, 109, 112, 117, 121, 123, 129,
  138, 141, 144–148, 167, 186, 195,
  200, 204–205, 207–210, 217, 221
Mussolini, Benito, 43, 123, 219
  discussing bust of Jesus with Hitler, 79
  visited by Hitler in 1938, 79
Münchener Beobachter (newspaper), 112
Münchener Post (newspaper), 154
Münchner-Kindl-Keller, 204

The Nation (newspaper), 165–166
National Socialism, 1, 3, 5, 7–8, 13–14,
  18, 20–24, 26–27, 31, 33, 40, 45, 48,
  51, 56, 61, 63, 65, 68, 71–75, 78,
  81–83, 90, 96–97, 100, 103–106,
  110, 116–117, 124, 134–135, 139,
  142, 145–146, 150, 153, 155,
  157–159, 166, 172, 180, 187–189,
  194–195, 198, 206–207, 209,
  216–217, 220–221, 227, 231–233,
  235–236, 238–242
  and "faith in race," 97
  and "life as struggle," 55
  and antisemitism, 45, 51, 56, 72, 75,
  99, 230, 232

275 / Index

and Anton Drexler's influence on
Hitler, 192
as antireligious, 26
as applied biology, 104
and Catholicism, 153, 189
and Christ as a worrior, 205
and Christ as an antisemitic warrior, 186
Christian ideas in propaganda, 72
and Christian productivism, 48, 228,
231, 239
Christian Socialist roots of, 34, 47–48,
50
and Christian theologians, 64
and Christianity, 53, 56, 73–74,
81–82, 149, 172, 184, 187, 200,
217
Christianity and racism, 64
and Christmas celebration, 205, 211
and the churches, 27
and creation of a state church, 69
and the *Deutsch Christen*, 72
Dietrich Eckart's influence on, 109,
118, 238
and ethical conservatism, 53
ethical foundations of, 20
as ethnotheism, 81
and Evangelical Christianity, 71
finishing Christ's work, 187
following in Christ's footsteps, 134
and God, 4, 147, 149, 237
history of, 3–5, 42, 82, 195
and Hitler's early sympathies with
Social Democracy, 192
Hitler's fanaticism, 99
Hitler's narrative control over his
beliefs, 120
and Hitler's political beginnings, 85
and Hitler's religious beliefs, 135
and Holocaust, 20–21
Houston Stewart Chamberlain's
influence on, 133
ideology of, 3, 14, 17, 24, 41, 48, 82,
146, 195, 242

and imperialistic expansion, 58
importance of Hitler's religiosity for,
133
influence of *Thule Gesellschaft* on, 112
as internally rational, 102
and Jesus, 1, 3, 7, 31, 33, 59–60, 80,
82–83, 131, 135–136, 138, 141,
145–147, 181, 196, 204–205, 208,
212, 220, 232, 235–238, 242
and Jesus' teachings in the Gospels, 61
and Jews and mammon, 202
lack of scientific basis for the concept
of race, 105
as lacking ideological purpose, 30
as love, faith, and hope, 201
as mass movement, 29
meaning of 'Socialism', 41
moral principles of, 229, 232, 235
and moral renewal, 149
and need for ethical reform, 53
as nihilistic, 235
and objective ethics and morality, 182
opposition to, 82
opposition to Darwinism and
evolution, 103–104
opposition to rationality and science,
102, 104
and the "people's church", 69
as political crusade, 214
and positive Christianity, 56, 150
and private property, 49–50
and privatization, 41
as punishment for the Jews, 230
and purging the Bible of Jewish
influences, 68
as quasi-religious or political religion,
28
as racial Christian community, 203
as radical evil, 20
rejection of humanism, 90–91
and religion, 5, 18
religion as propaganda, 33
as religious movement, 75

276 / Index

National Socialism (cont.)
  religious nature of, 5, 14, 19, 26–27, 29, 31, 75, 79, 82, 132, 168, 175, 198, 201, 215, 220, 229–230, 237, 241
  and renewal of German religious life, 69
  as revolutionary, 42–43
  right-wing nature of, 43
  right-wing origin of, 82
  right-wing roots of, 4–5, 39–40
  role of God in, 17, 20
  and Rosenberg's theology, 63
  and social Darwinism, 54
  and socialization/nationalization, 44
  sources of, 15
  and studies of Judaism, 66
  theology of, 150, 233
  as true Christianity, 63, 157, 182, 186, 190–191, 197, 204–205, 212–213, 216–217
  as true Socialism, 42, 157, 196
  as ultranationalism, 45
  understanding of biology, 104
  view of the soul, 98
  and willpower, 92
National Socialist German Workers' Party. *See* NSDAP
Naumann, Friedrich, 4, 34, 37, 39, 41–42, 47–48, 50, 53–55, 58, 231, 235
Nazi/Nazism. *See* National Socialism
Neu-Salems-Gesellschaft (New Salem Society), 110
Neu-Salem Verlag, 110
New Testament, 23, 52, 62, 67, 70, 73, 79, 88, 96, 111, 116–117, 127, 130, 137, 139, 141, 144, 152, 162, 165, 182, 186, 190–191, 196, 202, 211, 228, 232, 237, 241
Newton, Isaac (Sir), 104
Nietzsche, Friedrich, 38, 92, 101, 117
  Dietrich Eckart bitterly criticizing, 117

Night of Long Knives, 141
Nihilism, 20, 30, 235
Nolte, Ernst, 113
Nordin, Svante, 11
November Pogrom (November 9–10, 1938), 68
NSDAP, 4, 10, 13, 16, 24, 27, 32, 34–37, 40–41, 43–44, 46–48, 52, 56–57, 59, 63, 72–73, 77–78, 82, 90, 93, 99–100, 112, 116, 119–120, 124–125, 129–132, 136, 138–140, 142, 144–145, 147, 149–150, 153–154, 157, 161–162, 165–166, 174, 178–180, 182–184, 186–187, 195, 199–201, 203–208, 211–215, 217–220, 224, 231–232, 236, 238, 240, 242
  Hitler achieving dictatorial powers in, 115
  as true Socialists, 57
NSDAP party program, 41, 43, 45–48, 55–57, 74, 93, 111, 125, 131, 147, 150, 214, 231
NSDAP Teachers' Association, 103

Obergammau Passion Play, 123, 190
Old Testament, 62, 67, 70, 111, 115, 117, 230
  inspiring Dietrich Eckart to antisemitism, 117
The one who is unwilling to work shall not eat, 228
Operation Erntefest, 227
Operation Reinhard, 227

Paganism, 145, 155, 206–207, 240
Parsifal (opera, and character, by Richard Wagner), 89
Pasewalk, 85, 93, 154, 164–165, 167–168, 241
The Passing of the Great Race (book by Madison Grant), 100
Paul of Tarsus, apostle, 3, 6, 57, 62, 67, 78, 80, 86, 95–96, 107–108, 111,

114, 126, 133, 137, 152–153, 157, 160, 162–164, 166–169, 173–174, 177–178, 180, 241
corrupting teachings of Jesus, 57
Pauline epistles (in the New Testament), 62
Peer Gynt (by Dietrich Eckart), 110
Peniger Tageblatt (newspaper), 190
People's church, 63, 69–70
Peter's Letter to James (apocryphal early Christian text), 152
Pharisees, 37, 59, 98, 139, 202
Phayer, Michael, 18
Pilate, 228
Pinker, Steven, 29
Plato, 114, 121
Plewnia, Margarete, 112–113, 119–120
Plöckinger, Othmar, 191, 211
Ploetz, Alfred, 105
Poland, 79, 230
Political religion, 25, 31
Pope, the, 131, 154, 214
Popp, Joseph, 171
Posen, 226
Positive Christianity, 46, 56–57, 93, 111, 125, 131, 136, 150, 215
Price, Ward, 171
Propaganda, 6, 16, 21, 25, 33, 46, 71–72, 74–75, 82–83, 86, 99, 109, 112, 117–119, 121, 123, 142, 145, 149–151, 155, 157, 162, 166, 172, 176–178, 181–182, 184, 192–193, 200, 210, 216–217, 220–221, 241
Protestant Soldier's Song Book, 65
Protestantism, 5, 34, 39, 56, 63, 65, 69, 71–72, 74, 83, 103, 124, 131, 147, 154, 190, 215–216, 225
The Protocols of the Elders of Zion, 49, 203
Providence, 30–31, 58, 84, 92–94, 133, 156, 167, 175, 218
Pyta, Wolfram, 120–121, 161, 193, 225–226

Racial hygiene, 80, 91, 105, 107
Racism, 4–5, 17, 21–22, 28, 37, 40, 49, 51–52, 54, 56, 64, 74, 76, 80–81, 83, 86, 91, 95, 97, 100–101, 104–108, 110, 125, 128, 135, 146, 153, 159, 203, 220, 236–237
Rassenkunde des deutschen Volkes (book by Hans F. K. Günther), 105
Rassenschande, 17
Raubal, Geli
suicide of, 209
Rauschning, Hermann, 30, 33, 73, 108–109
Redles, David, 2, 113–114, 202, 231
Renan, Ernest, 38, 64, 77, 83
Riehl, Walter, 35, 37
Rißmann, Michael, 25, 162, 199–200
Ritter, Gerhard, 82
Rodbertus-Jagetzow, Carl, 39
Roder, Lorenz (Hitler's lawyer during trial), 154
Röhm, Ernst, 141
Rome, 43, 131, 154, 214
Hitler visiting, 79
Rosenberg, Alfred, 13, 47, 52, 56, 61, 66, 68, 70, 77, 88, 108–109, 112, 114, 122–124, 143, 155, 197–198, 219
hostility to science and rationality, 102
rejects the theory of evolution, 103
views of Jesus, 59–63, 69, 208, 236
writing as theologian, 63
Rosenheim, 77, 136, 202
Rosenheimer Tageblatt (newspaper), 136
Rothschild (Jewish banking family), 50, 230
Rousseau, Jean-Jacques, 104
Ryback, Timothy, 78, 95, 186

SA (*Sturmabteilung*), 71, 140–141, 149, 170, 195
Sachsenhausen (concentration camp), 231, 239

278 / Index

Satan, 37, 52, 59, 61, 77, 99, 111, 115–117, 127, 130, 197, 206, 216, 220
Sauckel, Fritz, 194
Schaub, Julius, 156
Schemm, Hans, 103
  our religion is Christ, 103
Schiller, Friedrich, 58, 101
Schmaus, Michael, 189
Schopenhauer, Arthur, 92, 101, 114
Schott, Georg, 225–226
  Hitler mentioning the Final Solution in 1924, 225
Schroeder, Christa, 94, 151
Schrönghamer-Heimdal, Franz, 59, 137–138
Sebald, Max, 76
Sebottendorff, Rudolf von, 40, 79, 90, 103, 111–112, 193, 236
  founder of *Thule Gesellschaft*, 112
Second World War, 4, 23–24, 240
Sermon on the Mount, 63, 91, 184, 202, 211
Siedler, Wolf Jobst, 9
Sobibor (death camp), 227
Social Darwinism, 17, 22, 54, 104, 228
Social Democracy, 4, 34, 37, 42, 192, 216
Social Democratic Party, 192
Socrates, 121
Sohm, Rudolf, 54
Solon, 147
Sonderweg (hypothesis), 4, 24
Soviet Union, 75, 215
Spandau prison, 96
Spandauer Tagebücher (book by Albert Speer), 9
Speer, Albert, 8–9, 30, 227
Spengler, Oswald, 40, 103–104, 228
Spicer, Kevin, 18, 119
SS (*Schutzstaffel*), 20, 71, 208, 210, 217, 233, 239

Stangl, Franz, 230
Steigmann-Gall, Richard, 18, 31, 57, 64, 142, 182
Stempfle, Bernhard, 119
Stoecker, Adolf, 4, 34, 37–39, 41, 47–48, 53
Straßer, Otto, 78, 95
Streicher, Julius, 194, 220–221
Swastika, 74, 90, 213–214
  as symbol for true Christianity, 212
  history of party emblem, 36

Talmud (collection of Jewish writings), 114, 191
  Hitler allegedly having read, 114
Theologians, 5, 22–23, 25, 38, 41, 52, 63–66, 71, 76, 78, 83, 87, 93, 97, 108, 126, 157, 159, 161, 178, 187, 189–190, 215, 232, 240
Theory of evolution, 102–104
  considered Jewish and materialist, 103–104
Theresienstadt (concentration camp), 231, 239
Third Reich, 1, 3, 8–9, 15, 18, 23–24, 28, 71, 83, 116, 124, 131, 135, 220, 233
Thirty Years War, 100
Thule Gesellschaft, 36, 79, 103, 112, 193
Tomberg, Friedrich, 11, 32–33, 144, 202, 216
Torah (the five books of Moses), 68, 98
Treblinka (death camp), 227, 230
Trevor-Roper, Hugh R., 2, 8, 29
Trinity, 116
  Hitler never mentioning, 117
Trützschler, Fritz von, 225
Turner, Jr., Henry Ashby, 198
Tyrell, Albrecht, 34–35, 46, 129, 181, 218

Ullrich, Volker, 234
Useless eaters, 230
USSR. *See* Soviet Union
Utopia, 29

279 / Index

Valhalla, 156
Varshizky, Amit, 68, 104, 106, 198
Vatican, 38, 131, 154
Verein für Sozialpolitik (Association for
Social Policy), 39
Vienna, 35, 53, 85, 87, 95, 102, 216, 224
Voegelin, Erich, 20, 25
Völkischer Beobachter, 10, 12, 36, 59,
77, 87, 104, 112, 116, 119,
122–124, 130–131, 136–137, 140,
167, 182–184, 191, 200, 204,
206–209, 211, 213, 217–218, 224
Volkskirche. See People's Church
Voltaire (François-Marie Arouet), 104
Vom Kaiserhof zur Reichskanzlei (book
by Joseph Goebbels), 13

Wagener, Otto, 170, 191, 195–200,
202–203
Wagner, Cosima (Richard Wagner's
second wife), 87
Wagner, Eva (daughter of Richard), 87, 95
Wagner, Richard, 38, 68, 76, 83, 87, 89,
95, 103

Wagner, Siegfried (son of Richard),
89
Wagner, Winifred (wife of Siegfried, son
of Richard), 209
Weber, Max, 19
Weber, Thomas, 4, 111, 122, 124, 129,
160, 164, 166, 172, 219, 223
Wehrmacht, 65, 93–94, 192
Weikart, Richard, 25–26, 143–144, 146,
148
Weininger, Otto, 124–125
Wie sah Christus aus? (book by Franz
Wolter), 61
Wirth, Christian, 230
Wolter, Franz, 61
Worte Christi (book by Houston Stewart
Chamberlain), 185
Wotan, 69, 215
Wrede, William, 65
Wüst, Walther, 64
Zentrum (Catholic political party), 55,
57, 116, 212–216

Zluhan, Otto, 110

Printed in the United States
by Baker & Taylor Publisher Services